Women and the Making of the Mongol Empire

How did women contribute to the rise of the Mongol Empire while Mongol men were conquering Eurasia? This book positions women in their rightful place in the otherwise familiar story of Chinggis Khan (commonly known as Genghis Khan) and his conquests and empire. It examines the best-known women of Mongol society, such as Chinggis Khan's mother, Hö'elün, and senior wife, Börte, as well as those who were less famous but equally influential, including his daughters and his conquered wives. Through this examination the book demonstrates the systematic and essential participation of women in empire, politics, and war. Anne F. Broadbridge also proposes a new vision of Chinggis Khan's well-known atomized army by situating his daughters and their husbands at the heart of his army reforms, looks at women's key roles in Mongol politics and succession, and charts the ways the descendants of Chinggis Khan's daughters dominated the Khanates that emerged after the breakup of the empire in the 1260s.

Anne F. Broadbridge is Associate Professor of the Department of History at the University of Massachusetts Amherst. She is a member of MESA (Middle East Studies Association) and CESS (Central Eurasian Studies Society). At UMass, she won the Outstanding Teacher Award, has been nominated three times for the Distinguished Teaching Award, and has taught approximately 2,500 students so far. Her previous book is entitled *Kingship and Ideology in the Islamic and Mongol Worlds* (Cambridge University Press, 2008).

Cambridge Studies in Islamic Civilization

Other titles in the series are listed at the back of the book.

Women and the Making of the Mongol Empire

ANNE F. BROADBRIDGE
University of Massachusetts Amherst

CAMBRIDGE
UNIVERSITY PRESS

CAMBRIDGE
UNIVERSITY PRESS

University Printing House, Cambridge CB2 8BS, United Kingdom

One Liberty Plaza, 20th Floor, New York, NY 10006, USA

477 Williamstown Road, Port Melbourne, VIC 3207, Australia

314–321, 3rd Floor, Plot 3, Splendor Forum, Jasola District Centre, New Delhi – 110025, India

79 Anson Road, #06–04/06, Singapore 079906

Cambridge University Press is part of the University of Cambridge.

It furthers the University's mission by disseminating knowledge in the pursuit of education, learning, and research at the highest international levels of excellence.

www.cambridge.org
Information on this title: www.cambridge.org/9781108424899
DOI: 10.1017/9781108347990

First published 2018

A catalogue record for this publication is available from the British Library.

Library of Congress Cataloging-in-Publication Data
Names: Broadbridge, Anne F., author.
Title: Women and the making of the Mongol Empire / Anne F. Broadbridge.
Description: Cambridge ; New York, NY : Cambridge University Press, 2018. | Series: Cambridge studies in Islamic civilization | Includes bibliographical references and index.
Identifiers: LCCN 2017059713| ISBN 9781108424899 (hardback) | ISBN 9781108441001 (paperback)
Subjects: LCSH: Genghis Khan, 1162-1227–Family. | Queens–Mongolia–History. | Daughters–Mongolia–History. | Women–Mongolia–History–To 1500. | Inheritance and succession–Mongolia–History. | Mongolia–Kings and rulers–Biography. | Mongolia–History–To 1500. | Mongols–History–To 1500. | Mongols–Biography. | Mongolia–Biography. | BISAC: HISTORY / Middle East / General.
Classification: LCC DS22 .B76 2018 | DDC 950/.209252–dc23
LC record available at https://lccn.loc.gov/2017059713

ISBN 978-1-108-42489-9 Hardback
ISBN 978-1-108-44100-1 Paperback

To Beatrice on the East Coast, and Tom on the West

Contents

Figures

Family Trees

Tables

Maps

Acknowledgments

It is a delight to thank the many people who helped me write this book.

First I mention Tom Allsen on the US West Coast, who persisted in believing that someone trained in the history of the Mamluk Sultanate could indeed have something to say about Mongol imperial women. I learned much from his conviction that the Mongol Empire was only part of the larger story of Eurasia, and from his refusal to consider petty limitations on this vision. I also benefited from his knowledge of the scholarship and sources, and always appreciated receiving a new reading list from him. He took particular joy in sending me references in German to keep me on my toes. Tom and his wife, Lucille, kindly hosted me at their home in Oregon for an intellectually stimulating and convivial visit, during which Tom and I walked and talked shop for hours, and Lucille joined us at meals for equally fascinating yet more general conversation. I will treasure the memory of that trip.

I am equally grateful to another scholar, this one on the US East Coast, whose influence on this book was as profound as Tom's: Beatrice Forbes Manz. She was extremely generous in lending me microfilms of manuscripts I desperately needed but did not possess, and trading other scholarly works as the occasion demanded. She kindly invited me to teach a class and give a talk at Tufts University, in both cases to lively and engaged audiences. Between these we spent many profitable hours talking shop, something we repeated, also at length, at conferences. Furthermore, I owe Beatrice a particular debt for the way she asked me so many hard yet essential questions, usually when I thought I had just aced an explanation: "Well, Anne, but what about soldiers? What about seniority? What about marriage negotiations? ... " She then insisted on repeating the hardest questions from meeting to meeting until I finally found responses to at least some of them. Without her keen eye and refusal to let me off the hook, this book would be much poorer.

Another scholar to whom I am grateful, and whose influence was early yet critical, was David Morgan, who invited me to present at the Burdick–Vary Symposium: The Mongol Empire and Its World, April 8–10, 2010, at the Institute for Research in the Humanities at the University of Wisconsin Madison. This stimulating event not only gave me the opportunity to try out ideas, but also introduced me to many of the people I now have occasion to thank. I have accrued another debt to Paul Buell, who not only undertook a translation of critical sections of the *Yuan Shi* for me, but also sent me references to women I had missed, comments on the Chinese sources, interesting questions, links to pertinent articles, and general good cheer, humor, and kindness. As if this were not enough, Paul read and commented helpfully on one of the chapters.

Other scholars have been equally important to this project: Ruth Dunnell was always ready to answer questions on the Tanguts or on the Chinese sources, and it was she who directed me to Paul as a translator. Similarly Tim May read and commented on a chapter, invited me to participate in Mongol panels at the Central Eurasian Studies Society Annual Meetings, and was always ready with references, articles, humor, and YouTube links to appropriate musical accompaniment for the Mongol Empire. Bruno De Nicola, whose own book on Mongol women came out before mine, generously let me read his page proofs, then himself read my entire work and made many excellent suggestions. Our fruitful correspondence on Mongol imperial ladies continues to this day. Emily Gottreich invited me to speak at the University of California–Berkeley to a wonderfully intense audience, whose questions led to a discussion that lasted longer than the paper I had presented. Chris Atwood sent me pertinent articles, made kind and helpful comments on Facebook, and, particularly critically, gave me the essential references to guides in Mongolia that made my 2016 research trip there such a success. Those guides also have my gratitude: these were Emma Hite and Karolina Zygmanowska, who with great cheer, expert knowledge in history (Karolina) and archaeology (Emma), and overall noteworthy competence spent three weeks taking me to museums, cultural programs, and critical historical sites across Mongolia. I owe another debt to Buldo, our truly masterful and perpetually sunny chef, and Nandiya, who, with the help of Emma's GPS, uncomplainingly took us to every remote location we wanted to visit, assured me that a particular wolf would not come into my tent at one campsite, and unfailingly repaired our vehicle when it broke.

I also thank Bettine Birge, my coauthor on an article on "Women and Gender Under Mongol Rule" for *The Cambridge History of the Mongol Empire*, with whom I spent a profitable afternoon of collaboration in Cambridge (MA), and with whom I exchanged many subsequent emails. I am grateful to my three anonymous readers, whose insights spurred me to shape the manuscript into its present form, which is far clearer than what they read. I also thank the excellent team at at the press, particularly my supportive editor, Maria Marsh, Cassi Roberts on production, Scarlett Lindsay, the sharp-eyed copyeditor, and Divya Arjunan, the manager who kept me on schedule. I owe gratitude to the Five-College History Seminar for providing me the very first venue to present my work on this topic. My trips to Oregon and Mongolia, and related research activities, were partly funded by the College of Humanities and Fine Arts at the University of Massachusetts Amherst, the Department of History, the Massachusetts Society of Professors, and the Center for Teaching and Development at UMass.

Finally I thank my family: my mother, Fran, for reading the entire manuscript with her excellent editorial eye and useful suggestions. I am also grateful to my husband, Dave, whose continued support and good cheer were all I could ask for, but whose greatest contribution came when he whisked our children away, first so I could go to Oregon and then Mongolia, and later so I could finish this project. Without him, you would hold nothing in your hands right now.

All omissions and errors remain, of course, my own.

Note on Transliteration

Mongolian names and terminology conform to the model set by J. A. Boyle in his translation of Rashid al-Din's *The Successors of Genghis Khan*, with the exception of the hybrid "Chinggis Khan."

Turkish employs the system used by the *Encyclopedia of Islam*, second edition, with some modifications: ch instead of ç, j instead of dj, q instead of k with a subscript dot, and no diacriticals suggesting long vowels (i.e., Qutlugh-Khanids not Quṭlugh-Khānids), but rather only the Turkish vowels (a, ı, o, u; e, i, ö, ü).

Arabic names and terminology conform to the standards set in *Mamluk Studies Review*; these also have been applied to Persian, although in this latter I have used "v" for "w" (i.e., Vaṣṣāf not Waṣṣāf) and "z" for "dh" (i.e., *Zayl-i Ta'rīkh-i Gūzidah* not *Dhayl-i Ta'rīkh-i Gūzidah*).

The few Armenian names follow the style of the American Library of Congress.

Chinese words use the Pinyin system, except in references to older works, in which cases Wade-Giles comes first, followed by Pinyin in brackets.

Dynasties and place names are written without diacritical marks, and conform to the most commonly recognized spelling, even if it is different from the systems mentioned above (i.e., Seljuk, Salghurid). Where possible, place names appear in English or other modern language versions (i.e., Cairo, not al-Qāhirah).

Dates in the text are in Common Era. A few in the bibliography are in Persian Solar (first) and Common Era (second).

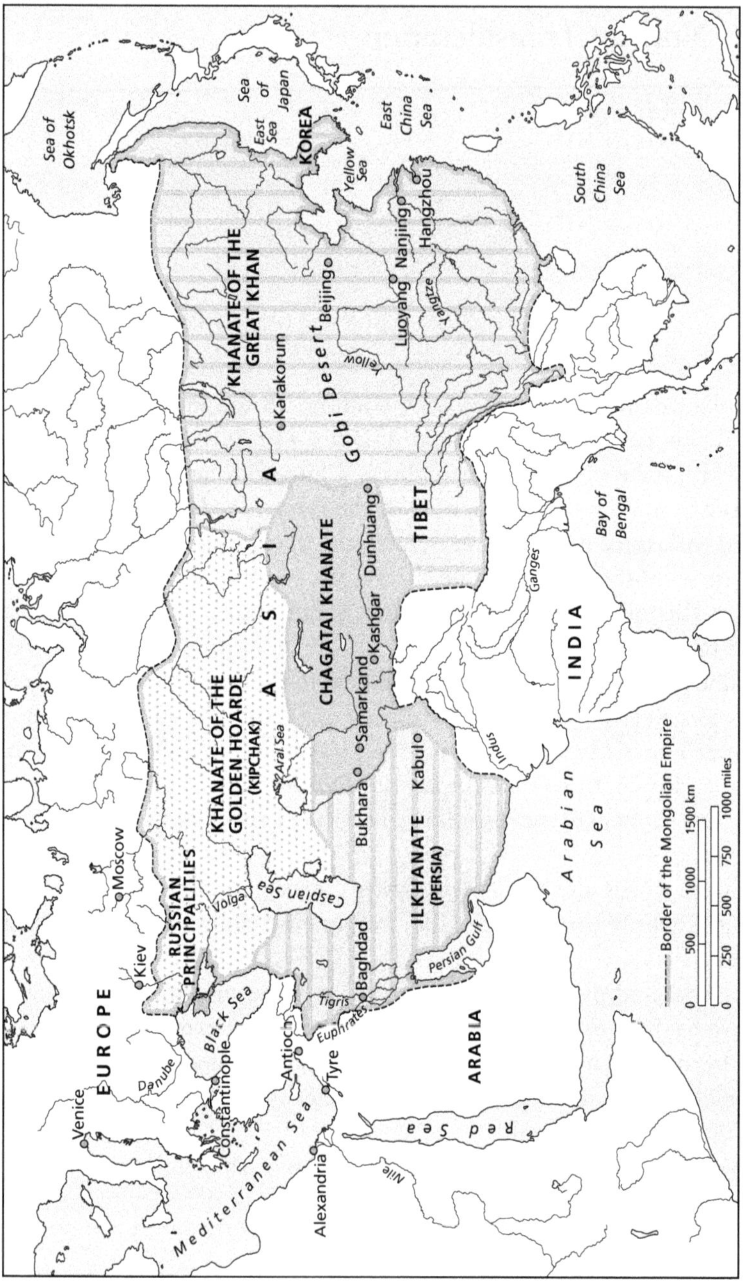

Map 1 The Mongol Successor Khanates

Introduction

Knowing the history of the Mongol Empire is central to understanding both the medieval and modern worlds, yet this history is frequently unfamiliar to more than a handful of specialists and aficionados. Furthermore, two phenomena have guaranteed that our view is dominated by men. First is the captivating personage of Chinggis Khan himself, who has become a household name worldwide and an unparalleled icon in popular culture, even though the actual man and his character are surprisingly difficult to know. Second are the Mongol military campaigns throughout Eurasia, which on the surface appear to have been largely conducted and accomplished by men. But one leader's charisma and the riveting actions of his warriors do not give us anything close to the whole picture. Rather, women played critical roles both in Chinggis Khan's life and in the development of the Mongol Empire. Although scholars have known and written on this for years, the story is larger than one might think, and has not yet been fully told.

This book seeks to fill the gap in our understanding by answering two questions: Where do women fit into the story of Chinggis Khan, the Mongol Empire, and the Mongol conquests? And how exactly did these women contribute to the development of that empire? It examines the lives and careers of particular women at the pinnacle of Mongol society, among them Chinggis Khan's mother, Hö'elün, and his senior wife, Börte, as well as three imperial widows who made a mark on succession to the grand khanate in the 1240s and 1250s: Töregene, Oghul-Qaimish, and Sorqoqtani. It describes overlapping categories of elite women: senior and junior wives, senior and junior princesses, daughters-in-law from illustrious consort houses, daughters-in-law from vanquished families. Then it situates them all in their proper places in Mongol history.

As this book will make clear, the roles that women played in the birth and expansion of the Mongol Empire were varied, yet always essential. Some roles were logistical: women managed the nomadic camps with their inhabitants, gear, and flocks; the biannual migrations between summer and winter camping sites; and irregular traveling camp movement during military campaigns. In the imperial case, senior wives ran camps with the assistance of servants and staff, while junior wives and concubines lived and worked under their seniors' supervision. Once the empire began to form, these staffs grew to hundreds or thousands of people, and imperial women began to cooperate with the imperial bodyguards, whose task was to safeguard them, the ruler, and their encampments, which formed the heart of a traveling city. Women's control of these establishments both when men were home, and when men went to war, was essential to the Mongol ability to field such extraordinary armies. That is to say, women's dominance on the "home front" is what enabled Mongol men to specialize in war, and to muster a larger percentage of men as warriors than any other contemporary society.

At the same time, women were key to the nomadic economy: they engaged regularly in trade both with their own property and with that of their husbands and children. During war they enjoyed portions of spoils, while during peace they acquired interests in tax revenues. Thus the highly placed women this book examines controlled significant human, animal, and material resources, and deployed them as well or as ill as their own training and savvy permitted.

Women were also critical to politics. First, select women made carefully chosen marriages with important political and military leaders, as when the five daughters of Chinggis Khan and Börte wedded their father's allies during the empire's expansion. These marriages brought political, military, and economic benefits to everyone involved. In later generations, strategic marriages between the Chinggisids and particular consort houses conferred similar benefits on Chinggis Khan and Börte's descendants. Women also acted as political advisors to men – their husbands, fathers, brothers, sons – and also to one another. Women attended, participated in, and supported persons and policies at nomadic assemblies (*quriltai*s). They engaged in diplomacy, both in cooperation with men and on their own. They interacted with military commanders and bureaucrats, patronized religions as they chose, and functioned as channels of intercession with men for petitioners. Some took up leadership after their husbands' deaths: the most openly active women in Mongol politics were widows. Moreover, women were central to succession even in this patriarchal society: when Chinggisid princes had children, it was the status of the mother and the father together that determined the likely trajectory of each child's life. To put it another way: the question in succession was not merely who was a child's father, but, rather, who was the mother?

It is also through women that we catch a glimpse of the losers in Chinggis Khan's wars, that is, the dispossessed peoples whose subjugation fueled the empire's extraordinary expansion. The memory of these lost peoples lived on in the secondary wives that Chinggis Khan acquired, all of whom were literally trophies of his success, and some of whom struggled to preserve what remained of their past and their people. Later marriages between Chinggis Khan's descendants and royal houses in Korea, Georgia, Seljuk and Byzantine Anatolia, Muscovy, Fars, and Kirman similarly demonstrated a map of vassalage, tribute and subjection, which could be sealed either by the dynamic presence of a Chinggisid princess at the vassal court, or the relocation of a vassal princess to the Mongol court.

THE BACKGROUND

Life on the steppe in the 1160s was cold, lawless, and politically unstable.[1] Steppe society was composed primarily of Turkish- or Mongolian-speaking horse- and sheep-herding nomads, although other animals were also in evidence (goats, Bactrian camels, cattle). This society was divided among groups of people who shared a common name and connections to a real or mythical ancestor, like the Merkits, Naimans, and Mongols themselves. Society was hierarchical, as seen in the existence of ruling lineages and subject peoples within each group. Nevertheless, internal structures could vary significantly, so that some groups boasted multiple ruling lineages and consequently a more egalitarian, consensus-driven ruling cadre, like the Qonggirats in eastern Mongolia. Others possessed few or only one ruling lineage, with the accompanying centralizing tendencies that that implied, like the Kereits or the Naimans to the

[1] Paul Ratchnevsky, *Genghis Khan: His Life and Legacy*, trans. Thomas Nivison Haining (Oxford, UK: Blackwell, 1992), 103.

Mongols' south and west.[2] Religion in this society was a patchwork of shamanistic practices side-by-side with Nestorian Christianity, Buddhism, and Islam.

Among the major players on the steppe at the time of Chinggis Khan's rise were the large, wealthy, and sophisticated Turkic polities of the Naimans and the Kereits, the settled Uighurs in the Tarim river basin and the Taklamakan desert, and the Öng'üts near the border of the Jin Empire in Northern China. Mongolian speakers included the wealthy yet politically disunited Tatars to the east of the Mongols, the Merkits east of Lake Baikal, and the Qonggirats close to the Öng'üts, to name only a few of the larger groups. The Mongols themselves in this period were without leadership and were poor: the last and least of their neighbors.

The birth of Temüjin (later Chinggis Khan) in the 1160s occurred against a backdrop of societal instability and disorder in general, and lawlessness and division within his own people in particular. Although his father, Yisügei, was a war leader from a ruling lineage, the family does not appear to have been wealthy, and in any case Yisügei's death when Temüjin was still young plunged Yisügei's widow, Hö'elün, and her children into a period of troubles. Over time Temüjin overcame these setbacks to rise on the steppe as a promising leader, but then suffered serious defeat at the battle of Dalan Balzhut in 1187 and disappeared for nearly 10 years. When he returned to the steppe in 1196 from Northern China leading an army for the Jin emperor, he began a second, more successful rise. By 1206 he had either destroyed or subsumed most of his Turkic and Mongolian neighbors, and was raised at a quriltai to the position of Chinggis Khan. After a pause to reorganize his military, and through it the rest of steppe society, Chinggis Khan set out on what became his world-famous campaigns: one against the Tangut Kingdom of Xi-Xia (1209–10), another against the Jin Empire in northern China (1211–15, with continuations in 1217–23, 1230–34), a third into the Khwarazm-Shah Empire in the Islamic lands to the west (1218–23), and a second campaign against the Tanguts in 1226–27, during which Chinggis Khan died.[3] At some point before or during these gigantic enterprises he acquired the ideology that helped fuel them and the later expansion of the

[2] Isenbike Togan, *Flexibility and Limitation in Steppe Formation: The Kereit Khanate and Chinggis Khan* (Leiden: Brill, 1998), 124–127.

[3] For his biography see Ratchnevsky, *Genghis Khan*; Ruth Dunnell, *Chinggis Khan: World Conqueror* (Boston: Longman, 2010); Michal Biran, *Chinggis Khan*, Makers of the Muslim World Series (Oxford: Oneworld, 2007).

empire: namely, that the overarching spirit of the Sky, the Enduring Blue Sky (*Gök Mönggke Tenggeri*) had commanded him to conquer the entire world, both steppe and settled.[4] After Chinggis Khan's death, his family used this ideology to continue his conquests through a multiyear invasion of Central Asia, Russia, the Caucasus, and eastern Europe in 1236–42; campaigns in southern China in the 1250s and again thereafter until 1279; and a second and final campaign into Iran, Iraq, and Anatolia (1253–60), among many, smaller ventures. While these campaigns were going on, the empire was also rocked by a series of contentious succession struggles in the 1240s and 1250s, which led eventually to the Mongol Civil War of 1260–64 and the political disintegration of the United Empire into multiple, warring successor states.

THE SCOPE

The majority of this book covers the period between the 1160s, when Chinggis Khan's mother Hö'elün was first kidnapped by and married to his father; through the establishment of the United Mongol Empire from the twelve-teens to 1230s; to the arrest and execution in the 1250s of the widow and regent, Oghul-Qaimish, by Chinggis Khan's grandson, the Grand Khan Möngke, less than a decade before the Mongol Civil War (1260–64) broke the empire apart. The final section addresses women and their activities in the successor khanates that emerged before and after the civil war, ending with a case study of women in politics in the Ilkhanate in Iran until the 1330s.

Because what we can glean from the historical sources varies tremendously, the chapters are far from uniform. Some follow the lives of individuals as they made their personal marks on the empire. Others describe larger systems of labor, marriage, the military, or politics in order to draw out trends within nomadic society that were propelled by women's behavior. Our story begins in Chapter 1 with an overview of the systems in which nomadic women operated. First was marriage, whether sanctioned or unsanctioned; levirate marriage (when a widow wedded her husband's junior kin after his death); and the question of seniority among wives. Next came women's labor as they managed their camps, and their economic roles as they controlled resources and interacted with merchants. Women's work also meant bearing children and bringing

[4] Anne F. Broadbridge, *Kingship and Ideology in the Islamic and Mongol Worlds* (Cambridge University Press, 2008), 6–10 with notes.

them up to understand the cultural intricacies and necessary hierarchies of nomadic society. Women then helped make strategic marriages for their children with other families, especially their own natal kin. Other important systems to which women contributed were politics, and, in ruling circles, succession. A last topic is women's loyalty – where it was assumed to go, and where it might actually lie, especially in the case of women who had been brought into a family by force.

With these major themes in place, we turn to the first two individual women to shape the empire: Chinggis Khan's mother, Hö'elün, and his senior wife, Börte. In Chapter 2 we examine not only the eventful specifics of their lives, but also the ways in which they represented larger systems of marriage, labor, and war. Then, since both women were tied inextricably to Chinggis Khan's rising star and the realities of triumph, we turn in Chapter 3 to Chinggis Khan's other women – his secondary wives – who only joined his family and empire after his conquest of their own families and peoples, and whose lives were therefore inexorably shaped by defeat. In their stories we see the profound effects of conquest on women, men, and populations, and the different ways that subjugation limited women's opportunities. We also catch a glimpse of the complexity of women's loyalties, and the effect these loyalties could have on women's behavior after their capture.

The next stories that emerged as the empire grew were those of systems and women's places in them, especially the military. Chapters 4 and 5 feature many women, chief among them the five daughters of Börte and Chinggis Khan, along with some of Chinggis Khan's daughters from lesser wives. The systems included Chinggis Khan's armies, the reorganization of which was far more closely tied to these princesses and their husbands than has previously been imagined. Chapter 4 also addresses the relationships between imperial wives and the imperial guard, as well as the hitherto unacknowledged influence of individual women on Chinggisid succession. In Chapter 5 we look at the gigantic project of the Mongol conquests, in which – contrary to general understanding – men and women participated together. Our focus here includes the individual contributions made by imperial sons-in-law and their princess wives to specific military campaigns.

After Chinggis Khan's death in 1227, and with the first round of conquests achieved by 1334, the narrative returns to the exploits of individuals. The late 1240s and early 1250s were the age of imperial widows, and were dominated by three: Töregene, widow of Grand Khan

Ögedei (r. 1229–41); Oghul-Qaimish, widow of Töregene's son, Grand Khan Güyük (r. 1246–48); and Sorqoqtani, widow of Chinggis Khan's son Tolui and mother of the Grand Khan who overthrew Güyük's descendants, Möngke (r. 1251–59). All three women have been inaccurately presented by historical sources that were eager to fit them into clear-cut molds of worthy and unworthy feminine behavior. We begin with Töregene in Chapter 6 and explore her high ambitions and correspondingly extraordinary accomplishments as she worked as regent after her husband's death, the challenges she faced from enemies and detractors as she sought to enthrone her unpopular son, the profound effect she had on the history of the empire, and the heavy toll all of this took on her health. Next we move to Oghul-Qaimish and Sorqoqtani in Chapter 7, who found themselves set in opposition to each other. In the deadly game that followed, Oghul-Qaimish lost and took her family down with her, while Sorqoqtani won and set her own son on the throne, but in victory badly damaged the empire itself.

The final section charts women's activities in the successor khanates that became independent states after the Mongol Civil War of the 1260s. Here in Chapter 8 we return to systems, this time systems of lineage, marriage, inheritance, and politics, which were populated by many women from many families. Important consort lineages star here, especially the Qonggirats, Oirats, and Kereits, and their connections to Börte's daughters are made clear – or not, in the case of the Kereit family, which was unrelated to any Chinggisid princess, and was therefore unique. This section concludes in Chapter 9 with a case study of women, politics, and consort families in the Ilkhanate in Iran, where the relatively plentiful evidence allows us to see patterns and make connections that are impossible for other regions.

This book is best understood as a contribution to an ongoing discussion – a building block in our construction of the many ways in which women shaped the history of the Mongol Empire. As all scholars drawn into the Mongols' fierce gravity know, the multiplicity of languages, scholarly literatures, and tricky historical sources present extreme technical challenges to all of us, which makes uncovering Mongol history into a cooperative venture by necessity, far more than is the case in, say, the history of sixteenth-century France. Thus although this book uses as many sources in as many languages or translations as were available, it does not claim to have included every single one known to the world. It also focuses exclusively on the stories of the elite, not ordinary subjects, since that is what the sources preferred to describe. Finally, this book does not aim to represent a definitive study of everything written on women in the Mongol Empire in all languages, and in no way dictates a final word on the subject. Rather, it is designed to inspire further discussion of this critical topic, in order to help us all better understand the extraordinary phenomenon of the Mongol Empire and the women who helped build it.

1

Women in Steppe Society

To date, scholarly and popular histories of the Mongols have been dominated by the seemingly masculine topic of Mongol warfare, which makes it easy to suspect that steppe women enjoyed little political, social, or economic power. Furthermore, Mongol society before Chinggis Khan's rise was not only impoverished but also tremendously unsettled, so that nomadic women were vulnerable to aggression, violence, and rape. This may especially have been the case among rank-and-file nomadic subjects, among whom harsh circumstances might weigh more heavily on women and girls than on men and boys.[1] Nevertheless, despite the dangers inherent in their society, many nomadic women enjoyed control and exerted influence in a wide range of arenas. As for women at the pinnacle of steppe society, such as the Chinggisids, the picture is one of wealth, responsibility and tremendous opportunity for those with intelligence and talent.

It is only possible to appreciate the authority that some women enjoyed and the contributions they made to Mongol history if we understand the general situation of women on the steppe. To do this, we must examine their lives in detail. We begin with marriage, since women's most

[1] Ratchnevsky notes the infanticide of girls, selling children in hard times, or making restoration for crime by giving girls to the aggrieved. Paul Ratchnevsky, "La condition de la Femme mongole au 12e/13e siècle," in *Tractata Altaica: Denis Sinor, sexagenario optime de rebus altaicis merito dedicata*, ed. W. Heissig et al. (Wiesbaden: Harrassowitz), 522. Aubin agrees on recompensing murder with a girl, but she argues that infanticide was rare, and took place primarily in areas influenced by Chinese traditions. Françoise Aubin, "Le statut de l'enfant dans la société mongole," *Recueils de la société Jean Bodin pour l'histoire comparative des institutions* 35 (1975): 482–3, 492.

extensive powers tended to appear after marriage through their status as wives, mothers, or widows. Next comes women's work, since they engaged all day long in a wide range of activities, which required the formation and maintenance of many complex relationships. Along with work, we must investigate women's economic opportunities, since their daily business included the management, control, and exploitation of animal, human, and other resources. An additional area of women's activity centered on hospitality and religious duties. Women also had a profound influence on the family: in the immediate sphere, they managed the upbringing of children with the help of others, while on a larger front, women were essential to the question of succession and inheritance, since a woman's own status shaped the options open to her children. Women also figured in politics in many ways, including as advisors to others, as political actors themselves, or as the critical links that joined allied families, among other roles. Finally, women's private, interior lives came to affect the empire in surprising ways, especially those conquered women brought into the Chinggisid house by force, whose loyalty to that house was never questioned, but perhaps should have been.

It is also necessary to remember that all women's lives were governed by status. Steppe society remained generally hierarchical in nature for women and men, even after Chinggis Khan upended existing social hierarchies to create a new, merit-based social and military system. We cannot understand the activities of women, and from them learn about their relationships and their control of resources, without locating these women in a hierarchy of rank of which nomads themselves were exquisitely aware.

BRIDE PRICE, LEVIRATE, AND SENIORITY AMONG WIVES

Although the Mongols were a polygynous people, wealth strongly shaped marriage, since rich men wedded more wives than poor ones.[2] One reason was that Mongol grooms paid a bride price to compensate a prospective

[2] Ratchnevsky sees no limitation in wives, but does not account for social class. Ratchnevsky, "La Femme," 514. Holmgren sees unlimited wives only for wealthy men, otherwise one or two. Jennifer Holmgren, "Observations on Marriage and Inheritance Practices in Early Mongol and Yüan Society, with Particular Reference to the Levirate," *Journal of Asian History* 16, rprt. in *Marriage, Kinship and Power in Northern China* (London: Variorum, 1995), 147; similarly Morris Rossabi, "Khubilai Khan and the Women in His Family," in *Studia Sino-Mongolica: Festschrift für Herbert Franke*, ed. Wolfgang Bauer (Wiesbaden: Franz Steiner), 155.

wife's family for the "loss" of their daughter.[3] Brides with wealthy parents could bring a dowry (*inje*) of household items, jewelry, livestock, and even servants and slaves to the union. But this was not always produced immediately – in some cases the delay could be as long as three years – and in any case seems to have been less than the sum provided by the groom.[4] Furthermore, when the dowry did appear it remained the woman's personal property, not the man's, and later went to her children: livestock to sons, cloth and jewels to daughters, and servants to both.[5] If a family could not afford a bride price, the groom might instead pay off his debt by working for his father-in-law for a period of time. Another option was to arrange a double marriage between two families, where each family provided a son and a daughter, which allowed both sides to dispense with bride price.[6] Nevertheless, for poorer men in the chaotic period before Temüjin's rise, the bride price may have been such a barrier to marriage, and the idea of labor so unappealing, that one affordable way to acquire a wife became to kidnap her, even though this eliminated any chance of a dowry.[7] Thus one scholar has suggested that Temüjin's

[3] John of Plano Carpini, "History of the Mongols," in *The Mongol Mission: Narratives and Letters of the Franciscan Missionaries in China and Mongolia in the Thirteenth and Fourteenth Centuries*, trans. by a nun of Stanbrook Abbey, ed. Christopher Dawson (New York: Sheed and Ward, 1955), 7; not in John of Pian de Carpine, *The Journey of William of Rubruck to the Eastern Parts of the World, 1235–55, as Narrated by Himself, with Two Accounts of the Earlier Journey of John of Pian de Carpine*, trans. W. W. Rockhill (London: Hakluyt Society, 1900); also C. de Bridia, *The Vinland Map and the Tatar Relation*, trans. and ed. R. Skelton, T. Marston, and G. Painter (New Haven: Yale University Press, 1965): §49.

[4] Holmgren, "Levirate," 129–31; Ratchnevsky, "La Femme," 511–2; George Qingzhi Zhao, *Marriage as Political Strategy and Cultural Expression: Mongolian Royal Marriages from World Empire to Yuan Dynasty*, Asian Thought and Culture, vol. 60 (New York: Peter Lang, 2008), 4 for a dissenting view. Also *Secret History* §43 for a servant as part of the *inje*. Miyawaki-Okada suggests that women brought substantial property into marriage, although its relationship to the husband's property is not clear. Junko Miyawaki-Okada, "The Role of Women in the Imperial Succession of the Nomadic Empire," in *The Role of Women in the Altaic World*, ed. Veronika Veit (Wiesbaden: Harrassowitz, 2007), 144–6. Aubin, "Enfant," 539 (the three-year delay). Also Bettine Birge, *Women, Property and Confucian Reaction in Sung and Yüan China (960–1368)* (Cambridge: Cambridge University Press, 2002), 206.

[5] Aubin, "Enfant," 541–3, 546–8; also *Secret History* §43 (a female servant becoming a son's concubine).

[6] Aubin, "Enfant," 535.

[7] Ratchnevsky, "La Femme," 516; Holmgren, "Levirate," 144–5; Herbert Franke, "Women under the Dynasties of Conquest," in *La donna nella Cina impeiale e nella Cina repubblicana*, ed. Lionello Lanciotti (Florence: L. S. Olschki, 1980), rprt. in *China Under Mongol Rule* (Brookfield, VT: Variorum, 1994), 36–7; Birge, *Confucian Reaction*, 204.

father, Yisügei, was himself relatively poor, first because he acquired Temüjin's mother, Hö'elün, by kidnapping her, not by negotiating an agreement with her parents; and second because he left their son Temüjin to work off the bride price for his fiancée, Börte, rather than simply providing the expected gift.[8]

The Mongols engaged in strictly exogamous marriages, which stipulated that individuals had to wed into a lineage other than their own.[9] Nomadic society was organized by larger groups (*oboq*, sometimes "tribes"[10]) descended from a real or mythical ancestor, and within these large groups, by smaller patrilineal descent groups (*uruq*), or lineages. One large group could contain multiple lineages, usually connected to one another by a cousinly relationship.[11] Marriages between descendants of related patrilineal groups were unacceptable, but loopholes did exist. In particular, the Mongols favored exchange marriages, where children married back into their mother's natal line. This could be a daughter marrying her mother's nephew "in exchange" for the mother's earlier marriage, or it could be a sister exchange, where a son and his male cousin married one another's sisters.[12] Such marriages were possible within the

8 See Chapter 2.

9 Zhao, *Marriage*, 15–21; Sechin Jagchid and Paul Hyer, *Mongolia's Culture and Society* (Boulder, CO: Westview Press), 92.

10 Recently scholars have suggested that the term "tribe" has become fraught because of its association with questionable ethnographic practices influenced by colonial policies. David Sneath, *The Headless State: Aristocratic Orders, Kinship Society and Misrepresentations of Nomadic Inner Asia* (New York: Columbia University Press, 2007), and Sneath, "The Headless State in Inner Asia: Reconsidering Kingship Society and the Discourse of Tribalism," in *Representing Power in Ancient Inner Asia: Legitimacy, Transmission and the Sacred*, ed. Isabell Charleux, Grégory Delaplace, Robert Hamayon, and Scott Pearce (Bellingham: Western Washington University), 365–415. Yet some of the historical sources from the Mongol period use "tribe" to categorize the peoples they discuss. Rashīd al-Dīn in particular uses "*qom*" (Persian, from Arabic *qawm*), which can indicate a "tribal group" of related individuals. This book will take a stance midway: it acknowledges that "tribe" can be problematic when used in the modern world, replaces it with "lineage" to indicate the ruling families of large groups and "subjects" or "people" to indicate those ruled by the lineages in question, but retains the "tribal" names associated with particular groups (the Merkits, Kereits, etc.), since these are the markers used throughout the sources.

11 Buell and Kolbas, "Ethos," 48.

12 Two forms of exchange existed: (1) When "in exchange for" his wife a man married a daughter to his wife's brother's son and (2) When he then married a son to his wife's niece at the same time; this latter was considered sister-exchange since the two grooms had "exchanged" sisters. Nobuhiro Uno, "Exchange-Marriage in the Royal Families of Nomadic States," in *The Early Mongols: Language, Culture and History: Studies in Honor of Igor de Rachewiltz on the Occasion of His 80th Birthday*, eds. Volker

rules of exogamy because of the patrilineal quality of nomadic lineages, which meant that the bloodlines of fathers, not mothers, determined the relationship between two prospective partners.[13] Thus a couple could marry their daughter or son to the mother's nephew or niece without qualm, since the fathers in question – the man, his wife's brother – were not related by blood. By modern standards these marriages would be consanguineous on the mother's side, but this was not a concern for the Mongols.[14] Although consanguinity may have contributed to the poor health that plagued the Chinggisids in the later decades of their empire, it should not be seen as the sole cause.[15]

Although details on the negotiation process are scant for the early period, mothers are likely to have been actively involved in pairing their own children with those of their siblings. Certainly mothers shaped their children's marital futures through the preference for the woman's relatives as partners. It is reasonable to assume that women were also somehow involved in the negotiations for their children, especially since later marriage manuals point to the active participation of both sets of parents in the wedding ceremonies.[16] Fathers and mothers together might accompany their daughters to their new homes after the wedding.[17]

If a woman's husband died, the widow usually engaged in a second, levirate marriage to a junior kinsman of her deceased husband, such as a younger brother, nephew, or son from another wife.[18] Levirate marriage gave the widow a protector, and kept her from seeking remarriage outside the husband's family, taking his children and any property she controlled

Rybatzki et al. (Bloomington: Indiana University Press), 176, 179–80. Zhao prefers "one-way" marriages (a lineage only provided husbands to the Chingizids) and "two-way" marriages (a lineage provided husbands and accepted wives). Zhao, *Marriage*, 24–5, 102–10 (Qonggirats).

13 Zhao, *Marriage*, 16.

14 Zhao, *Marriage*, 16, 18–24; Jagchid and Hyer, *Culture and Society*, 92.

15 Broadbridge, "Toluid-Oirat Connection," 122; John Masson Smith, "Dietary Decadence and Dynastic Decline in the Mongol Empire," *JAH* 34, no. 1 (2000): 35–52.

16 H. Serruys, "Four Manuals for Marriage Ceremonies among the Mongols, Part I," *Zentralasiatische Studien* 8 (1974): 248 (texts can be dated to 1904–8, but originals are "much older"), 294–6 (presence of both male and female parents in wedding ceremonies). Jaghchid and Hyer, *Culture and Society*, 83.

17 See the example of Börte's mother Chotan, who went to Temüjin's camp with her while Börte's father, Dei Sechen, turned back. *Secret History*, §94–6.

18 Holmgren, "Levirate," 152–3; Ratchnevsky, "La Femme," 517; and Paul Ratchnevsky, "The Levirate in the Legislation of the Yuan Dynasty," in *Tamura Hakushi shoju Toyoshi ronso*, (Kyoto: Kyoto University, 1968), 45–62.

with her.[19] Despite the levirate's origin as a nomadic practice, it later appeared in the Mongol Empire among subject peoples as well, even though at times it conflicted with existing, non-Mongol legal practices.[20] But although levirate marriage was widespread on the steppe, a few imperial widows of Chinggisid princes managed to avoid remarriage, and thus formed one important exception to this rule.[21]

Scholars have claimed that wealthy men with many wives treated their wives equally.[22] Even if this delightful theory were possible to carry out, it did not mean that wives were equal to one another in status. Rather, nomadic society distinguished clearly between wives according to rank, even though all wives had their own dwelling, servants, income, and husbandly attention. The senior wife was the most important, and was often the first woman the husband married. She controlled the largest and wealthiest camp (*ordo*). At the same time, a few other high-status wives controlled secondary camps. The junior wives and concubines then lived in the establishments of either the senior wife or the lesser camp-managing wives and answered to them.[23] A senior wife could be displaced if she had no children or died, in which case another woman would become the next senior wife through marriage and the bestowal of the senior wife's camp on her. If the second senior woman had been a junior wife, a reassignment of the main camp might take place; if she already had her own camp, she would simply increase in honors, respect, and ceremonial to reflect her new status.[24] Historical sources from China suggest that each Mongol khan had four main wives with four main camps, but sources for the

[19] Holmgren, "Levirate," 151–4; Ratchnevsky, "La Femme," 517.

[20] Ratchnevsky, "Levirate," 45–6, 57–8; Birge, *Confucian Reaction*, chapter 4.

[21] Holmgren, "Levirate," 159–63; Birge, *Confucian Reaction*, 205–6. For imperial widows who remained single – Töregene, Oghul Qaimish, and Sorqoqtani – see Chapters 6 and 7. Bruno De Nicola suggests that the sons' importance also affected their mothers' ability to avoid remarriage. Email correspondence, June 2017.

[22] Ratchnevsky, "La Femme," 516.

[23] *Yuan Shi*, 14:2693–6, 2698, 2701, Table of Empresses (unpublished trans. Buell). Bruno De Nicola, *Women in Mongol Iran: The Khatuns, 1206–1335* (Edinburgh: Edinburgh University Press, 2017), 130–2, 132–9, and his "Ruling from Tents: Some Remarks on Women's Ordos in Ilkhanid Iran," in *Ferdowsi, the Mongols and the History of Iran: Art, Literature, and Culture from Early Islam to Qajar Persia*, ed. Robert Hillenbrand, A. C. S. Peacock, and Firuza Abdullaeva (London: I. B. Tauris, 2013), 128. For Ilkhanid examples see Chapter 9.

[24] For Töregene displacing Ögedei's senior wife, Oghul-Qaimish, see Chapter 6. For Chabi displacing Qubilai's senior wife, see Chapter 8. See Chapter 9 for Hülegü (two senior wives), Abaqa (three), Arghun (two), and Geikhatu (two).

Western Khanates beginning in the mid-thirteenth century do not always specify a fixed number of camps.[25] Spatially, wifely dwellings within each camp formed a line arranged in strict hierarchy of rank, with the managing wife at the westernmost position, and the most junior wife at the eastern end.[26] Younger children lived with their mother, older children had their own gers (yurts, or round, felt-walled tents) behind her, and servants inhabited lesser quarters behind the family they served.[27] (Concubines were also positioned behind the wives, but in front of the gers of the bodyguard and officials.[28]) We may assume that when several camp-managing wives were together, the camps were lined up in order of the status of the mistresses. Once the Chinggisids had established their empire, all of the imperial gers became marvels of gleaming white felt outside and gold brocade inside, strewn with carpets and decorated with gems and pearls to mark the imperial status of the inhabitants.[29] The khan may have possessed his own establishment, and also a larger pavilion, which held the thrones for him and his senior wife.[30] But for daily living, the husband appears to have moved from ger to ger among his wives, accompanied by his guards (*keshig*).[31] Additional guards were responsible for the safety of the entire family compound, which was further protected by lines of carts, and an open space in front of the imperial gers.[32] Above and

[25] The *Yuan Shi* stated that Chinggis Khan's wives had four camps, managed by Börte, Qulan, Yisüi, and Yisügen. *Yuan Shi*, 14:2693–6, 2698, 2701, Table of Empresses, and 21:2422–7, Annual Gifts (unpublished trans. Buell); also Marco Polo, *Marco Polo: The Description of the World*, ed. and trans. A. C. Moule and Paul Pelliot (London: Routledge), §82; De Nicola, "Ruling from Tents," 127–30.

[26] William of Rubruck, *The Mission of Friar William of Rubruck: His Journey to the Court of the Great Khan Möngke, 1253–55*, trans. Peter Jackson (London: Hakluyt Society, 1990), 74 (Batu's wives), 188 (Möngke's wives).

[27] For size of dwellings according to rank see Rubruck, *Mission*, 74, 95, 178.

[28] *Hei-Ta Shih-lüeh* [*Hei Da shi lü*], trans. P. Olbright and E. Pinks (Wiesbaden: Harrassowitz, 1980), 104.

[29] Thomas T. Allsen, *Commodity and Exchange in the Mongol Empire: A Cultural History of Islamic Textiles* (Cambridge: Cambridge University Press, 1997), 13–16.

[30] The existence of a "male" ordo is a challenge to extract from the sources. More work is certainly needed. For now see De Nicola, *Khatuns*, 138, 152, 155–9, 161–5.

[31] Carpini *History*, 17–18 (not in Rockhill); Marco Polo (1938), *Description*, §82.

[32] Andrews, *Felt Tents*, 325–9; this additional contingent is unspecified, although half the nightguards guarded the camp when Chinggis Khan went hunting. *Secret History*, §232, de Rachewiltz, Commentary, 835–9. Also Charles Melville, "The Keshig in Iran: The Survival of the Royal Mongol Household," in *Beyond the Legacy of Genghis Khan*, ed. Linda Komaroff (Leiden: Brill), 135–64.

beyond the imperial guard, some women may have had their own guardsmen, although in smaller numbers than the *keshig*.[33]

In addition to holding the most prestigious place in the wifely line, the senior wife spent more time with the husband than did the junior wives, which may explain why senior wives often had many children (between five and nine), whereas junior wives and concubines tended to have one or two.[34] Although a junior wife enjoyed precedence over her co-wives during drinking-parties at her dwelling if her husband attended, otherwise the senior wife sat closest to the husband at ceremonies and receptions, and received other courtesies: at feasts in thirteenth-century Yuan China, for example, Qubilai (r. 1260–94) sat at a raised table with his senior wife, while the junior wives sat at a lower table so that their heads were level with the senior wife's feet.[35] (See Figure 1.1.) In the royal encampments of the Jochid khanate along the Volga River, the khan's throne had space for two – the khan and the senior wife – and was situated on a platform raised three steps off the floor.[36] Less vertical yet equally telling

[33] Ibn Baṭūṭah, *Travels*, 498, states that Özbek's third wife had 300–500 of her own troops, in addition to those provided by her husband. When Töregene was regent and Temüge advanced upon her to seize the throne, she sent word that the people and the soldiery (*lashkar va ulūs*) were upset, which suggests that she indeed had warriors at hand. Her emissary was accompanied by his own followers, also probably serving as soldiers: Juvaynī, 'Alā' al-Dīn 'Aṭā'-Malik, *The History of the World-Conqueror*, trans. J. A. Boyle (Cambridge, MA: Harvard University Press, 1958), 244 (omitting any reference to Töregene's people, but then "retinue and troops" for her emissary); but in Rashīd al-Dīn, *Jāmi'*, 802 ("*lashkar wa ulūs* " for Töregene's people, then "*aqvām va atbā'* " for the emissary's men), trans. Thackston, 391 (both "soldiery and ulus," and "ulus and army," then "clans and followers" for the emissary), trans. Boyle, 178 ("whole army and ulus," then "people and followers" for the emissary). See also footnote 63 in Chapter 5 on princess Alaqa holding the home front while her husband was out hunting.

[34] Carpini, *History*, 18 (not in Rockhill); Rubruck, *Mission*, 196, on Möngke's fourth, least-visited wife; Ibn Baṭūṭah, *Travels*, 2:486. For Yisügei's senior wife, Hö'elün, and her five children, see Chapter 2. For Chinggis Khan's senior wife, Börte, and her nine children, see Chapter 2, and Chapter 3 for his junior wives. Ögedei's most influential wife, Töregene, had five sons; see Chapter 6. Tolui's senior wife Sorqoqtani had four sons and possibly a daughter; see Rashīd al-Dīn, *Jāmi'*, 969, trans. Thackston, 471, albeit claiming five sons (sic). Note also De Nicola, *Khatuns*, 38–9, on status and children among wives.

[35] Marco Polo, *Description*, §86; *Hei-Ta Shih-lüeh* [*Hei Da shi lü*], trans. P. Olbright and E. Pinks, 105; Rubruck, *Mission*, 76 (the precedence of the wife of the day in drinking parties).

[36] Carpini, *History*, 57 and trans. Rockhill, 10; also Rubruck, *Mission*, 132, and see Chapter 8 (Jochi and his probable senior wife, Sorghan).

Figure 1.1 An enthronement scene from the Diez Albums, Iran (possibly Tabriz), early fourteenth century, ink, colors, and gold on paper. Staatsbibliothek zu Berlin-Prussischer Kulturbesitz, Orientabteilung, Diez Album, fol. 70, S. 22.

ceremonial distinctions appeared during fourteenth-century Jochid social gatherings, where the khan walked to the doorway of an imperial pavilion to welcome his senior wife and seat her. He then met the junior wives in order after they had entered the pavilion, not at the doorway.[37] On the grimmer end of womanly duties in the steppe, widows in general and certainly senior widows in particular usually survived their husbands' funerals, whereas concubines could be dispatched – by strangulation, immolation, or live burial – to serve their master in the afterlife, along with male servants and livestock. Although wives were expected to rejoin their husband after death, they generally escaped being sent after him immediately, since duties to their live children, and to their new husband if they remarried through the levirate, outweighed duties to their dead spouse for the time being.[38]

WOMEN AND WORK

We can best imagine steppe women's lives by examining the work they did every day.[39] The Franciscan Friar Carpini, who traveled through the Mongol Empire in 1245–7, and his later counterpart, Friar William of Rubruck in 1253–5, both noted that women's responsibilities were extensive.[40] Friar William in particular catalogued the separate duties of women and men: men made gers and wagons, but women managed the journeys between summer and winter camps by loading the gers on to the wagons, driving the wagons to the next site, and unloading them again.[41] Gender similarly shaped livestock duties: women cared for cattle, men tended horses and camels, and both took care of sheep and goats. In addition, men fermented mares' milk (*qumiz*), fashioned weapons and tack, and cured skins; women made butter, cooked, and sewed clothes from the skins the men had cured.[42] As one scholar puts it, women handled all work relating to the hearth, to dairy production except from horses, and to childrearing (which will be discussed later); men handled

[37] Ibn Baṭūṭah, *Travels*, 483 (the Jochids).

[38] Jean-Paul Roux, "La veuve dans les sociétés Turques et Mongoles de l'Asie Centrale," *L'Homme* IX, no. 4 (1969): 61. Note Ögedei's decision to sacrifice forty "moonlike virgins," (concubines?), not his father's wives, for Chinggis Khan's funeral. Juvaynī, *World-Conqueror*, 189.

[39] Note Rossabi's important treatment of this topic in "Women," 153–5.

[40] Carpini, *History*, 18 (not in Rockhill); Rubruck, *Mission*, 90–1; Polo, *Description*, §69, and de Bridia, *Tatar Relation*, §49.

[41] Rubruck, *Mission*, 90–1, 73–4. Carpini explains that small gers were dismantled and carried on animals, while large ones were kept whole and moved on wagons. Carpini, *History*, 8 (not in Rockhill); also Rossabi, "Women," 153; *Hei-Ta Shih-lüeh* [*Hei Da shi lü*], trans. P. Olbright and E. Pinks, 105.

[42] Rubruck, *Mission*, 90–1; Rossabi, "Women," 153.

hunting, fighting, and horses; and both cooperated to manage small animals, make felt, and preserve meat at butchering time.[43] The interiors of Mongol dwellings reflected the clear division of labor, with different sections designated for men and women, the tools they needed, and specific kinds of work.[44]

But Friar William's otherwise useful description overlooks both the way a woman's status determined her labor, and the question of overall management, which was the responsibility of wives in general and a senior wife in particular. Women maintained their camps both when men were present, and when they departed to hunt or fight, which they did regularly.[45] These were non-combatant camps (*a'ughruq / a'uruq*, sometimes called *ordo* as well).[46] Whenever the man was absent from the non-combatant camp, the senior wife supervised everything.[47] During military campaigns, a different kind of camp (potentially and confusingly also called *ordo*),[48] was also run by a woman with staff, but these accompanied the armies as they traveled.[49] When Chinggis Khan set out on his conquests, he took one wife with him to manage the traveling

[43] Barbara Frey Näf, "'Compared With the Women the ... Menfolk have little Business of their own': Gender Division of Labour in the History of the Mongols," in *The Role of Women in the Altaic World: Permanent International Altaistic Conference, 44th Meeting, Walberberg, 26–31 August 2001*, ed. Veronika Veit (Wiesbaden: Harrassowitz, 2007), 71.

[44] Caroline Humphrey, "Appendix: Inside a Mongolian Tent," in *Nomads: Nomadic Material Culture in the Asian Collections of the Horniman Museum*, ed. Ken Teague (London: Horniman Museum and Gardens), 88.

[45] Ratchnevsky, "La Femme," 509–10; Rossabi, "Women," 154; Valentin Riasanovsky, *Fundamental Principles of Mongol Law*, Uralic and Altaic Series 43 (Bloomington, IN: Indiana University Publications, 1965), 84; Franke, "Dynasties of Conquest," 36.

[46] Rashīd al-Dīn / Thackston, (glossary) 765; Gerhard Doerfer, *Türkische und mongoischen Elemente im Neupersischen* (Wiesbaden, 1963–75), entry 496.

[47] For an example see Chih-Chang Li, *The Travels of an Alchemist: The Journey of the Taoist Ch'ang-ch'un from China to the Hindukush at the Summons of Chingiz Khan, Recorded by His Disciple, Li Chih-Ch'ang*, trans. Arthur Waley (Westport, CT, 1931, rprt. 1976), 70–1, at Chinggis Khan's *ordo*, run by the "Empress," while Chinggis Khan himself was on the Western campaign.

[48] Ordo could refer, confusingly, to an imperial camp during peacetime. Rashīd al-Dīn / Thackston (glossary) 765; Doerfer, *Neupersischen*, entry 496; also see Christopher Atwood, "Ordo," *Encyclopedia of Mongolia and the Mongol Empire* (New York: Facts on File, Inc., 2004), 426–7.

[49] Bruno De Nicola, "Women's Role and Participation in Warfare in the Mongol Empire," in *Soldatinnen: Gewalt und Geschlecht im Krieg vom Mittelalter bis heute* (Paderborn: Ferdinand Schöningh, 2010), 108.

camp, while the other wives remained in Mongolia to manage the noncombatant camps.[50] In addition to this routine management, some wives took on extra responsibilities temporarily or even permanently if their husbands died.[51]

The writings of the fourteenth-century Muslim North African visitor to the Mongols, Ibn Baṭūṭah (d. 1377), reveal further details of the labor of imperial women (*khatuns*, "ladies" or "queens"), gained when he met the wives and married daughter of the Jochid ruler Özbek Khan (r. 1313–41) in the grasslands near the Volga River.[52] Like Friar William, Ibn Baṭṭuṭah described royal women as they engaged in domestic activities, but unlike Friar William, he mentioned their managerial roles. Thus when Özbek's senior wife received Ibn Baṭṭuṭah, she was both personally cleaning a tray of cherries, and overseeing fifty female servants doing the same. Similarly, whereas Friar William suggested that all women sewed clothes, Ibn Baṭṭuṭah instead found another royal wife reading aloud to thirty ladies as they performed skilled embroidery for her.[53]

In the case of the wives of Chinggisid princes, the question of management became further complicated by the presence of the imperial bodyguards (*keshig*) after 1203.[54] A certain number of the guards were responsible for important household tasks that overlapped the wifely domain. Guards supervised some male and female household attendants, managed the care of some animals, maintained weapons, carts, and hunting equipment; supplied, staffed, and ran the kitchens, and helped distribute certain kinds of spoils.[55] Although clearly some of these responsibilities related to their military duties, others, especially food

[50] Qulan ran Chinggis Khan's traveling camp during the Western Campaign of 1218–23, while Yisüi did the same during the second Tangut Campaign of 1226–7. See Chapters 3 and 5.

[51] This happened in both nomadic and sedentary families. David M. Farquhar, "Female Officials in Yüan China," *Journal of Turkish Studies* 9 (1985): 21–5. See also Sorqoqtani in Chapter 7.

[52] The wives were with Özbek; the daughter was 6 miles away. Ibn Baṭūṭah, *Travels*, 489. Also De Nicola, *Khatuns*, 138–9.

[53] Ibn Baṭūṭah, *Travels*, 487–8.

[54] See Chapter 4.

[55] *Secret History* §192, §232, §234, §278; also Andrews, *Felt Tents*, 324; Thomas T. Allsen, "Guard and Government in the Reign of the Grand Qan Möngke, 1251–59," *Harvard Journal of Asiatic Studies* 46, no. 2 (1986): 515; Timothy May, *The Mongol Art of War* (Yardley, PA: Westholme, 2007), 35; Melville, "Keshig," 139; Samuel Grupper, "A Barulas Family Narrative in the Yuan Shih: Some Neglected Prosopographical and Institutional Stories on Timurid Origins," *Archivum Eurasiae Medii Aevi* 8: 39–41; Ch-i-Ch'ing Hsiao, *The Military Establishment of the Yuan Dynasty* (Cambridge, MA: Council of East Asian Studies, Harvard University, 1978), 93–4.

preparation, intertwined with women's work. Officers in the *keshig* appear to have answered both to the Chinggisid prince they guarded, and to the wife in whose camp they were assigned. For example, the Tangut Buda, who was a commander of a hundred in Chinggis Khan's personal unit of a thousand, reported militarily to Chinggis Khan, and domestically to his senior wife, Börte, as her personal camp commander (*amīr*-i *ordo* in later sources). The position of camp commander in an imperial woman's establishment became standard in the decades after Chinggis Khan.[56] Wives were responsible not only for working with the camp commander, but also for coordinating additional areas of activity that were not under the camp commander's purview, such as some animal care, children's needs, clothing and wardrobe, religious rituals like the mourning of the dead, trade and political advice (both of which will be discussed later). In addition to the camp commander, a set of male and female administrative officers reported to each imperial wife and helped manage her retinue.[57] The activities, equipment, and personnel a woman and her staff had to supervise could be extensive, as shown in a financial decision made by Ghazan (r. 1295–1304) in the Ilkhanate: "funds for the ladies' board, provisions, necessities of wardrobes and mounts would be assured, as would be funds for supplies for the department of potables and stables, for camels and pack horses, and for wages of maids, eunuchs, custodians, kitchen help, caravan drivers, muleteers, and other servants and retinue [of each lady] as necessary."[58] Even concubines formed part of the domestic work force: Marco Polo remarks that concubines on duty at Qubilai's court not only had sex with Qubilai, but also prepared and served food and drink. At the same time, other women spent their time sewing or "cut[ting] out gloves and ... other genteel work."[59]

According to Friar William, one imperial woman might possess 200 wagons of belongings, as well as servants to tend to them.[60] Indeed, one of Chinggis Khan's secondary wives, the Kereit princess Ibaqa, came into

[56] The *amir-i ordo* was a routine post among the Ilkhanids, and could be a commander, or even a lesser Chinggisid (i.e., the son of a concubine). The duties of this officer are not entirely clear; note De Nicola, *Khatuns*, 137–8 and "Ruling from Tents," 131–2. For examples of *amīr-i ordo*s see Chapter 4, footnote 16.

[57] These included female chamberlains. Ibn Baṭūṭah, *Travels*, 485–6.

[58] Rashīd al-Dīn, *Jāmi'*, 1508, trans. Thackston, 746; also Rashīd al-Dīn, "The Third Portion of the History of Gāzān Xān in Rasīdu 'D-Dīn's Ta'rīx-e Mobārak-e Gāzānī," trans. Peter Martinez, *Archivum Eurasiae medii aevi* 6 (1986), 118.

[59] Polo, *Description*, §82.

[60] Rubruck, *Mission*, 74, 114, 131; Ibn Baṭūṭah, *Travels*, 482.

the marriage with at least 200 servants and 2 stewards (and the corresponding wagons), as well as slaves and followers, horses and cattle, and equipment and stores that included golden dishes.[61] Later the Jochid prince Sartaq (r. 1257) married 6 wives, whose wagons numbered 1,200 when gathered together.[62] In China under Qubilai, each of the 4 most important wives had her own dwelling and 300 ladies-in-waiting, male and female servants, and staff to help her manage all this, so that each establishment might number as many as 10,000 people.[63] In the fourteenth century Volga grasslands, each of Özbek's wives attended Friday court ceremonies with 370 attendants.[64] When Özbek's third wife, a Byzantine princess, returned to Constantinople to give birth, she took a retinue of about 500 people (servants and troops), 400 wagons, 2,000 horses, and 500 oxen and camels. Not only was this merely a fraction of her own people, but it did not even include the 5,000 additional warriors her husband sent to escort her.[65] In addition to their immediate retinues, some women controlled peoples given to them as spoils, such as the 3,000 Olqunu'ut subjects that Chinggis Khan gave to his mother, Hö'elün, in 1206, or the Tanguts he bestowed on his wife Yisüi during his final campaign in 1226–7.[66] Women's subjects, dependents and retinues could therefore be numerous, especially among women in the ruling elite. Some visitors to the Mongols were astonished to reach settlements as large as cities, whose inhabitants were mostly female; these were the establishments of imperial women.[67] When a Chinese visitor arrived at Chinggis Khan's home camp in summer 1221, he found an enormous moveable city – "hundreds and thousands of wagons and tents."[68] This was managed by the highest-ranking wife, the Empress (possibly Börte) while

[61] De Nicola, *Khatuns*, 143; *Secret History*, §208; Rashīd al-Dīn, *Jāmi'*, 304, trans. Thackston, 149.
[62] Rubruck, *Mission*, 114.
[63] Polo, *Description*, §82; also De Nicola, *Khatuns*, 133–4, 138.
[64] Ibn Baṭūṭah, *Travels*, 2:484. [65] Ibn Baṭūṭah, *Travels*, 2:498.
[66] For Hö'elün see Chapter 2. For Yisüi see *Secret History*, §268; also Peter Jackson, "From *Ulus* to Khanate: The Making of the Mongol States, c. 1220–c. 1290," in *The Mongol Empire and Its Legacy*, ed. Morgan and Amitai-Preiss (Leiden: Brill, 1999), 19; De Nicola, "Warfare," 105–7.
[67] Rubruck, *Mission*, 74, 100.
[68] Li, *Alchemist*, trans. Waley, 71. Also Noriyuki Shiraishi, "Avraga Site: The 'Great Ordū' of Genghis Khan," in *Beyond the Legacy of Genghis Khan*, ed. Linda Komaroff (Leiden: Brill, 2006), 83–93 and esp. 84.

Chinggis Khan was campaigning thousands of miles to the west, based in a traveling camp run by his junior wife Qulan.[69] Indeed, nomadic men were free to specialize in warfare to such a high degree precisely because nomadic women managed camps with such skill.

ECONOMICS, HOSPITALITY, AND RELIGION

Given women's extensive control of animal, human, and other resources, it comes as no surprise that they were economically important to the families into which they married. Any aristocratic wife acquired through negotiation (not kidnap or capture) had her dowry in livestock, cloth, jewels, household items, and servants. A senior wife also received a portion of her husband's wealth after marriage, often in livestock, which she managed for him during his lifetime and held after his death for their youngest son to inherit.[70] (Junior wives also held part of their husband's wealth, but the amounts relative to the share of the senior wife are unknown.)[71] Thus when a woman emerged from her ger every morning she might gaze on both her own animals and those of her husband; it is probable that she kept close track of which animals were whose over generations of livestock. Women could also employ Muslim, Chinese, or other merchants (*ortaq*s) to act as financial agents and engage in sales, purchases, or investments with capital that the woman supplied. Such merchants furnished women with interest, profits from enterprises, and gifts from third parties.[72] Even as the empire was forming, personal merchants soon became standard among imperial wives.[73] Thus, for example, in 1218 Chinggis Khan ordered all the princesses, princes, and major commanders to send agents with ingots of precious metal to trade in the Khwarazm-Shah Empire.[74]

But other than the dowry, the husbandly grant, and the potentially shrewd uses to which women put these assets, women did not receive a

[69] This was the Western Campaign (1218–23); see Chapter 5.

[70] Holmgren, "Levirate," 129–31; in contrast to Ratchnevsky, "La Femme," 511–2. Also Rossabi, "Women," 155.

[71] Aubin, "Enfant," 547.

[72] Thomas T. Allsen, "Mongolian Princes and Their Merchant Partners, 1200–1260," *Asia Major, 3rd ser.*, 2, no. 2 (1989): 85, 88–9, 91; Elizabeth Endicott-West, "Merchant Associations in Yüan China," in ibid., 129, 132, 140–1; De Nicola, *Khatuns*, 145–9, 153–4.

[73] Rashīd al-Dīn, *Jāmi'*, 1507, trans. Thackston, 745; Allsen, "Merchant Partners," 88–9, 91, 111, 117, 119.

[74] Allsen, "Merchant Partners," 87–92; Endicott-West on merchants as spies in "Merchant Associations," 134.

regular income from men.[75] Instead men provided occasional gifts in the form of spoils from warfare by distributing goods, animals, territories, and peoples both to male followers, and also to wives, mother, sisters, and daughters, not to mention stepmothers, aunts, and daughters-in-law. After Chinggis Khan conquered Northern China, for example, he gave all his wives lands there, which became their own possessions, not his.[76] Similarly in 1219 he parceled out artisans captured at Samarqand to "officers, commanders and ladies."[77] At the quriltais where Grand Khans were elected, the princesses, princes, generals, and administrators were rewarded by the new ruler with handsome gifts.[78] Once the Mongol Empire was established, wives of rulers could expect to receive gifts from subject rulers or their envoys, or from ministers and officials working directly for the Chinggisids.[79] In later decades, imperial women acquired access to tax monies raised from conquered populations.[80] Overall this meant that the female kin of a steppe leader could control herds, deposits of ore or other natural resources, artisans and craftspeople, and even portions of industries.[81]

Yet a wife's duties hardly stopped with the practical matters of managing personnel and exploiting resources. According to a maxim attributed to Chinggis Khan, a wife bore the weighty responsibility of promoting her husband's public reputation by maintaining the hospitality of their home for guests, especially when the husband himself was away.[82] Thus in the case of the Chinese visitor to Mongolia in 1221, the Empress chose her guest's lodging site within the great camp and

[75] Rashid al-Dīn, *Jāmi'*, 1507, trans. Thackston, 745; trans. Martinez, 114–15; Allsen, "Redistribution in the Mongol Empire, Comparisons and Implications" (unpublished article), 6, 11; also Polo, *Description*, §69.

[76] Ratchnevsky, "La Femme," 518; Allsen, "Merchant Partners," 110–1, Rashīd al-Dīn, *Jām'*, 1507, trans. Thackston, 745.

[77] Rashid al-Din, *Jāmi'*, 503, trans. Thackston, 249. Note *Secret History* §215, where Chingiz Khan rewarded his daughters and their offspring, but the text has been excised, probably for political reasons; de Rachewiltz, Commentary, 807. See Chapter 6.

[78] Juvaynī, *World-Conqueror*, 254–5; also De Nicola, *Khatuns*, 150 (gifts).

[79] Carpini, *History*, 39 (not in Rockhill); Allsen, "Redistribution," 13. The Mamluk embassy of the early 1280s to the Jochid Khan Möngke-Temür included gifts for his wives. Muḥyī al-Dīn Ibn 'Abd al-Ẓāhir, *Tashrīf al-Ayyām wa-al-'usūr fī sīrat al-malik al-Manṣūr*, ed. Murād Kāmil (Cairo: al-Sharikah al-'Arabīyah lil-ṭibā'ah wa al-nashr, 1961), 17.

[80] Rashid al-Dīn, *Jāmi'*, 1507–8, trans. Thackston, 745–6; trans. Martinez, 116–18.

[81] Rashid al-Din, *Jāmi'*, 77, trans. Thackston, 43 (Chinggis Khan's daughter-in-law Sorqoqtani trying to exploit silver deposits).

[82] Rashīd al-Dīn, *Jāmi'*, 584, trans. Thackston, 295–6.

demonstrated her hospitality by sending him melted butter and clotted milk every day, while her co-wives, the Jin and Tangut princesses, dispatched gifts of clothing, millet, and cash (silver).[83] Similarly in 1246 it was the wives of the new Grand Khan Güyük (r. 1246–8) who arranged a welcome for Friar Carpini and his companions when they arrived at the imperial camp.[84] Social status and rank further shaped hospitality, just as it did the rest of Mongol society. Thus, when in 1254 Friar William paid calls on Möngke's family, he first met with Möngke and his senior wife in her personal gold-hung ger, went next to Möngke's oldest son, and then called on Möngke's other wives and daughter in order by rank.[85] Ibn Baṭṭuṭah similarly took careful note of seniority while paying his respects to Özbek's wives and daughter in the 1330s.[86] During such visits, wives could favor individuals by giving them bowls of *qumiz* with their own hands, or sitting and looking on while they ate; by contrast, less privileged guests were waited on by servants.[87]

Imperial women also acted as participants in and patrons of religion, whether shamanism, Taoism, Nestorian Christianity, Islam, Tibetan Buddhism, or a combination of several.[88] Women learned not only to practice religion but participate in religious ceremonies, and sometimes preside over them.[89] Some imperial women were known for the portable houses of worship that accompanied them everywhere, while others patronized a range of religions financially.[90] Imperial hostesses also facilitated religious events, as seen in the example of Özbek's daughter, who summoned the Muslim personnel in the camp so that Ibn Baṭṭuṭah and his companions could meet them. Similarly the senior wife of Grand Khan Möngke (r. 1251–9) attended Christian services, then hosted a meal that Friar William attended.[91]

[83] Li, *Alchemist*, trans. Waley, 70–1. [84] Carpini, *History*, 60 and Rockhill, *Journey*, 17.
[85] Rubruck, *Mission*, 192–6. [86] Ibn Baṭūṭah, *Travels*, 487.
[87] Ibn Baṭūṭah was welcomed by Özbek's Muslim wives and given drink from their own hands (Ibn Baṭūṭah, *Travels*, 487, 488), but the less-respected Friar William did not enjoy such personal treatment. Rubruck, *Mission*, 194–6.
[88] See the extensive work of De Nicola, *Khatuns*, Chapter 5.
[89] Temüjin's mother Hö'elün and the Naiman queen Gürbesü were (or tried to be) involved in shamanistic ceremonies. See Chapters 2 and 3; also De Nicola, *Khatuns*, 186.
[90] De Nicola, *Khatuns*, 193 (Dokuz), 208–22 (patronage in the Ilkhanate) and E. W. Budge, *The Monks of Kublai Khan, Emperor of China*, 202; also see Chapter 7 for Sorqoqtani.
[91] Ibn Baṭūṭah, *Travels*, 489; Rubruck, *Mission*, 189–91; Bruno De Nicola, "The Ladies of Rum: A Hagiographic View of Women in Thirteenth- and Fourteenth-Century Anatolia," *Journal of Sufi Studies* 3, no. 2 (2014): 152–3 (the Seljuk example).

Thus it is clear that although in a very small household a woman's duties might not exceed the activities that Friar William described, in larger establishments women had to oversee the coordination of significant resources (herds, flocks, subjects) as well as people (shepherds, stewards, craftspeople, household servants, and armed retainers). It is surely no accident that another of Chinggis Khan's maxims described an ideal steppe girl as not only naturally beautiful without "combs or rouge," but also spry and efficient.[92] Friar Carpini claimed that the reality matched Chinggis Khan's ideal: "In all their tasks they [the women] are very swift and energetic."[93] To keep up with their many responsibilities, they would have to be.

WOMEN, CHILDREN, INHERITANCE, AND SUCCESSION

In addition to the work they performed on a daily basis, women in general and mothers in particular had the potential to shape steppe society through childbearing, childrearing, and inheritance. Although mothers played a central role in bringing up children, childrearing was a joint endeavor shared by all adults.[94] This communal approach was strengthened by existing practices: some mothers sent their children out for extended visits with other branches of the family, while in all cases women with the means to do so employed wet nurses and attendants when children stayed at home.[95] Later during the independent khanates, tutors and religious officials taught the royal young, along with co-wives and others.[96] To gain a better understanding of childrearing in the Mongol period, scholars have combined a modern anthropological approach with careful mining of the historical sources to propose the following: young people seem to have been taught to have a sense of

[92] An ideal boy was brave, manly, wise, and clever. Rashid al-Din, *Jāmiʿ*, 588, trans. Thackston, 299.

[93] Carpini, *History*, 18 (not in Rockhill). [94] Aubin, "Enfant," 504–5.

[95] Princes sent out to stay with other women include Grand Khan Möngke (r. 1251–9), who lived with Ögedei's wife Ang-hui, and the ilkhan Ghazan (r. 1295–304), who lived with his father's wife Bulughan Khatun, not his concubine mother Qultaq. *Yuan Shih*, trans. Abramowsky, 16 (Möngke); Rashīd al-Dīn, *Jāmiʿ*, 1213, trans. Thackston, 592 (Ghazan). Note Sorqoqtani's choice of two different wet nurses (a Naiman and a Tangut) for Qubilai, and the case of two nurses (a Muslim and a Sino-Jurchen) for the later Chinggisid prince Ananda (Bruno De Nicola, "The Role of the Domestic Sphere in the Islamization of the Mongols," in *Islamisation: Comparative Perspectives in History*, ed. A. C. S. Peacock [Edinburgh: Edinburgh University Press, 2017]: 360).

[96] De Nicola, "Domestic Sphere," 361 on the Ilkhanate.

Figure 1.2 The modern game of turtle, Chinggis Khan Monument ger camp museum, Dadal, Mongolia (author's image).

honor, a respect for hierarchy, admiration for elders, and an appreciation for working with others.[97] Children were also encouraged to develop a certain "agility of spirit."[98] This could be achieved through games like chess, which taught strategy; or riddles, which were fun and also helped children learn to use metaphors and metonyms in place of taboo objects (See Figure 1.2).[99] Literature was oral among the Mongols at least until they acquired a script in the 12-aughts thus children not only memorized existing maxims, songs, stories, and epics, but were encouraged to produce new pieces extemporaneously, since the ability to create literature on the spot as occasion demanded was highly valued in steppe society.[100] Children furthermore learned rules, practical advice, and genealogy, which helped them follow the regulations of exogamous marriage.[101] In

[97] Aubin, "Enfant," 507–8.
[98] The phrase is Aubin's in "Enfant," 508.
[99] Aubin, "Enfant," 508–9.
[100] Aubin, "Enfant," 508–9; for adults learning poetry and maxims see Larry V. Clark, "From the Legendary Cycle of Činggis-qaγan: The Story of an Encounter with 300 Tayičiγud from the Altan Tobči (1655)," *Mongolian Studies* 5 (1978/1979): 12–13.
[101] Aubin, "Enfant," 507–9.

addition to these abstract forms of knowledge, children learned how to care for specific animals – goats, sheep, horses, cattle, camels – at specific ages as they themselves matured.[102]

To date, scholars have focused on the way mothers interacted with sons: they have noted that nomadic society expected women to promote peace and cooperation among their boys, and, when the mothers were high in status, rear their sons to be leaders.[103] One mother in Chinggis Khan's family was celebrated by contemporary authors and modern scholars alike for the way she taught her four sons Mongol customs, beliefs, and military practices, as well as the religions, beliefs, and habits of the sedentary peoples they controlled.[104] Certain mothers within the Mongol empire themselves held great political importance: Chinggis Khan's mother, Hö'elün, helped her oldest son establish himself, while others were instrumental in maneuvering their sons onto a throne they should not have held at all.[105]

In literature, including *The Secret History of the Mongols*,[106] mothers appear as responsible for harnessing the tremendous violence expected of males in Mongol society, and directing their sons' aggression outward against enemies, not against one another. The most famous example of such a portrayal was the ancestral Mongol mother, Alan-qo'a, who appeared in the *Secret History* using the example of individual arrows versus arrows tied together to teach her sons that cooperation would make them a force to be reckoned with: "If, like the five arrow-shafts just now, each of you keeps to himself, then, like those single arrow-shafts, anybody will easily break you. If, like the bound arrow-shafts, you remain together and of one mind, how can anyone deal with you so easily?"[107] Scholars caution us to view such stories of mothers and sons as folkloric motifs designed to teach lessons about the high costs of disunity among brothers, not as historical reality.[108] Nevertheless, such stories at least

102 Aubin, "Enfant," 507–9. 103 Ratchnevsky, "La Femme," 510.

104 This was Sorqoqtani, wife of Tolui and mother of Möngke, Qubilai, Hülegü, and Ariq Böke. Rossabi, "Women," 161–2, but see Chapter 7 for an alternate view. Also Rashid al-Din, *Jāmi'*, 791–2, trans. Thackston, 386, trans. Boyle, 169.

105 I.e., Töregene and Sorqoqtani, for whom see Chapters 6 and 7.

106 Anonymous, *The Secret History of the Mongols*, 2 vols., ed. and trans. Igor de Rachewiltz (Leiden: Brill, 2006).

107 *Secret History*, §20–2.

108 Larry Moses, "The Quarrelling Sons in the Secret History of the Mongols," *The Journal of American Folklore* 100, no. 395 (1987): 63–9 and esp. 63–4; he charts this motif in the stories of Temüjin murdering his half-brother Bekter and disputing with his brother Qasar, along with the argument between Chaghatai and Jochi in 1218.

indicate that the author and audience of the *Secret History* were likely to see women as appropriate teachers on moral questions like proper sibling behavior. A later historian, writing without the arrow motif, described another woman in a similar vein: "she exerted herself to raise and educate them [her sons] and teach them skills and manners. She never allowed even an iota of disagreement to come between them."[109]

But scholars of the Mongol empire have paid little attention to the upbringing of girls.[110] Surely, however, steppe women worked as hard at raising their daughters as they did at everything else, since the competent wives, mothers, and widows who crowd Mongol history did not come from nowhere. A close look at the historical sources reveals that traces of their education can indeed be found. Thus Friar William observed women making and breaking camp, driving, cooking, sewing clothes, and tending animals, from which we may deduce that girls learned these activities when young.[111] Since many historical observers saw women riding and shooting, it is logical to assume that girls acquired these skills, too, probably with instruction given the danger involved for a novice – Friar Carpini notes that children began to ride at the age of two or three.[112] If we accept Chinggis Khan's maxim on a wife's duty to provide good hospitality, then we may infer that girls were taught about the proper reception of guests.[113] If we observe that most senior wives used a range of techniques to manage their people, herds, and property – possibly including memorizing their animals' strengths, weaknesses, and bloodlines[114] – then it is reasonable to conjecture that women began to acquire management skills as girls, and further that they probably passed them on to their daughters.[115] The ample evidence we see of women's religious involvement similarly indicates that girls learned to participate in

109 This was Sorqoqtani. Rashīd al-Dīn, *Jāmi'*, 790, trans. Thackston, 386, trans. Boyle, 168.

110 A welcome exception is De Nicola, "Domestic Sphere," 353–76, although even De Nicola must comment more on boys than girls because of the limitations of the sources.

111 Rubruck, *Mission*, 90–1.

112 Carpini, *History*, 18 (not in Rockhill); Rubruck, *Mission*, 89; also Rossabi, "Women," 154; Yoni (Jonathan) Brack, "A Mongol Princess Making *ḥajj*: The Biography of El Qutlugh Daughter of Abagha Ilkhan (r. 1265–82)," *Journal of the Royal Asiatic Society* 21, no. 3 (2011): 333.

113 Rashid al-Din, *Jāmi'*, 584, trans. Thackston, 295–6.

114 On the indispensability of this skill among modern British shepherds see James Rebanks, *The Shepherd's Life: Modern Dispatches from an Ancient Landscape* (New York: Flatiron, 2015), 117–8, 127–8, 153–7, 165–8, 199–200, 259–62, 281–2.

115 On control of property in particular see Holmgren, "Levirate," 152–3.

shamanistic ceremonies and rituals, or those of other religions.[116] In addition, politically successful women had husbands who listened to their advice and rewarded them for it with spoils; they must have figured out how best to advise others, as when Chinggis Khan's Tatar wife Yisügen convinced him to look for her sister and marry her, and when the sister, Yisüi, later persuaded him to make a partial reconstitution of his Tatar enemies.[117]

Another arena in which women played a critical role was that of inheritance, especially succession to a throne. On the steppe, succession was a complex, contrary, and contradictory process: a ruler could be followed by a senior male member of his family (uncles, brothers), a son, grandson or nephew that he chose himself (ruler's choice), or a widow acting as regent for a son.[118] Or the next ruler could be his oldest son (primogeniture) or his youngest (ultimogeniture), as long as their mother was his senior wife – sons of junior wives were not candidates for succession.[119] But Chinggis Khan narrowed the options for succession to his empire by limiting himself to the four sons of his senior wife, Börte, and cutting out his brothers, uncles, and nephews, as well as his sons from junior wives. His descendants similarly preferred their offspring as heirs. Thus whereas the senior wife of any steppe leader knew her sons might inherit rule from their father but had competition from other men in the family, the senior wife of a Chinggisid knew her sons' chances were much better because succession was so limited.[120]

As for daughters: these often married their father's political allies or vassals.[121] One theory is that the great nomadic empires that preceded the Mongols were confederations of various peoples led by rulers who maintained their alliances chiefly through marriage ties.[122] Although Chinggis Khan is widely credited with dismantling the confederation system, he did

[116] De Nicola, *Khatuns*, Chapter 5; Ratchnevsky, "La Femme," 521. [117] See Chapter 3.

[118] Peter Jackson, "The Dissolution of the Mongol Empire," *Central Asiatic Journal* 22 (1978): 186–244, reprinted in Peter Jackson, *Studies on the Mongol Empire and Early Muslim India* (Farnham, Surrey and Burlington, VT: Variorum, 2009), 193–5 (ultimogeniture, primogeniture, and seniority). Ratchnevsky, *Genghis Khan*, 125–6 (all but ruler's choice even though Chinggis Khan favored this method). Juvaynī, *World-Conqueror*, 40 (favoring children based on mother's age); Polo, *Description*, §83; Holmgren, "Levirate," 148–9; De Nicola, *Khatuns*, 50 (women regents).

[119] De Nicola, *Khatuns*, 39; one rare exception was Abaqa (r. 1265–82) in the Ilkhanate. See Chapter 9.

[120] Holmgren, "Levirate," 146–7; 149.

[121] Holmgren, "Levirate," 164–7. Also see Chapter 4.

[122] Miyawaki-Okada, "Imperial Succession," 143.

actually make confederation-style marriages himself, as seen in Chapter 4. It should come as no surprise that the most important of these alliances were reserved for children of his senior wife. Börte's five daughters, all of whose names are known to posterity, made good or even brilliant marriages in terms of wealth and status, and their husbands were important figures or major vassal rulers linked politically to Chinggis Khan.[123] Furthermore, Chinggisid princesses who married vassal lords and produced sons could expect to see their sons succeed to the vassal's throne.[124] Striking examples of the impact of Chinggisid princesses on succession appeared in Korea, first in 1298, when a ruler was deposed for refusing to have sex with his Mongol princess wife, and again in the thirteen-teens, when a Korean king requested three Chinggisid wives in succession, despite the fact that he had sons from other women.[125]

In contrast to the benefits heaped on the children of senior wives, the offspring of junior wives could expect lesser favors, as could the children of concubines. Chinggis Khan's junior children had respectable careers, but they were less brilliant than those of their senior half-siblings, despite claims to the contrary.[126] Daughters of junior wives made good marriages but not brilliant ones, while junior sons enjoyed military careers, but could not even dream of ruling.

WOMEN AND POLITICS

Women and men both played active roles in steppe politics. High-ranking women in particular joined men in the public expression of political

[123] For Börte's daughters see Chapters 2, 4 and 5. [124] Holmgren, "Levirate," 164–7.

[125] These were King Ch'ungsŏn (r. 1298) and King Ch'ungsuk (r. 1313–30, 1332–9). George Q. Zhao, "Control through Conciliation: Royal Marriages between the Mongol Yuan and Koryŏ (Korea) in the 13th and 14th Centuries," *Cultural Interaction and Conflict in Inner and Central Asia* 6 (2004): 3–26 and esp. 4–6, 22–3; Louis Hambis, "Notes sur l'histoire de Corée à l'époque mongole," *T'oung-pao* 45 (1957): 196–201; David M. Robinson, *Empire's Twilight: Northeast Asia under the Mongols* (Cambridge, MA, and London: Harvard University Asia Center for the Harvard-Yenching Institute, 2009), 101–2, 122.

[126] Carpini, *History*, 17 (not in Rockhill), claiming no distinctions between sons of wives or concubines; but Marco Polo, *Description*, §83, applied strict primogeniture to inheritance in Qubilai's family, yet also acknowledges the lesser sons' careers. Herbert Franke argues that nomadic children of wives or concubines had equal status, which contradicts the specific Mongol examples. Franke, "Dynasties of Conquest," 37. But Rossabi, "Women," 155, acknowledges that children of lesser wives or concubines received smaller inheritances, while Zhao, *Marriage*, 74, cites the *Yuan Shi* that sons of concubines should not inherit the throne.

power by attending and participating in political ceremonies, while decrees could be issued jointly through the authority of a man and his wife or wives.[127] Many women made strategic marriages and thereby participated in networks of personal and political connection, as will be discussed shortly. Women with access to political information could use it to advise others or shape policy. Finally, and as mentioned previously, women managed the essential activities of everyday life, which allowed men to engage in their specialties of raiding and war.

Women in the Mongol Empire and the successor khanates participated most visibly in politics at formal ceremonies like quriltais, coronations, and receptions of ambassadors. Visitors particularly noted the presence of women at official gatherings. As elsewhere in Mongol life, physical space was assigned to each gender: men sat to the right of the ruler, women to the left. Usually all of an important man's wives attended these ceremonies, but only the senior wife sat next to her husband, often on a raised dais, while the others sat below on designated benches or other seats.[128] (See Figure 1.3.) Thus for example the senior wife of the Jochid prince Sartaq received Friar William with her husband, and together they examined an incense burner and psalter that Friar William showed them.[129] Other women present at political events could be the daughters, sisters, aunts, and mothers of important men.[130] Ambassadors also routinely met with women independently from their meeting with the ruler, and might be given food, drink, and gifts by the wife or her servants.[131] In later centuries, nomadic wives usually received diplomats a few days before their menfolk. It has been suggested that the women were vetting the visitors in order to help men prepare for a later audience.[132] Unfortunately the existing information is too scant to tell us whether there was a Mongol precedent to this behavior.

Women also attended informal political meetings: if a man discussed politics inside any ger other than his own ceremonial pavilion, the ger

[127] See footnote 138. [128] Rubruck, *Mission*, 210, 132; Ibn Battuta, *Travels*, 483.
[129] Rubruck, *Mission*, 117.
[130] Juvaynī, *World-Conqueror*, 184–8, 249–52; Carpini, *History*, 64–5, trans. Rockhill, 24; Rashīd al-Dīn, *Jāmiʿ*, 839, trans. Thackston, 409, trans. Boyle, *Successors*, 215 (Chinggis Khan's sisters-in-law at the 1251 quriltai).
[131] Carpini met Töregene separately from Güyük in *History*, 61, 65, 69, trans. Rockhill 19, 26, 30; Friar William met Möngke's wives in *Mission*, 190, 195–6, 204 (wives giving presents). Also Brack, "Mongol Princess," 340–7.
[132] Tom Allsen, referring to Muscovite diplomatic reports in the sixteenth to eighteenth centuries, covering the Noghai, Kalmuks and Khalka khanates, email correspondence, summer 2016.

Figure 1.3 A recreation of a man's and woman's thrones with wolfskins, Chinggis Khan Monument ger camp museum, Dadal, Mongolia (author's image).

always belonged to a wife, who would be there waiting on (or directing servants to wait on) her husband and his guest as well as participating in or listening to their conversation. In this way women's roles in hospitality could involve them in politics. One such highly informal interaction took place between Temüjin and his youngest brother Temüge when the latter burst in late at night after a set-to with the shaman Kököchü. Since Temüjin was in Börte's ger, she participated in the conversation.[133]

Some women were therefore well-positioned to gain valuable knowledge of politics, personalities, and current events, which they could then use to advantage. But women rarely seem to have employed their political acumen openly for themselves; rather, historical and literary evidence suggests that they shared their ideas with men, many of whom deliberately sought out and followed women's advice.[134] Thus on one occasion Temüjin asked both his mother and wife about a cryptic comment that his friend Jamuqa had made, and decamped with all his followers as a result

[133] See Chapter 2. [134] Tom Allsen, email correspondence; also De Nicola, *Khatuns*, 38.

of Börte's political advice.[135] Similarly both Hö'elün and Börte provided important political analyses and advice when Temüjin faced rivals, while the Tatar wife Yisüi is credited with convincing Temüjin to settle the question of succession to his throne.[136]

In addition to acting as advisors to their immediate contacts, women could interact extensively with a wide range of political players. A description of the Chinggisid princess Kelmish Aqa illuminates the networking practices of a politically active Chinggisid woman:

Toqta [of the Jochids, (r. 1291–1312)] and the other princes hold her in a position of great importance. Since she is the offspring of [Chinggis Khan's son] Tolui Khan, she shows a constant affection to the Padishah of Islam [Ghazan in Iran (r. 1295–1304)] and continually sends emissaries to inform him of events that transpire in that realm. It is due to her that friendship has been maintained and strife and enmity avoided between Toqta and Jochi's Khan's other offspring and Tolui Khan's house. When [Qubilai's son] Nomoghan was surprised and seized by his cousins and sent to Möngke-Temür, the ruler of Jochi Khan's *ulus* [land and peoples], Kelmish Aga exerted herself to have him sent back to his father with honor in the company of some of the princes and great amirs [commanders].[137]

Nevertheless, few women ruled openly, and then only under certain circumstances. As noted above, more often women shared rule with their husbands by participating in government and enjoying inclusion on official decrees, most clearly among the fourteenth-century Golden Horde, Chaghatayids, and Ilkhanids.[138] Or, when a lesser Chinggisid or other important Mongol man died, his widow could administer his personal territory and continued to receive his revenues, income, gifts, and other resources.[139] A third possibility was for a woman to rule as a regent on behalf of a son for a limited period of time. This was the case for Börte's third daughter, Alaqa, who governed Öng'üt territory for a son; for Töregene, who ran the entire empire after Ögedei's death until enthroning her own son Güyük; and for Chinggis Khan's granddaughter, Orqīna, who ruled the Chaghatayid Khanate for a decade, also on behalf of a young son.[140]

[135] See Chapter 2. [136] See Chapters 2 and 4.

[137] Rashid al-Din, *Jāmi'*, 779–80, trans. Thackston, 382, trans. Boyle, 160.

[138] al-'Umarī, *Masālik*, 67, trans. Lech, 136.

[139] Carpini, *History*, 60, and trans. Rockhill, 17, on Orda's widow running his territory. See also Chapter 8.

[140] See Chapter 5 for Alaqa, Six for Töregene and Eight for Orqīna; also De Nicola, *Khatuns*, 50; Carole Hillenbrand, "Women in the Saljuq Period," in *Women in Islam: From the Rise of Islam to 1800*, ed. G. Nashat and L. Beck (Urbana, IL: University of Illinois Press, 2003), 114–15 (Seljuk women).

Women also contributed to steppe politics by marrying the allies of their menfolk. Typically men formed certain kinds of alliances and friendships with other men. When enough such relationships were established among individuals, families, or lineages, larger organizations could result, among them confederations, as outlined above. But although scholars have focused on the political links among men, it is vital to remember that in most confederations these male alliances were matched by marriage ties between the two sides, which equally helped hold confederations together.[141]

This was the realm of in-laws. Among the Mongols, the word *quda* referred to in-laws in a general sense: when negotiating the marriage between Temüjin and his senior wife Börte, for example, the fathers in question, Yisügei and Dei Sechen, referred to one another as *quda*.[142] (A son-in-law earned a special name: *küregen*.)[143] The relationship of *quda* was one of mutual affection and assistance between the marital partners, and between their families. In this way it differed from other forms of political alliances between men, which only linked individuals.[144] Marriage negotiations were conducted with the assumption that both sides would benefit from the match, especially if the families involved had political standing.[145] Some benefits were long-term, as when a woman married a man expected to hold political power in the future. This was the case when the previously mentioned leader Dei Sechen engaged his daughter Börte to the young Temüjin, who could be expected to take over his father Yisügei's position as war leader.[146] Other benefits were more immediate, such as when the Kereit leader Jaqa Gambu married his loveliest daughter to the Tangut ruler Weiming Renxiao (r. 1140–93, Renzong) in return for immediate status in Tangut lands, or when Jaqa Gambu's brother Ong Qan matched his own daughter, Huja'ir, with the Merkit leader Toqto'a in return for protection in exile.[147] At other times marriage obligations could be perilous – the Mongol-Tatar feud that shaped Temüjin's early life began as a disagreement between the

[141] Miyawaki-Okada, "Imperial Succession," 143; also De Nicola, *Khatuns*, 40; C. Hillenbrand, "Women," 108.

[142] *Secret History*, §62–3, §65–6; Atwood, "Quda," Encyclopedia, 460–1.

[143] Rashīd al-Dīn / Thackston, glossary, 767; Doerfer, *Neupersischen*, entry 340.

[144] Chih-Shu Eva Cheng, "Studies in the Career of Chinggis Qan" (PhD dissertation, School of Oriental and African Studies, University of London, 1996), 212–7.

[145] Cheng, "Career," 217; Ratchnevsky, "La Femme," 511.

[146] Cheng, "Career," 218.

[147] Cheng, "Career," 43, 219.

Qonggirats and the Tatars, not the Mongols, but expanded to include the Mongols because of their in-law connections with the Qonggirats.[148]

Particularly among political families, strategic marriages created a network of female and male informants across a confederation, whose loyalties were multiple and complex, and who were well-positioned to gather political information and send it where it could be useful.[149] Women could therefore draw on their birth families, their children, and sons- or daughters-in-law, and even their co-wives for information. Thus, for example, Temüjin's divorced Kereit wife Ibaqa traveled to Mongolia from China each year to consult with her sister Sorqoqtani, host parties for the major political players in the realm, and confirm her political and social connections at the heart of the empire.[150] Women with rank, privilege, and wealth also controlled additional networks of servants, staff and retainers. The daughters of such women must have learned both political savvy and the best ways to express political advice from their mothers, grandmothers (and perhaps stepmothers), then later applied them as situations warranted.

A nomadic lord could use the in-law relationship and the networks it created to promote and maintain his own power. One simple way to do this was to make a political subordinate into a son-in-law, which honored him, elevated him politically, and also guaranteed his service. Chinggis Khan did this with his Turkic sons-in-law from Qara-Khitai territory in 1211.[151] Less benevolently, a strong nomadic ruling family might seek to control the people ruled by the lineage into which it had married. This was the secret fear of Ong Khan of the Kereits when Temüjin proposed a double marriage between their families: the Kereits had endured unwanted in-law meddling before, and so Ong Khan saw the matches as a prelude to a takeover and refused to cooperate. Temüjin soon proved these fears to be well-grounded when he conquered the Kereit people and subjugated its rulers, albeit without the sanction of the in-law connection that he himself had suggested.[152]

[148] Cheng suggests that the feud began with the Mongol Qabul Qan, whose sister married the Qonggirat Sayin-Tekin. When the Qonggirats attacked the Tatars over a shaman's failure to cure Sayin-Tekin's illness, Qabul Qan participated as a brother-in-law, which sparked the Mongol-Tatar feud. Cheng, "Career," 214–15.

[149] Cheng, "Career," 212, 223 (an "eyes and ears" network).

[150] See Chapter 3.

[151] See Chapters 4 and 5.

[152] See Chapter 2; also Cheng, "Career," 20–7 (the precedent-setting earlier takeover); Togan, *Flexibility and Limitation*, 69–70.

Later, Chinggis Khan used the ties of obligation and affection enshrined in the in-law relationship to bring other nomadic or semi-nomadic peoples, like the Öng'üts, Oirats, Uighurs, and Qarluqs under his control without actually having to conquer them; unlike in the case of the Kereits, however, he left their subject people and their realms intact.[153] These "conquests" took place through the marriages of Chinggis Khan's daughters and granddaughters to these rulers, which made the brides into general managers of people, property, and resources for their princely husbands, according to steppe custom. These women were thus perfectly positioned to act both as local informants for Chinggis Khan, and as political advisors for their husbands, while their husbands gained political rights and privileges among the Chinggisids.[154] This reliance on the political network formed by in-law or consort families became business-as-usual throughout Mongol territory; indeed, after the Mongols were driven out of China in 1368, their Ming successors implemented a policy of restricting the activities, power, and influence of in-law families, which may have been a response to Chinggisid customs.[155]

WOMEN'S LOYALTIES

Whereas steppe women's marriages, work, and childrearing have commanded some scholarly attention, no attention has yet been paid to the larger question of women's mental energy, especially their loyalty, its focus, and the way it affected their behavior. The historical sources and literature mention loyalty in passing, usually when praising a woman for demonstrating it in a socially acceptable way. Thus the mother who worked herself to the bone for her children, the senior wife who remained sexually faithful to her husband, or the junior wife who advised her husband wisely were directly or indirectly lauded as exemplars of women's loyalty and its proper expression.[156] But the realities of women's experiences, and the ways they actually behaved, suggest that their real loyalties were far more complex than has been previously assumed.

[153] Cheng, "Career," 226. See also Chapter 5. [154] See Chapters 4 and 5.

[155] This began in 1425. Although the author overlooks the Yuan dynasty, it is reasonable to assume that the Ming knew of Mongol practices. E. Soulliere, "Imperial Marriages of the Ming Dynasty," *Papers on Far Eastern History* 37 (1988): 20.

[156] *Secret History*, §73–5, §254; Rashid al-Din, *Jāmi'*, 71–2, 94, 299–300, trans. Thackston, 41, 53, 146.

It is helpful first to consider women whose loyalties were straightforward, that is, women who grew up in one family, married into another, and bore children, all without encountering abduction, captivity, rape, violence, or other hardship along the way. Scholarship on nomadic marriage has suggested that the bride price system limited married women's contact with their birth families, since once the bride price was paid the woman was no longer her family's responsibility; the levirate only exacerbated this situation, since a widow was a concern for her in-laws alone.[157] The resulting conclusion is that a married woman's loyalty was directed solely at her immediate family – her husband and children. Or was it? In contrast to scholarly claims, the historical sources suggest that daughters of steppe leaders maintained a sense of responsibilities that extended beyond their own wifely households to the peoples their parents ruled; that is, they retained their loyalty to their birth families and subjects even after marriage, and even as they developed new loyalties to their husbands and children. A famous poetic passage from the *Secret History* suggests that a well-placed steppe wife was entrusted not just with managing her husband's wealth and their family, but with protecting her own parents, kin, and people. The passage describes Qonggirat women, who were famed for their beauty:

> With us, the Qonggirat people, from old days,
> To have the good looks of our granddaughters
> And the beauty of our daughters is enough:
> We do not strive for dominion …
> We lift our good-looking daughters,
> We have them ride on a carriage with front seat;
> We harness a dark male camel,
> We lead them off to the qa'an,
> And seat them on the throne, at his side.
> From old days, the Qonggirat people
> Have the qatuns as shields,
> Have their daughters as intercessors.[158]

These lines imply that a woman who married a leader was expected to keep her family and people in mind even after she rode off to a new

[157] Birge, *Confucian Reaction*, 204–5; Holmgren, "Levirate," 151–2.

[158] *Secret History*, §64, de Rachewiltz, Commentary, 332; Isenbike Togan, "The Qongrat in History," in *History and Historiography of Post-Mongol Central Asia and the Middle East: Studies in Honor of John E. Woods*, ed. Judith Pfeiffer, Sholeh A. Quinn, and Ernest Tucker (Wiesbaden: Harrassowitz, 2006), 70–2; see also the *Altan Tobci*, 12–13.

life, regardless of the mechanics of bride price or levirate.[159] Accordingly, then, even if a woman had only limited contact with her birth family after her marriage, out of sight was not supposed to mean out of mind.

Additional Chinggisid examples suggest that women in advantageous positions might continue to interact with their families after marriage, sometimes extensively. Although the tremendous political power Chinggis Khan wielded after 1206 certainly facilitated the abilities of his wives or mother to contact their families, it was not the only factor at play, since concepts of loyalty to birth family joined Mongol preferences for exchange marriages with a wife's relatives. One example was Temüjin's mother Hö'elün, whose relatives were not even on terms with her kidnapper husband Yisügei. Nevertheless, Yisügei deliberately chose Hö'elün's Olqunu'ut family as the one in which to find a wife for their son Temüjin, and the patterns of exchange marriage suggest that the bride would have been one of Hö'elün's close relatives.[160] Although ultimately Temüjin's bride (Börte) came from the Qonggirats instead of the Olqunu'uts, Yisügei's original intent might have enabled Hö'elün to reestablish contact with her family. Later after Yisügei's death, Hö'elün's youngest son, Temüge, did marry an Olqunu'ut woman, which Hö'elün probably helped arrange.[161] Thereafter Chinggis Khan's unique position further supported Hö'elün's renewed contact with her people, since he gave her the Olqunu'ut subjects to command in 1206; at the same time her male relatives became commanders of a thousand in Chinggis Khan's army and married among Chinggis Khan's junior daughters.[162]

Börte also interacted with her family after marriage, although the Qonggirats profited far more from Börte's position than the Olqunu'uts did from that of Hö'elün. Although we know nothing about Börte's early contact with her people, the Qonggirat submission to Temüjin in 1203 certainly facilitated her (re-) connection to her relatives. Thereafter Chinggis Khan made some of Börte's male kin into commanders of a thousand in his army.[163] He and Börte also married one daughter to a

[159] De Rachewiltz, Commentary, 332, interprets this as "when the daughters and granddaughters of the Onggirat [Qonggirat] marry powerful chiefs and become *qatuns* they serve as shields against the Onggirat's enemies; and by the requests they make to their husbands, they obtain favors for the Onggirat."

[160] Uno, "Exchange-Marriage," 179–80.

[161] Rashid al-Din, *Jāmiʿ*, 280, trans. Thackston, 137.

[162] See Chapters 2, 4, and 5.

[163] *Secret History*, §176 (Qonggirat submission); Ratchnevsky, *Genghis Khan*, 86; also see Chapter 4.

Qonggirat man (a nephew or adopted nephew), and two sons to Qonggirat women.[164] It is reasonable to assume that both families were involved in the negotiations, and that both attended the weddings and the installment of the brides with their new husbands. Later the Qonggirats became the most important consort lineage for the Chinggisids, which further facilitated exchange between the families.[165]

Additional examples of contact between steppe wives and their birth families include those of Chinggis Khan's daughters who left Mongolia once they married.[166] Some of these women may well have encountered their father again during his conquests, since the Mongol armies crossed their territories, and their husbands joined Chinggis Khan's forces with their own warriors.[167] The princesses who married among Chinggis Khan's own followers were even more likely to see their natal family, since their husbands continued to work for their father.[168] Furthermore, even when a Chinggisid woman held the uneasy role of representing the Golden Lineage in a vassal country, as in Korea beginning in the 1260s, princesses were able to go back home for visits (in the Korean case, to Yuan China).[169]

But it is even more likely that women maintained multiple loyalties in cases where their lives were interrupted by hardship, despite the fact that these loyalties are harder to prove. Particularly in the violent and chaotic period before the rise of Chinggis Khan, steppe women were especially vulnerable to capture, rape, or other trauma. For a captured wife or daughter, then, where was her loyalty to go? In theory, to her new husband, even if he had just had her family and people killed. In reality, who can say? We cannot know the thoughts of people from such a different world, and the historical sources breathe no word of conflicts raging within these women's minds. But they were still humans as we are, and we can at least imagine that some captives may have harbored anger, resentment, or hatred. Many of Chinggis Khan's own women in the early years were daughters of conquered peoples, among them his wives Qulan, Ibaqa, Yisüi, and Yisügen, as well as the Jin and Tangut princesses, while conquered women who married his sons and grandsons included Töregene, Oghul Qaimish, and Sorqoqtani.[170] Unfortunately the historical sources, and the scholars, have generally not thought even to question

[164] See Chapters 4, 5 and 8.
[165] Zhao, *Marriage*, 94, 99, 101–18 especially tables 3, 4 and marriage lists 1, 2.
[166] See Chapter 4. [167] See Chapter 5. [168] See Chapters 4 and 5.
[169] Hambis, "Corée," 180, 186, 203; see also Zhao, "Conciliation," 3–26.
[170] See Chapters 6 and 7.

where these women's hearts lay, or have assumed that their husbands or their children became their all.[171]

A clear example of women's contested loyalties does appear in the case of Chinggis Khan's Tatar wives, Yisüi and Yisügen, who went to Temüjin as part of the spoils when he annihilated the Alchi Tatars in 1202. As daughters of a leader, the sisters became Chinggis Khan's wives, not concubines; they then used their position to help those Tatars left alive. They contrived to rescue a few survivors almost immediately, then later maneuvered to gather the others in a remarkable, albeit extremely partial, reconstitution of their destroyed people.[172] The sisters thus maintained a sense of responsibility to their former subjects, alongside their new responsibilities in the households they were forced to establish with Chinggis Khan.

It is therefore essential to consider the question of women's mental energy, and particularly their loyalty, in order to understand their lives in nomadic society. The wide varieties in women's experiences, and the specifics of their behavior, suggest that their loyalties were multiple, complex, and sometimes hidden. Although the scholarly assertion that women were cut off from their families after marriage may be useful as a general rule, it must be tempered by the reality of measurable contact between a woman and her people, as shown in many Chinggisid examples.

CONCLUSION

Before we turn to specific women in the Mongol empire, it has been vital to investigate the general realities of steppe women's lives. This investigation has focused on married women, since it was particularly after marriage and childbirth that women were best positioned to exercise their powers. They then spent their lives engaged in a tremendous variety of activities: caring for animals, raising children, supervising workers of many kinds, and carefully husbanding or exploiting the human, animal, or other resources they controlled. Women were an economic mainstay for the families into which they married, and bore heavy responsibilities. Without their logistical, managerial, and economic contributions, to say nothing of their daily labor, steppe life could not have functioned: men

[171] One exception is Rossabi, who posits Sorqoqtani's difficult relationship to her husband, "Women," 160.

[172] See Chapter 3.

would not have been free to raid, or to fight, or even hunt, and the histories of the great steppe empires would be very, very short. In what follows we will examine the individual women important in the life of the greatest empire-builder of them all, Chinggis Khan, and will consider their unique contributions to Mongol history in the specific light of their womanly training, abilities, world-view, and circumstances.

2

Hö'elün and Börte

Although historians have focused on Temüjin's rise to the position of Chinggis Khan in 1206 and his astonishing conquests until his death in 1227, his womenfolk had their own narratives, which illuminated and shaped Temüjin's better-known one. Women were numerous in Temüjin's life, but two towered above the others in their contributions to his success: his mother, Hö'elün, and his senior wife, Börte. By focusing on the intertwined lives of these two women, this chapter illuminates their participation in Temüjin's career, and the larger roles they played in Mongol history. Investigating the particulars of their experiences also illuminates certain critical themes: women's need for resilience in hard circumstances and the toll those circumstances took on them, the social and economic problems caused by irregular kidnap marriages, the question of wealth in Temüjin's family and its relationship to his political career, and the way different kinds of women's work – logistical, economic, advisorial, reproductive – were essential to his rise. Hö'elün and Börte also shaped Temüjin's life by participating, albeit unwillingly, in a saga of kidnap and retribution entwined with the Merkit people, the political, military, social and familial repercussions of which affected several generations.

HÖ'ELÜN: THE KIDNAPPED WIFE AND TENACIOUS MOTHER

The first woman in Temüjin's life was his mother, Hö'elün. A retelling of her story here demonstrates that she possessed a notable resilience, which enabled her to survive a life filled with difficulties, but it also shows that

Figure 2.1 The modern statue of Hö'elün across from the monumental Chinggis Khan equestrian statue, Mongolia (author's image).

her irregular marriage to Temüjin's father through kidnap caused long-term social and economic weaknesses for her and her children, as well as political and military repercussions for later generations. Furthermore, the details of Hö'elün's tribulations are found largely in the *Secret History*, and are at best just barely corroborated by other sources. Because the *Secret History* contains poetry and elements of epic along with what we might discern as actual history, we must therefore interrogate every episode carefully in order to extract useful ideas about Hö'elün's life from it. (See Figure 2.1.)

Hö'elün has been described as possessing a strong will, great determination, clear awareness of responsibility, and, at times, a flashing temper. She emerged in the historical record as an unusually beautiful young Olqunu'ut woman whose parents arranged a good marriage for her to Yeke Chiledü, a brother to the Merkit leader Toqto'a. This means that

Chiledü's family negotiated properly for her and paid an appropriate bride price. Chiledü may have spent time living with his parents-in-law. He and Hö'elün are likely to have wed in a formal ceremony complete with rituals, poetry, and festive refreshments.[1] At the time, Hö'elün was perhaps fifteen years old.[2] But after the wedding, while Hö'elün and Chiledü were traveling from her home to his, they were attacked by hunters – Yisügei and his brothers from the Borjigin people – who abducted Hö'elün because of her striking looks and physical indications of fertility.[3] A poetic description shows the spirit and initiative for which Hö'elün later became known: she is said to have given Chiledü her scent-imbued shirt to remember her by, then urged him to flee since their attackers would kill him, but not her.[4]

Yisügei brought Hö'elün back to his camp and "took [her] into his tent" as a wife.[5] This method of bride acquisition was known in the steppe in this period, but was nevertheless irregular and unsanctioned by the bride's family. It must have contrasted markedly with the formal wedding festivities Hö'elün had just undergone with the approved groom who had paid her family a proper bride price.[6] Yisügei's kidnap marriage thus created a weakness for Hö'elün and, later, her offspring: no evidence suggests that her new husband ever reconciled with her family (or even met them), and perhaps as a result she was not in a position to call on her relatives for support when she needed it, or to even contact them, for years.

In Yisügei's camp, Hö'elün discovered that her new husband already had a woman, the mother of his oldest son, Bekter, who later bore

[1] Henry Serruys, "Four Manuals for Marriage Ceremonies among the Mongols, Part I," *Zentralasiatische Studien* 8 (1974): 247–331. In *Secret History*, §155, the wealthy family of the Tatar princess Yisüi, "a bridegroom for her (Yisüi) was taken into our family as a son-in-law." If we surmise that they did not even consider an impoverished man, then in some cases, living with a bride's parents may have allowed a man simply to come to know them before departing with their daughter.

[2] Louis Hambis, "Un episode mal connu de l'histoire de Gengis-Khan," *Journal des Savants* (January–March 1975): 3–46.

[3] *Secret History*, §54; the more practical *Altan Tobchi*, §11, says that the hunters saw a spot where Hö'elün had peed on the ground and deduced from the color that she would bear strong sons (!).

[4] *Secret History*, §54–6, and de Rachewiltz, Commentary, 508–9.

[5] *Secret History*, §56.

[6] Sławoj Szynkiewicz, "On Kinship Symbolics among the Western Mongols," in *Religious and Lay Symbolism in the Altaic World and Other Papers. Proceedings of the 27th Meeting of the Permanent International Altaistic Conference, Wlaberberg, Germany, June 12–16, 1984*, ed. Klaus Sagaster and Helmut Eimer (Wiesbaden: Harrassowitz, 1989): 379–85.

another, Belgütei.[7] Nevertheless, Hö'elün became the senior wife for reasons that are not entirely clear. Perhaps it was the respectability of her status and training, which we may deduce from the fact that Chiledü's family had requested her as the wife for a ruler's brother, that made Yisügei now think she would be a better mother for his children and manager of his camp than the other woman, whose upbringing and abilities are unknown.[8]

In the camp Hö'elün also met other important figures, who shared in her struggles after Yisügei's death and later became key supporters for Temüjin. These were Charaqa of the Qongqotan, a family retainer, and his adult son Mönglik. One scholar highlights the way researchers have generally overlooked questions of women and family by suggesting that Charaqa and Mönglik were not just servants – as they usually appear – but rather that they enjoyed a special relationship to Yisügei because of an unrecorded marriage between Mönglik and a sister or half-sister of Yisügei. Some of the evidence for this theory can be found in the fact that Yisügei's family addressed Charaqa with the respectful epithet of *ebügen* (forefather, ancestor, old man, elder[9]), which could be understood as "grandfather" and indicate an elderly in-law.[10] If so, then this family connection might explain both men's later behavior: Charaqa's support of Hö'elün, and Mönglik's complex relationships with both Hö'elün and Temüjin (see the following discussion in this chapter).

After her arrival, the teenaged Hö'elün faced the first test of her noted resilience. She was at first very much alone, cut off as she was from both her first husband and her parents. Perhaps she wondered about Chiledü. Despite his brother's important position among the Merkit, however, he never tried to rescue the bride for whom he had negotiated and paid, and married in a formal ceremony with proper observances. Did Yisügei's reputation as a warrior dissuade them from attack? If so, the crime was nevertheless not forgotten, and the Merkits later sought vengeance. In this way, Hö'elün's kidnap became the catalyst for a chain of events that stretched long past Yisügei's lifetime

[7] Ratchnevsky cites Pelliot naming this woman as Suchigu, but himself suggests the servant Qoaqchin (who appears in *Secret History*, §98). Ratchnevsky, *Genghis Khan:* 15–16 and note 95, without clear reference to Pelliot's work.

[8] The other woman's marriage to an ordinary Merkit (see the subsequent discussion of the Merkit raid in this chapter), not a leader, implies that she was not high in status.

[9] Hambis, "Episode," 31; de Rachewiltz, Commentary, 236, 339, 489 for the translation.

[10] Hambis, "Episode," 35–6.

and into subsequent generations, touching Hö'elün's son Temüjin, his wife and their children, as well as countless Merkit subjects. Rather than being a mere poetic passage in the *Secret History*, therefore, Hö'elün's kidnap demonstrates the long-term social weaknesses caused by the irregular acquisition of women in this period: anger and a desire for revenge (among the Merkits) and a lack of communication (between Hö'elün and her Olqunu'ut relatives).

We do not know how soon Hö'elün adjusted to living with a husband whom neither she nor her parents had approved. But we may assume that she immediately had enough work to occupy herself: as senior wife she took up authority over the household and hearth, and she would have been in a position to direct the other woman, servants, and retainers. Also as senior wife, Hö'elün probably received a portion of Yisügei's wealth to manage in the form of herds. Nevertheless, it is unclear that she ever collected any dowry in animals, cloth, and jewelry, which would have been intended for her marriage with Chiledü.[11] If not, then this points to the economic problems of irregular kidnap unions, which compounded the social problems mentioned previously.

At the time of Hö'elün's kidnap, the Mongols were engaged in a long-standing feud with their Tatar neighbors to the east. The Tatars were numerous, and their leaders' control of silver deposits, and their position as vassals to the Jurchen dynasty of the Jin in Northern China, made them both wealthy and powerful. Although the Mongols sought to rival the Tatars, a series of largely unsuccessful struggles between the two left the Mongols without leadership, but with an axe to grind.[12] Hö'elün's new husband was among those who participated in the feud, and he named their first son Temüjin after a Tatar leader he had defeated.[13] The infant was said to have emerged clutching a blood clot the size of a knucklebone in his hand; in Asian folkloristic belief, this indicated future

[11] See Chapter 1, footnote 4.

[12] Ratchnevsky, *Genghis Khan*, 4–5; Ruth Dunnell, *Chinggis Khan: World Conqueror* (Boston: Longman), 16–18, 20. Rashīd al-Dīn, *Jāmi'*, 80–3, 252–9, trans. Thackston, 45, 128 (the feud); *Secret History*, §53; also De Nicola, *Khatuns*, 40.

[13] This was Temüjin Üge. *Secret History*, §59; Anonymous (2), *Historie des campagnes de Gengis Khan: Cheng wou ts-in-tcheng lou*, trans. and ed. Paul Pelliot and Louis Hambis (Leiden: E J. Brill, 1951), §1. Clark argues that this name made Temüjin a "living memorandum" of the Mongol-Tatar feud. Larry V. Clark, "The Theme of Revenge in the *Secret History of the Mongols*," in *Aspects of Altaic Civilization II: Proceedings of the XVIII PIAC, Bloomington, June 29–July 5, 1975*, ed. Larry V. Clark and Paul Alexander Draghi (Bloomington, IN: Asian Studies Research Institute, Indiana University, 1978), 36. Also Dunnell, *Chinggis Khan*, 20.

Figure 2.2 The birth of a Mongol prince. Staatsbibliothek zu Berlin-Prussischer Kulturbesitz, Orientabteilung. Diez Album, fol. 70, S. 8.

greatness.[14] Scholars disagree on the date of Temüjin's birth, with one school preferring 1162 and another favoring 1167; this book will use 1162[15] (see Figure 2.2). Yisügei and Hö'elün went on to have four more children, for a total of five in nine years. These were four sons: Temüjin, Jochi-Qasar, Qachi'un, and Temüge, and a daughter, Temülün.[16] For companionship Hö'elün's children had their half-brothers, Bekter and Belgütei, the seven sons of Mönglik and his unnamed wife, and the children of Yisügei's Tayichi'ut followers. Hö'elün seems to have appreciated the presence of children: she is credited with adopting and raising orphan boys who later served her son. Although some scholars dismiss this as an epic literary trope, this seems unnecessary: these orphans did in fact become important

[14] For the blood clot see *Secret History*, §59, §78; Anonymous (2), *Campagnes*, trans. Pelliot and Hambis, §1; Rashīd al-Dīn, *Jāmi'*, 310–1, trans. Thackston, 152. For the folklore motif see Jagchid and Hyer, *Culture and Society*, 75; de Rachewiltz, Commentary, 321; Dunnell, *Chinggis Khan*, 21.

[15] See the discussion in de Rachewiltz, Commentary, 320–1, 410–1; also Peter Jackson, *The Mongols and the Islamic World: From Conquest to Conversion* (New Haven, CT: Yale University Press, 2017), 63; for 1167 see Ratchnevsky, *Genghis Khan*, 17–19 and esp. 18; Dunnell, *Chinggis Khan*, 21.

[16] *Secret History*, §60.

companions for Temüjin, and raising them would have accorded with the Mongol belief that abandoned children were gifts from the Sky.[17]

TEMÜJIN'S MARRIAGE AND YISÜGEI'S DEATH

When Temüjin was old enough for an engagement (nine), Yisügei and Hö'elün invoked the steppe tradition of exchange marriage, in which children married out of their father's family but into their mother's kin. This tradition indicated that they should seek a wife for Temüjin among Hö'elün's Olqunu'ut relatives.[18] Yisügei thus had no qualms about approaching Hö'elün's parents, despite having wrested her from the husband they had approved, and failing ever to pay a bride price. Or did he? The *Secret History* notes that Yisügei and Temüjin set out to meet the Olqunu'ut. (Hö'elün stayed at home to run the camp despite her actual connections to her relatives.) But on the way the travelers chanced upon a group from the Qonggirats, the parent people to which the Olqunu'ut belonged, and as a result never completed their journey to Hö'elün's people.[19]

According to the *Secret History*, the encounter that ensued was dramatic: the Qonggirat leader, Dai Sechen, inquired about Yisügei's purpose for traveling. Upon hearing it, he revealed that the previous night he had dreamed auspiciously of a white falcon that brought him the sun and moon. He suggested that the dream foretold Yisügei's arrival with his son, noted that Qonggirat girls were beautiful enough to marry steppe leaders, and proposed that Yisügei consider his ten-year-old daughter, Börte, as a bride for Temüjin. After further discussion, in which the fathers agreed their children had "fire in their eyes and light in their faces," Yisügei let Dai Sechen put them up for the night. In the morning Yisügei agreed to a betrothal. Then Yisügei gave Dai Sechen a horse to seal the engagement, left Temüjin with him for a set term of service, and set out alone for home.[20]

[17] Anonymous (2), *Campagnes*, trans. Pelliot and Hambis, §17 and commentary 375; *Secret History*, §114 and de Rachewiltz, Commentary, 433; Aubin, "Enfant," 471–2; Ratchnevsky, "Šigi Qutuqu," 75–6.

[18] Uno, "Exchange-Marriage," 176, 179–80.

[19] Atwood argues that these were Bosqur, who later rose to control all the Qonggirats. Christopher P. Atwood, "Chigü Küregen and the Origins of the Xiningzhou Qonggirads," in *Archivum Eurasiae Medii Aevi 21: Festschrift for Thomas T. Allsen in Celebration of His 75th Birthday*, ed. P.B. Golden, R. K. Kovalev, A. P. Martinez, J. Skaff, and A. Zimonyi (2014–15), 21.

[20] *Secret History*, §61–6. Also Togan, "Qongrat," 61–83.

Some scholars suggest that the Secret Historian embellished this story, since it appears in no other historical source, and it enjoys unusually beautiful imagery and an epic style.[21] And yet the story is not entirely preposterous, and should not be dismissed out of hand. All sources agree that Börte became Temüjin's senior wife. In order for them to marry, some initial negotiations must have taken place. Furthermore, since Yisügei was actually heading for Hö'elün's Olqunu'ut relatives, his encounter with Dai Sechen can be seen as unplanned. Börte was a Qonggirat, not an Olqunu'ut. Choosing Börte was therefore a deviation from tradition and from Yisügei's own intention, but it did allow him to avoid meeting his own wife's family and arranging a connection with them. This again hints at the social weaknesses caused by the irregular marriage pattern of kidnap. As for the poetic exchange between the fathers: it does not seem especially improbable that the fathers are recorded as describing their children poetically in the context of a union. At that time Mongol children themselves were brought up to compose poetry extemporaneously as part of their education.[22] Even in the twentieth century, Mongolians expected both sides at an engagement or wedding to produce complex passages of spontaneous poetry in friendly competition.[23] Portraying a potential bride and groom in heightened language would thus have been simple and fun for twelfth-century Mongols with their entirely oral and often impromptu literature.[24] Even if the poetry is a later creation by the anonymous Secret Historian, it may still capture the spirit of the occasion, regardless of whether it differs in actual words from what was said. The passage thus should not be discarded simply because of the poetry's presence.

The next dramatic episode in the *Secret History* to illuminate Hö'elün's life began with Yisügei's journey home from Dai Sechen's camp, where he had left Temüjin. On his way, Yisügei is said to have encountered a group of feasting Tatars, whom he joined out of need. The laws of steppe hospitality required them to serve him.[25] Because they recognized him, however, they tampered with his food, so that by the time he reached his camp, he was dying. One of his last acts was to ask Mönglik to bring

[21] See de Rachewiltz, Commentary, 337.
[22] Aubin, "Enfant," 508–9; also de Rachewiltz, Commentary, 661, on the use of alliteration in a message to make it easy to understand.
[23] Jagchid and Hyer, *Culture and Society*, 84–5.
[24] Jagchid and Hyer, *Culture and Society*, 84–5; Aubin, "Enfant," 508–9.
[25] Ratchnevsky, *Genghis Khan*, 21; Dunnell, *Chinggis Khan*, 23; Biran, *Chinggis Khan*, 33–4.

Temüjin home and take care of Hö'elün and the children. Yisügei's language here suggested that Mönglik could indeed have been his brother-in-law: "Mönglik, my boy ... You take care of your younger brothers, the little ones that I leave behind, and of your widowed elder sister-in-law [Hö'elün]. Go quickly and bring back my son Temüjin, Mönglik my boy!"[26]

Here again, some question the *Secret History*, with one scholar suggesting that this episode was created out of whole cloth merely to highlight the Tatar-Mongol feud.[27] But the Tatars may well have had a hand in Yisügei's demise. Their feud with the Mongols predated Yisügei and is recorded in other historical sources than merely the *Secret History*.[28] More significantly, Temüjin treated the Tatars very badly when he conquered them decades later.[29] Furthermore, other historical sources confirm that Yisügei died young, although without mentioning how. Scholars suggest that these sources may have omitted the cause of death in order to avoid smearing the father of the Conqueror with the scandal of murder.[30]

For Hö'elün, Yisügei's death was a logistical calamity, and must have set a new challenge for her resilience. Yisügei's absence deprived her of a man to hunt game for food and to raid people for spoils, while his Tayichi'ut followers were left without a war leader. It soon became evident that they would not transfer their allegiance to Temüjin, who was the oldest of Hö'elün's sons, yet still too young to lead fighting. This became clear when Hö'elün was excluded from an important ceremony of ancestor reverence by the other women in the camp. Thereafter the matter worsened when the Tayichi'uts abandoned the family entirely, which amounted to a death sentence in the cold and unforgiving steppe.[31]

But the Tayichi'uts did not go unmolested, since the two senior members of the camp both sought to prevent their departure: these were Charaqa in his capacity as an important retainer and also perhaps an in-law, and Hö'elün as the senior wife. First Charaqa pursued the

[26] *Secret History*, §67–8.

[27] And between the Tatars and the Borjigin Mongols in particular. Clark, "Revenge," 36–7.

[28] Anonymous (2), *Campagnes*, trans. Pelliot and Hambis, §21; Rashīd al-Dīn, *Jāmi'*, 80–3, 252–9, trans. Thackston, 45–6, 128.

[29] See Chapter 3.

[30] Anonymous (2), *Campagnes*, trans. Pelliot and Hambis, §3; and Rashīd al-Dīn, *Jāmi'*, 80–3, 185, 311, 562, trans. Thackston, 45–6, 99, 153, 285. Rashīd al-Dīn describes the Tatars as "murderers and enemies of Genghis Khan and his forefathers," on p. 82 (trans. Thackston, 46). He could have been referring to Yisügei, Ambaqai, or both.

[31] This was under Ambaqai Khan's grandson Tarqutai Kiriltuq. *Secret History*, §71–2; de Rachewiltz, Commentary, 346. Note also De Nicola, *Khatuns*, 45–7, 186.

Tayichi'uts, but he was speared in the spine and staggered back to die in camp.[32] Then Hö'elün caught up her husband's war standard, itself a sign of authority, and chased the fleeing followers. Although she returned unharmed with some of them, they soon deserted again, this time for good.[33] Things worsened when Charaqa's son Mönglik absconded with his own family after bringing Temüjin home, contrary to Yisügei's explicit deathbed request.[34] This left Hö'elün at the age of perhaps twenty-five to manage the affairs of five children (the youngest still an infant), another woman with two more children, a few servants and retainers, and a scattering of stock, without the protection or food and goods that a man was expected to supply.

Thus impoverished, they scraped a miserable existence from small game, fruit, vegetables, and fish, which was famine fare in the eyes of their hearty meat-loving, plant-scorning society. But why were they so poor? Some believe the *Secret History* exaggerated the depths to which the family sank in order to make the most of Temüjin's rise thereafter.[35] Yet it is also possible that Yisügei was never wealthy. The sources agree that he was a successful warrior with followers, and he therefore cannot have been destitute.[36] Despite his martial achievements, however, peculiarities about his life suggest that he was not a rich man. One peculiarity was his method of acquiring both his wife and daughter-in-law. Some scholars believe that Yisügei could have paid a bride price, but that he was dissuaded from seeking a wife through the usual channels because of the dangers of the long-distance travel required to fulfill the rules of exogamy. If so, then his kidnap of Hö'elün was happenstance: the pleasant surprise of bringing home a lovely, fertile, and energetic woman rather than dinner.[37] But Yisügei was willing to travel on Temüjin's behalf when it

[32] *Secret History*, §73; Anonymous (2), *Campagnes*, trans. Pelliot and Hambis, §3; Hambis, "Episode," 35–6.

[33] *Secret History*, §73–4; also Michael Hope, *Power, Politics and Tradition in the Mongol Empire and the Ilkhanate of Iran* (Oxford, 2016): 28.

[34] Hambis, "Episode," 23. [35] Ratchnevsky, *Genghis Khan*, 22.

[36] The descriptions of him vary. He is a successful warrior with some followers (*Secret History*, §59 [a warrior], §72 [followers]), a lord with many followers (Anonymous (2), *Campagnes*, tr. Pelliot and Hambis, §3, §4), and the ruler over many clans and obedient relatives (Rashīd al-Dīn, *Jāmi'*, 274, trans. Thackston, 134). One Chinese source describes him as the son of a commander of 10 men (i.e., a minor commander, not a major lord). *Meng-ta pei-lu [Meng Da bei lu]*, trans. Olbricht and Pinks, 3. Ratchnevsky believes he was an aristocratic and brave warrior with followers, but makes no comment on his wealth. Ratchnevsky, *Genghis Khan*, 15, 22.

[37] *Secret History*, §54–6. See also Ratchnevsky, *Genghis Khan*, 15–16, also Dunnell, *Chinggis Khan*, 20.

was his turn to wed. This suggests that the journey was not the problem, and implies that Yisügei's acquisition of a senior wife by kidnap smacks more of poverty than an aversion to travel.[38] This possibility is reinforced by Yisügei's decision to let Temüjin pay Börte's bride price in labor, which was a method used at times when families could not produce a bride gift in livestock.[39] If a lack of wealth was the true reason Yisügei kidnapped Hö'elün and left Temüjin to work for Börte, then Yisügei's death must have left Höelun living well below what she could have expected materially in long-ago days as Chiledü's wife.

Another question then arises: since Hö'elün as the senior wife managed her husband's livestock, where were the herds? The family seems to have owned few horses, the most valuable animal on the steppe. The *Secret History* implies that Temüjin and his people were primarily sheepherders, and it states outright that they only had a handful of horses, while the thirteenth-century Persian historian who worked for the Ilkhanids in Iran, Rashīd al-Dīn (d. 1317), relates that Temüjin still possessed relatively few horses as late as 1203–4.[40] Hö'elün could have scraped by with 100–20 animals, especially if most were sheep.[41] Did she have to? The family's paucity of stock reinforces the likelihood that Hö'elün never received a dowry, since she otherwise would have used it to ameliorate their situation. Poverty is further implied by the fact that neither of Yisügei's brothers married Hö'elün through the levirate, which they should have rushed to do for a wealthy widow.[42] Nevertheless, the *Secret History* 's claim that the family was entirely abandoned must be seen as an exaggeration.[43] Although the Tayichi'ut followers deserted them, Yisügei's younger brother Daritai did not, while his nephew Quchar, a skilled

[38] Holmgren, "Levirate," 134; Ratchnevsky counters that the danger of making long trips for a bride might convince even wealthy men to kidnap likely women if possible. Ratchnevsky, *Genghis Khan*, 15.

[39] Holmgren, "Levirate," 132–5; Zhao's dissenting view in *Marriage*, 5–9, albeit with some flaws. Also see footnote 1 for a counter case where a son-in-law lived with his wife's parents to get to know them, not pay off a high bride price.

[40] For the few horses see *Secret History*, §77, §90; Rashīd al-Dīn, *Jāmi'*, 419, trans. Thackston, 203. For the implication that they were sheep-herders see Ratchnevsky, *Genghis Khan*, 37–8; also *Secret History*, §118, and de Rachewiltz, Commentary, 441–2.

[41] A small family (4–5 people) needed a minimum of 50 or 60 animals to survive, mostly sheep. Hö'elün would therefore have required twice this number to feed the children and adults in her care. Dunnell, *Chinggis Khan*, 2.

[42] Holmgren, "Levirate," 132–5, esp. 134–5. Ratchnevsky believes that Hö'elün may have refused a levirate marriage. Ratchnevsky, *Genghis Khan*, 22; Dunnell, *Chinggis Khan*, 24.

[43] The author of the *Campaigns* skips these troubles. Rashīd al-Dīn mentions them vaguely, in Rashīd al-Dīn, *Jāmi'*, 294, trans. Thackston, 144.

archer, brought some warriors to support them during these difficult years, although neither man was present all the time.[44]

It was thus Hö'elün's responsibility as senior widow to keep the family together and alive, possibly aided by the junior widow. The *Secret History* provides beautiful poetic descriptions of Hö'elün's struggles to feed the children – an endless and draining task, especially with little stock and few men to go hunting. But almost all the children in Hö'elün's care made it to adulthood, which was no mean feat with limited food, especially in the case of the youngest and only girl, Temülün, who was a vulnerable infant when their troubles began. Hö'elün's contributions to the survival of Temüjin's brothers gave him a few good men on whom to rely throughout his career, while Temülün grew up to wed one of her brother's early followers, Butu of the Ikires, and form the first link in a network of strategic political marriages that radiated outward from Temüjin himself.

During this lean period, the family faced many challenges, including suffering attacks by thieves and raiders.[45] (Their horses, and Temüjin himself, were abducted.)[46] It was Hö'elün's task to maintain a place to which stolen people and animals could return. Another challenge was strife among the children, who squabbled and fought, sometimes badly. As a single parent for her own five children, and the senior parent in the camp, Hö'elün was forced to assume greater authority in order to offset Yisügei's absence. But if one of her tasks as a mother was to channel her sons' violence, she sometimes failed. One especially dire moment came when Temüjin and Qasar flouted their mother's direct orders and murdered their older half-brother Bekter. The disagreement was framed around competition over a fish, but it was probably an attempt to eliminate Bekter as Temüjin's rival, since Bekter was not only Yisügei's oldest son, but could have asserted a claim to marry Hö'elün through the levirate.[47]

44 He was son of Yisügei's older brother Nekün Taishi. Rashīd al-Dīn, *Jāmi'*, 269, 271, trans. Thackston, 132, 133; Ratchnevsky, *Genghis Khan*, 22.

45 *Secret History*, §74–93.

46 *Secret History*, §90–3 (horse theft), also Ratchnevsky, *Genghis Khan*, 28–31, Dunnell, *Chinggis Khan*, 25–6.

47 *Secret History*, §77–8; Ratchnevsky, *Genghis Khan*, 23–4; for this incident as one in a series of didactic episodes in the *Secret History* see Larry Moses, "The Quarrelling Sons in the Secret History of the Mongols," *The Journal of American Folklore* 100, no. 395 (January–March 1987): 65. For the levirate see Dunnell, *Chinggis Khan*, 24–5, including an interesting discussion of the way Temüjin heard his mother's advice on cooperation

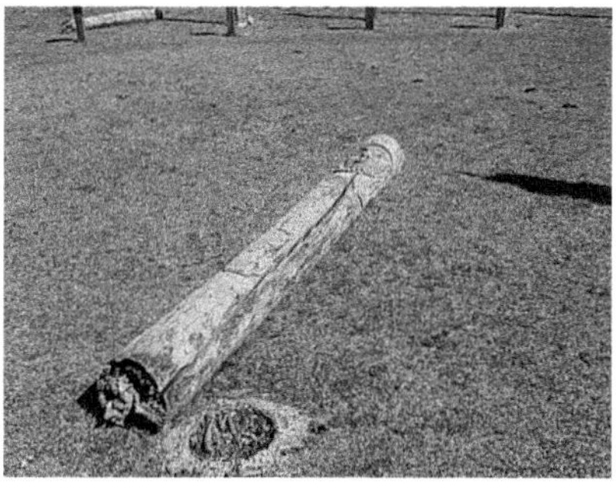

Figure 2.3 A wooden statue of Hö'elün (fallen) from the modern installation at Dark Blue Lake of the Black Heart, Mongolia (author's image).

This wearying period in Hö'elün's life is better known through Temüjin's activities: in these years he formed key relationships, including one with an important sworn companion, Jamuqa, a leader of the Jadirat people. The frequent kidnappings Temüjin suffered during this period honed his character, while he may also have spent some useful time as a "hostage" at the court of the Kereit lord Ong Qan, a sworn friend (*anda*) of his father.[48] Nevertheless it was on Hö'elün's strength and stamina that the anxiety and toil of these years made the greatest demands. She bore the responsibility of keeping the family alive, but in a smaller community shaped by far fewer resources and little protection against danger. This situation surely made great inroads on her store of resilience. (See Figure 2.3.)

BÖRTE: THE IMMENSELY INFLUENTIAL WIFE

The second major woman in Temüjin's life was his wife, Börte, the Qonggirat girl with "fire in her eyes," whose name can be translated as "blue-grey" or even "Celeste."[49] (See Figure 2.4.) Despite Hö'elün's crucial role in bearing Temüjin, keeping him alive during the time of troubles, and raising him to adulthood, Börte soon emerged as the single

among the boys, took it by sparing Belgütei, then asserted himself as a leader by killing Bekter. Also see May, *Art of War*, 7.

[48] Many abductions appear only in the *Secret History*, but other sources confirmed these obliquely. On Ong Qan see Togan, *Flexibility and Limitation*, 75–6, noting that Jamuqa was also present; also Ratchnevsky, *Genghis Khan*, 31–2; Dunnell, *Chinggis Khan*, 27.

[49] Igor de Rachewiltz, "A Note on the Word Börte in *The Secret History of the Mongols*," *East Asian History*, 13/14 (1997): 155; also Dunnell, *Chinggis Khan*, 23.

Figure 2.4 A wooden statue of Börte (standing) from the modern installation at Dark Blue Lake of the Black Heart, Mongolia (author's image).

most important woman in Temüjin's life, and she made unparalleled contributions to his political career and the establishment of the empire. Her influence began immediately upon their marriage, and continued uninterrupted until the moment in 1226 when he chose one of her sons to succeed him as ruler. No other woman in Temüjin's life ever compared to Börte, although a few later rivaled her central role in the history of the empire.

Initially Börte appeared to be simply a good choice for a wife. She first met Temüjin at her parents' camp, then grew to know him better while he worked there until Yisügei's deathbed summons cut this short. Although Dai Sechen let Temüjin leave when Mönglik came to collect him, he urged his son-in-law to return soon. But Temüjin never did.[50] The repercussions

[50] *Secret History*, §69.

of this emerged when he was about fourteen and ready to marry Börte (in perhaps 1178).[51] Dai Sechen appears to have been angry at his son-in-law: one author claims that he opposed the marriage entirely, and only the intervention of Börte's brother made it happen.[52] Another states that the wedding took place as planned, but that when Dai Sechen and his wife, Chotan, set out to escort their daughter to her new home, Dai Sechen turned back early because he was disgruntled about Temüjin's failure to discharge his full duties.[53] In either case, Dai Sechen's behavior supports the contention that Yisügei was not wealthy, and that Temüjin's truncated term of service left Börte's bride price partially unpaid.

But the two did marry, which was a signal achievement for Temüjin. Their union marked Börte's first contribution to his political career, since her marriage and the new in-law connection she represented gave Temüjin official, public recognition from a respectable outside family. Only after the wedding was Temüjin able to build the network of close companions who helped him in his rise, which he started immediately.[54] Even Dai Sechen's resentment did not last, and later he became a strong ally.[55] Börte's contribution to Temüjin's future was also material, since she brought independent wealth into her marriage in the form of a luxurious sable coat, which she gave her mother-in-law as a gift.[56] (This contrasts sharply with Hö'elün, who brought only herself to her forced union with Yisügei.) The coat immediately proved its worth, since Hö'elün let Temüjin use it to establish a political alliance with Ong Khan of the Kereits.

51 Ratchnevsky, *Genghis Khan*, 31; on the 1178 date, see footnotes 104–7 of this chapter.

52 Rashīd al-Dīn would not have portrayed Temüjin as irresponsible for having failed to complete his service. Rashīd al-Dīn, *Jāmi'*, 159, trans. Thackston, 85; Ratchnevsky accepts the claim of intercession by Börte's brother Alchi at face value. Ratchnevsky, *Genghis Khan*, 21.

53 Holmgren, "Levirate," 133–4, noting that the *Altan Tobci*, §20, explained Dai Sechen's failure to go to Temüjin's camp as a result of fever, and arguing that this was a coverup for the real reason, resentment.

54 Cheng, "Career," 220; also Dunnell, *Chinggis Khan*, 26.

55 They joined Temüjin in 1203 after opposing him earlier, but this opposition was because of an ill-conceived attack on them made by Temüjin's brother Qasar, which Temüjin later held against him. See Ratchnevsky, *Genghis Khan*, 61, 71–2; Dunnell, *Chinggis Khan*, 39, 43; Biran, *Chinggis Khan*, 37.

56 *Secret History*, §96; also Urgunge Onon, *The Secret History of the Mongols: The Life and Times of Chinggis Khan* (Richmond, Surrey: Curzon, 2001), §189, note 425, citing Eldengtei, Oyuundalai, and Asaraltu, *Menggu Mi Shi* and *Chihui Xuan Shi* (selected translation of the vocabulary of *The Secret History of the Mongols*) (Ulaanbaatar, 1980), 148–9.

Finally and perhaps most critically, gaining Börte as a wife put Temüjin in a position to "start his own family line."[57]

Börte's contributions to the marriage were also logistical. In her new role as wife, she can be assumed to have taken over some tasks from her mother-in-law, although Hö'elün is likely to have remained responsible for supervision, and the two must have worked closely together. In the years that followed, these key women cooperated to manage the camp's economy and its human and animal resources, which allowed Temüjin to pursue his political and military career. After a time Börte became pregnant with a daughter, Qojin, who was born perhaps as early as 1179 or 1180, and who was the first of Börte's nine children (see the following discussion in this chapter).[58] In addition to her managerial support, these children were another important resource that Börte provided for Temüjin's empire building: her four sons played central roles in Temüjin's campaigns of conquest and inherited his territories, while her five daughters married his key political allies.

Then came a series of events crucial to understanding Temüjin's career and the history of his rise: the Merkit raid on Hö'elün's camp, and the kidnap and return of Börte. Unfortunately this is perhaps the most controversial sequence in Temüijin's story: contemporary authors either contradicted one another wildly about it, or simply failed to mention it.[59] The *Secret History* is the most detailed report, and claims that early one morning an elderly servant named Qo'aqchin awakened the camp because she heard the approach of three hundred horses, ridden by several Merkit leaders and their fighting men. Hö'elün's family fled, but they did not have enough horses for everyone, and therefore left behind Börte, Qo'aqchin, and Yisügei's second widow. The widow's actions are unknown, but Qo'aqchin hid Börte in an ox cart and fled until it broke

[57] Cheng, "Career," 220.

[58] For the date see text below, and footnotes 104–7. Scholars often neglect Börte's five daughters and mention only her four sons. For Qojin see Rashīd al-Dīn, *Jāmi'*, 164, 301 (302 her sisters), trans. Thackston, 88, 146–7, trans. Boyle, 97 (her status as eldest overall); *Secret History*, §165, and de Rachewiltz, Commentary, 596–7; Anonymous (2), *Campagnes*, trans. Pelliot and Hambis, §5 and commentary, 49–50; *Meng-ta pei-lu* [*Meng Da Bei lu*], trans. Olbricht and Pinks, 24 and note 14 on 30–1 (her status as eldest daughter).

[59] The story appears only in the *Secret History* and Rashīd al-Dīn (for references see below). The *Campaigns* and *Yuan Shi* avoid anything unflattering to Temüjin. Juvaynī leaves it out in *World-Conqueror*, 40, perhaps because he skips Temüjin's early life entirely, and furthermore identifies Chinggis Khan's senior wife as Yesünjin (Yisüi?), not Börte. See Ratchnevsky, *Genghis Khan*, 34–7.

down.[60] Ultimately the Merkits captured all three women. They also hunted Temüjin on nearby Mount Burqan Qaldun but failed to seize him, and they eventually rode off with their prizes, triumphant over their revenge for Yisügei's earlier theft of Hö'elün.

To seal that revenge, Börte and Yisügei's widow were both made to marry Merkit men. The widow's husband was an ordinary Merkit subject, but Börte married Chilger Bökü, a younger brother of Hö'elün's deceased first husband, Chiledü, in recompense for Chiledü's earlier loss of Hö'elün's herself.[61] This put Börte in the same position as her mother-in-law sixteen-odd years earlier: surrounded by armed men and lacking any means of escape. Even if she had slipped away, the steppe was no place for a lone traveler. Börte must have wondered whether she would see Temüjin (and Qojin) again, just as Hö'elün had once wondered about Chiledü. Like Hö'elün, Börte probably worked to adjust to her new life with Chilger, since she had no reason to expect a rescue. Thus she showed the resilience so important among successful steppe women, and which her mother-in-law had already demonstrated so well.

But unlike Chiledü all those years ago, Temüjin did plan a rescue. He therefore sought help from Ong Qan and his relative Jaqa Gambu, and Temüjin's sworn friend Jamuqa.[62] All three men joined Temüjin with their soldiers in a retaliatory campaign against the Merkits. Although the joint offensive was probably a series of events,[63] the *Secret History* presents it as a single, daring, nighttime attack, during which Temüjin called out for his wife as the Merkits scrambled to flee. She heard him, ran toward him, and fell into his arms in the moonlight. Qo'aqchin was also rescued, but Yisügei's second widow, shamed by her lowly marriage to an ordinary man, disappeared. Some time after the rescue Börte gave birth to her second child (and first son), Jochi, whose paternity was forever doubted, even though Temüjin accepted him as his own.[64]

[60] *Secret History*, §100, §111, §112. Ratchnesvky argues that Qo'aqchin may have been the second wife in *Genghis Khan*, 15–16. He does not fully acknowledge her rescue with Börte in *Secret History* §110.
[61] *Secret History*, §111.
[62] *Secret History*, §107–8 (the participants); also de Rachewiltz, Commentary, 409; Togan, *Flexibility and Limitation*, 78–80.
[63] Ratchnevsky, *Genghis Khan*, 36; Anonymous (2), *Campagnes*, trans. Pelliot and Hambis, §14, and commentary 266.
[64] *Secret History*, §254 (her pregnancy must be inferred from the reference to Jochi as a "Merkit bastard"); Rashīd al-Dīn, *Jāmi'*, 72, 94, 299, 708–9, trans. Thackston, 41, 53, 146, 347.

But Rashīd al-Dīn tells a wildly different story: First that Börte was pregnant when the Merkits abducted her; then, that she never married Chilger. Instead, since the Merkits were friendly with Temüjin's Kereit patron, Ong Khan, they sent Börte to him as a captive.[65] But he chivalrously refrained from having sex with her because of his former friendship with Temüjin's father. As for the raid: Rashīd al-Dīn mentions no such thing, and certainly not the thrilling and perhaps dubious moonlit rescue. Rather, he claims that Temüjin sent a trusted follower, Sebe, to retrieve Börte from her extended stay with Ong Qan. On the way home Börte went into labor unexpectedly, and Jochi was born on the road. Because it was dangerous to stop for long, Sebe made a soft dough out of some flour, encased Jochi with it, and thus kept him safe for the rest of the ride.[66]

Both stories are rife with problems. First the *Secret History*, which has received the lion's share of attention: One scholar argues that the three Merkit leaders would not personally have led three hundred warriors against an enemy so poor as to only possess a few horses.[67] Another suggests that the episode comes from an epic about feuds over women, not an actual historical event.[68] A third accepts the initial raid but dismisses the rescue as a romantic fabrication, based on problems in the dating; he also points out that only the *Secret History* records Temüjin's retaliatory campaign against the Merkits, and is therefore suspect.[69] The artistry of the rescue passage has also come under fire.[70] I note that we

[65] Ratchnevsky, *Genghis Khan*, 34–5.

[66] Rashīd al-Dīn, *Jāmi'*, 72, 94, 299, 708–9, trans. Thackston, 41, 53, 146, 347.

[67] Hidehiro Okada, "The Secret History of the Mongols, a Pseudo-Historical Novel," in *Ajia Afurika Gengo Bunka Kenkyu* [*Journal of Asian and African Studies*] 5 (1972): 62–3. Okada also denounces (p. 63) the claim the Merkits were annihilated in Temüjin's attack "down to the offspring of their offspring" (*Secret History*, §112) since Temüjin was not free of the Merkits until 1217–18 (*Secret History*, §236; Rashīd al-Dīn, *Jāmi'*, 457, trans. Thackston, 226–7; Ratchnevsky, *Genghis Khan*, 116). But I respond that *Secret History* §112 only claims that the [300] Merkits who attacked Temüjin were destroyed, and further states that others escaped, including their leaders (§110–14).

[68] Clark, "Revenge," 38.

[69] Anonymous (2), *Campagnes*, trans. Pelliot and Hambis, §14, and commnentary, 265–7. He assumes that Jochi, Chaghatai, and Ögedei were born in 1184, 1185, and 1186, but this does not account for Qojin's earlier birth. Nor does it account for natural spacing of children, which is linked to the hormones regulating fertility and nursing (breastfeeding), and does not permit three children in three years. See footnote 106.

[70] De Rachewiltz, Commentary, 407, citing L. Lörincz, "Ein historisches Lied in der Geheimen Geschichte der Mongolen," in *Researches in Altaic Languages*, ed. L. Ligeti (Budapest, 1975), 117–26; and Clark, "Revenge," 38 (also citing Lörincz).

should, in addition, question Chilger's poetic lament about how wrong he was, being lowly, to lay hands on a lady of Börte's status, since he was actually an important Merkit while Börte was a poor man's wife.[71]

Rashīd al-Dīn's story is equally troublesome.[72] First, it is unlikely that the Merkits gave Börte to Ong Qan. They did have in-law ties to him since his daughter had married the Merkit leader Toqto'a, and one scholar believes this makes Rashīd al-Dīn's tale more convincing.[73] But another points out that turning Börte over to a sworn friend of Yisügei, i.e., a friend of the man who had stolen Hö'elün, meant the Merkits were abandoning their long-held desire for vengeance, which seems highly unlikely.[74] Rashīd al-Dīn's insistence that Börte was pregnant before the raid is also out of character, since he never discussed the timing of her other eight pregnancies, or those of other women.[75] The inclusion of the flour used to make the dough cushioning Jochi is equally suspect, since in the 1180s the meat-and-dairy-eating Mongols are unlikely to have been consuming or producing this plant derivative.[76] Why then did a messenger carry enough of such a rare substance to encase a newborn in dough? The report also raises medical questions about Jochi's birth. Even if it was truly "unexpected" (i.e., early), Jochi could only have survived if Börte had reached a late stage in her pregnancy (week 34 or later of

[71] *Secret History*, §111.

[72] Similarly Anonymous (2), *Campagnes*, trans. Pelliot and Hambis, §14, §19, and commentary, 266, 413. But Ratchnesvky, *Genghis Khan*, 35, finds Rashīd al-Dīn's version of Börte's return to be implausible, accepts the *Secret History* engagement story, but critiques its rescue story.

[73] Cheng, "Career," 29–31. [74] Ratchnevsky, *Genghis Khan*, 35.

[75] The exception is in a single comment about Chinggis Khan's final Tangut campaign, which Tolui joined late because his senior wife was pregnant. Rashīd al-Dīn, *Jāmiʿ*, 537, trans. Thackston, 261.

[76] The Mongols seem to have eaten meat, dairy products, and occasional wild plants into the Empire period, but sources differ on the question of flour and bread. The 1221 report of Li Chi-Ch'ang suggests that flour consumption was significant by 1221 (see Allsen, "Merchant Partners," 93, and De Nicola, *Khatuns*, 144). But in 1245–7 by contrast, Carpini observed a limited diet, "They have neither bread nor herbs nor vegetables nor any thing else, nothing but meat ... " *History*, 16 (not in Rockhill). Similarly, ambassadors for King Louis IX returned from the Mongols in 1251 and reported that, "The Tatars' lifestyle was such that they did not eat bread at all, and lived off meat and milk." Joinville, *Life*, trans. Smith, §487. The Georgian chronicle claims that the Mongols " ... did not know the taste of bread and nourished themselves only with meat and the milk of animals ..." M. Brosset, *Histoire de la Georgie*, 5 vols. in 4 (St. Petersburg, 1849), 485, text 317. Jagchid and Hyer, *Culture and Society*, 41, find no evidence of Mongol grain consumption before the Yüan period.

40–2 weeks).[77] Since Jochi was her second child, her condition would have shown much earlier than the first time; if so, then Ong Qan would not have let her travel.[78] A related medical question is whether a woman who had just given birth could have so easily gotten back onto a horse.

The two sources agree on the problem of Jochi's parentage: was Temüjin the father, or Chilger? Although the *Secret History* ignores Börte's pregnancy when recounting her dramatic rescue, it later describes Jochi as a "Merkit bastard."[79] At the same time, and despite claiming that Börte was pregnant before the raid and that Ong Qan never slept with her, Rashīd al-Dīn explained that Jochi always quarreled with his brothers Chaghatai and Ögedei, but not his youngest brother Tolui, "who never taunted him *but considered him legitimate*" (emphasis added).[80] Although in many steppe societies a woman's child was attributed to her husband's family even when the father was another man, the fact that Jochi was passed over as a successor to Chinggis Khan implies that some Mongols doubted his paternity, and that Chinggis Khan knew it.[81]

What can we conclude from the problematic sources and the scholarly ink that has been spilled over them? Several things. First, some Merkits raided Temüjin's camp and rode away with Börte, although their precise number is unknown. Second, this happened early in Temüjin and Börte's

[77] A full-term pregnancy is 38–42 weeks. Modern statistics suggest that babies born prematurely at 30 weeks (2.5 months early) have a survival rate of 96% or better, but these assume the baby will be in a Neonatal Intensive Care Unit (NICU), often on a respirator, in an incubator, and with a feeding tube. Note that "survival" means only that the baby is alive, and says nothing about standard complications of prematurity in the lungs, digestive system, eyes, brain, etc., some of which can lead to death in later months or years. Premodern premature babies are unlikely to have fared as well as they do today. For modern prematurity see: www.marchofdimes.com/professionals/14332_1157.asp. Accessed December 2011.

[78] The muscles and ligaments of the midsection stretch in the first pregnancy, and are then looser (and stretch again and "show" sooner) in subsequent pregnancies. (Roger W. Harms, ed., *Mayo Clinic Guide to a Healthy Pregnancy* [HarperResource, 2004], 63). Jagchid and Hyer note that a woman would ordinarily stay in camp, not travel, in the later stages of pregnancy (*Culture and Society*, 75).

[79] *Secret History*, §254; Igor de Rachewiltz, "On the Expression Cul Ulja'ur, (?= Čol Olja'ur) in #254 of the *Secret History of the Mongols*," *Journal of Turkish Studies* 9 (1985): 213–18, esp. 213–17, esp. 217.

[80] Emphasis added. Rashīd al-Dīn, *Jāmi'*, 709, trans. Thackston, 348 and note 1.

[81] Aubin, "Enfant," 465, 467–8, pointing out that a child born before a marriage took place or after it was over (i.e., after a husband had died) was still linked to the husband's family. For Jochi and succession see Ratchnevsky, *Genghis Khan*, 37; also Qu, Dafeng and Liu, Jianyi, "On Some Problems Concerning Jochi's Lifetime," *Central Asiatic Journal* 42, no. 2 (1998): 283–90.

marriage – i.e., around 1180 or 1181 – since Jochi was Börte's second-born, and the "natural spacing" of Börte's children makes 1182 most likely for his birth.[82] Third, it is reasonable to suspect that this was a revenge abduction, since such events made enough sense to the Mongols to figure in their literature, and probably at times happened for real.[83] Fourth, since for unknown reasons the Merkits failed to retrieve Hö'elün immediately after Yisügei kidnapped her, it makes sense that they waited to retaliate until Temüjin married, as this allowed them to injure Yisügei's oldest son just as Yisügei had injured Chiledü. If we doubt the Merkits sent Börte to the Kereits, it becomes likely that she married a Merkit man and slept with him. There is no doubt at all that Börte became pregnant at some point close to the Merkit raid, although, like the Mongols, we will never know the timing of conception or the truth about Jochi's parentage. But Temüjin considered the Merkits his enemies and spent years trying to destroy them. The Merkit treatment of his wife was surely a factor, even though his marriage with Börte survived well enough to result in seven more children. In this way an outrage perpetuated against one woman (Hö'elün) led to an avenging outrage against another (Börte), repercussions down the generational line (Jochi) and violence against an entire people (the Merkits). This was a heavy price to pay for Yisügei's self-serving abduction of Hö'elün all those years earlier.

As for Temüjin's retaliatory campaign: The lack of record outside the *Secret History* does not indicate the absence of a campaign, since other sources clearly repressed this episode or referred to it only vaguely.[84] And if Temüjin's uncle Daritai or cousin Quchar were present, their soldiers could have participated in the endeavor, since Temüjin had none.[85] We may assume that Ong Qan contributed to Börte's return, and possibly

82 For the natural spacing of 18–24 months between births see the subsequent discussion in this chapter, and especially footnotes 104–8. Rashīd al-Dīn suggests this raid happened in the 1190s, but Jochi could not have been born this late. Rashīd al-Dīn could have been inserting this event into later reports about hostilities in order to hide Börte's rape and protect Temüjin's reputation as a husband. Rashīd al-Dīn, *Jāmiʿ*, 94, trans. Thackston, 52–3. De Rachewiltz posits Temüjin's birth in 1162, marriage in 1180, the raid in 1181, and the rescue campaign and Jochi's birth in 1182. *Secret History*, §59, de Rachewiltz, Commentary, 320–1, 411. But this does not allow for the earlier birth of Qojin, for which reason I propose moving the marriage back to perhaps 1178 in order to posit Qojin's birth in 1179 or 1180 (Börte was 18 or 19).

83 Clark, "Revenge," entire.

84 Anonymous (2), *Campagnes*, trans. Pelliot and Hambis, §14, and commentary, 265–7.

85 For Quchar see the previous text in this chapter.

Jamuqa and Jaqa Gambu as well, even if the details are unclear. Certainly this was the first successful joint military action undertaken by Temüjin and several important allies. Their success gave him the chance to practice his leadership, and to work with other men in a shared endeavor. It also improved Temüjin's material situation through spoils, which thereafter allowed him to raise his political standing through gift-giving.[86]

DALAN BALZHUT AND ITS AFTERMATH

The *Secret History* claims that Ong Qan returned to his own activities after the rescue of Börte, but Jamuqa and Temüjin lived together as sworn friends (*anda*) for nearly two years.[87] While with Jamuqa, Temüjin encountered new people and gained followers, helped by the spoils from the Merkit campaign, which he distributed generously.[88] As Temüjin increased in stature, so did Hö'elün, for whom these years may have marked an easing of deprivations and toil. The influx of wealth from the Merkit raid must also have improved material conditions for the entire family.

But then Temüjin and Jamuqa had a falling-out. As the *Secret History* would have it, one afternoon Jamuqa said something cryptic during a routine interaction over where to camp.[89] Temüjin immediately sought advice from both his mother and his wife. In the narrative Börte is credited rather dramatically with answering first and thereby forestalling her mother-in-law's response, which led Temüjin to break immediately with his friend and depart.[90] But the point of this episode is not its drama – rivalry between Börte and Hö'elün, and a breakup between Temüjin and Jamuqa, all in one section. Rather it demonstrates the general role of women as advisors and the particular advisorial role played by both Hö'elün and Börte: Temüjin clearly valued the opinions of his female kin since he sought them out first in a moment of uncertainty, then followed the advice Börte gave. In the end, the two men not only parted company forever, but became rivals. Thereafter Temüjin's followers elected him khan of the Mongol Borjigin people in perhaps 1185.[91] An

86 *Secret History*, §117; also Ratchnevsky, *Genghis Khan*, 40.
87 *Secret History*, §116–17; Rashīd al-Dīn, *Jāmi'*, 202, 204, 332–3, 611–2, and to a lesser degree 185, 372, trans. Thackston, 106, 108, 162, 281; also 99, 180.
88 Ratchnevsky, *Genghis Khan*, 39–40. 89 *Secret History*, §118.
90 De Nicola, *Khatuns*, 47–8.
91 Ratchnevsky, *Genghis Khan*, 42–4, and chronology, 281.

exchange of horse theft and retaliation thereafter led to the battle of Dalan Balzhut between Temüjin and Jamuqa in about 1187, which Temüjin lost badly.[92] After the battle Jamuqa treated some of Temüjin's men very cruelly indeed.[93]

For both Temüjin and Hö'elün, the catastrophe of Dalan Balzhut had a silver lining: Jamuqa's behavior provoked some followers to defect in disgust, among them Mönglik of the Qonqotan, who had abandoned Hö'elün's family so many years earlier. Although Mönglik must have been aware that Temüjin and Jamuqa were together, he appeared only after Dalan Balzhut, possibly reasoning that Temüjin and Hö'elün needed him badly enough to overlook his earlier abandonment.[94] They did so, and welcomed Mönglik back warmly. If Mönglik had not been an in-law before, he became one now: to seal the reunion Hö'elün married him, making him her third and final husband, although some sources obscured this, perhaps to make her appear as a chaste widow rather than a thrice-married woman.[95] If Mönglik had indeed been Yisügei's brother-in-law, then this new wedding with Hö'elün was both reminiscent of the levirate, and meant that Mönglik was finally fulfilling Yisügei's deathbed request.[96] Thereafter Temüjin addressed Mönglik as *echige* ([step-] father), as he had once called Mönglik's father Charaqa *ebügen*.[97] Thus Hö'elün not only gained her final husband, but the families experienced a general reunion of Mönglik's sons with Temüjin and his siblings. Mönglik and several of his sons went on to serve Temüjin later.

In the years after Dalan Balzhut, Hö'elün continued to act as both mother and father to her children. It was she who helped decide to hold a celebratory feast with their Jürkin relatives, possibly to mark new alliances formed after Dalan Balzhut. At the feast she was seated in Yisügei's

92 Ratchnevsky, *Genghis Khan*, 45–7, *Secret History*, §128–9.
93 Ratchnevsky, *Genghis Khan*, 46–7 (Jamuqa's savagery and the sources on it).
94 Hambis, "Episode," 33.
95 We know of the marriage, although not its timing, but Hambis implies that it was at or after the reconciliation after Dalan Balzhut. Hambis, "Episode," note 39 on 23, also 19, 31, 36; he observes that the Chinese sources omit Hö'elün's third marriage since they viewed it as inappropriate, for which see 33. For source references, some slight, see *Secret History*, §130; de Rachewiltz, Commentary 339; Anonymous (2), *Campagnes*, trans. Pelliot and Hambis, §3, and commentary, 21–2; Rashīd al-Dīn, *Jāmi'*, 166, trans. Thackston, 89. Otherwise see Ratchnevsky, *Genghis Khan*, 98; Dunnell, *Chinggis Khan*, 57.
96 Hambis, "Episode," 19.
97 "Grandfather, respected elder, ancestor." Hambis, "Episode," 31; de Rachewiltz, Commentary, 236, 339, 489 for the translation.

place, not with the other women, in a nod to her unusual position.[98] In Yisügei's absence Hö'elün is likely to have arranged the marriage between her daughter, Temülün, and Temüjin's companion, Butu of the Ikires. It also seems probable that she helped negotiate another marriage between her son, Temüge, and an Olqunu'ut relative, even though the evidence is lacking. If she did, this signals her first rapprochement in years with the family she left behind.[99]

Unfortunately, many events from this period are difficult to date, and Temüjin's whereabouts for much of the late 1180s and early 1190s are unknown. Scholars have offered various theories, among them that Temüjin was near or in China, possibly in the Jin Empire.[100] His patron Ong Qan also suffered reversals, in part because of Temüjin's defeat at Dalan Balzhut, and was overthrown as leader of the Kereits by a brother and driven into exile for several years.[101] Nor do we know where Temüjin's family spent this period, although when he emerged in 1196 supporting a Jin army against the Tatars and began to reestablish himself in steppe politics, at least some of his family was with him.[102]

We can be sure that Börte at least was never separated from Temüjin, as her childbearing makes clear, and as scholars have overlooked. This is because of the natural spacing of her children. If we imagine that she married in perhaps 1178, then she could have borne Qojin a year or two later in 1179 or 1180 (Börte was 18 or 19). We must recall, however, that natural spacing usually results in 18–24 months between births (as in the case of Hö'elün, whose children were all two years apart in age[103]).[104]

[98] This was the feast with the Jürkin. Note that a pitcher of kumis was poured first for Hö'elün, her sons Temüjiin and Qasar, and Sacha Beki of the Jürkin, then another pitcher was poured for the women, which suggests that Hö'elün was not seated with the women. *Secret History*, §130–2.

[99] See Chapters 4 and 5 (Qojin); Rashīd al-Dīn, *Jāmi'*, 280–1, trans. Thackston, 137 (Temüge, whose wife was Sandaqchin).

[100] Ratchnevsky, *Genghis Khan*, 49–50, 52–3; Dunnell, *Chinggis Khan*, 34.

[101] For Ong Qan's troubles see Togan, *Flexibility and Limitation*, 80–90; Cheng, proposing some innovative dating in "Career," 85–103, 120–3; also in brief Ratchnevsky, *Genghis Khan*, 49–50; Dunnell, *Chinggis Khan*, 35; Biran, *Chinggis Khan*, 36.

[102] Ratchnevsky, *Genghis Khan*, 52–3. *Secret History*, §132–5 (the 1196 campaign, including a reference to Höelün in §135).

[103] *Secret History*, §60.

[104] In modern women, nursing (i.e., breastfeeding) hormones suppress fertility hormones for 6–24 months after a birth. Thus only 7% of nursing mothers return to fertility by 6 months, 37% in 6–12 months, 48% in 12–24 months, and 8% over 24 months. www.kellymom.com/bf/normal/fertility.html#transition. Accessed August 9, 2017. (Obviously premodern statistics are unavailable.) To produce babies in rapid succession (one per year), or in other words, for a woman to conceive again three

This meant that Börte probably had only four (or five) children by the time of Dalan Balzhut in 1187: Qojin (1179 or 1180; Börte was 18 or 19), Jochi (1182; Börte was 21), Chaghatai (late 1183 or 1184; Börte was 22 or 23), Ögedei (1186, the only verifiable date;[105] Börte was 25), and perhaps her second daughter, Checheyigen (late 1187 or 1188?; Börte was 26 or 27).[106] She then must have borne her last four children during the troubled years, which means that she remained with Temüjin: Alaqa (late 1189 or 1190?;[107] Börte was 28 or 29), Tümelün (1192?; Börte was 31), Tolui (1194?; Börte was 33), and Al Altan, the youngest (1196?; Börte was 35).[108] (See Family Tree 2.1.) This assumes that Börte was not

months after giving birth, nursing hormones must be interrupted (i.e., the woman cannot breastfeed) so that fertility hormones can resurge. In cases where nursing hormones are not interrupted (i.e., the woman breastfeeds her children), according to modern fertility rates, only 7% of women can get pregnant in the first *six* months, to say nothing of the first three. The interruption of hormones is accomplished through using wet nurses (historically) or infant formula (today). Thus if Börte was nursing her babies – and we have no evidence of a wet nurse, see footnote 109 – she could not have become pregnant once a year, even if she were in the atypical 7% of women who can conceive again within *six* months, assuming her fertility corresponded with modern rates.

105 Ögedei died at the age of 56 by Chinese historical standards (55 by modern Western standards) in 1241, meaning he was born in 1186. See Anonymous (2), *Campagnes*, trans. Pelliot and Hambis, §14, and commentary, 266, although his assertion that Börte could have borne three boys in three years does not accord with modern research on fertility and breastfeeding. See footnote 104.

106 Checheyigen's birth order is not entirely clear, but if Ögedei was born in 1186, there was no time for her between Jochi, Chaghatai, and Ögedei, so she may have come after Ögedei and before Alaqa.

107 De Rachewiltz, Commentary, 856–7, suggests a birth date around 1191.

108 If Börte had been separated from Temüjin, she could not have begun to produce their four later children until 1196. This is unlikely for several reasons: first, she would have given birth four times when between the ages of 35 to 43 – medically possible then and now, but still difficult and dangerous in the premodern world. Second, waiting would mean that her eighth child, Tolui, was born around 1200, but this is unsupportable since he married Sorqoqtani in 1203. If instead he was born in 1194, he would have been 9 at the wedding (perhaps an engagement?), which is young but still possible for a male. For all of Börte's offspring see Rashīd al-Dīn, *Jāmi'*, 299–302, trans. Thackston, 146–8; for birth order (including trans. Boyle) see pages in the following parentheses. Qojin was the oldest child overall (i.e., older than Jochi, *Jāmi'*, 708, trans. Thackston, 347, trans. Boyle, 97); Alaqa was younger than Ögedei but older than Tolui (*Jāmi'*, 132, trans. Thackston, 71), Tümelün was also older than Tolui (*Jāmi'*, 160, trans. Thackston, 86). Rashīd al-Dīn places Al Altan last (the youngest daughter), but does not relate her to Tolui, so we must guess she was Börte's last child. Also *Secret History*, §186 (Tolui's marriage); Ratchnevsky, *Genghis Khan*, 80, 282 (chronology) and "Šigi Qutuqu," 77–8 (Tolui's age). See also Rashīd al-Dīn, *Shu'āb-i Panjgānah*, MS III Ahmet 2937, fol. 107a; *Yuan Shi*, 13:2757–61, Table of Imperial Princesses (unpublished trans. Buell).

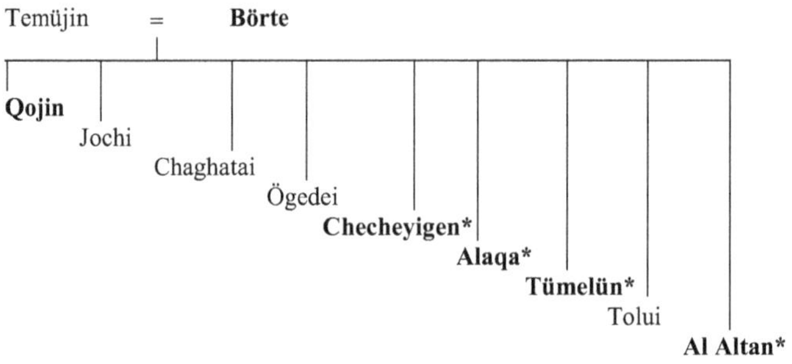

Family Tree 2.1 Temüjin and Börte's children.
All women are in **bold.**
* Indicates that birth order is not wholly clear.

in a position to employ a wet nurse (which could change the timing of births), even though we know that later imperial women used them.[109]

THE QURILTAI OF 1206

The period after Temüjin's reemergence in 1196 was one of intense struggle leading to hard-won triumphs. It included his campaigns against coalition armies and powerful individual peoples like the Tatars (1202), Temüjin's former Kereit allies (1203), and the Naimans (1204). This phase culminated in the assembly (*quriltai*) of 1206 when Temüjin's followers proclaimed him Chinggis Khan.[110] The aftermath of 1206 should have been an equally triumphant period for Temüjin's most important womenfolk. Börte in particular was in her element: she had been in touch with her own family again, at least since their alliance with her husband in 1203. No other woman possessed such political clout: Börte's brothers and cousins worked for her husband as commanders of a thousand, and during these years she celebrated weddings for many of her sons and daughters. Several of her children married her Qonggirat nieces and nephews, which further strengthened ties between her family and the Chinggisids.[111] She can be assumed to have helped arrange matches for

[109] I assume that Börte's circumstances during the 1180s and '90s (poverty before the Merkit raid, a move to China [?] after Dalan Balzhut) precluded the regular employment of wet nurses.

[110] On the quriltai as an institution see Florence Hodous, "The Quriltai as a Legal Institution in the Mongol Empire," *Central Asiatic Journal* 56 (2012/2013): 87–102.

[111] See Chapters 4 and 5.

all her children. These marriages simultaneously served Temüjin's political interests, and provided Börte's daughters with husbands who offered security and wealth, and her sons with capable and talented wives.[112]

But for Hö'elün the aftermath of 1206 was less triumphant. Temüjin's transformation into Chinggis Khan should have marked the culmination of her years of hard work. Instead his success led her to hard losses, and placed her in conflict with her third husband, Mönglik, and his family. As usual, the story is not entirely clear. Sources suggest that the problems began with the rewards that Temüjin handed out to family, followers, and fighting men from the possessions, herds, and subjects of his defeated enemies. According to the *Secret History*, Temüjin gave the largest group of subjects to Hö'elün, which demonstrated his appreciation for her support. But when she discovered that the grant included subjects both for her and for her son Temüge, she secretly felt that she had received less than she deserved, and became deeply unhappy.[113] Meanwhile, Temüjin had contrarily singled out Hö'elün's husband Mönglik for reward: he promised to consult Mönglik "yearly and monthly," and designated him to sit on his right – the most elevated position after Temüjin's own – which made Mönglik the second man in the empire.[114] Mönglik was the very first commander of a thousand to be named in the *Secret History*, and three of his sons became commanders as well.[115] It is possible that the disparity in rewards put the relationship between Hö'elün and Mönglik under some strain.

New developments then pitted Hö'elün's sons against one another, and against Mönglik's sons. First one rivalry over leadership developed between Temüjin and his brother Qasar,[116] followed by another between Temüjin and Mönglik's son, the shaman Kököchü or Teb Tengri (Most

[112] See Chapters 4 and 5.

[113] The number is 10,000, but some were for Temüge. *Secret History*, §242–3. De Rachewiltz observes that 10,000 seems inflated (Commentary, 863–4). For 3,000 (for Hö'elün) and 5,000 (for Temüge) see Rashīd al-Dīn, *Jāmi'*, 611–2, trans. Thackston, 281; also De Nicola, *Khatuns*, 133, 142.

[114] The service included the time that Mönglik had saved Temüjin from a Kereit ambush in 1202. *Secret History*, §204; Hambis, "Episode," 36.

[115] *Secret History*, §202; the sons were Tolon, Süyiketu, and Kököchü. Also see Hambis, "Episode," 40–6.

[116] For Temüjin's fear of Qasar as a rival see de Rachewiltz, Commentary, 873–4. The grudges included Qasar's failure to execute all the Tatar men assigned to him in 1202, and his unprovoked attack on the Qonggirats that had made them ally with Temüjin's enemies before reconsidering and joining him in 1203. Rashīd al-Dīn, *Jāmi'*, 83 (Tatars), trans. Thackston, 46; Ratchnevsky, *Genghis Khan*, 99 (the Qonggirats).

Heavenly, a title).[117] To make matters worse, Kököchü and his brothers became involved in separate altercations with both Qasar and Temüjin's youngest brother, Temüge.[118] Meanwhile, Hö'elün and Börte both appeared in the *Secret History* narrative: Börte as an advisor, who encouraged her husband to take decisive action and contain Kököchü's threat,[119] and Hö'elun as a disciplinarian, who intervened angrily with Temüjiin in his quarrel with Qasar.[120] Nevertheless Hö'elun ultimately failed to control her son, since Temüjin surreptitiously reduced Qasar's dependents from 4,000 to 1,400 and thereby contained the threat that Qasar posed.[121] Then, to eliminate the second rivalry with Kököchü, Temüjin let Temüge kill the shaman in a rigged wrestling match. Although Temüjin did not harm anyone else, and Mönglik and his remaining sons continued to serve him, their prominence was certainly reduced.[122]

What may we conclude from this latest series of dramatic events? The months before and after the quriltai of 1206 can be understood as a time when Chinggis Khan was finally establishing himself for good, both by rewarding those who had supported him in his long journey to the top, and by eliminating rivals who might challenge his newly won position. With this in mind, it is reasonable to conclude that something was indeed amiss with the rewards, either those for Hö'elün or Qasar, since the *Secret History* turns this into a full dramatic narrative of lost tempers, while Rashīd al-Dīn in equally telling fashion obscures the situation: he includes Hö'elün but omits Qasar from his description of troop distribution, and notes only a modest allotment given not to Qasar but to his offspring, which implies that something about the handout was worth hiding. The combination of drama in one source and reticence in the other – the *Secret History* elaborates at length on Mönglik's special treatment, while Rashīd

[117] Reasons for the rivalry included Temüjin's unpopular military reforms, Kököchü's ambitions, and political intrigue. Ratchnevsky, *Genghis Khan*, 98–9 (including the title), 100–1; Hambis, "Episode," 8, 16–17, 19.

[118] Only *Secret History*, §244 mentions the beating. Rashīd al-Dīn, *Jāmi'*, 167, trans. Thackston 90, conflates it with Kökochü's wrestling match with Temüge and substitutes Qasar as the victor. Hambis argues that some Chinese sources omit this episode because it showed Chinggis Khan arguing with a subject, which was undignified. Hambis, "Episode," 26.

[119] *Secret History*, §245.

[120] *Secret History*, §244; Rashīd al-Dīn, *Jāmi'*, 166–7, trans. Thackston, 89–90; also De Nicola, *Khatuns*, 48.

[121] *Secret History*, §244.

[122] *Secret History*, §245–6; Hambis, "Episode," 40–6; Ratchnevsky, *Genghis Khan*, 100–1.

al-Dīn barely mentions it – further suggests that the different rewards for Hö'elün and Mönglik may have caused tension. There was also clear ill will between Kököchü and Chinggis Khan, which ended in Kököchü's death. Finally, the *Secret History* claims that the drama sent Hö'elün into a rapid decline and death, but this detail has been critiqued as an epic motif, not an actual event.[123] Rashīd al-Dīn mentions no illness, but if Hö'elün died for real and not just for poetic effect, he might not have addressed it for fear of appearing to critique Chinggis Khan in a history written for his proud descendants.[124] In any case, if by contrast Hö'elün did weather the troop handout and her sons' infighting, she still had to respond to Köküchü's execution and Mönglik's crippling grief, to which the sources attest.[125] It is to be wondered whether she had much left in her famous stores of resilience by the time of these latest trials. Although we cannot know for certain what happened to Hö'elün after 1206, we do know that two later imperial mothers, Töregene and Sorqoqtani, also worked terribly hard to help their sons to the throne, and passed away shortly after achieving this goal. Raising a son to be khan was a wearying ordeal.

CONCLUSION

Despite the compelling quality and greater familiarity of Temüjin's narrative, the stories of the two most important women in his life, his mother and his wife, deserve investigation on their own merits. As this chapter has shown, Hö'elün's contributions to the history of the Mongol Empire included her early care of the conqueror and his siblings despite daunting odds, her shepherding of limited resources, and her years' worth of support. The irregularity of her marriage and the problems it caused also had a long-term impact on her family. Meanwhile, Börte provided Temüjin with important family connections to a Qonggirat lineage, numerous offspring to play military and political roles in the empire, and her own brand of counsel and guidance. The two women cooperated to support Temüjin logistically and economically, and freed him to pursue his ambitions while they ran the rest of his life around him. They also joined, inadvertently, in a uglier story of kidnap and pregnancy entwined with

[123] *Secret History*, §244 and de Rachewiltz, Commentary, 869–78; Moses, "Quarrelling Sons," 66.
[124] Rashīd al-Dīn, *Jāmi'*, 611–2, trans. Thackston, 281.
[125] *Secret History*, §245; Rashīd al-Dīn, *Jāmi'*, 167, trans. Thackston, 90.

the Merkits, which shaped Temüjin's military goals, strengthened his early relationships with important men, provided him with new followers through the distribution of Merkit wealth, affected his decisions about the ultimate fate of steppe rulers and subject peoples (the Merkits among them), and probably influenced his relationship with Börte's oldest son. The experiences of both women also make it clear why steppe wives needed resilience, given the challenges of their circumstances, and why some women became greatly strained by the demands made on their abilities. Nevertheless, these stories were ultimately marked by triumphs. In the next chapter we will investigate Temüjin's many other women, whose lives were marked irrevocably by defeat.

3

Conquered Women

Whereas investigating the two most important women in Temüjin's life illuminates his rise to power, studying his other women reveals the losing side of the equation, and has been largely overlooked by scholars.[1] This chapter explores the stories of Temüjin's most prominent secondary wives in order to recover the vanished history of the conquered. Such an exploration provides new insights into several topics. The Merkit, Tangut, and Jin princesses show the roles of female hostages on the steppe as compared to male hostages. The Tatar sisters demonstrate the complexity of women's loyalties. The Kereit sisters clarify the networks of informants that some conquered women controlled. The Jin princess highlights the ways that some women consoled themselves when faced with an absent husband and no children. Finally, the Naiman and Khwarazm-Shah cases illuminate the waste of female talent that accompanied conquests. At best, the stories of Temüjin's secondary women give us glimpses of the dispossessed; at worst, they remind us that the reverse of Temüjin's triumphal narrative was the ugly fate of the defeated.

BÖRTE AND THE OTHER WIVES

Although Börte was Temüjin's senior wife, she was certainly not the only one. Temüjin acquired other wives during his second rise in steppe politics, which was after Börte had finished childbearing: her ninth and

[1] Exceptions include de Rachewiltz, Commentary to the *Secret History*; Cheng, "Career;" Togan, *Flexibility and Limitation*, and discussions of the Mongol-Naiman battle of Chakirma'ut, which usually include Gürbesü Khatun.

final child, a daughter, Al Altan, was born in perhaps 1196. Thereafter Chinggis Khan's offspring came from other women. Börte had been the steady, reliable partner who cooperated with Hö'elün in the careful management of camp logistics that freed Temüjin to pursue his political goals. Börte had also produced enough sons to help Temüjin in his wars and to ensure inheritance of his patrimony, and enough daughters for Temüjin to form the alliances necessary to a political confederation when the time came. By contrast, the wives that Temüjin acquired between 1195 and 1215 represented something different: these were conquered women, and they demonstrated both the gradual fulfillment of Temüjin's political goals, and his military ascendance over enemies. They were all princesses or queens: the Kereit, Ibaqa; the Tatar sisters, Yisüi and Yisügen; the Uhaz Merkit, Qulan; Gürbesü, wife of the Naiman khan; the Tangut, Chaqa;[2] the Jin princess Qiguo;[3] and the Khwarazm-Shah queen mother, Terken,[4] although she did not become a wife. Some of these women produced children, but these were all younger than and junior to Börte's offspring, and although their career paths served their father, their lives were less glamorous than those of their half-siblings.

Despite the differences among them, all of Temüjin's secondary wives were characterized by certain similarities. They did not all live in the same establishments, since some controlled entire camps (*ordos*) that were similar to, but lesser than, the one managed by Börte, while others simply resided in camps run by others. Nevertheless, when gathered together, their gers must all have been sited in proximity to one another, possibly in the long east-west line described by Friar William.[5] Although Börte managed the wives and concubines who lived in her own camp, it is unclear how much she had to do with the affairs of the secondary wives who ran their own camps. But certainly all the wives met on festive or ceremonial occasions to drink and eat together. Temüjin presumably moved from ger to ger in some sort of rotation, and may have spent more time with his younger wives once Börte passed her childbearing years. But if so, none received the lion's share of attention that Börte had, since no junior wife bore anywhere near as many children with Temüjin as the

[2] Probably meaning "Child" (Mongolian), and not her Tangut name, which is lost. De Rachewiltz, Commentary, 904.

[3] This was a title; we do not know her name. I thank Anonymous Cambridge Reader 3 for pointing this out.

[4] This was also a title; see the subsequent discussion under the section "The Jin Princess," and also footnote 91.

[5] See Chapter 1.

nine that Börte produced.[6] In fact, none of Temüjin's secondary wives or concubines seem to have had more than one or two children.[7] We may also assume that Temüjin still visited Börte regularly, since her camp was the largest and most prominent, and was staffed with his own military officers.[8] Börte also had political advice to offer, children to discuss, and a long shared history with the conqueror.

Like Börte with her connections to her natal family, these later conquered wives were characterized by multiple loyalties; unlike Börte, they were rarely able to act on them. None of the conquered wives married Temüjin without suffering crushing loss, whether of family alone, or family and people. The most successful wives soon demonstrated an overt commitment to their husband and his empire, but may still have kept their first loyalties underneath. Nevertheless, although they began their married lives as captives, these women were not completely isolated. Thus even after the devastation of the Tatars in 1202, the sister-wives Yisüi and Yisügen were still alive, each commanding her own camp, along with the remaining women of their people, who had been parceled out among the Mongols. The sisters thus met for occasions when all wives were present, and perhaps for private visits as well. Similarly, when Temüjin took over the Kereits in 1203 with far less destruction, the senior Kereit men were killed, but the younger princes were not, while the Kereit royal women married into the Chinggisid family and formed a network there, supported by servants and retainers. In fact, very few conquered wives were truly isolated – even the Jin and Tangut princesses brought entourages when they married Chinggis Khan later in his career, and they may have kept contact with home through intermediaries.

Some of Chinggis Khan's conquered women also served as hostages. But although hostages were common among steppe nomads, most were men.

[6] Carpini notes that a senior wife always spent more time with her husband than the other wives. See Carpini, *History*, 18 (not in Rockhill).

[7] His named sons include Kölgen, son of the Merkit wife, Qulan; Cha'ur, son of the second Tatar wife, Yisügen; Orchan, son of the Tatar concubine, and Jürchedei, son of a Naiman concubine. There were allegedly many others. None of his named daughters – Töre, Chalun / Chabun, Alajai, and Ikires – have identifiable mothers. See Rashīd al-Dīn, *Jāmi'*, 141 (Alajai), 302–5 (Chinggis Khan's sons), trans. Thackston, 76, 148–9; *Meng-ta Pei Lüeh* [*Meng Da bei lu*] trans. Olbricht and Pinks, 24 (the sons and general proliferation of Chinggis Khan's offspring), albeit mentioning an unnamed son, older than Jochi (?), who died during the Jin campaign); *Yuan Shi*, 13: 2757–61 Table of Imperial Princesses (unpublished trans. Buell); also 109: 2761 for Töre, as cited in de Rachewiltz, Commentary, 843.

[8] For Börte's staff vs. those of the other wives, see Chapter 4, footnotes 8–16.

Chinggis Khan's numerous male hostages were relatives of army commanders or subject rulers, and they often joined the imperial guard. This gave them special proximity to Chinggis Khan, and could offer career opportunities.[9] By contrast, the roles, experiences, and importance of female hostages were far more limited. Chinggis Khan's hostage women all became his wives – the Merkit princess Qulan, the Tangut princess Chaqa, the Jin princess Qiguo. Their status as wives implied that these women enjoyed greater influence over Chinggis Khan than did the imperial guardsmen, since there were far fewer wives than guards. But their access to the conqueror actually gave these women few concrete gains, since – with the exception of Qulan – they themselves only mattered politically during the negotiations that led to their weddings, which sealed the interactions between Chinggis Khan and their families. Thereafter most hostage wives served symbolic roles at best, and had little influence on events, even those involving their natal families.

One final way in which conquered women differed from Börte was by representing significant losses of political talent and managerial experience. Although loss was an integral part of all conquest, these women's talent disappeared because it was left deliberately unused once the conquest ended (unlike the talent of conquered royal men, which was actively destroyed through death or exile). Thus, in her heyday, Gürbesü, senior wife of the Naiman ruler Tayang Khan, controlled and deployed far greater human, animal, and other resources than either Hö'elün or Börte, and was an independent force in Naiman politics. But the dismantling of the Naiman lineage, the distribution of Naiman subjects among the Mongols, and Gürbesü's forced marriage to Temüjin in 1204 limited her to managing whatever truncated allotment of servants, staff, and flocks she was permitted, while her political clout was reduced to nothing. She does not even seem to have gained her own camp. Similarly, Terken, queen mother of the Khwarazm-Shah Empire, lost an even higher position as an empress – her stature, wealth, and power far outshone anything possessed by Chinggis Khan's other women, even the daughter of the Jin emperor. This may have been a fortunate loss for Terken's subordinates, since some reports damned her as a tyrant, but the fact remains that Terken's considerable experience, connections, wealth, savvy, and skill became utterly useless in her new (and miserable) life once she was reduced to a symbol of conquest among the ranks of Chinggis Khan's lesser women.

[9] Lien-Sheng Yang, "Hostages in Chinese History," in *Studies in Chinese Institutional History*, ed. Lien-Sheng Yang, Harvard-Yenching Institute Studies 20 (Cambridge, MA: Harvard University Press), 43–57, esp. 48–9, 53–4 (Chinese and Mongol hostage systems).

THE KEREIT: IBAQA

The first major conquered wife was the Kereit princess Ibaqa, whose story sheds light on a network of Kereit relatives, retainers, and servants that came to exist within the Chinggisid family. But this was only after conquest. At first, the Nestorian Christian Kereits were a numerous, wealthy, powerful, and sophisticated people with many divisions, all subject to the ruling family under Ong Qan.[10] The Kereits were probably bilingual in Turkish and Mongolian, and their lands were near the Kerülen and Onon Rivers. This was in a region of semiarid grasses and scrub that blanketed wide valleys between low mountains extending south toward China and west to the upper Tula River.[11] Temüjin's father, Yisügei, had been Ong Qan's ally, and supported Ong Qan's often bloody attempts to rule the Kereits, despite the disapproval of some of Yisügei's fellow Mongols.[12] Temüjin himself may have spent part of his youth at Ong Qan's court; he later served as Ong Qan's follower.[13] It is likely that Temüjin modeled his imperial guard on a Kereit precedent.[14]

Temüjin had a separate relationship to Ong Qan's younger brother or perhaps young uncle, Jaqa Gambu (a Tangut title, "Great Commander of the Region"[15]), who seems to have had his own subjects, separate from those of Ong Qan, and who also lived for years in the Tangut Kingdom of Xi-Xia and was connected to the Tangut royal family by marriage.[16]

[10] Ong Qan had a golden tent (brocade?), and golden dishes in *Secret History*, §184–5, §187; even if this was poetic exaggeration, the implication of wealth is clear. Also Togan, *Flexibility and Limitation*, 63–4 (Kereits in general), 103 (wealth); Cheng, "Career," 36–37. For Kereit Christianity see De Nicola, *Khatuns*, 189–90.

[11] Togan, *Flexibility and Limitation*, 62–4.

[12] This was Qutula Qan; see Togan, *Flexibility and Limitation*, 70–74. Cheng suggests that Qutula was not leader of all Mongols, but only a war-leader on a particular campaign. This meant that Yisügei was free to help Ong Qan if he wanted. Cheng, "Career," 51–5.

[13] Togan, *Flexibility and Limitation*, 75–6, 120–21.

[14] Ratchnevsky, *Genghis Khan*, 84.

[15] I modify Cheng's translation in "Career," 77; also Togan, *Flexibility and Limitation*, 109, note 248, citing Pelliot who translates this roughly as "vastly accomplished." See also Ruth Dunnell, "The Fall of the Xia Empire: Sino-Steppe Relations in the Late 12th to early 13th Centuries," in *Rulers from the Steppe: State Formation on the Eurasian Periphery* , ed. Gary Seam and Daniel Marks (Los Angeles: Ethnographic Press, 1991), 163 and note 9.

[16] He was first a captive (hostage?), then earned a governorship, married, and wedded his most lovely daughter to the Tangut ruling family. Togan, *Flexibility and Limitation*, 76–7; she notes (p. 64) that the Tübe'en branch of the Kereits had close ties with the T'o-pa branch in Tangut realms, which may have helped Jaqa Gambu live there. Also Cheng, "Career," 74–9.

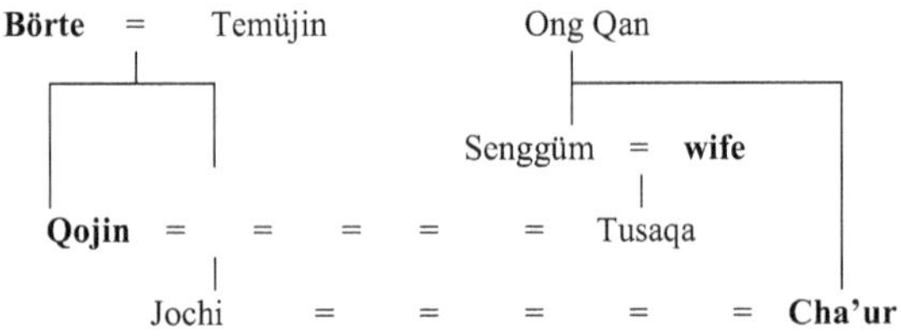

Family Tree 3.1 The proposed Chinggisid–Kereit double marriage.
All women are in **bold.**

Unfortunately, little is known about Jaqa Gambu's career or his interactions with Temüjin, in part because the early sources seem to be suppressing material.[17] But we can at least say that the relationship between the two men was long-standing and, at times, strong.

Nevertheless the main alliance was between Temüjin and Ong Qan. When Ong Qan was driven into exile by a brother (not Jaqa Gambu), it was Temüjin who helped him reclaim rule of the Kereits in the late 1190s.[18] As time passed, however, Temüjin's subservience seemed to wane, while disagreements over battles and spoils complicated matters.[19] Although ultimately a break between Temüjin and Ong Qan became inevitable, it arose ostensibly out of conflicts over questions of family, women, and status. At first, Temüjin had focused on creating a network of followers from within the Mongol people.[20] But in 1202 he proposed a double marriage (a sister exchange): Börte's daughter Qojin would marry Tusaqa, a son of Senggüm and thus a grandson of Ong Qan, while Börte's son Jochi would marry Ong Qan's daughter Cha'ur (Senggüm's sister).[21] (See Family Tree 3.1). This was clearly a foray into the larger world of nomadic confederations, in which two ruling lineages linked themselves through marriages between key principals.[22]

[17] Togan, *Flexibility and Limitation*, 77, note 112; for her reconstruction about Jaqa Gambu see 76–80, 95–7. Also Cheng's reconstructions of the relationship, with innovative dating, in "Career," 74–9; 85–6, 91; 96–101; 110–113.

[18] Togan, *Flexibility and Limitation*, 87–90; also Cheng with innovative dating in "Career," 78, 85–103, 120–23.

[19] It is possible that the two experimented with a dual kingship, but if so, this was short-lived. Togan, *Flexibility and Limitation*, 90–103, and 118–19 (desertions and battlefields); also Ratchnevsky, *Genghis Khan*, 67–83; Cheng, "Career," 123–36.

[20] Cheng, "Career," 119.

[21] *Secret History*, §165 and de Rachewiltz, Commentary, 596–7; Ratchnevsky, *Genghis Khan*, 67; Togan, *Flexibility and Limitation*, 99–101, 118–19; Cheng, "Career," 137–9.

[22] Miyawaki-Okada, "Imperial Succession," 143.

At first glance the proposal looked respectable: these were the two oldest children from Temüjin's senior wife.[23] But the Kereits feared it was really a maneuver to take over, and refused, insulting Temüjin, Börte, and their children.[24] Relations deteriorated immediately.[25] Then, however, the Kereits did an about-face and invited Temüjin to what looked like a betrothal feast. Temüjin started out with only a few men, unsuspecting, but spent the night on the way with Hö'elün's third husband, Mönglik, who guessed rightly that this was a trap, and dissuaded him from attending.[26] (Mönglik may have been warned by his son Kököchü, Temüjin's cousin, who had married a Kereit woman.[27]) Although Temüjin abandoned his journey and escaped, battle with the Kereits became inevitable. The two armies met first at Qalaqaljit Sands in 1203, but Temüjin failed to win the day and retreated to an emergency camp at Baljuna Lake. Some months later he returned to his regular camp, regrouped his forces, and gained new ones, including Börte's relatives and many other Qonggirats. He then attacked the Kereits again and defeated them, plundered their rank and file, and redistributed them among the Mongols.[28] Both Ong Qan and Senggüm fled and were later killed by other nomadic groups, and Temüjin assumed rule over the Kereits, exactly as Ong Qan had feared.[29]

23 At this point Qojin was about 23 – older for a Mongol bride – and Jochi perhaps 21.

24 Cheng, "Career," 137–8; Togan, *Flexibility and Limitation*, 99–100; also Ratchnevsky, *Genghis Khan*, 67–9; Biran, *Chinggis Khan*, 37; Dunnell, *Chinggis Khan*, 42; De Nicola, *Khatuns*, 44. The refusals revolved around concerns about women's status. Thus Senggüm complained that the proposal would not give Cha'ur and Qojin equal rank in *Secret History* §165: "If a kinswoman of ours [Cha'ur] goes to them, she would have to stand by the door and only face towards the back of the tent [the least honorable place]; but if a kinswoman of theirs [Qojin] comes to us, she would sit in the back of the tent and face towards the door [the most honorable place]." Elsewhere Ong Qan was furious: "How has not [Temüjin] great shame to ask for my daughter for wife [sic, for Jochi]? Does he not know that he is my man and my slave? But go back to him then and tell him on my part that I would have my daughter burnt sooner than I would give her him for wife [sic]." (Polo, *Description*, §65.) Both responses suggest Kereit apprehensions about Temüjin's political ambitions, which could be expressed in the guise of outrage over potential insults to Cha'ur. Also Rubruck, *Mission*, 124–5.

25 *Secret History*, §165.

26 *Secret History*, §168; Ratchnevsky, *Genghis Khan*, 67–9; Biran, *Chinggis Khan*, 37–8; Dunnell, *Chinggis Khan*, 42–3; also Togan, *Flexibility and Limitation*, 101; Cheng, "Career," 143.

27 Ratchnevsky, *Genghis Khan*, 69; Cheng, "Career," 222.

28 Ratchnevsky, *Genghis Khan*, 67–83; Biran, *Chinggis Khan*, 38; Dunnell, *Chinggis Khan*, 42–3.

29 Ong Qan by a Naiman who did not recognize him, and Senggüm by Temüjin's agents. Ratchnevsky, *Genghis Khan*, 67–83; Biran, *Chinggis Khan*, 38; Dunnell, *Chinggis Khan*, 42–3 and "Fall of the Xia," 164 for Senggüm; Atwood, "Tibet," 23–4.

But Jaqa Gambu was not present during this showdown, since he had earlier taken refuge with the Naimans after a falling out with Ong Qan. Then, after Temüjin defeated the Naimans in 1204, Jaqa Gambu joined him and received very special treatment. This was because Jaqa Gambu had four daughters, which allowed Temüjin to achieve a version of the marriages he had sought with the Kereit royal family, albeit with different brides. Jaqa Gambu's eldest daughter, Ibaqa, married Temüjin; her sister Begtütmish married Jochi, and a third sister, Sorqoqtani, became Tolui's senior wife, while their cousin, Dokuz, became one of Tolui's junior wives.[30] (See Family Tree 3.2).

They brought with them dowries of their own retainers, servants, and flocks, while their father kept his people and possessions by virtue of being an in-law.[31] These women thus formed a Kereit network, complete with subordinates and dependents, within the Chinggisid family. It is likely that they exchanged news and information with one another and with their father that furthered their single and common interests, and, in difficult times, may have been critical to their survival. Certainly the later close relations between the descendants of Jochi and Tolui have been attributed in part to the sisterly relationship between Begtütmish and Sorqoqtani.[32] But two Kereit women disappeared: one was Jochi's original intended, Ong Qan's daughter Cha'ur, whose fate is mentioned by no historical source; the other is Jaqa Gambu's fourth daughter, whose name is unknown, and who had already married among the Tanguts and vanished from historical view.[33] (By contrast, Qojin did not benefit from the Kereit downfall like her brothers; instead she married Butu of the

[30] Rashīd al-Dīn, *Jāmi'*, 118–19, 303, 361, 969, trans. Thackston, 64, 148, 175, 471; *Secret History*, §186 (only two daughters, Ibaqa and Sorqoqtani). Togan suggests that Begtütmish, Jochi's wife, may have been excised from the *Secret History* in order to promote Toluid interests, in *Flexibility and Limitation*, 77, note 112; also Ruth Dunnell, "Fall of the Xia," 163.

[31] *Secret History* §186, §208 (Jaqa Gambu; Ibaqa's possessions and staff), also Rashīd al-Dīn, *Jāmi'*, 197, 304, trans. Thackston, 104, 149; also Togan, *Flexibility and Limitation*, 104–5, arguing that the in-law relationship between Chinggis Khan and Jaqa Gambu was less important than their brief attempt to share kingship.

[32] Jackson, "Dissolution," 196.

[33] *Secret History*, §186 (Ibaqa and Sorqoqtani); Rashīd al-Dīn, *Jāmi'*, 118, 361, trans. Thackston, 64, 175 for the fourth daughter. She is said to have married into another people – the Önggüt (118 or trans. Thackston 64) or the Tangut (361, or trans. Thackston 175), and Temüjin later sought her unsuccessfully. Also Anonymous (2), *Campagnes*, trans. Pelliot and Hambis, 237, preferring Önggüts, and Atwood, "Tibet," 24, note 11, noting the confusion.

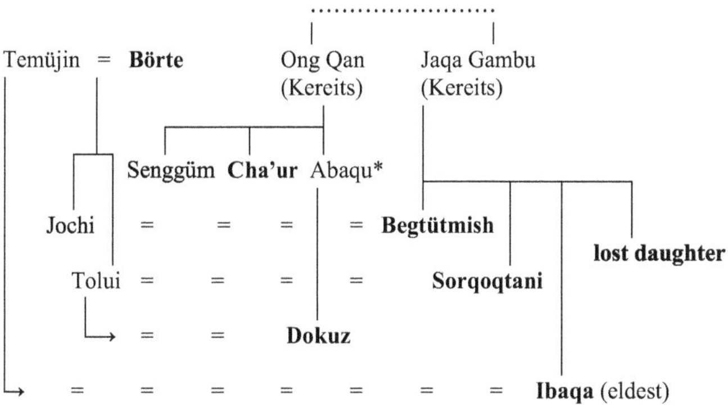

Family Tree 3.2 The Kereits and the Chinggisids.
All women are in **bold.**
Dotted line indicates unclear relationship.
* Indicates unclear birth order.

Ikires, her father's longstanding follower and the widower of her aunt Temülün.)[34]

Although one of these Kereit women, Sorqoqtani, later rose to tremendous power in the empire, the sister with the highest place did not enjoy it for long: this was Ibaqa, who stayed with Temüjin for only a few childless years until Temüjin abruptly remarried her in 1206 to a trusted follower, the Uru'ut Jürchedei.[35] The explanations for this sudden move are various yet unsatisfactory. The *Secret History* claims that when Temüjin rewarded his followers in 1206 he thanked Jürchedei for two special services: wounding Ibaqa's cousin Senggüm at Qalaqaljit Sands and killing Ibaqa's father Jaqa Gambu, who had turned against Temüjin some time after 1204.[36]

[34] *Secret History,* §202 (listing Butu as Chinggis Khan's son-in-law but without identifying his wife), and de Rachewiltz, Commentary, 446–7; Hambis, *Chapitre CVIII*, 29–30, citing the *Yuan wen-lei* (25, 6a–7b) and the *Yuan Shi* (118, 8b), also Table 4; Anonymous (2), *Campagnes*, trans. Pelliot and Hambis, 49–50; Rashīd al-Dīn, *Jāmi'*, 161–2, (garbled) 164, 301, 600, trans. Thackston, 87–8, 147, 276; also see Cheng, "Career," 221–2.

[35] He left Jamuqa for Chinggis Khan after Dalan Balzhut; he fought in the vanguard at Qalaqaljit Sands and wounded Senggum there, and later killed Jaqa Gambu. *Secret History*, §130, §171, §176, §185, §208. Rashīd al-Dīn confused Jürchedei with his son Kehetei (Ketei), who with his brother Bujir succeeded their father. Rashīd al-Dīn, *Jāmi'*, 196–7, 599–600, trans. Thackston, 104, 276; also de Rachewiltz, Commentary, 792.

[36] *Secret History*, §208; also Togan, *Flexibility and Limitation*, 100–106 on Temüjin and Jaqa Gambu's brief, failed dual kingship or alliance. Also Christopher P. Atwood, "Alexander, Ja-a Gambu and the Origins of the Image of Jamugha in the Secret History of the Mongols," in *Neilu Ouya lishi wenhua guoji xueshu yantaohui lunwenji*, ed. Teligeng [Terigün] and Li Jinxiu (Beijing: Nei Menggu renmin chubanshe, 2015), 164–170.

Jürchedei's reward included marriage to Ibaqa, which gave him the son-in-law privilege of command of a large military unit (4,000 men instead of 1,000) composed of soldiers who were Uru'uts like him, not strangers.[37] Temüjin thus thanked his follower in an exceptional way and guaranteed himself a lifetime of service. He also – inadvertently or deliberately? – weakened the network of royal Kereit women by moving its central character out of his own sphere.

By contrast, Rashīd al-Dīn explains this unprecedented repudiation as the result of a nightmare: when Temüjin awoke he told Ibaqa that God had commanded him to give her away, and he immediately did so to the first available man – the guard outside the tent, who happened to be Jürchedei. But this may be another of Rashīd al-Dīn's pious fictions designed to whitewash something unpleasant, like his insistence on Börte's pregnancy before the Merkit raid. Was something wrong with Ibaqa, or between her and Temüjin? Temüjin never renounced any other wife. Why was Ibaqa the exception? If Temüjin had wanted to make Jürchedei an in-law, he and Börte could have offered him a daughter, three of whom were unwed in 1206.[38] But instead he gave Ibaqa away to the man whose greatest service had been violence toward Kereit men. One theory is that Temüjin entered into a political alliance with Jaqa Gambu after marrying Ibaqa, but Jürchedei coveted Jaqa Gambu's place of honor, and attacked and killed him in 1204, either out of ambition, or in response to Jaqa Gambu's growing dissatisfaction with and distance from Temüjin. Ibaqa then became the reward for Jürchedei's service to Temüjin.[39] If Jaqa Gambu did turn against Temüjin it helps explain Rashīd al-Dīn's fiction, since he would not portray Sorqoqtani's father and the maternal ancestor of the entire Toluid branch of the Chinggisids as disloyal. Another theory is that Jürchedei had earned his new wife and position as a reward for general services to Chinggis Khan, and that Ibaqa's role would be to actively cement the alliance between the two men, and the cooperation of their many soldiers.[40]

Nevertheless, it seems that Temüjin suffered a guilty conscience about Ibaqa. In the *Secret History* he promised that he still cared for her, invoked the principle of proper social order (which he was maintaining by rewarding Jürchedei for his service), explained that she would keep her

[37] See Chapter 4 for in-law privileges.
[38] These were Checheyigen, Alaqa, and Al Altan. For their marriages, and those of their sisters and half-sisters, see Chapter 4.
[39] Togan, *Flexibility and Limitation*, 104–5.
[40] Buell and Kolbas, "Ethos," 51.

status and position as his wife even in her new marriage, and asked her to leave a token of her dowry by which he could remember her.[41] In Rashīd al-Dīn he begged her not to be angry (although he asked Jürchedei not to be afraid).[42] Ibaqa had no choice in the matter, but married Jürchedei, with whom she had children and later moved to northern China.[43] Furthermore, despite the damage that Ibaqa's second marriage surely did to the network of royal Kereit women within the Chinggisid family, the network itself remained active. Ibaqa exemplified this by returning to Mongolia every year to renew her connections at court, host parties, and confer with her sister Sorqoqtani (at least until the latter also moved to northern China).[44] Later Jürchedei repaid Temüjin's trust by playing an active military role in China.[45]

Thus the Kereits represented Temüjin's foray into the world of nomadic confederations through the proposed double marriage. After this failed, Temüjin's relationships with his former friends, allies, and patrons deteriorated so far that he eventually conquered and dismantled the Kereit ruling lineage and scattered their subjects among his own. By doing so he accidentally created a network of Kereit women and their dependents at the highest political levels among the Chinggisids, which provided these conquered women with unexpected resources and political connections. Furthermore, despite his failure to forge an initial confederation with the Kereits through marriage, it was, ironically, Temüjin's Kereit wife Ibaqa whose second marriage to Jürchedei turned her into an important member of a later Chinggisid confederation that Chinggis Khan used to conquer his empire.[46]

THE ALCHI TATAR SISTERS: YISÜI AND YISÜGEN

The next two conquered women to enter Temüjin's family were the Tatar sisters, Yisüi and Yisügen. They best exemplify the complexity of women's loyalties, which we can see in unusual detail because of unexpected revelations about their activities in one historical source. The tale began with the Tatar people and their leaders' long-standing feud with the Mongols, as first mentioned in Chapter 2. This led the Tatars to oppose

41 *Secret History*, §208; also Buell and Kolbas, "Ethos," 51; De Nicola, *Khatuns*, 143.
42 Rashīd al-Dīn, *Jāmi'*, 304, trans. Thackston, 148.
43 Rashīd al-Dīn, *Jāmi'*, 673, trans. Thackston, 330, trans. Boyle, 65–6.
44 Rashīd al-Dīn, *Jāmi'*, 673, trans. Thackston, 330, trans. Boyle, 65–6. Later Sorqoqtani also gained possession of lands in China. See Chapter 7.
45 See Chapter 5 for the campaigns. 46 See Chapters 4 and 5.

Temüjin bitterly as he struggled to establish himself on the steppe. The Tatars surely also mistrusted Temüjin's connections to their Jin overlords when he returned to the steppe leading a Jin army in 1196 after his mysterious absence. Temüjin in turn needed to eliminate the Tatars because of their wealth, strength, and numbers, which represented a serious threat despite the Tatars' political disunity. Temüjin therefore fought the Tatars at least twice, and in the autumn of 1202 defeated them for good at Dalan Nemurges.[47] After the battle Temüjin and his relatives decided to "measure the Tatars against the linchpin."[48] In the idiom of the steppe this meant that males descended from a common ancestor were literally measured against the linchpin of a cart (about 2 feet or nearly 2/3 meter high), and those taller than the linchpin – all but babies or short toddlers – were slain.[49] In this way Temüjin defeated his enemies, avenged the Tatar betrayal of his ancestor Ambaqai Khan decades earlier, and the murder of his father, Yisügei, more recently. He also acquired the Tatars' considerable wealth, especially in silver, for his own purposes.[50]

Although Rashīd al-Dīn claims that Temüjin also killed Tatar women and girls, this was dramatic overstatement; instead they and a few very young boys became part of the spoils.[51] Among the survivors was a young woman, Yisügen, a daughter of the executed Tatar leader, Yeke Cheren. Because of her status, Yisügen went to Temüjin, who slept with her. The *Secret History* claims that while in bed together, Yisügen asked Temüjin to treat her well and not discard her; when he seemed amenable to this, she recommended her missing older sister Yisüi as a wife for him. Temüjin, perhaps a little surprised, asked Yisügen if she would cede her place to her sister if the latter proved to be as remarkable as promised. But Yisügen agreed willingly. Temüjin therefore sent men out to hunt for Yisüi, who was soon discovered in the woods, fleeing with her husband. The man ran away, but Yisüi was brought to Temüjin, who found her every bit as pleasing as promised. Yisügen then stepped down in rank to let her sister take her place.[52]

[47] The battles were in 1196 and 1202. Ratchnevsky, *Legacy*, 52–4, 66–7.

[48] *Secret History*, §154 and de Rachewiltz, Commentary, 571.

[49] *Secret History*, §154, and de Rachewiltz, Commentary, 571; for a similar story see the Qangli Turks at Bukhara, Juvaynī, *World-Conqueror*, 106; Rashīd al-Dīn, *Jāmi'*, 500, trans. Thackston, 247. Biran, *Chinggis Khan*, 37, on the height of the linchpin.

[50] For silver "vessels and implements" see Rashīd al-Dīn, *Jāmi'*, 77, trans. Thackston, 43; for the orphan Shigi Qutuqu in gold-stitched silk and fur see *Secret History*, §135.

[51] Rashīd al-Dīn, *Jāmi'*, 83, trans. Thackston, 46; de Rachewiltz, Commentary, 571, for a corrective.

[52] *Secret History*, §155.

What to make of this story? Was it yet another dramatic exaggeration? Not necessarily so. Although it is unlikely that the author of the *Secret History* was present while Temüjin and Yisügen were (first?) having sex and (later?) conversing, those men sent to seek Yisüi probably pieced together some of the details from their orders. Certainly the story does not ring untrue. Yisügen had just seen her menfolk slaughtered, and in a mixture of desperation and resilience must have been grasping at straws to save her female relatives. Despite the daunting emotional cost of sleeping with Temüjin, she had no choice about doing so; furthermore, time spent in his bed also represented opportunity, which Yisügen seized. Yisügen must have feared for her sister's chances, alone with her husband, a hunted man, in reach of the Mongol army as the weather turned toward winter. Clearly Yisügen's loyalties were entirely to her family, and she adeptly used her new position to convince Temüjin to send troops after what little remained of it.

When Yisüi and Yisügen were reunited, they found themselves left with one another and the remnants of their people – the other bereaved mothers, wives, sisters, and daughters who had been parceled out among the Mongols. Their men were dead, their livestock divided, their tents and belongings given to others. As the daughters of the dead chief, Yisüi and Yisügen had to sleep with the man who had just had their relatives killed. Their situation was thus traumatic, and they were fortunate to have one another, and a third Tatar woman, who became Temüjin's concubine.[53] Meanwhile Temüjin's brother, Jochi-Qasar, also had a Tatar wife (possibly acquired at this time). Later, yet another high-ranking woman named Boraqchin – a descendant? A young sister or cousin? – married Jochi's son Batu.[54] Finally, both Yisüi and Yisügen were placed in charge of camps, which demonstrates their abilities.[55] Nevertheless, such trauma made tremendous demands on captive women's resilience, and it is unreasonable to expect major achievements from them, especially not ones that highlight the true state of their hidden loyalties.

And yet Yisüi and Yisügen are credited with such achievements. A curious story recounts that the sisters asked their husband for two young Tatar brothers who had escaped the slaughter. Apparently pleased with his new wives, Temüjin granted their request, and the boys went to work in Yisüi's kitchen. Later they achieved modest careers: the older one,

53 Rashīd al-Dīn, *Jāmi'*, 89, 304; trans. Thackston, 49, 149.
54 Rashīd al-Dīn, *Jāmi'*, 88–9, 304; trans. Thackston, 48–9, 149.
55 *Yuan Shi*, 14: 2693–6, 2698, 2701, Table of Empresses (unpublished trans. Buell).

Quli, worked for Temüjin in a minor capacity, and later served Börte's fourth son, Tolui, then Tolui's tenth and least son, Sübügetei. The younger brother, Qara Mönggetü Uha, did not distinguish himself under Temüjin, but his offspring rose to respectable positions under Tolui's first son, Möngke (r. 1251–9), under Möngke's brother Hülegü (d. 1265), and finally under Hülegü's descendants, the Ilkhanid dynasty in Iran (1258–1335).[56]

Some time later Yisüi made another request of her husband. She praised the brothers for their dependable service, then asked Temüjin to reward them by collecting their remaining family: "Quli Noyan and his brother Mönggetü Uha have grown up, are in attendance on you, and enjoy your trust. If you so order, let their relatives and clansmen be assembled from wherever they may be."[57] Yisüi timed her request well. Perhaps she made it after successfully advising Temüjin on the matter of succession to his position as grand khan, as will be discussed in Chapter 4. Or she waited until her sister Yisügen gave birth to Temüjin's son Cha'ur, and thus took advantage of what may have been Temüjin's celebratory mood on the arrival of a new child. Less likely, she could have coordinated it with the pregnancy of the Tatar concubine, who bore another son, Orchan. Or perhaps she selected some other felicitous event of which the sources record no trace.[58] Regardless of the details, Yisüi clearly chose a good moment because Temüjin was amenable and allowed her to collect the few remaining Tatars. Lest the story seem like only a charming fable, it should be noted that thirty families descended from these rescued Tatars were living in Iran in 1306, with other Tatar families among the Jochids in Central Asia, where the aforementioned Alchi Tatar woman, Boraqchin, had gone.[59]

This tale raises important questions about women's loyalties. Although ostensibly Yisüi was helping two downtrodden orphans, her real goal must be understood as larger and more subversive: to ameliorate the

[56] Neither appears in the *Secret History*. Quli had a modest career: he ran the camp of Tolui's junior son Sübügetei, whose mother was a lesser wife. Rashīd al-Dīn, *Jāmi'*, 86, 779, 783; trans. Thackston, 48, 381, 383; trans. Boyle, 159, 162.

[57] Rashīd al-Dīn, *Jāmi'*, 88; trans. Thackston, 49.

[58] Rashīd al-Dīn claims that both sons died as babies in *Jāmi'*, 303–4, trans. Thackston, 148–9, but Boyle points out that Rashīd al-Dīn cannot be trusted, since Orchan actually participated during the second Tangut campaign (1226–7), i.e., as an adult. Juvaynī, *World-Conqueror*, 180–81 and footnotes, esp. note 7.

[59] Rashīd al-Dīn, *Jāmi'*, 88; trans. Thackston, 49.

wretched situation of her people, the Tatars her father had ruled and her mother had managed. She was thus using her status as Temüjin's wife and her position in his favor to act on her first loyalties, which were certainly not to him. She laid the groundwork for this perilous behavior by convincing Temüjin to give her the orphans as dependents, then built on that foundation by collecting those Tatars still alive among Temüjin's peoples under the guise of restoring the orphans' families.

Nor could this unexpected achievement have happened without Yisüi's training as a young woman. Steppe society expected a woman who married a ruler to remember the needs of her family and people even in her new life.[60] As daughters of a leader, Yisüi and Yisügen had been raised to wed rulers and manage both their husbands' resources and their own, not just those of a small household. At the same time, their status meant that Temüjin married them (rather than making them concubines) as a visible expression of his ascendance over their father, the dismemberment of the Tatars, and the beginning of a new order. (They also represented his due reward.) This meant that as wives, and in Yisügen's case, the mother of a son, they were both trained and positioned to make a partial reconstitution of their dispersed subjects, despite their own original status among the enemy.

Nor were the sisters alone. Initially Temüjin had assigned executions of the Tatars to his followers, among them some to his brother Qasar. But a wife of Qasar's, herself a Tatar, is said to have interceded and saved half the men allotted to her husband. This suggests her own divided loyalties, and paralleled Yisüi's efforts. Temüjin later discovered Qasar's failure to kill his entire allotment and held this lapse against his brother (unfortunately his view of his sister-in-law is unrecorded).[61] Thus although in theory the annihilation of a steppe people was final, in reality some few might be saved. If so, then captured women with their hidden loyalties could be the ones to do it, but only if they were well trained and placed, like Yisüi, Yisügen, or Qasar's wife, and only if they possessed the necessary resilience, and daring, to try. Other women in this position, like the Merkit wife Qulan, either did not make this dangerous effort, or failed to achieve anything.

[60] See Chapter 1, footnote 158, referring to the poem: "From old days, the Qonggirat people / Have the qatuns as shields, / Have their daughters as intercessors." *Secret History*, §64, and de Rachewiltz, Commentary, 332; Togan, "The Qongrat," 70–72.

[61] *Secret History*, §154 (without Qasar's wife). Rashīd al-Dīn, *Jāmi'*, 83, trans. Thackston, 46.

THE MERKIT QULAN

The Merkit Qulan was Temüjin's next major known wife after Börte, Ibaqa, and the Tatar sisters. Her position was at first the uncomfortable one of a hostage. She appeared in Mongol history when her father, Dayir Usun of the Uhaz branch of the Merkits, submitted to Temüjin in the winter of 1203–4 and offered him his daughter.[62] But at least according to the *Secret History*, Qulan and her father were detained on the way by Naya'a, one of Temüjin's officers, who was ostensibly trying to protect them from nearby Mongol soldiers. After their arrival three days late, Temüjin became suspicious that Naya'a's intentions had been more carnal in nature than anyone was admitting. While Temüjin was interrogating Naya'a, Qulan spoke up in his defense and boldly invited Temüjin to inspect her personally for virginity, which apparently pleased him.[63] In the end Temüjin accepted both Dayir Usun's submission and Qulan herself as a wife. But by this point unexpected damage may have been done, since upon arriving in Temüjin's camp Dayir Usun had noted how few horses Temüjin had.[64] This may have convinced him to change his tune: he soon threw off his submission, but he and his subjects were subdued, his possessions plundered, and he himself killed.[65] This left Qulan stranded: when her father reneged on the alliance she was meant to seal, Qulan was ensconced in her new life, and had nowhere to go.[66] To make matters worse, Temüjin then pursued all branches of the Merkits until their final dispersal in 1218.

Despite the limitations of her position, Qulan managed to achieve meaningful status in her new life with Chinggis Khan. She was an able manager: she controlled one of the big wifely camps, in which other wives, concubines, children, staff, and animals lived under her aegis.[67] She earned enough respect – perhaps by demonstrating the executive skills she used to run the camp – that Chinggis Khan chose her to manage his traveling camp on the Western Campaign (1218–23) as well.[68] To further suggest the positive regard with which her husband viewed her, it should be noted that Qulan's brother worked as a mid-level commander directly for Chinggis Khan, and also served Qulan in her own camp in an

[62] *Secret History*, §197. [63] *Secret History*, §197.
[64] Rashīd al-Dīn, *Jāmi'*, 419, trans. Thackston, 203.
[65] Rashīd al-Dīn, *Jāmi'*, 96 (plunder), 620 (Dayir Usun's death), trans. Thackston, 53, 304.
[66] Rashīd al-Dīn, *Jāmi'*, 96, 419, trans. Thackston, 53, 203.
[67] *Yuan Shi*, Table of Empresses, 2693–6, 2698, 2701 (unpublished trans. Buell).
[68] *Secret History*, §257. Also see Chapter 5.

unspecified capacity.[69] Qulan may well have had a hand in finding him this position.

On a more simple, human level, Chinggis Khan liked her: his appreciation seems to have led him to spend time with her, which allowed her eventually to emerge as a imperial childbearer when she became pregnant with a son, Kölgen. Kölgen grew safely to adulthood, and went on to participate with Börte's sons in their father's campaigns, and in a later campaign to Russia.[70] We cannot doubt that Kölgen was an important junior son, since he inherited substantially from his father – his personal troop numbers resembled those of Börte's sons, which underscores his mother's status.[71] Nevertheless, although Kölgen and his descendants attended important assemblies (*quriltai*s) in which succession was decided, he was never a candidate for rule, since Qulan was not Chinggis Khan's senior wife.[72] Furthermore, Qulan herself is not noted for special resilience or extraordinary achievement, nor is there any record that she shaped Temüjin's treatment of the Merkits, or engaged in subversive efforts on their behalf like Yisüi and Yisügen with the Tatars.[73] Thus although she rose admirably above the initial limitations of her position, she should still not be compared to the most influential women in the history of the empire.

GÜRBESÜ AND THE NAIMANS

Having conquered his way steadily through the Alchi Tatars, Kereits, and Uhaz Merkits and acquired at least one wife each time, Temüjin turned to the next threat on the steppe, the Turkic Naimans under the leadership of Tayang Khan (a title from the Chinese *taiwang*, Great King; his name was Baibuqa[74]). Like the Kereits mentioned above, the Naimans formed a large, wealthy, powerful, and sophisticated polity, which was located to the west of Mongol territory. Tayang Khan first prepared to attack Temüjin in 1204, and invited Alaqush, prince of the Öng'üt Turks, to

[69] Rashīd al-Dīn, *Jāmi'*, 96, 593, trans. Thackston, 54, 273 Rashīd al-Dīn calls him Jamal Khwaja, a Muslim name that seems unlikely for a Merkit in this period.
[70] Rashīd al-Dīn, *Jāmi'*, 96, 302, 537, 609, 666, 668, trans. Thackston, 53–4, 148, 261, 280, 325, 327; Juvaynī, *World-Conqueror*, 180, 269; also Dunnell, *Chinggis Khan*, 45.
[71] Rashīd al-Dīn, *Jāmi'*, 609, trans. Thackston, 281.
[72] Juvaynī, *World-Conqueror*, 180–81, 568 (Kölgen's sons at the 1251 quriltai).
[73] By contrast Cheng argues that the Uhaz Merkit were not destroyed, but distributed among the Mongols because of Qulan's position. Cheng, "Career," 236.
[74] Ratchnevsky, *Genghis Khan*, 83.

join him. The Öng'üts lived along the border with the Jin Empire, and many were Nestorian Christians. Their ruling family was connected by marriage to the Naimans.[75] But Alaqush assessed the situation and decided to ally himself with Temüjin, not Tayang Khan. To this end Alaqush sent a warning of Tayang Khan's intentions to Temüjin, which allowed him to prepare for and win a battle that he might otherwise have lost. Temüjin later showed his appreciation for Alaqush's timely notice by marrying Börte's third daughter, Alaqa, into the Öng'üt ruling family.[76]

The conquered woman who came to Temüjin after he defeated the Naimans was not herself a Naiman, but was Tayang Khan's stepmother and wife, a woman of unknown origin, Gürbesü, who had married Tayang Khan through the levirate after the death of his father, Inanch Khan.[77] Among the conquered women, Gürbesü is the first example of the way female talent was wasted in the aftermath of a military victory. Talent she had: she was clearly Tayang Khan's senior wife, since she wielded considerable authority among the Naimans. Tayang Khan is said to have loved her deeply (and may even have quarreled with his brother Buiruk Khan about her),[78] which could have contributed to her status and position.[79] Her sophistication is unquestioned: when the decapitated head of the Kereit Ong Khan was brought to the Naiman court, it was Gürbesü who recognized it and ordered her daughters-in-law to honor it with appropriate mourning rituals that included homage, wine libations, and song.[80] It is worth wondering whether she was a Kereit herself, since such another large group of Turkic Nestorians would be a logical place for

[75] Buell, "Prolegomena," 45; also Atwood, "Öng'üt Case," 515–16, 520–1.

[76] See Chapters 4 and 5.

[77] She is described in the *Secret History* as Tayang Khan's mother, but this should be understood as stepmother, then wife. Ratchnevsky, *Genghis Khan*, 83; *Secret History*, §189, and de Rachewiltz, Commentary, 569–70; Anonymous (2), *Campagnes*, trans. Pelliot and Hambis, 308–9. De Nicola, *Khatuns*, 44–5, on the contradictory references to her marriages.

[78] Anonymous (2), *Campagnes*, trans. Pelliot and Hambis, 308.

[79] Rashīd al-Dīn, *Jāmi'*, 127, 304, trans. Thackston, 68–9, 149.

[80] Less believably the text claims that the head laughed, which caused Tayang Khan to stomp on it. *Secret History*, §189, de Rachewiltz, Commentary, 680–81 (the laughing effect); De Nicola, *Khatuns*, 186. Note Carpini, *History*, 13 (not in Rockhill), on the task of women to "burn bones for the men's souls." For general duties of daughters-in-law, see Urgunge Onon, *The History and the Life of Chinggis Khan* (E. J. Brill: Leiden 1990), 93, note 236, repeated verbatim in Onon (2001), *The Secret History of the Mongols: The Life and Times of Chinggis Khan*, (Curzon: Richmond, Surrey), §189, note 425. Also F. W. Cleaves, "Uighuric Mourning Regulations," *Journal of Turkish Studies* 1 (1977): 69, for daughters-in-law among Uighurs, who mourned by donning white garments and loosening their hair.

Inanch Khan to find a wife, and might explain why she knew Ong Qan's face. At least according to the *Secret History* she was accustomed to authority: she not only helped convince Tayang Khan to attack Temüjin, but later a disgruntled commander griped that Gürbesü should be in charge of the Naiman army, not Tayang Khan, since the latter was not acting boldly enough for the commander's liking.[81] Gürbesü is also credited with a fine sense of her own elevation: the *Secret History* describes the contempt she expressed for the uncultured, dirty, and smelly Mongols, with which Temüjin later taunted her after she was brought as a captive to join his ranks of wives.[82] (The argument that she became a concubine is untenable.)[83] Thereafter another high-ranking woman from the conquered Naimans married Börte's son Tolui.[84]

Whereas Temüjin's previous conquered women had all been talented, often spirited, but otherwise relatively inexperienced daughters of important leaders, Gürbesü was in another category entirely, having been the senior wife of two khans in a row (Inanch and Tayang), both of whom controlled one of the largest and most cultured steppe peoples. With her came the Naimans' considerable wealth as spoils, but Gürbesü herself could no longer deploy it as she once had done: that task fell to Temüjin, who parceled his gains out among his womenfolk, commanders, and followers. Thus Gürbesü's sophistication and administrative experience did her no good alongside the management of Hö'elün and Börte, even though Gürbesü had certainly controlled far greater resources than they.

It would be instructive to know more about Gürbesü's mental state. As a twice-married woman, to a father and then a son, and as a woman

81 This was Tayang's advisor Qori Sübechi. *Secret History*, §194. Alternatively, this passage may be so heavily infused with entertaining and instructive literary devices that it cannot be accepted at face value. Paul Kahn, "Instruction and Entertainment in the Naiman Battle Text: An Analysis of 189 through 196 of *The Secret History of the Mongols*," in *Cultural Contact, History and Ethnicity in Inner Asia*, ed. Michael Gervers and Wayne Schlepp (Toronto: Joint Center for Pacific Studies, 1996), 95–106.

82 *Secret History*, §189, §196. Kahn reads this interaction as pure literary invention.

83 She is described as Temüjin's wife in *Secret History*, §196, and Rashīd al-Dīn, *Jāmi'*, 304, trans. Thackston, 149, but the *Yuan Shi* 2:106, 2693–7 does not list her as a wife, as cited in de Rachwiltz, Commentary, 723; also *Yuan Shi*, 2693–6, 2698, 2701 (unpublished trans. Buell). See also W. Hung, "Three of Chi'en Ta-hsin Poems on Yuan History," *HJAS* 19 (1956): 31–2, footnote 7, on a confusing reference to her and to concubines in the same sentence. Given Temüjin's habit of marrying socially prominent conquered women like the Tatar sisters or Ibaqa, rather than making them concubines, there is no reason to think he treated Gürbesü differently. De Nicola accepts the concubine hypothesis in *Khatuns*, 45.

84 This was Küchlüg's daughter, Lingqun. See Chapter 8, footnotes 30, 32.

who – if reports are accurate – had precipitated a major political break between Tayang Khan and his brother Buiruk Khan, she was hardly some ingénue without experience or resilience.[85] But her reaction to the conquest of her husband's people and to her reduction to a trophy remains unknown. Did she miss not only the people she had known, but also the powers she had enjoyed and the events she had shaped? What effect did conquest have on the mind of a once-powerful person? Soon after her absorption into the ranks of Temüjin's womenfolk, Gürbesü vanished from historical view. No record indicates that she worked to care for the remnants of the Naiman people themselves, scattered now among the Mongols. It is also unknown how often Temüjin visited Gürbesü, while if she had children with her new husband, they went unmentioned by all historical sources.

WOMEN FROM CONQUERED EMPIRES

Three final conquered women represented Chinggis Khan's transformation from a regional ruler commanding steppe nomads to a terrifyingly adept subduer of empires. Whereas the wives he acquired in 1202–4 symbolized his success over other nomads, these later women publicly demonstrated his dominance over sedentary states. They were Chaqa, a Tangut princess from the small kingdom of Xi-Xia southwest of the Mongols; Princess Qiguo, a daughter of the Jin emperor in Northern China, and Terken Khatun, queen mother in the empire of the Khwarazm-Shah, which encompassed the Islamic territories of Transoxiana, Khwarazm, Khurasan, and Iran. Chaqa and Princess Qiguo joined the ranks of Chinggis Khan's wives, but although both were honored and treated well, they were little more than hostages during the negotiations that were sealed by their marriages, and, thereafter, living reminders of their husband's ascendance over their homelands and families. Occasionally they exerted themselves to receive important visitors, especially those coming from home, but otherwise we hear little of their activities. Neither is known to have borne children with Chinggis Khan, and it seems unlikely that he visited them more often than decency required. As for Terken Khatun, who was older than her Tangut and Jürchen counterparts: it is unclear whether she became a wife, but certainly she suffered

85 Anonymous (2), *Campagnes*, trans. Pelliot and Hambis, 308.

tremendous reversals to her power, and eked out a miserable existence in Mongolia for long years until she was released by death.

CHAQA THE TANGUT PRINCESS

Chaqa[86] was the first of Chinggis Khan's imperial conquests, and the best illustration of the powerlessness of female hostages in steppe society. Chaqa married Chinggis Khan at the end of his first major campaign into the sedentary society of the Tangut kingdom of Xi-Xia (1209–10) on the far side of the inhospitable Gobi Desert. Chaqa's father was the Tangut king, Weiming Anquan (r. 1206–11). The campaign was a logistical challenge for the Mongols because it was the first time they had to besiege cities, and although they comported themselves well enough, it was not a dazzling success: ultimately they were forced to sue for peace when their camp was flooded during an important siege.[87] But in the end Weiming Anquan agreed to become a vassal, send costly tribute, and provide supplies for future military campaigns.[88] He also sent Chaqa, who became one of Chinggis Khan's junior wives. Nothing suggests that she had a camp of her own, which means that she must have resided under another woman's auspice. Nor do sources mention any children, or a political role for her; all we know is that when possible she spent her time welcoming important guests from China.[89]

Unlike in the case of the first hostage wife, Qulan, who overcame her father's uprising to become an important figure in Chinggis Khan's life, Chaqa's value seems to have been limited to the negotiations in which her father and husband came to terms. Thereafter Chaqa's position may have declined when her father's reign ended only a year after she was sent to Chinggis Khan, and rule shifted to a collateral line under Weiming Zunxu (r. 1211–23, Shenzong).[90] Power never returned to Chaqa's immediate family, since when Weiming Zunxu abdicated he was followed by his son, Weiming Dewang (r. 1224–6, Xianzong), then one final relative, Weiming Xian (r. 1226–7).[91] Since Weiming Dewang and Weiming Xian were both covertly or, at times, overtly hostile to the Mongols, we may deduce that

86 Probably meaning "Child" (Mongolian), and not her Tangut name, which is lost. De Rachewiltz, Commentary, 904.

87 See Chapter 5. 88 Dunnell, *Chinggis Khan*, 64.

89 *Secret History*, §249, and de Rachewiltz, Commentary, 903–4; see also Chaqa's 1221 welcome of the Taoist master Li, Chang-chun, in, *Travels*, 70–71.

90 I.e., a cousin to Weiming Anquan. Dunnell, "Xi-Xia," 171.

91 Dunnell, "Xi-Xia," 175, 177.

Chaqa's position had little effect on their policies. It is also worth wondering whether her familial distance from them – she was a cousin, not a sister – encouraged a certain disregard from them. Or perhaps they knew the limitations of her marriage, and thus discounted her presence among the Mongols entirely. We do not hear that she acted as an intermediary between her husband and her people, which was a marked contrast with steppe wives like Börte, who was busy linking the Chinggizids and the Qonggirats along with a host of other duties, or the tenacious Yisüi, who spent her energies caring covertly for stray Tatars.

THE JIN PRINCESS

The second imperial conquest was Princess Qiguo (a title; we do not know her name[92]), a daughter of the Jin emperor, Wanyan Yongji, a.k.a. Xingsheng, a.k.a. (posthumously) Wei Shao Wang (r. 1209–13).[93] Like Chaqa, she demonstrated the lack of influence that female hostages exerted on events; unlike Chaqa, Princess Qiguo seems to have consoled herself by building a reputation as a hostess later in life. She entered the history of the Mongol Empire during Chinggis Khan's campaign against the Jurchen dynasty of the Jin in Northern China. As Chinggis Khan advanced, representatives of the Jin government offered him a series of gifts designed to convince him to go away, among them Princess Qiguo herself. This was during the siege of the northern Chinese city of Zhongdu in 1214–15, another technical challenge for Chinggis Khan's armies, which were again trying to master a relatively unfamiliar form of warfare (siegecraft), and also struggling with sickness. But the Jin government was itself in a state of weakness, since Princess Qiguo's father the emperor had been overthrown and murdered by the general Zhizong in September 1213.[94] It was therefore the subsequent Emperor Xuanzong (r. 1213–23), a nephew of his predecessor, who came to an agreement with Chinggis Khan and sent him extensive tribute. Included with these riches was Princess Qiguo as a hostage wife. This was an impressive piece of marital diplomacy from Xuanzong, who made it appear that he was capitulating to terms of humiliation, but adroitly paid little personal cost since Princess Qiguo was his cousin, not his sister or daughter. We note that none of Xuanzong's close female relatives ever married Chinggis Khan, despite

[92] Report from Anonymous Cambridge Reader 3.
[93] I.e., "Prince Shao of Wei."
[94] Martin, *North China*, 161–2.

the Jin government's continued troubles as the Mongol invasion continued into the 1220s and beyond.

But although Princess Qiguo was a helpless pawn and a living symbol of Jin humiliation, the formalities were beautifully observed. She thus was dispatched to her fate with an impressive retinue of 500 servants; then, after marriage, she ranked highly among Chinggis Khan's wives.[95] She is remembered in one historical source as not at all beautiful – a pejorative detail that was widely repeated – but she was treated with respect because she represented the Jin Empire.[96] Nevertheless, like the Tangut princess Chaqa, Princess Qiguo's usefulness as a hostage was limited because her family had been dispossessed with the murder of her father. Surely few if any at the new Jin court spared a thought for her while planning their next reactions to Mongol aggression.

Also like Princess Chaqa, Princess Qiguo is not known to have borne children, even though she was probably young at the time of her marriage (she lived until the 1260s).[97] Given her age, this lack of offspring suggests that her busy husband may not have visited often. But despite her childlessness or any overt political role for her in Mongol interactions with the Jin, she does appear to have made a name for herself in hospitality. This was in part due to the efforts of one of her retainers, an Örmüg woman trained as a steward whose fame became widespread, probably by arranging the dinners and parties that the Mongols so loved.[98] Along with Princess Chaqa, Princess Qiguo made a special effort to welcome the Taoist sage Changchun, who visited the enormous imperial camp in summer 1221, by sending him millet, silver, and clothing.[99] These details suggest that Princess Qiguo enjoyed a certain reputation as a hostess, which surely increased the respect with which she was treated.

TERKEN KHATUN

The third and last major conquered imperial woman was Terken Khatun, queen mother to the Khwarazm-Shah ruler Muḥammad b. Tekish

95 Martin, *North China*, 170–71 and note 42; Rashīd al-Dīn, *Jāmi'*, 303, 450; trans. Thackston, 148, 221 (her rank and treatment).

96 Rashīd al-Dīn, *Jāmi'*, 302, trans. Thackston, 148, states that the respect stemmed from her father's importance (sic); he apparently was unaware that her father was no longer emperor (nor alive) when she married Chinggis Khan.

97 Rashīd al-Dīn, *Jāmi'*, 302, trans. Thackston, 148; Dunnell, *Chinggis Khan*, 67.

98 Rashīd al-Dīn, *Jāmi'*, 302, trans. Thackston, 148.

99 Li, *Alchemist*, trans. Waley, 70–71; also De Nicola, *Khatuns*, 188.

(r. 1200–20). As is so often the case, we do not know her name – Terken was a title ("princess"; "khatun" meant "lady" or "queen").[100] Like Gürbesü, Terken represented the loss of female experience and ability that accompanied a conquest; but unlike Gürbesü or indeed any other woman in Chinggis Khan's life, Terken also demonstrated the tremendous power that the mother of a ruler could hold. In this way she contrasted sharply with Hö'elün, since Terken succeeded in many places where Hö'elün did not. Nevertheless, perhaps because of her great elevation itself, Terken's downfall was possibly the hardest of any conquered woman.

Terken appears to have enjoyed substantial authority all her life until the Mongols came along. She was a Turk, either a Qangli (from north of Khwarazm), a Qipchak (from the eastern Volga region), or a member of the Baya'ut branch of the Yemek (from the Ural area).[101] Regardless of her affiliation, her father was a ruler, which allowed her to become the senior wife to Sultan Tekish (r. 1172–1200), ruler of the vast Khwarazm-Shah Empire. Because of her position, it was her son, Muḥammad, who inherited his father's empire.[102] Contemporary historians credited Terken with wielding tremendous power, often tyrannically.[103] Some were highly critical of her, but it is unclear whether this was because she was actually oppressive – she was accused of known executions and suspected

[100] Anonymous (2), *Campagnes*, trans. Pelliot and Hambis, 89–90.

[101] Juvaynī, *World-Conqueror*, 465 (she was a Qangli Turk; also see Boyle's summation in footnote 2). Also Minhāj [al-Dīn] Sirāj Juzjānī (1963), *Ṭabaqāt-i Nāṣirī*, ed. 'Abd al-Ḥayy Ḥabībī (Kabul), 2:300, 306, 313 (she was the Qipchak Khan's daughter), and Minhāj Sirāj Juzjānī (1881, rprt. 1970), *Ṭabaqāt-i-Nāṣirī: A General History of the Muhammadan Dynasties of Asia, Including Hindustan; from A.H. 194 (810 AD) to A. H 658 (1260 AD) and the Irruption of the Infidel Mughals into Islam*, trans. Major H. G. Raverty (Asiatic Society of Bengal), 240, 254, 279; Nasawī, *Mangubartī*, ed. Ḥamdī, 71, 99, trans. Houdas, 44, 72 (she was from the Baya'ut branch of the Yemek). Also Anonymous (2), *Campagnes*, trans. Pelliot and Hambis, 95 (the relationships among the Yemek, Qipchak and Qangli), 82–89 (the Bayaut), 107–110; Minorsky, *Ḥudūd al-'Alam*, 304–10, 315–17.

[102] The sources garble her relationship to Muḥammad: most claim that she was his mother, but some state that she was his "mother" and/or wife, which suggests a levirate marriage. Similar confusion marks her relationship to Muḥammad's heir, where Terken is either his grandmother (and his mother is Terken's relative), or Terken herself is the heir's mother. This section will assume that Terken was Muḥammad's mother, and that her relative was the mother of the heir. Juvaynī, *World-Conqueror*, 79, 336, 378, 466; Juzjānī, *Ṭabaqāt*, 2:306, 313, trans. Raverty, 253, 279–80. Nasawī, *Mankubartī*, ed. Ḥamdī, 71, 120, trans. Houdas, 44, 93; Rashīd al-Dīn, *Jāmi'*, 474, 478, 510, trans. Thackston, 234, 236, 252.

[103] Juzjānī, *Ṭabaqāt* 2:300, trans. Raverty, 239–40; Juvaynī, *World-Conqueror*, 465–66.

murders – or because she engaged in activities (the executions and murders, as well as high-level diplomacy), that, in the eyes of these conservative Muslim authors, were too prominent (and bloodthirsty) for a woman, even though they would have been acceptable from her husband or son.[104] But her dominance was real: she had her own court, officials, and sources of income, and she also enjoyed some control over her son's state apparatus, including the empire's finances.[105] One historian claimed that she issued imperial decrees, some of which superseded those of her son.[106] Later, however, this same power helped bring about her downfall, since Chinggis Khan is said to have used forged letters revealing an ostensible rivalry between Muḥammad and his mother to turn Muḥammad against his maternal relatives and weaken Terken's position.[107]

Terken illustrates what a woman could do on behalf of her son's career when she was properly positioned. The thirteenth-century Persian-language historian Juzjānī describes her as someone who "acquired great celebrity in the world, and rose to great eminence."[108] Her power surely came in part from her close relationship to her natal family, especially once Muḥammad took over as Khwarazm-Shah, after which Terken actively brought her relatives and their subjects to work in his empire. Some of her male relatives became important officials for Muḥammad. These included Inalchuk, governor of the border city of Otrar by the Jaxartes River, whose massacre of merchants in that city led to Chinggis Khan's invasion in the Western Campaign (1218–23); Közli, governor of the ancient and lovely city of Nishapur; Tört-Aba, military supervisor (*shahnah*) at the sophisticated capital of Samarqand in Transoxiana; and Khumar, an army commander at the second capital of Urgench in Khwarazm, who became sultan temporarily after Muḥammad fled the Mongol invasion.[109]

[104] Juvaynī, *World-Conqueror*, 465 (her family was cruel, violent, and wicked) and 466 (Terken's destruction of princely houses and murder of hostages). Also Juzjānī, *Ṭabaqāt*, 2:301, trans. Raverty, 240, although his story that she almost killed her husband in an overheated bathhouse out of jealousy over a concubine, then suffered no repercussions, seems hardly credible.

[105] Juvaynī, *World-Conqueror*, 466; also Nasawī, *Mangubartī*, ed. Hamdi, 76, trans. Houdas, 50 (her son's obedience to her).

[106] Nasawī, *Mangubartī*, ed. Hamdi, 99, trans. Houdas, 73, claiming that if decrees came from her and Muḥammad on the same topic, officials would follow the most recent.

[107] Nasawī, *Mangubartī*, ed. Hamdi, 92–3, trans. Houdas, 65.

[108] Juzjānī, *Ṭabaqāt*, 2:300, trans. Raverty, 240 (citation).

[109] Juvaynī, *World-Conqueror*, 79 (Inalchuq aka Ghāyir Khan), 124 (Khumar Tegin), 336–9 (Közli), 349 (Tört-Aba); and with fewer details, Rashīd al-Dīn, *Jāmiʿ*, 474, 478, 513, trans. Thackston, 234, 236, 253.

Terken's male relatives in particular acted as companions to the sultan and were described as being "in the ascendancy" during Terken's lifetime, while the subjects they brought with them formed major units in the Khwarazm-Shah armies.[110]

Terken also lavished opportunity on her female relatives: the mother of Muḥammad's heir was from Terken's family, which suggests a version of exchange marriage (the daughter-in-law married in "exchange" for Terken's earlier marriage). It was furthermore Terken who convinced Muḥammad to choose this son (her grandson) as heir, even though he was not the oldest of the princes.[111] Another of Terken's female relatives married the vassal ruler of Fars, which tied him effectively to Terken's ruling house, while a third married the petty ruler of Yazur (?), which enabled Terken to take it over when he died.[112] When compared with Hö'elün, therefore, Terken demonstrated the power of a highly placed wife, mother, and widow who also enjoyed close relations to her natal family. By contrast, Hö'elün's relative isolation underscored the weakness of a wife whose marriage was unapproved, and who had to live bereft of family connections. Certainly it was only late in her life that Hö'elün could do for her own family a few of the favors that Terken bestowed liberally on hers for years. Terken therefore stands out as an example of the awesome capabilities of a well-connected imperial mother who lived well into the reign of her child.

Terken also differed markedly from Börte. Börte's sons were automatically favored with military opportunities because of her status, and became the only contenders for succession to the empire.[113] Although Börte surely appreciated these benefits for her children, she is not known to have exercised any particular control over their careers once they were established in life. By contrast, Terken, a woman of strong temperament, was perfectly willing to undertake a range of actions to benefit her son, even after he became ruler. Thus once when Muḥammad was absent on campaign, Terken personally received an embassy from her overlord, the Gür Khan of the Qara-Khitai Empire that lay to the east, and paid the necessary tribute. This allowed Muḥammad to pretend he was still

110 Juvaynī, *World-Conqueror*, 378, 465 (citation); Rashīd al-Dīn, *Jāmi'*, 505–6, trans. Thackston, 250.

111 Juzjānī, *Ṭabaqāt*, 2:313, trans. Raverty, 279; Nasawī, *Mangubartī*, ed. Ḥamdī, 71, trans. Houdas, 44.

112 Nasawī, *Mangubartī*, ed. Ḥamdī, 62 (Fars, the Atabek Sa'd b. Zangi), 95 (Hindu Khan of Yazur); trans. Houdas, 34, 67.

113 See Chapter 4.

the Gür Khan's vassal, although later he asserted his independence and his mother's face-saving fiction was revealed.[114] On another occasion Terken refused to let her granddaughter's new husband depart after a royal wedding, claiming that she needed him to stay longer in order to ensure that all parties received proper respect. Since the husband in question was the ruler of Transoxiana and himself a vassal of the Gür Khan, this again touched on diplomacy.[115] But at times Terken's zeal to uphold her son's position turned ugly. She is said to have overthrown "many an ancient house" in order to protect Muḥammad from rivals.[116] After the Mongols erupted onto the scene and Terken fled Urgench before them, she had twelve royal or noble hostages in her keeping murdered (perhaps drowned), which was probably unnecessary treatment, and which disgusted the general population of Urgench.[117] She also made enemies, among them other women: she passionately hated Ay Chichek, who was the mother of Muḥammad's son Jalāl al-Dīn Mangubertī but not one of Terken's own relatives. Terken refused to flee to Ay Chichek for protection after the empire began to crumble, even though this might have helped her escape the Mongols.[118]

Because of her extraordinary prominence within the Khwarazm-Shah Empire, Terken's downfall at the hands of the Mongols was particularly hard. First her son failed to protect his empire and fled in ignominy in 1220, abdicating his power to anyone who wanted it. This must have been humiliating for her, and was surely only compounded by her grief over his death in exile. Terken herself initially escaped the Mongols with Muḥammad's harem and young sons by taking refuge in a fortress in Mazandaran, but the general Sübedei soon captured the imperial family and sent it to Chinggis Khan. He in turn executed all of Terken's grandsons, regardless of age, which devastated their grandmother.[119] As if the

[114] Juvaynī, *World-Conqueror*, 357–8.
[115] Juvaynī, *World-Conqueror*, 393–4. This was Sultan Osman of Transoxiana, who married Muḥammad's daughter, but wanted to take her home before the end of his year at Muḥammad's court. Juvaynī claims that would be disrespectful, but it is unclear of whom. On her, see Jean Richard, "La conversion de Berke et les débuts de l'islamisation de la Horde d'Or," *Revue des études islamiques* 35 (1967): 173–84, although the question of whether she was the mother of Berke Khan of the Jochids remains contested. See Chapter 8.
[116] Juvaynī, *World-Conqueror*, 466.
[117] Nasawī, *Mangubartī*, ed. Ḥamdī, 94–5, trans. Houdas, 66–7; Juvaynī, *World-Conqueror*, 466; Juzjānī, *Ṭabaqāt*, 2:313, trans. Raverty, 279–80.
[118] Nasawī, *Mangubartī*, ed. Ḥamdī, 96–7, trans. Houdas, 69.
[119] Juvaynī, *World-Conqueror*, 468; Nasawī, *Mangubartī*, ed. Ḥamdī, 97, trans. Houdas, 70 (claiming piously that this was divine retribution for Terken's mistreatment of others).

failure and death of her son and the murders of her grandsons were not enough, Terken's granddaughters were distributed among the Chinggisid family as spoils: one married Jochi, two went to Chaghatai as concubines, not wives, while the rest married Chinggis Khan's secondary sons.[120] Later, Terken and the other imperial Khwarazmian women accompanied the Mongol forces to the remains of Samarqand, where, in an exquisite example of humiliation, Chinggis Khan ordered them to sing a dirge on the fate of their empire while his troops paraded past them.[121] Ultimately Terken went to Mongolia. Her status was not high, and it is unclear whether Chinggis Khan married her, or just took her as a symbol of his victory. One author claims that she occasionally attended banquets, at which she took away food to survive on for days thereafter, while another says she "existed wretchedly" until her death in 1232 or 1233.[122]

CONCLUSION

Whereas the lives of Hö'elün and Börte illuminate Temüjin's rise to power, those of his other women tell us about the losers in his battles – the conquered and defeated whose history is largely unknown. This chapter has demonstrated how the behaviors and activities of these women bring fresh insights into several important topics: the situation of female hostages on the steppe, the complexity of women's loyalties, the networks of informants that some conquered women controlled, the secondary outlets of expression with which women might console themselves, and the waste of female talent that marked successful conquests. Despite their relative weakness, a few of these conquered women managed to contribute to the formation of Chinggisid institutions, or to the history of the imperial conquests. Among these were Ibaqa, Qulan, and Yisüi, although their roles were nothing compared to what they could have been had the circumstances of their marriages been happier. And certainly not one of these women ever held a candle to Börte and her daughters, to whom we turn next.

120 Juvaynī, *World-Conqueror*, 468. See Chapter 8 for Khan-Sultan's (contested) marriage to Jochi; also Nasawī, *Mangubartī*, ed. Ḥamdī, 97 and 300–1 (other women wedded to Chinggis Khan's lesser sons), trans. Houdas 70, 305.

121 Juvaynī, *World-Conqueror*, 468; Rashīd al-Dīn, *Jāmi'*, 530, trans. Thackston, 258.

122 Nasawī, *Mangubartī*, ed. Ḥamdī, 97 (banquets), trans. Houdas, 70; Juvaynī, *World-Conqueror*, 468 (wretchedness).

4

Women and the Guard, the Army, and Succession

The quriltai of 1206 was a triumphant political moment for Chinggis Khan, representing both his ascendance among his own followers and the culmination of his campaigns against many steppe peoples. Nevertheless, despite the symbolism of this single date, it was actually in the years immediately surrounding 1206 that he critically reorganized his military. This resulted not only in a massive restructuring of steppe society, but also in the establishment of a set of institutions that powered the expansion of the empire through a remarkable series of conquests into the Tangut Kingdom and the Jin Empire in northern China, and the Khwarazm-Shah Empire in Transoxania, Khwarazm, Central Asia, and Iran. During these conquests, Chinggis Khan also took the time to determine the matter of succession to his position as ruler, and the inheritance of the empire after his death.

Despite the importance of these years and the interest they have inspired, scholars have thus far focused largely on the roles of men in the creation of Chinggisid institutions, not on the contributions made by women, even though women were in fact instrumental to shaping and structuring these institutions. This chapter therefore investigates the critical connections between imperial women and three important Chinggisid systems: the imperial guard, the atomized army, and succession to the Grand Khanate. The chapter first outlines the interactions between Chinggis Khan's wives and his imperial guard, and the way that guards' duties overlapped with women's responsibilities for their camps. Next it reinvestigates the atomized army. Although the innovation of the atomization process has been seen as the heart of Chinggis Khan's genius, a radical revision of steppe militaries, and the key to his conquests, scholars have not acknowledged that Chinggis Khan's new imperial army actually retained an older, confederation style of organization overlaid on top of the atomized units. This confederation model is outlined here for the first time through a close study of the relationships between Chinggis Khan's female kin and their husbands on the one hand, and the atomized army units on the other. Once this updated vision of the new imperial army is established, Chapter 5 will explore that army in action during Chinggis Khan's major campaigns.

The final institution studied here is succession. Certainly rule was at least outwardly the province of men, but women significantly shaped succession in ways that have hitherto been overlooked. First and foremost was maternity: the critical question in succession was less the identity of a candidate's father than of his mother. Thus, in the case of Chinggis Khan's offspring, it was the mothers whose status determined whether a son was eligible or ineligible for rule, regardless of the fact that Chinggis Khan enjoyed paternity. Second, many women shaped succession as political advisors or even as independent political actors, often to their own will and in contravention of the aspirations of Chinggisid men. That discussion begins here and continues in Chapters 6 and 7. In sum, examining women's roles in the context of empire building greatly enriches our understanding of all of the institutions for which Chinggis Khan is best known, and brings out the hitherto unseen centrality of key women to their formation.

CHINGGISID MILITARY REFORMS

Although Chinggis Khan rose to lead great numbers of nomads like such famous conquerors as Attila the Hun or Toghrul the Seljuk, he did not do so – as they did – through the vehicle of a confederation. Rather, he is best known for dismantling existing social and political structures on the steppe through wide-reaching organizational changes to the Mongol army between 1204 and 1209.[1] Scholars have meticulously established the outlines of his reorganization. Previously many steppe militaries had been formed of leading families as commanders and their subjects as

[1] 1204–9 were Chinggis Khan's organizational years, although Togan suggests that he actually began the atomization process as early as the 1180s. Togan, *Flexibility and Limitation*, 132–4. Also see Ratchnevsky, *Genghis Khan*, 90–6, 101; May, *War*, chapter 2; Dunnell, *Chinggis Khan*, 50–2; Biran, *Chinggis Khan*, 41–2. For general comments see Nicola di Cosmo, "State Formation and Periodization in Inner Asian History," *Journal of World History* 10, no. 1 (1999): 17–19.

soldiers, but some also employed a decimal system, with units of 10, 100, 1,000, and 10,000.[2] (A standard scholarly assumption is that each unit of a thousand contained no more than perhaps 60 percent of its capacity, but the ideal of a thousand will be used in this discussion.[3]) Chinggis Khan adopted this decimal arrangement, creating 95 units of 1,000 soldiers (Mongolian *tümen*, pl. *tümet*) in his army, but then destroyed the unity of steppe peoples by dismantling ruling lineages and scattering their subjects throughout the units instead of leaving them with their relatives. To enhance this new "atomized" system, he imposed rigid discipline so that soldiers could not leave their units without permission from their officers, and officers could not congregate without authorization.

THE IMPERIAL GUARD (*KESHIG*)

The commanders of the thousands were all men on whom Chinggis Khan could rely: his companions from early days, his sworn followers, or men who had performed special services for him.[4] Chinggis Khan further ensured discipline among these commanders by taking their family members as hostages, who then worked directly for him in his other major new institution, the imperial guard (*keshig*), which also contained some of his closest and most loyal followers. The imperial guard was formally created in 1203 with 1,150 members, but Chinggis Khan increased the organization in size to ten thousand in 1206.[5] Irregularly, guard members were chosen for special assignments and campaigns.[6] Otherwise, members worked not only as day and night guards, but also as quiverbearers, doorkeepers, grooms, equerries, scribes, wagoners, herders, and so on. Night guards in particular acted as stewards, cooks, and supervisors of household staff.[7] Men in the imperial guard therefore combined household and military duties.

[2] Ratchnevsky, *Genghis Khan*, 84 (but without commanders of 10,000), 90–2; May, *War*, 31.

[3] May, *War*, 27. [4] Ratchnevsky, *Genghis Khan*, 92; also May, *War*, 31–2.

[5] It may have originated as early as the 1180s. Allsen, "Guard and Government," 514; Charles Melville, "The *Keshig* in Iran: The Survival of the Royal Mongol Household," in *Beyond the Legacy of Genghis Khan*, ed. Linda Komaroff (Leiden: Brill, 2006), 136–7; Grupper, "Barulas Family Narrative," 39, 41; May, *War*, 32–6.

[6] Allsen, "Guard and Government," 509–10.

[7] For the combination of household and imperial activities see *Secret History*, §192, §232, §234, §278; Allsen, "Guard and Government," 510–13, 515; May, *War*, 33–5; Andrews, *Felt Tents*, 324; Hsiao, *Establishment*, 37, 92–4; Melville, "Keshig," 139; Hope, *Ilkhanate*, 37–8; note the Mughal parallel in Stephen P. Blake, "The Patrimonial-Bureaucratic Empire of the Mughals," *The Journal of Asian Studies* 39, no. 1 (November 1979): 82–3.

Despite the excellent scholarship to date on this important institution, scholars have not yet integrated their view of the guards' activities with wifely activities, even though the two appear to have been inextricably linked. When all the wives were assembled together, the imperial palace ger compound could be enormous, composed as it was of individual encampments of ger clusters, each of which was itself surrounded on two or three sides by walls of wagons, which separated these establishments from one another. The *keshig* 's general task was to guard all these clusters of gers and the walls of wagons. At the same time, guards had to pay particular attention to the individual ger and encampment in which the Khan slept, which could change from night to night as he visited different wives.[8] In addition, some guards were assigned directly to particular camps managed by wives like Börte, Yisüi, or Qulan, each of which contained junior wives, concubines, children, and staff. In these cases officers seem to have reported to both Chinggis Khan and to the managing wife, although not for the same tasks.[9] Further complicating the picture is the fact that Chinggis Khan's *keshig* included his own personal unit of a thousand, in addition to the day and night guards.[10] The eight commanders of a hundred within that thousand were also stationed in the senior wives' camps, in assignments that clearly reflected the wifely hierarchies of rank.[11] Five of these eight officers were positioned with Börte: one was her camp commander (*amīr-i ordo* in later

[8] On guards in general, see Andrews, *Felt Tents*, 325–9. Note that half of the night guards remained in the camp to guard it when Chinggis Khan went hunting. *Secret History*, §232 and de Rachewiltz, Commentary, 835–9. For the Khan's movement from wife to wife see Carpini, *History*, 17–18 (not in Rockhill); Polo, *Description*, §82 (Qubilai going to the wife or summoning her to him); also Rubruck, *Mission*, 178, 195 (Möngke receives Friar William's party in a deceased wife's residence).

[9] The highest ranking officer was the camp commander; see Chapter 1. The first of these was the Tangut Buda (or perhaps Chagan and then Buda, see footnote 10), who was Börte's camp commander. Rashīd al-Dīn attributes this position to the inception of the *keshig*, and observes that it was standard among the Ilkhanids as well, where camp commanders answered directly to the wife. For the Ilkhanid examples of Hülegü's wives Qutui and Öljei see Chapter 9. Rashīd al-Dīn, *Jāmiʿ*, 1126, 1130, 1170–1, trans. Thackston, 549, 551, 570–1, and De Nicola, "Ruling from Tents," 131, and *Khatuns*, 142.

[10] Atwood remarks that this unit and its commander, Chagan of the Tangut, appear in Rashīd al-Dīn and the *Yuan Shi* (10/120: 2955–6), but were excluded from the *Secret History*, §202, §232, §234. Christopher P. Atwood, "Titles, Appanages, Marriages and Officials: A Comparison of Political Forms in the Zhüngar and Thirteenth-Century Mongol Empires," in *Imperial Statecraft: Political Forms and Techniques of Governments in Inner Asia, Sixth-Twentieth Centuries*, ed. D. Sneath (Bellingham, 2006), 214 and note 6.

[11] Rashīd al-Dīn, *Jāmiʿ*, 593–4, trans. Thackston, 272–3.

sources), two were cooks, one an equerry, while the last held unspecified duties.[12] The sixth officer worked as Yisüi's camp commander,[13] while the seventh may have been attached to Qulan, who was his sister,[14] and the eighth served as a kind of overseer for the camps of several wives at once.[15] The *keshig* system was subsequently copied by Chinggis Khan's offspring, as was the position of the camp commander.[16] Thus in later generations multiple *keshig*s were stationed throughout the empire or the successor khanates, with camp commanders and other staff reporting both to the prince and to the wife.[17]

Although a full study of the overlap between the *keshig* and the wives' activities is beyond the scope of this book, one is certainly needed. Until such a study is available, however, one can at least imagine a hypothetical situation: on any given morning, Börte could wake up in her brocade-lined ger, open the heavy wooden door, perhaps greet the guards standing

[12] None of these officers appear in the *Secret History*, for which see Atwood's comments about deliberate omission in footnote 10. Rashīd al-Dīn lists the officers in Börte's camp: (1) The adopted Tangut son, Buda, who replaced the Tangut Chagan in this position. Buda "was the commander of Börte Füjin's great *ordo*" and three others as well (!). (2) The Dörben Yürki (?), father of the famed Bolad Aga, who was a cook (*ba'urchi*) for Chinggis Khan, and was stationed with Börte (*az urdu'yi Börte*). (3) The Sönit El Temür was another cook for Börte. (4) The Kereit Elenger was attached to her camp, but his responsibilities are unspecified. (5) The Tatar Yesün To'a was an equerry (*atakhchi*), but should not be confused with the Uriangqat Yisün Te'e, a quiverbearer in the *keshig* and son of Chinggis Khan's servant Jelme. Rashīd al-Dīn, *Jāmi'*, 574, 137, 197, 75, 89, trans. Thackston, 272 and 74 (Buda), 104 (Yürki), 43 (El Temür and Elenger), 50 (Yesün To'a). For Bolad Aqa see Thomas T. Allsen, "Two Cultural Brokers of Medieval Eurasia: Bolad Aqa and Marco Polo," in *Nomadic Diplomacy, Destruction and Religion from the Pacific to the Adriatic*, ed. Michael Gervers and Wayne Schlepp, Toronto Studies in Central and Inner Asia 1 (Toronto: University of Toronto Press, 1994), 64.

[13] This was Qongqiyadai or Kingqiyadai, an Olqunu'ut commander of a thousand in the right wing, perhaps identifiable with the Kinggiyadai found in *Secret History*, §202 and de Rachewiltz, Commentary, 765. Rashīd al-Dīn, *Jāmi'*, 595, trans. Thackston, 273–4; see also Table 1B: footnote a.

[14] Jamal Khwaja (Qucha?) was Qulan's brother. His camp assignment is not entirely clear. Rashīd al-Dīn, *Jāmi'*, 96, 593, trans. Thackston, 54, 273.

[15] The Jalayir Oldai was a military supervisor (*shahnah*) for all four camps. Rashīd al-Dīn, *Jāmi'*, 593, trans. Thackston, 273.

[16] On multiple *keshigs* see Melville, "*Keshig* in Iran," 161; also Grupper, "Barulas Family Narrative," 60. It is my assertion that the camp commander held the highest liaison position, since it is a generalist job, whereas the other posts reported are as cooks or stewards, both of which are specialists. Note Di Cosmo, "State Formation," 23, on the proliferation of retinues among nomadic royal families, and De Nicola, *Khatuns*, 137–9.

[17] This position could be held either by a noyan (commander or lord), or a lesser Chinggisid prince (son of a concubine). For examples see Rashīd al-Dīn, *Jāmi'*, 137, 593, 967, 1126–7, 1130, 1144–5, 1170–1, 1264, trans. Thackston, 74, 272, 474, 549, 551, 558, 570–1, 631; Qāshānī, *Uljaytū*, 8.

at attention, and survey any flocks pastured across from the imperial encampment. A household servant might appear with her breakfast, which could have been prepared by guardsmen in the kitchens situated behind her cluster of gers (or, in inclement weather, on Börte's own hearth). When Börte wanted to change her robe, the new one would be brought by her servants, who might have extricated it either from a chest inside the ger, or the storage carts that the guardsmen protected. At least once if not multiple times, Börte would speak with Buda, her camp commander, in order to review any unfinished business and discuss work for the day. Directly or through Buda, she could receive reports from shepherds about her and Temüjin's flocks and herds; from her servants about clothing, children, grandchildren, and dependents; from the stewards in the guard about meals and entertainment; from bureaucrats about administrative or judicial matters. Directly or through Buda, she could give orders on any number of topics. She could consult with religious officials – shamans, in her case – about religious duties or ceremonies. She would almost certainly exchange daily messages with some of the other wives. She would regularly communicate with the merchants she employed, and would periodically receive emissaries. In order to reach her, all visitors would have to pass the guards to enter her camp, then the guards at the door to her ger. If Börte attended any kind of ceremony, she is likely to have been accompanied by the guardsman designated as bearer of her imperial parasol, plus a military escort. If she went riding, she would not have gone alone; if she went to check on animals, she might be attended by her ladies, her guardsmen, the shepherds. And above all this activity, at some point she is certain to have interacted with her husband about family, politics, animals, trade, or otherwise, even if he had stayed in the ger of one of the other wives, unless he was absent on a campaign.

The imperial guard outranked and counterbalanced the regular army units, provided men to lead major campaigns, and formed a ruling class that was personally linked to Chinggis Khan over what became the empire.[18] Together, these changes to the army and to the imperial guard created a well-balanced military force, with the imperial guard at the top and the atomized army at the bottom, all beautifully checked by internal balances and maintained with such rigorous discipline that the possibly of insurrection was essentially eliminated.

[18] Ratchnevsky, *Genghis Khan*, 94; Allsen, *Mongol Imperialism*, 73–4; May, *War*, 32–4.

But these reforms were unpopular, dramatic, and, for some, painful. Why then did Chinggis Khan undertake them? This is a complex issue. One possibility is that Chinggis Khan sought to replace the existing social system of ruling lineages and their subjects with an artificial one composed of his new army units. This made the commander-in-chief – Chinggis Khan himself, and after him Börte's male descendants – the sole recipient of loyalty and obedience from every soldier, and, by extension, that soldier's family.[19] And yet even as Chinggis Khan dispersed some peoples, he kept others together. Another suggestion is therefore that Chinggis Khan retained groups where the internal structure was egalitarian and leadership was shared among many (the Qonggirats, Ikires, Qorulas), as well as those dominated by others (the Jalayirs, Uru'uts, Baya'uts, etc.), but dismantled peoples where leadership was dynastic (the Kereits, the Merkits, the Naimans).[20] This eliminated royal families that could rival the Chinggisids.[21]

THE CHINGGISID CONFEDERATION

To date, discussions of Mongol military restructuring and the societal changes that resulted from it have either downplayed or overlooked the contributions of Chinggis Khan's female kin. But these women critically shaped the Mongol military by marrying leaders from ruling lineages, who then worked directly for Chinggis Khan as special army commanders of a thousand, or as commanders of auxiliary forces. These strategic marriages were a critical element of Chinggis Khan's reforms, and challenge the view that atomization was the main process to shape the army. Rather, the use of marriages to form alliances was reminiscent of earlier political practices (as seen in Chapter 1), where nomadic confederations were held together both by political bonds between men, and by the corresponding marriages involving women. Although as stated previously Chinggis Khan is best known as the exception to the confederation model of empire associated with steppe nomads, we can now see that that he did not dispense with confederation politics as much as has been thought. Rather, strategic matches between Chinggisid women and certain men actually created a small confederation (or very large extended family)

[19] Morgan, *Mongols*, 79. [20] Togan, *Flexibility and Limitation*, 137–8.

[21] A third argument is that he used marriage to control peoples whose submission was unreliable (although this begs the question of why he did not simply dismember them through atomization). Zhao, *Marriage*, 40.

within the empire – the Chinggisid confederation – even while the rest of nomadic society was being atomized through the army reforms. Furthermore, in clear contrast to the atomization that took place among soldiers in the standard units, the soldiers of imperial sons-in-law were allowed to remain unified as a people. The marriages of Chinggisid women thus permitted Chinggis Khan to bring major steppe peoples under his control and keep them intact without spending the lives of Mongols to subdue them violently and atomize them.[22] Among those "conquered" in this way were the Qonggirats, the Olqunu'uts, the Uru'uts, the Oirats, the Öng'üts, the Uighurs, and the Qarluqs.

The marriages of Börte's daughters – the senior princesses – were the backbone of the Chinggisid political confederation. These women wedded important and powerful men – rulers or their sons – then took on the management of their husbands' camps, property, and other resources, at least in part (depending on the presence of other wives). In addition to the senior princesses, other women contributed to the confederation: Börte maintained extensive links to the Qonggirats, Hö'elün supervised the Olqunu'uts, and the Kereit Ibaqa strengthened the connection between Chinggis Khan and her second husband, Jürchedei, and his Uru'ut soldiers. (But other than Ibaqa, Chinggis Khan's conquered wives did not add to the confederation since they had no menfolk left.)

The junior princesses, i.e., those from junior wives or concubines, also promoted their father's career and empire through marriage, even though far less is known of these nine (or probably more) daughters. Often, junior princesses supported the senior ones, since the Chinggisids liked to contract multiple marriages – a constellation – with certain, favored lineages. This fit steppe habits of exchange marriages, where multiple connections between two families were preferred.[23] In a marriage constellation, the senior marriage would be for one of Börte's daughters, whose own rank would be highest overall, and whose husband would be the most important. A second marriage could then take place between one

[22] Cheng, "Career," 226, 234; Atwood, "Comparison," 225 and note 16; in brief Hope, *Ilkhanate*, 38.

[23] See Uno, "Exchange-Marriage," 176, 179–80; also Chapter 1. Exchange marriages took place between the Chinggisids and the Qonggirats, where the marriage partners were Börte's relatives. However, early marriages with the Oirats and the Öng'üts were "exchange-like," since Chinggis Khan had neither an Oirat nor an Öng'üt wife (that we know of) to provide nieces and nephews. Later marriages with these groups were genuine exchanges since the descendants of the first marriages were cousins to other branches of the Chinggisid line.

of Chinggis Khan's junior daughters (or a granddaughter), and another man from the consort lineage. This provided the Chinggisids with two princess-agents in a consort house, one with greater and one with lesser status. To seal the arrangement, marriages between Börte's sons, or Chinggis Khan's sons from other wives, were also encouraged in standard exchange style, particularly for desirable lineages like the Qonggirats, the Ikires, and the Oirats.[24]

After marriage, all of these women were well positioned to shape their husbands' political and military relationships with their father (or grandfather). The judicious distribution of princesses across the empire provided Chinggis Khan with a useful network of agents, both daughters and sons-in-law. Thus after allying himself with these key ruling families and "subduing" their peoples without bloodshed, Chinggis Khan was then able to conquer less amenable peoples in bloodier fashion with the help of his sons-in-law, and finally administer an empire in which swathes of territory were controlled by these sons-in-law and their Chinggisid wives (see Map 2 in Chapter 5).

THE CONFEDERATION, THE ARMY, AND THE CONSORT HOUSES

The formation of the Chinggisid confederation also helped shape the reorganization of the atomized army. Its influence was most clear among the commanders of a thousand, where only eighty-eight men led ninety-five units. This discrepancy occurred because a few commanders had larger units, containing anywhere from two thousand to five thousand men. In addition to this privilege of numbers, these exceptional commanders chose their subordinate commanders of a thousand, and kept their own people as soldiers.[25] Scholars have

24 These were "two-way" marriage relationships, where the consort houses both provided husbands to and accepted wives from the Chinggisids. Zhao, *Marriage*, 24–5, 102–10 (Qonggirats), 122–3 (Ikires), 128–31 and 137–9 (Oirats).

25 Rashīd al-Dīn mentions certain larger, special units of a thousand (*minqan*, pl. *minqat*) and makes a point that their leaders were permitted to choose their own sub-commanders of a thousand: the Oirats, Uru'uts, Ikires, Ba'arins, and the Jurchid after the first China campaign. Choosing subordinate commanders *of a thousand* seems to be exceptional, although May points out that an ordinary commander of a thousand did choose his own subordinate officers (of 100 or 10). Rashīd al-Dīn, *Jāmi'*, 595–602, trans. Thackston, 274–7; May, *War*, 89.

identified the recipients of this special treatment as leaders who submitted voluntarily to Chinggis Khan, or men who performed special services for him.[26] Another suggestion has been that some of these peoples possessed egalitarian internal structures that made them worth keeping together.[27]

But when the question of army reform is related directly to the Chinggisid confederation, it becomes immediately clear that the privileges of large units, uniformity of soldiers, and the right to choose certain officers most often appeared among commanders of a thousand who were also in-laws to the Chinggisids. Thus of eighty-eight total commanders in the army, a certain number had larger, unified thousands. In the *Secret History* these were five, of whom four were in-laws, while in Rashīd al-Dīn these special commanders numbered eleven, of whom seven were in-laws.[28] In other words, and regardless of which text is consulted, more than half of the special, large, homogenous thousands in the atomized army were commanded by men married to Chinggisid women. See Tables 1A–1C.

Who then were these favored military commanders and their princess wives, who together formed the Chinggisid confederation? Here we will identify them as participants in a system. Then in Chapter 5 we will turn to the politics of each son-in-law's entry into the confederation, and the participation of sons-in-law and daughters in the giant project of the Mongol conquests.

The Ikires (see Family Tree 4.1): The first princess to support Chinggis Khan's career through marriage was his sister Temülün, who wedded her brother's follower, Butu of the Ikires, in the late 1180s or early 1190s when she was in her mid-teens, but then died in her 20s of unknown

[26] This is the reasoning in *Secret History*, §203–14; also Rashīd al-Dīn, *Jāmi'*, 598 (the Öng'üts and their voluntary submission), 599–600 (the Uru'uts and their commanders' service), 601 (the Ba'arin and their voluntary submission), trans. Thackston, 275–7. Also see Dunnell, *Chinggis Khan*, 52; Ratchnevsky, *Genghis Khan*, 93; May does not discuss these exceptions. Atwood mentions them without further comment. Atwood, "Comparison," 219.

[27] I.e., they shared leadership among many, not just one man or one family. Togan, *Flexibility and Limitation*, 136–8.

[28] These were Alchi and his adopted son Chigü, both leading the Qonggirats; Butu of the Ikires, and Alaqush of the Öng'üts. The fourth was Qorchi of the Ba'arin, whose right to control extra peoples is in §207, not §202. *Secret History*, §202, §207, §212, §213, §218, §221; note that in §202 the text excludes the Oirats and other Forest Peoples. Also Rashīd al-Dīn, *Jāmi'*, 596, trans. Thackston, 274. Hsiao, *Establishment*, 11.

Table 1A Special Commanders in the Atomized Army (according to the *Secret History*)

Unit	Troops	Leader	Connection	Wife	Source
Ikires	2,000	Butu	Marriage	Temülün; Qojin	*SH* §202
Öng'üts	5,000	Alaqush; Jingüe, others	Marriages	Alaqa	*SH* §202
Qonggirats (1)	3,000	Börte's brother Alchi	Börte's family	Börte	*SH* §202
Qonggirats (2)	1,000	Chigü, Börte's adopted nephew	Marriage	Tümelün	*SH* §202
Uru'uts	4,000	Jürchedei	Marriage	Ibaqa	*SH* §208
Olqunu'uts	[1,000?]	Olar	Hö'elün's family, marriage	Junior Princess	*SH* §202
Baya'uts (1)	[1,000?]	Buqa	Marriage	Junior Princess	*SH* §202
??	[1,000?]	Ashiq	Marriage	Junior Princess	*SH* §202, §207
Qonggirats (3)	[1,000?]	Qadai	Marriage	Junior Princess	*SH* §202
Qongqotans	[1,000?]	Tolun Cherbi	Marriage of Mönglik	Hö'elün	*SH* §212
Ba'arins	3,000	Qorchi	Prophecy	–	*SH* §207
Negüs	[1,000?]	Narin To'oril	Father's death for Chinggis Khan	–	*SH* §218
Baya'uts (2)	1,000	Önggür	Service to Chinggis Khan	–	*SH* §213
Besüts	[1,000?]	Jebe	–	–	*SH* §221
Urianqats	[1,000?]	Sübedei	–	–	*SH* §221

Dark shading: commanders with marriage ties and large, homogenized units.
Light shading: commanders with marriage ties but smaller units.
No shading: commanders with homogenous soldiers but no marriage ties.
Source: *Secret History*, trans. Igor de Rachewiltz.

Table 1B Special Commanders in the Atomized Army (according to Rashīd al-Dīn)

Unit	Troops	Leader	Connection	Wife	Source
Ikires	3,000	Butu	Marriage	Temülün, Qojin	Text 600, tr. 276
Oirats	4,000	Qutuqa	Multiple marriages	Checheyigen, Qolui	Text 596, tr. 274
Öng'üts	4,000	Alaqush; Jingüe, others	Marriages	Alaqa	Text 598, tr. 275
Qonggirats (1)	5,000	Börte's brother Alchi	Börte's family	Börte	Text 600–1, tr. 276–7
Qonggirats (2)	1,000–4,000	Chigü, Börte's adopted nephew	Marriage	Tümelün	Text 603, tr. 278
Uru'uts	4,000	Kehetei and Bujir, sons of Jürchedei	Marriage	Ibaqa	Text 599–600, tr. 276
Olqunu'uts(?)[a]	[1,000–3,000?]	Olar's son Taichu	Hö'elün's family, marriage	Junior Princess	Text 597, 611, tr. 275, 281
Jalayirs	3,000	Muqali	Service to Chinggis Khan	–	Text 599, tr. 275–6
Ba'arins (1)	3,000	Naya'a	Service to Chinggis Khan	–	Text 601, tr. 277
Ba'arins (2)	2,000	Qorchi	–	–	Text 596, tr. 274
Mangquts	[1,000?]	Quyildar and sons	Service to Chinggis Khan	–	Text 601, tr. 277
Qiyat	10,000	Köki (?), Mögetü	Chinggis Khan's own people	–	Text 598, tr. 265

[a]Rashīd al-Dīn explains that Taichu was a commander, and that Hö'elün received 3,000 Olqunu'uts whose commanders' names were unknown. He does not spell out that (either Hö'elün's father Olar or after him) Taichu commanded Hö'elün's soldiers. The *Secret History* clarifies that Olar was a son-in-law, but gives no troop numbers. We can hypothesize that Olar and Taichu commanded Hö'elün's forces by virtue of their natal relation to her, but we cannot be sure. Rashīd al-Dīn mentions another Olqunu'ut commander, Kingqiyadai, possibly the Qongqiyadai mentioned in the *Secret History*, but does not note special troops for him. Rashīd al-Dīn, *Jāmi'*, 595, 597, 611, trans. Thackston 273–4, 275, 281; *Secret History*, §202.

Dark shading: commanders with marriage ties and large, homogenized units.
Light shading: commanders with marriage ties but smaller units.
No shading: commanders with homogenous soldiers but no marriage ties.
Source: Rashīd al-Dīn, *Jāmi'* (marked "Text") and trans. Thackston (marked "tr.").

Table 1C Special Commanders in the Atomized Army (according to the *Secret History* and Rashīd al-Dīn Combined)

Unit	Troops	Leader	Connection	Wife	Source
Ikires	2,000–3,000	Butu	Marriage	Temülün, Qojin	*SH* §202, RD 600, tr. 276
Oirats	4,000	Qutuqa	Multiple marriages	Checheyigen, Qolui	RD 596, tr. 274
Öng'üts	4,000–5,000	Alaqush; Jingüe, etc	Multiple marriages	Alaqa	*SH* §202, RD 598, tr. 275
Qonggirats (1)	3,000–5,000	Börte's brother Alchi	Börte's family	Börte	*SH* §202, RD 600–1, tr. 276–7
Qonggirats (2)	1,000–4,000	Chigü, Börte's adopted nephew	Marriage	Tümelün	*SH* §202, RD 603, tr. 278
Uru'uts	4,000	Jürchedei son of Kehetei	Marriage	Ibaqa	*SH* §202, RD 599–600, tr. 276
Olqunu'uts[a]	[1,000–3,000]	Olar, then Taichu	Hö'elün's family, marriage	Junior Princess	*SH* §202, RD 597, 6611, tr. 275, 281
Baya'uts (1)	[1,000?]	Buqa	Marriage	Junior Princess	*SH* §202
??	[1,000?]	Ashiq	Marriage	Junior Princess	*SH* §202
Qonggirats (3)	[1,000?]	Qadai	Marriage	Junior Princess	*SH* §202
Qongqotans	[1,000?]	Tolun Cherbi	Marriage of Mönglik	Hö'elün	*SH* §212
Jalayirs	3,000	Muqali	Service to Chinggis Khan	–	RD 599, tr. 275–6

Table 1C (*cont.*)

Unit	Troops	Leader	Connection	Wife	Source
Ba'arins (1)	3,000	Naya'a	Service to Chinggis Khan	–	RD 601, tr. 277
Ba'arins (2)	2,000–3,000	Qorchi	Service to Chinggis Khan	–	*SH* §207, RD 596, tr. 274
Negüs	[1,000?]	Narin To'oril	Father's death for Chinggis Khan	–	*SH* §218
Baya'uts (2)	1,000	Önggür	Service to Chinggis Khan	–	*SH* §213
Mangquts	[1,000?]	Quyildar and sons	Service to Chinggis Khan	–	RD 598, tr. 265
Qiyats	10,000	Köki (?), Mögetü	Chinggis Khan's own people	–	RD 598, tr. 265

[a]See Table 1B: footnote a.
Dark shading: commanders with marriage ties and large, homogenized units.
Light shading: commanders with marriage ties but smaller units.
No shading: commanders with homogenous soldiers but no marriage ties.
Sources: *Secret History* (marked *SH*) and Rashīd al-Dīn, *Jāmi'* (marked RD), and trans. Thackston, (marked "tr.").

causes (childbirth? illness?).[29] Next, Butu married Börte's oldest daughter, princess Qojin, some time after her proposed marriage into the Kereit lineage had failed in 1203.[30] Later, Butu and Princess Qojin's son married a late-born junior daughter of Chinggis Khan in exchange for Qojin herself.[31] Certainly by 1206 Butu ranked as a son-in-law in the *Secret History*.[32] As such, Butu commanded a unit of a "thousand" in the atomized army composed of two thousand soldiers from his own Ikires people, and his sons with Princess Qojin inherited this position.

The Oirats (see Family Tree 4.2): Another in-law to Chinggis Khan and Börte was Qutuqa Beki, ruler of the Oirat forest people to the southwest of Lake Baikal. The Oirats enjoyed a constellation of marriages: the first between one of Qutuqa Beki's sons and Börte's second daughter, Princess Checheyigen. This was supported by a second marriage between Qutuqa Beki's other son and Jochi's daughter Qolui, and a third between Qutuqa Beki's daughter Oghul-Qaimish and Tolui (then Möngke through the levirate).[33] Thereafter, Qutuqa's relative Tankiz

29 Temülün was nine years younger than Temüjin. *Secret History*, §60, also §120 (Butu), and de Rachewiltz, Commentary, 324, 447, positing that Temülün was 14 or 15 at her marriage; Ratchnevsky, *Genghis Khan*, 18–19, from which we can assume that she was born around 1171. Hambis, *Chapitre CVIII*, 30, citing the *Yuan Shi*, 118, 8a, mentioning her marriage to Butu and death before his marriage to Qojin. Also *Yuan Shi*, 13:2757–61, Table of Imperial Princesses (unpublished trans. Buell); *Meng-ta pei-lu* [*Meng Da Bei lu*], trans. Olbricht and Pinks, 24. Allsen theorizes that Temülün wedded in the 1180s in "Merchant Partners," 86 and footnote 13.

30 *Secret History*, §202 (Butu as a son-in-law without identifying his wife), and de Rachewiltz, Commentary, 446–7; Hambis, *Chapitre CVIII*, 29–30, citing the *Yuan wen-lei* (25, 6a–7b) and the *Yuan Shi* (118, 8b), also his Table 4; Anonymous (2), *Campagnes*, trans. Pelliot and Hambis, §5 and commentary 49–50; Rashīd al-Dīn, *Jāmi'*, 161–2, 164 (garbled), 301, 600, trans. Thackston, 87–8 (garbled on 88); 147, 276; Ratchnevsky, *Genghis Khan*, 93; Cheng, "Career," 221–2; Allsen, "Merchant Princes," 86 and footnote 13 (hypothesizing on the date).

31 Qojin's son, Temegen, married Chalun / Chabun. Rashīd al-Dīn, *Jāmi'*, 164, trans. Thackston, 88 ("Chabun"); Hambis, *Chapitre CVIII*, 30 (and table 4) ("Chalun"), and *Yuan Shi*, 13:2757–61, Table of Imperial Princesses (unpublished trans. Buell).

32 *Secret History*, §202; also Ratchnevsky, *Genghis Khan*, 67–73, 75–8.

33 The *Secret History* claims that Checheyigen married Qutuqa's younger son, Inalchi, §239; de Rachewiltz, Commentary, 849, 852, 854–5 (on Qolui); Paul Pelliot, *Notes Critiques d'histoire Kalmouke*, I–II (Paris, 1960), I:5 and note 59 on 61–2. Rashīd al-Dīn claims Checheyigen married Töralchi in *Jāmi'*, 100, 301, 964, trans. Thackston, 55, 147, 472, while Juvaynī, *World-Conqueror*, 506, says she married "a chief" of the Oirats. Also see Broadbridge, "Ilkhanid-Oirat Connection," 123–4. Ishayahu Landa cites Bai Cuiqin to assert that she married Törelchi in "Imperial Sons-In-Law on the Move: Oyirad and Qonggirat Dispersion in Mongol Eurasia,"*Archivum Eurasiae Medii Aevi*, ed. P. D. Golden et al., (2016), 175, note 85, also 195, table 2. The Oirat princess Oghul-Qaimish should not be confused with the Merkit wife of Güyük Khan. She may

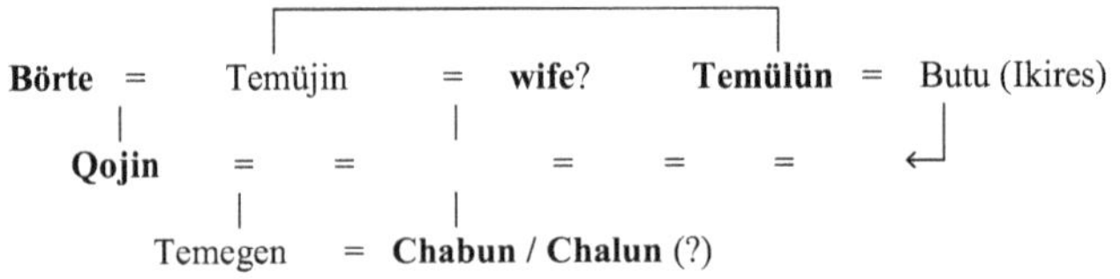

Family Tree 4.1 The Ikires and the Chinggisids.
All women are in **bold.**

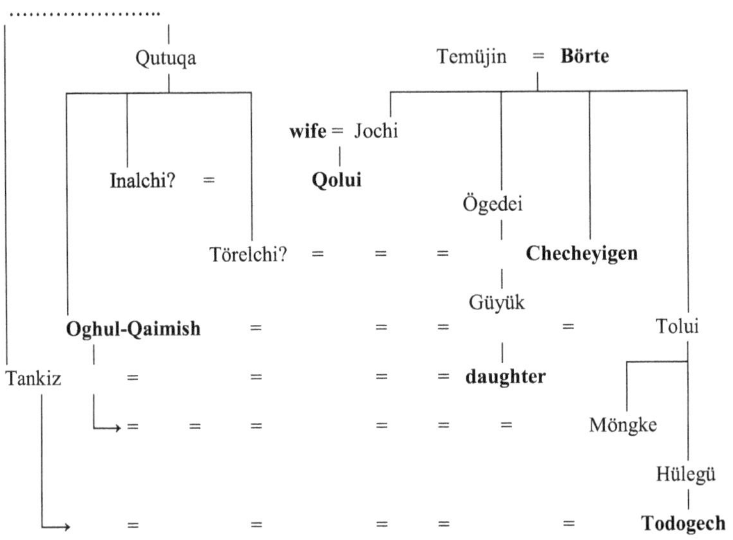

Family Tree 4.2 The Oirats and the Chinggisids.
All women are in **bold.**
Dotted line indicates unclear relationship.

married a daughter of Ögedei, followed by a daughter of Hülegü.[34] As a brother-in-law, Qutuqa Beki was granted the right to lead four thousand of his own Oirat soldiers in battle, but his unit functioned as an auxiliary to Chinggis Khan's atomized army, not an integral part of it.[35]

have been engaged or married to Tolui first, then later to Möngke. Rashīd al-Dīn, *Jāmi'*, 100, trans. Thackston, 55; Pelliot, *Kalmouke*, I:61 note 59; Zhao, *Marriage*, 137–9; also Cheng, "Career," 233, and De Nicola, *Khatuns*, 190, on her Christianity.

34 Rashīd al-Dīn, *Jāmi'*, 101, 971, trans. Thackston, 56, 476.

35 The Oirats do not appear in the *Secret History* list of commanders. *Secret History*, §202 and de Rachewiltz, Commentary 766, 787, 849–54; Rashīd al-Dīn, *Jāmi'*, 596, trans. Thackston, 274.

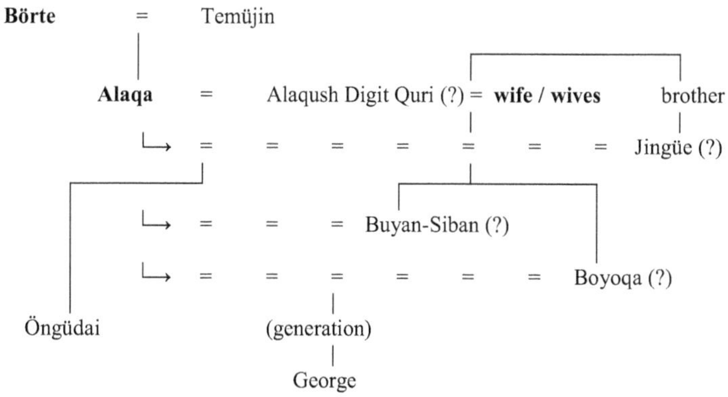

Family Tree 4.3 The Öng'üts and the Chinggisids.
All women are in **bold.**
All of Alaqa's marriages are possible, but not confirmed.

The Öng'üts (see Family Tree 4.3): Börte's third daughter, Alaqa, married into the Nestorian Christian Turkic Öng'üts, who lived on the border with the Jin Empire, and whose four or five thousand men were commanded initially by their ruler, Alaqush, and were listed among the ranks of the atomized army as one of the special thousands.[36] In the Öng'üt case no immediate second marriage with a junior princess is recorded, but since Alaqa herself was frequently widowed and therefore ultimately married several Öng'üt rulers in succession, perhaps another link was seen as superfluous. Later a daughter of Tolui did marry into the Öng'üts, and thereafter this lineage maintained marriage ties with the Chinggisids over time.[37]

The Qonggirats (See Family Trees 4.4 and 4.5): Not surprisingly, Börte's relatives were especially prominent among the special commanders of a thousand in the atomized army. The story of Börte's fourth daughter, Princess Tümelün, is less clear: recent scholarship suggests that she was first engaged to Terge Amal, leader of the Nirgin branch of the Qonggirats, whose rejection of a marriage alliance resulted in his death. Later she married his son, Chigü, who may have been adopted by her uncle Alchi in an attempt to unify Terge Amal's followers with his own.[38]

36 Rashīd al-Dīn, *Jāmi'*, 598, trans. Thackston, 275, with 4,000; the *Secret History*, §202, has 5,000. It is not clear who Alaqa married; for possibilities, see Chapter 5, footnote 32.
37 She married Negüdei, a son of Jingüe. See Pelliot, *Kalmouke*, 63.
38 Atwood, "Chikü *Küregen*," 16–23; Togan, "Qongrat," 71–4 (Terge and the Nirgin Qonggirats). The *Secret History*, §141, §176, mentions a Terge Emel who joined the

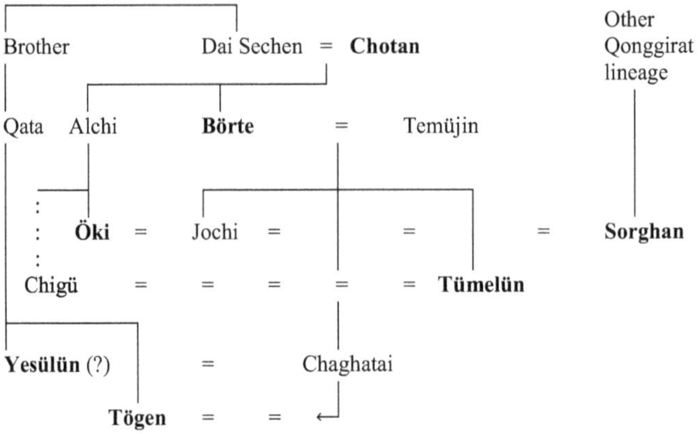

Family Tree 4.4 The Qonggirats and the Chinggisids (senior line).
All women are in **bold.**
: Indicates adoption.

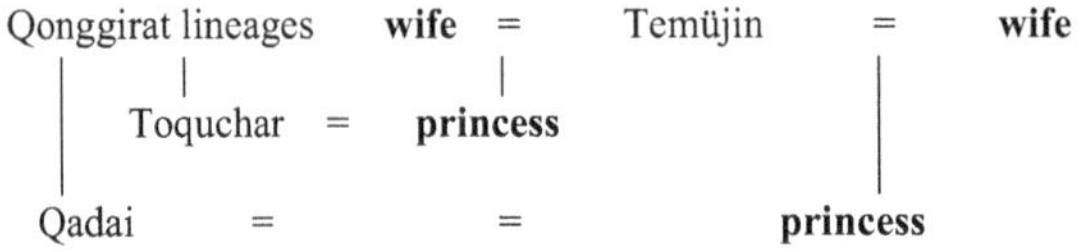

Family Tree 4.5 The Qonggirats and the Chinggisids (junior lines).
All women are in **bold.**

The adoption created an exchange-like marriage (an exchange for Börte), but if indeed Chigü was adopted then the marriage was not quite the standard arrangement for blood relatives.[39] In any case, both Chigü and Alchi led Qonggirat units (Alchi as a brother-in-law), with a total of between three thousand and five thousand soldiers, or more.[40] At the

1201 coalition against Temüjin, then submitted to Temüjin with the Qonggirats in 1203. Rashīd al-Dīn claims that Terge "El" (not Emel) refused a marriage because the bride was "a frog and a turtle. How can I take her?" This allegedly caused Chinggis Khan to execute him; certainly Terge El / Emel vanishes from the historical sources after 1203. Rashīd al-Dīn, *Jāmi'*, 159, trans. Thackston, 85.

39 Rashīd al-Dīn, *Jāmi'*, 159–60, 302, 603, trans. Thackston, 86–7, 147, 278; *Yuan Shi*, Table of Imperial Princesses, 13:2757–61 (unpublished trans. Buell); Zhao, *Marriage*, 109; Boyle's hypothesis that she married Toquchar cannot be supported; see Juvaynī, *World-Conqueror*, 174–5, note 11; for Chigü see *Secret History*, §202, §251 (as Chügü), de Rachewiltz, Commentary, 765, 914.

40 *Secret History*, §202, where Alchi commands a large unit, but Chigü does not. Chigü received four thousand Qonggirat troops for a later campaign in Tibet, and then

same time, Börte's sons Jochi and Chaghatai married one or more Qonggirat brides, and the two families went on to exchange their children in marriage for many subsequent generations.[41]

Other men from Börte's family, or from additional lineages among the Qonggirats, worked as military commanders for Chinggis Khan and earned son-in-law status by marrying Chinggisids. (See Family Tree 4.5.) Thus the Qonggirat Toquchar, who was not a commander of a thousand but nevertheless played an important role in the Western Campaign, became a son-in-law by marrying a junior princess.[42] The Qonggirat commander Qadai married a different junior princess.[43]

The Uighurs (See Family Tree 4.6): Börte's fifth and youngest daughter, Al Altan, married the wealthy *iduqut* of the Uighur Turks, Barchuk.[44]

remained there with them. Rashīd al-Dīn, *Jāmiʿ*, 603, trans. Thackston, 278; also Atwood, "Chikü *Küregen*," 13, 15–16, 22, and his "Tibetans," 31–4.

41 Jochi married Sorghan, then Börte's niece Öki in an exchange marriage. Chaghatai married Yesülün (sic), then Tögen, daughters of Börte's cousin Qata. See Chapter 8; also Nobuhiro, "Exchange-Marriage," 179–80; Zhao, *Marriage*, 109.

42 Juvaynī, *World-Conqueror*, 177; in note 18 Boyle misidentifies her as Princess Tümelün. Also see Chapter 5.

43 *Secret History*, §202. Qadai's unit appears to have been standard in size (one thousand), but its composition, and his wife's name, are unknown. Pelliot wonders whether he was Börte's paternal cousin from her uncle, Daritai, or an unrelated Qonggirat named Qadai about whom less is known. Pelliot, "Sur un passage," 924–5, n. 4, and 930, n. 20.

44 For *iduqut* or rather *iduq qut*, meaning "holy fortune" or "luck," see Allsen, "Uighurs," 246 and note 15.

Al Altan also appears as Altalun and Altaluqan. The identity of her husband is confused. Given her execution for murdering Ögedei (see Chapter 6), it seems likely that sources edited or excised information about her. On her marriage: *Secret History*, §238 (and de Rachewiltz, Commentary, 846–9), has her marrying the *iduqut* in about 1211 when she would have been fifteen – a good age for marriage. Also *Yuan Shi*, Table of Imperial Princesses, 13:2757–61 (unpublished trans. Buell); Hambis, *Chapitre CVIII*, 130–1 and footnote 9 on 133; also table 11. J. A. Boyle cites F. W. Cleaves claiming that he saw no evidence in the *Yuan Shi* that Al Altan did *not* marry Barchuk. (Juvaynī, *World-Conqueror*, 47 and note 17). Martin accepts that she married Barchuk in *North China*, 111. By contrast, de Rachewiltz, Commentary for *Secret History* §202 on 764–5 uses Rashīd al-Dīn to suggest that she married Hö'elün's father, Olar, then his son Taichu through the levirate.

The Persian sources greatly obscure Al Altan's marriage, with Rashīd al-Dīn the worst offender. He first claims that Al Altan married her uncle Taichu of the Olqunu'uts, but then asserts that her oldest sister, Qojin, married him. But even if Al Altan had married Taichu, she would not have then (re)married outside the Olqunu'ut into the Uighurs as the *Yuan Shi* and *Secret History* have it, and as the Persian sources themselves go on to suggest. At the same time, Qojin's marriage to Butu of the Ikires is also known, and cannot be confused with a marriage into the Olqunu'uts. The Olqunu'uts thus seem to be a red herring. Rashīd al-Dīn, *Jāmiʿ*, 141, 162, 274, 302, 597–8, trans. Thackston, 76, 87, 134, 147–8, 275; trans. Boyle, 198; Juvaynī, *World-Conqueror*, 47–8.

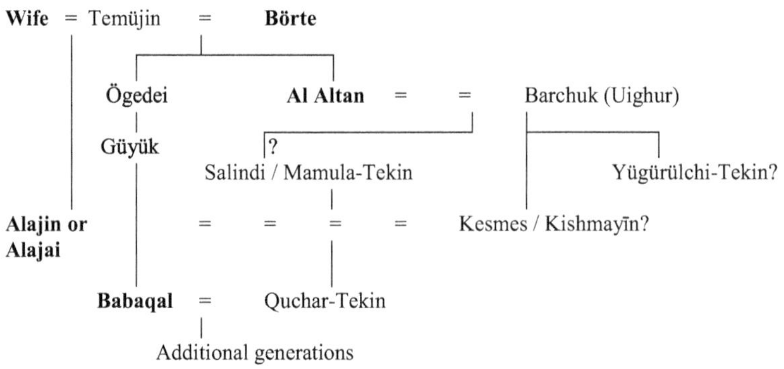

Family Tree 4.6 The Uighurs and the Chinggisids (tentative).
All women are in **bold.**
|? Denotes that parentage is uncertain.

Barchuk's forces were not in the atomized army; rather, he commanded an auxiliary of eighteen thousand of his own men, who fought in the

Juvaynī and Rashīd al-Dīn also claim that Barchuk was engaged to an unnamed daughter of Chinggis Khan in the late 1220s, but did not marry her because Chinggis Khan died. Next, allegedly, Ögedei did in fact engage Al Altan to Barchuk (again, casting great doubts on the possibility that she had earlier married into the Olqunu'uts), but she died while he was traveling to the wedding. Thereafter Ögedei engaged Barchuk to a princess named Alajin Beki (El Egetei, in Rashīd al-Dīn), but this time it was Barchuk who died before the wedding; thereafter (finally!) his son married her. (Juvaynī, *World Conqueror*, 47–8; Rashīd al-Dīn, *Jāmiʿ*, 141, trans. Thackston, 76). Rashīd al-Dīn complicates matters by claiming in a family tree that the *iduqut* delayed marrying El Egetei because of a determined wife at home (150; also Jackson, *Friar William*, 283–4 [appendix VII]). I cannot imagine Chinggis Khan accepting this insult on behalf of any daughter. (Cheng follows these sources and sets Barchuk's marriage to another daughter, not Al Altan, in the late 1220s, in "Career," 228–9.) Rashīd al-Dīn's claims are further confused by his statement that Al Altan was killed by the Jalayir commander Eljigidei, who was then executed during Möngke's reign (Rashīd al-Dīn, *Jāmiʿ*, 69, trans. Thackston, 39). See Chapters 6 and 7. I find it hard to believe that Al Altan died (once) of natural causes soon after Chinggis Khan's death, and then (again) so late that her killer was punished in the 1250s.

To sum up: it is improbable that Al Altan married into both the Olqunu'uts and the Uighurs, or that she died and was later killed, or that Chinggis Khan promised the *iduqut* a lesser daughter (Alajin, El Egetei) and then put off the wedding for fifteen years. Allsen notes the confusion about Al Altan's husband but focuses on Chinggis Khan's promise of "Altalun" to the *iduqut*, regardless of when or whether the marriage took place. He also notes that later marriages did happen between Chinggisid princesses and the *iduqut* 's descendants. Thomas T. Allsen, "The Yüan Dynasty and the Uighurs of Turfan," in *China among Equals: The Middle Kingdom and Its Neighbors, 10th–14th Centuries*, ed. Morris Rossabi (Berkeley and Los Angeles: University of California Press, 1983), 248.

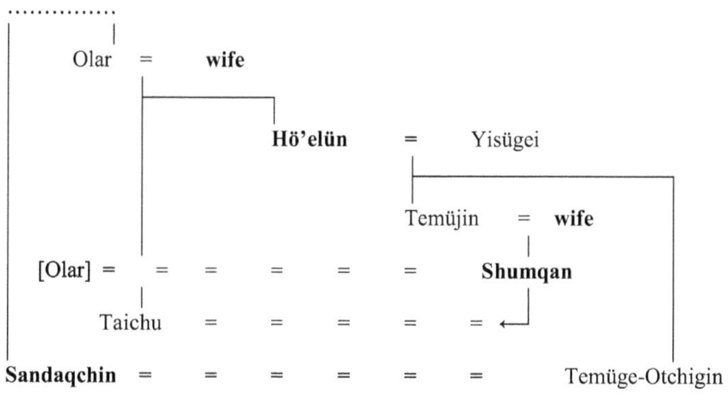

Family Tree 4.7 The Olqunu'uts and the Chinggisids.
All women are in **bold.**
.... Denotes undetermined relationship (cousins?).

Western Campaign.[45] Later one of his sons, Kesmes or Kishmayin, married a new Chinggisid princess in the 1240s.[46]

The Olqunu'uts (See Family Tree 4.7): Chinggis Khan's mother Hö'elün also contributed to her son's atomized army through members of her natal family, and through the Olqunu'ut subjects, whom Chinggis Khan had given her to rule. Thus Hö'elün's father Olar became a son-in-law by marrying a junior Chinggisid princess named Shumqan, and was also made a commander of a thousand.[47] That said, it is unclear whether he had a regular (atomized) thousand, or control of the oversized Olqunu'ut unit of a "thousand" belonging to Hö'elün, which actually contained three thousand Olqunu'ut soldiers.[48] In any case, after Olar's death, Hö'elün's brother Taichu inherited both Shumqan as wife and

[45] For Barchuk see Hambis, *Chapitre CVIII*, footnote 9 on 133. For numerous men (i.e., warriors) but without numbers, see Abū al-Ghāzī, *Shajarah-yi Türk-i Abū al-Ghāzī / Histoire des Mongols et des Tatares*, ed. and trans. Petr I. Desmaisons (St. Petersburg, 1871–4, rprt. Amsterdam, 1970), 100, trans. 108; also Ratchnevsky, *Genghis Khan*, 129.

[46] Alajin Beki in Juvaynī, *World-Conqueror*, 47–8, but Alajai Beki in Rashīd al-Dīn, *Jāmi'*, 141, trans. Thackston, 76; *Yuan Shi*, 13:2757–61, Table of Imperial Princesses (unpublished trans. Buell) for Princess Babaqal; also Hambis, *Chapitre CVIII*, 130–2 and table 11.

[47] *Secret History*, §202 and de Rachewiltz, Commentary, 764–5.

[48] See Table 1B: footnote a.

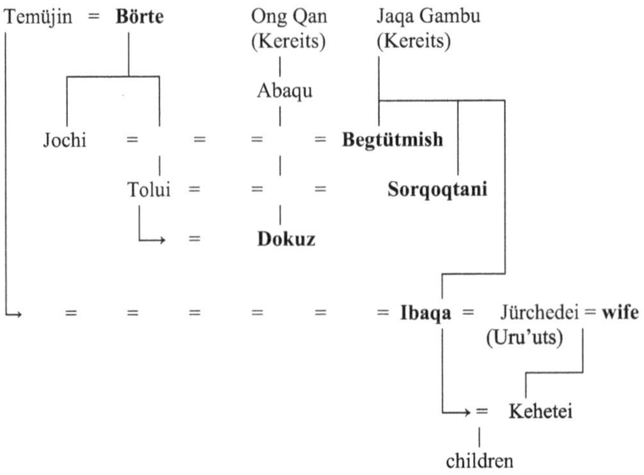

Family Tree 4.8 The Kereits, the Chinggisids, and the Uru'uts. All women are in **bold.**

his father's command.[49] (This princess was deliberately misidentified by Rashīd al-Dīn as Börte's fifth daughter, Al Altan.[50]) Hö'elün further strengthened the links between her natal lineage and the Chinggisids by marrying her youngest son, Temüge, to an Olqunu'ut relative named Sandaqchin, in an exchange for herself.[51]

The Uru'uts (See Family Tree 4.8): Chinggis Khan's Kereit wife Ibaqa married Jürchedei after Chinggis Khan set her aside. Jürchedei thus not only enjoyed an in-law relationship with the Chinggisids, but, as mentioned, had the right to command a unit of four thousand Uru'uts in the atomized army, with homogeneity among his soldiers.[52]

The Qarluqs of Qayaliq and Almaliq (See Family Tree 4.9): The most prominent junior princess may have been named Töre, who made a good match that was similar to (but lesser than) those of Börte's daughters when she married the Qarluq Arslan Khan and acted as the primary link

[49] *Secret History*, §202; de Rachewiltz, Commentary, 765; Rashīd al-Dīn, *Jāmi'*, 162, 274, 302, 597, trans. Thackston, 87, 134, 147, 275, Rashīd al-Dīn consistently claiming that Taichu married Al Altan. See footnote 44; for Shumqan see Atwood, "Evolution," 171.

[50] See footnote 44.

[51] Rashīd al-Dīn, *Jāmi'*, 280, trans. Thackston, 137.

[52] *Secret History*, §186 (the Kereits), §208, de Rachewiltz, Commentary, 787–92; Rashīd al-Dīn, *Jāmi'*, 118–19, 303–4, 361, 969, trans. Thackston, 64, 148–9, 175, 471.

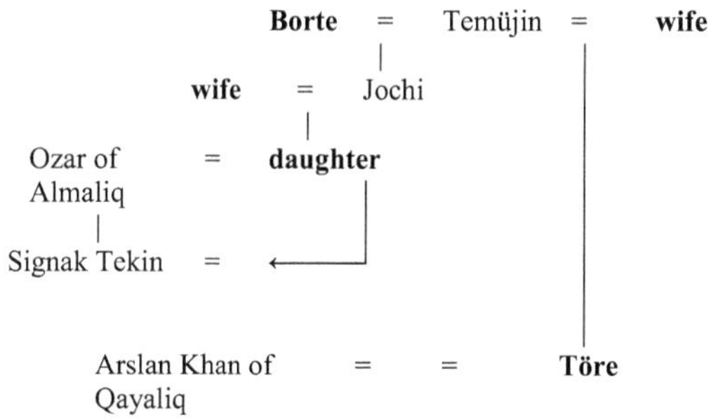

Family Tree 4.9 The Qarluqs of Almaliq and Qayaliq and the Chinggisids. All women are in **bold.**

between him and her father.[53] In any case, Arslan Khan commanded six thousand men.[54] Meanwhile a different Qarluq Turk, Ozar of Almaliq, married a daughter of Jochi, and commanded an unknown number of soldiers.[55] The military units of both Qarluq leaders were auxiliaries to the atomized army, not an integral part of it, as was true for their neighbor, the Uighur *iduqut* Barchuk.

The others: Several other sons-in-law to Chinggis Khan appear in the historical sources, but little is known about them, and nothing about their Chinggisid wives. One, "Fiku" (?), was a military leader in the Western Campaign.[56] Three other sons-in-law were commanders of a thousand: the Baya'ut Buqa; a man named Qadai who was perhaps another Qonggirat, as mentioned previously; and an unknown, Ashiq, who served under the favored Ba'arin leader Qorchi (see subsequent text) on a campaign.[57] Unfortunately the size and composition of their units is

[53] Töre's mother is unknown, and she herself may have been a granddaughter of Chinggis Khan, not a daughter. *Secret History*, §235 (she is unnamed), de Rachewiltz, Commentary, 842–3, citing the *Yuan Shi*, 109:2761 to establish that Töre married not the first Arslan Khan (a title), but rather his son (Yesü-Buqa, a second Arslan Khan), perhaps a remarriage through the levirate? Juvaynī, *World-Conqueror*, 75–6 (Arslan Khan marries a "royal maiden"). Also Ratchnevsky, *Genghis Khan*, 118–19.

[54] Juzjānī, *Ṭabaqāt*, 2:112, trans. Raverty, 1004; for Signak Tekin's warriors see Juvaynī, *World-Conqueror*, 82; Abū al-Ghāzī, *Shajarah-yi Türk*, 100, trans. Demaisons, 108 (numerous men); Ratchnevsky, *Genghis Khan*, 129.

[55] Juvaynī, *World-Conqueror*, 75–6 (Jochi's daughter marries Ozar) and 76 (Signaq Tekin receives his father's royal office and is "given one of Tushi's [Jochi's] daughters to wife," presumably the same daughter through the levirate?).

[56] For Fiku see Chapter 5.

[57] *Secret History*, §207, and de Rachewiltz, Commentary 787.

unclear, while their Chinggisid partners appear to have been junior princesses whose names have been lost.[58]

To reiterate the military distribution of these in-law commanders from the Chinggisid confederation: Many were commanders of a thousand in the atomized army, among them Butu of the Ikires; Alaqush of the Öng'üts; Chigü, Alchi, and possibly Qadai of the Qonggirats; Olar and then Taichu of the Olqunu'uts; Jürchedei of the Uru'uts; and Buqa of the Baya'uts, along with a few others whose affiliations are not known (Ashiq, Fiku). With the exception of Ashiq and Buqa, whose wives were junior Chinggisids and whose units were ordinary in size, these men all commanded "thousands" that were in fact larger than that number.[59] But although the Chinggisid confederation overlapped the atomized army, it was not a perfect match, since some members of the confederation functioned in the army as auxiliary fighting units. These in-laws were Qutuqa Beki of the Oirats; Barchuk of the Uighurs, both Qarluqs – Altan Khan and Ozar; and finally, Toquchar of the Qonggirats.

THE OTHER SPECIAL COMMANDERS OF A THOUSAND

As for the special commanders of a thousand within the atomized army whose divisions enjoyed homogeneity but who were not related to Chinggis Khan by marriage: Many had performed some special service for Chinggis Khan, and some units were as large as those of the in-laws. Thus Muqali, one of Chinggis Khan's "four steeds"[60] and commander-in-chief of the left wing, led three thousand Jalayirs.[61] Similarly either Qorchi or Naya'a commanded the three thousand Ba'arins, and both men served

58 Buqa: Rashīd al-Dīn suggests he was the chief of the Baya'ut, and that they fought at Dalan Balzhut (albeit with Önggür commanding) in *Jāmi'*, 180, 330, trans. Thackston, 96, 161; *Secret History*, §202 (Buqa, Ashiq, Qadai), §278 (Qadai), and de Rachewiltz, Commentary, 852 (Buqa), 1022 (Qadai as a possible Qonggirat, for which also Pelliot, "Sur un passage," 924–5, note 4 and 930, note 20). Some believe that the Olqunu'ut Kinggiyadei (*Secret History*, §202, commander number 80) and the Tayichi'ut Quril (commander number 82) were also sons-in-law, but de Rachewiltz rejects this in Commentary, 764–5; Atwood, "Comparison," 225 and note 16, accepts Kinggiyadai as an in-law.

59 The exception is Fiku; see Chapter 5.

60 These were Muqali, Bo'orchu, Boroqul, and Chila'un. *Secret History*, §163, §177, §209; de Rachewiltz, Commentary, 591–2, 792–3.

61 Rashīd al-Dīn, *Jāmi'*, 599, trans. Thackston, 275–6; Igor de Rachewiltz, "Muqali (1170–1223), Bōl (1197–1220), Tas (1212–39), An-T'ung (1245–93)," in *In the Service of the Khan, Eminent Personalities of the Early Mongol-Yüan Period (1200–1300)*, ed. Igor de Rachewiltz et al. (Wiesbaden, 1993), 5; also see Hope, *Ilkhanate*, 36.

Chinggis Khan militarily.[62] Smaller homogenous units included the Negüs, led by Narin To'oril, whose command was earned by his father's death for Temüjin at Dalan Balzhut.[63] The respected Baya'ut steward Önggür earned a similar privilege (up to one thousand homogenous soldiers).[64] The Mangqut also stayed together under Quyildar Sechen, who had played a crucial role at the battle of Qalaqaljit Sands in 1202, and who died of his wounds and bequeathed his privileges to his heirs.[65] Others leading their own people were Jebe of the Besüt and Sübedei of the Uriangqat, both important generals for Chinggis Khan and considered among his "four hounds,"[66] while Tolun the Qongqotan, son of Hö'elün's third husband, Mönglik (himself another commander), was allowed to control people he and his father had collected.[67] (Rashīd al-Dīn also mentions homogeneity for the Qiyats (or Qiyan or Borjigin), but these were simply the people to whom Chinggis Khan belonged.[68]) See Table 2.

THE ROLE OF THE CHINGGISID CONFEDERATION

The existence of the Chinggisid confederation within the empire in general and the reorganized army in particular was beneficial to many. First, some leaders saw which way the wind was blowing, and in the years

[62] The *Secret History* mentions Qorchi, who commanded a major expedition against the Forest Peoples, but Rashīd al-Dīn singles out Naya'a, who submitted early to Chinggis Khan and had a distinguished career. *Secret History*, §207; Rashīd al-Dīn, *Jāmiʿ*, 601, trans. Thackston, 277. Sometimes these men are seen as hereditary servants, for which see Christopher P. Atwood, "Mongols, Arabs, Kurds and Franks: Rashīd al-Dīn's Comparative Ethnography of Tribal Society," in *Rashīd al-Dīn as an Agent and Mediator of Cultural Exchanges in Ilkhanid Iran*, ed. Anna Akasoy, Ronit Yoeli-Tlalim, and Charles Burnett (London: Wartburg Institute), 239–43.

[63] *Secret History*, §218; Ratchnevsky, *Genghis Khan*, 92; Atwood, "Comparison," 220.

[64] *Secret History*, §213; Ratchnevsky, *Genghis Khan*, 92; Atwood, "Ethnography," 220; Rashīd al-Dīn, *Jāmiʿ*, 180, trans. Thackston, 96.

[65] Rashīd al-Dīn surely meant Quyildar's descendants, since Quyildar died before 1206 from wounds gained in Temüjin's service. *Secret History*, §175; Rashīd al-Dīn, *Jāmiʿ*, 601, trans. Thackston, 277. Also Ratchnevsky, *Genghis Khan*, 47, 69–70.

[66] These were Qubilai, Jelme, Jebe, and Sübedei, not to be confused with the four steeds (see footnote 62). For the hounds see *Secret History*, §209, and de Rachewiltz, Commentary, 792–3.

[67] For Jebe and Sübedei see *Secret History*, §221; for Tolun see §212 and de Rachewiltz, Commentary, 797–8.

[68] Rashīd al-Dīn, *Jāmiʿ*, 44, 145, 148–51, 270–1 (the Qiyat), 598, trans. Thackston, 26, 79, 80–1 and 133, 275; Atwood on this group in "Comparison," 218, note 9, and 219; de Rachewiltz, Commentary, 290–1, 297–9, 328–9, 445.

Table 2 Non In-Law Special Commanders in the Atomized Army (Rashīd al-Dīn and *Secret History* Combined)

Unit	Number	Leader	Connection	Sources
Jalayir	3,000	Muqali	Service to Chinggis Khan	RD 599, tr. 275–6
Ba'arin	3,000	Qorchi or Naya'a	Service to Chinggis Khan	*SH* §207, RD 601, tr. 277
Negüs	??	Narin To'oril	Father's death for Chinggis Khan	*SH* §218
Baya'uts	1,000	Önggür	Service to Chinggis Khan	*SH* §213, RD 180, tr. 96
Mangquts	??	Quyildar and sons	Service to Chinggis Khan	RD 601, tr. 277
Besüts	??	Jebe	Service to Chinggis Khan	*SH* §221
Uriangqats	??	Sübedei	Service to Chinggis Khan	*SH* §221
Qiyats	??	Köki (?), Mögetü	Chinggis Khan's own people	See footnote 70

Sources: *Secret History* (marked *SH*), Rashīd al-Dīn, *Jāmiʿ* (marked RD), and trans. Thackston (marked "tr.").

surrounding 1206 chose to join the Mongol juggernaut as in-laws while it formed, rather than scramble later to escape it. Because Chinggis Khan was willing to engage in old-fashioned confederation politics even while atomizing his military units, he was able to reward the early submission of some in-laws with special positions in the reorganized army. When other men submitted and became in-laws after the reorganization was finished, as will be detailed in Chapter 5, Chinggis Khan simply harnessed their militaries as auxiliaries without disrupting the atomized army at all. In any case, whether the submissions were early or late, in-laws may have acted as extra checks in the overall check-and-balance system of the Mongol military. They also could be subject to the same system, since Chinggis Khan occasionally took the relatives of these sons-in-law as hostages, as he did with regular commanders of a thousand.[69] The relationship of the Chinggisid confederation to the other military wings can be seen in Table 3:

[69] One such was the young Boyoqa of the Öng'üts, whose cousin Jingüe fought in China with Muqali while Boyoqa went on the Western Campaign. See Martin, *North China*, 237–8.

Table 3 The Chinggisid Confederation, Atomized Army and Imperial Guard

Imperial Guard (10,000 men)		
(1) Chinggisid Confederation leaders with auxiliaries (28,000–? soldiers)	(2) Chinggisid Confederation leaders with army units (15,000–24,000 soldiers)	(3) Non Confederation special commanders of 1,000 (17,000–? soldiers)
(4) **Total Confederation and Special Commanders of 1,000 (60,000–? soldiers)**		
(5) Regular Atomized Army commanders of 1,000 (61,000–73,000 soldiers)		

(1) *Chinggisid Confederation leaders with auxiliaries*: These were the Oirats (4,000), the Uighurs (18,000), the Qarluqs of Qayaliq (6,000) and the Qarluqs of Almaliq (troop numbers unknown), and the troops of Toquchar (unknown).
(2) *Chinggisid Confederation leaders with army units*: These were the Ikires (2,000–3,000), the Öng'üts (4,000–5,000), the Qonggirats (3,000–5,000 and 1,000–4,000), the Olqunu'uts (1,000–3,000), the Uru'uts (4,000), the Baya'uts (under Buqa; troop numbers unknown), and the three ill-known commanders with junior wives (see Table 1C for Buqa, Ashiq, and Qadai).
(3) *Non Confederation special units*: These were units of those special commanders who were not sons-in-law. They include the Jalayirs (3,000), the Ba'arins (3,000–5,000 under both Qorchi and Naya'a), the Negüs (troop numbers unknown), the Baya'uts (1,000 under Önggür), the Mangquts (troop numbers unknown), the Besüts (troop numbers unknown), the Uriangqats (troop numbers unknown), the Qiyats (10,000). In cases where there is a choice, the lower number is used to make the total.
(4) *Total Confederation and Special Commanders of 1,000*: Add up the lower numbers from categories 1–3 above for 60,000.
(5) *The Atomized Army number ranges*: The *Secret History* range for atomized soldiers who were not assigned to special units can be derived thus: Begin with the 95,000 in §202 as shown in Table 1A, then subtract those commanders with marked larger units (Butu with 2,000, Alaqush with 5,000, Alchi with 3,000, for a combined total of 10,000), for 85,000. Then subtract the other special commanders and their units at 1,000 each as implied by §202 (Chigü, Jürchedei, Olar, Buqa, Ashiq, Qadai, Tolun Cherbi, Qorchi, Narin To'oril, Önggür, Jebe, Sübedei, or a combined total of 12,000 [even though some, like Jürchedei, were allotted more than 1,000 in sections after §202]). The total is 73,000.
For Rashīd al-Dīn as shown in Table 1B: Begin with 101,000 (text 592, trans. Thackston, 272), then subtract all commanders with special units (using lower numbers in cases with a choice: Butu with 3,000, Qutuqa with 4,000, Alaqush et al. with 4,000, Alchi with 5,000, Chigü with 1,000, Jürchedei's sons with 4,000, Olar's son Taichu with 1,000, Muqali with 2,000, Naya'a with 3,000, Qorchi with 2,000, Quyildar et al. with 1,000, and the Qiyats with 10,000 for combined total of 40,000), for a total of 61,000.
Sources: *Secret History* (marked *SH*), Rashīd al-Dīn, *Jāmiʿ* (marked RD), and trans. Thackston (marked "tr.").

Thus the confederation provided an intermediate military unit between the imperial guard and the atomized army. The confederation overlapped the army, but not perfectly, since some confederation leaders commanded army units, but others commanded auxiliaries. Furthermore and as mentioned above, several additional special commanders of a thousand had performed special services, but were not also in-laws. Below all of these special cases were the regular commanders of a thousand with the atomized army units.

It is important to note that additional political benefits accrued to members of the confederation, beyond their clear military advantages. Whereas Butu and Jürchedei had been Chinggis Khan's early companions, most sons-in-law had no history of service to him. Marriage to a daughter, especially one of Börte's, gave these relative latecomers a closer relationship to Chinggis Khan than was otherwise possible. Some sons-in-law may also have lived with their new wife's relatives for a period as part of the engagement rituals, which gave both Chinggis Khan and Börte (and the other wives) an opportunity to acquaint themselves more fully with them.[70] Marriage to an imperial woman was a great honor, and created ties of mutual obligation on top of the ties ordinarily created when any man became a follower or vassal. Sons-in-law who were rulers continued to command their own realms, but now with their Chinggisid wives in place as general managers, political advisors, and potential informants for both their husbands and their father. In-laws also gained access to imperial quriltais, and they and their princess wives could marry their children at the top of the empire's political hierarchy.[71]

It is probable that Chinggis Khan and the women who advised him were also thinking like parents when arranging these matches. This brought its own benefits. The marriages of Börte's daughters were brilliant by steppe standards because of the wealth, status, and power involved, while Chinggis Khan's position as an overlord had the potential to provide all his daughters with protection from bad husbandly behavior.[72] Furthermore, although a steppe woman generally

[70] Cheng, "Career," 238–9.

[71] See Broadbridge, "Toluid-Oirat," entire and esp. 123–4; also De Nicola, *Khatuns*, 40 (on the importance of in-laws even before Chinggis Khan), 42–9 on women as political advisors; Zhao, "Conciliation," 24; Atwood, "Comparison," 226, with a dissenting view; also Chapter 1.

[72] On protection from husbands see De Nicola, *Khatuns*, 40 (although the protection failed in the case he mentions).

decamped to her husband's people after marriage, in the case of the Chinggisid princesses this does not mean they never saw their family again. Rather, Chinggis Khan summoned his sons-in-law to join him on his campaigns of conquest. Since women and families frequently accompanied fighting men on campaigns, some of these sons-in-law may have brought a wife or wives with them.[73] It seems most likely that a son-in-law would bring his Chinggisid wife when fighting with her father, although the sources name no names. But if so, this would give the princesses opportunities to interact personally with their father, mother, or stepmother and siblings during the campaigns, which could be useful to all parties.

SUCCESSION

In addition to bearing, educating, and helping to marry the five most important princesses in the Chinggisid confederation, Börte made her mark on the leadership of the empire, and the inheritance of it after Chinggis Khan's death, when the position of Great Khan became the province of her sons alone. Unlike in the case of a confederation, where existing mechanisms promoted known types of political connections, the restriction of succession to Börte's sons was a political innovation, and it proved to be immensely damaging to the empire as a whole.

In general, steppe succession was a complex process, since many different candidates could legitimately claim the right to rule. Some did so by invoking the principle of seniority, according to which a ruler was followed by a senior member of his family (uncles, brothers), or a senior widow acting as regent for a son (this last may have been a later addition).[74] But a man's oldest son also had a claim to rule (primogeniture),

[73] For source references on the presence of women during campaigns see Chapter 5. For scholarship see Brack, "Mongol Princess," 337–8 and note 38; 356–7; Rossabi, "Women," 154; Peter B. Golden, "War and Warfare in the Pre-Chinggisid Western Steppes of Eurasia," in *Warfare in Inner Asian History (500–1800)*, ed. Nicola Di Cosmo (Leiden, 2002), 130–1; Michal Biran, *The Empire of the Qara Khitai in Eurasian History* (Cambridge University Press, 2005), 166.

[74] Jackson, "Dissolution," 193–5; Wittfogel and Feng, *History of Chinese Society: Liao (907–1125)* (Philadelphia, American Philosophical Society, 1949), 398–400. Ratchnevsky, *Genghis Khan*, 125–6 (all but ruler's choice); also De Nicola, *Khatuns*, 54, 56, hypothesizing that the Mongols adopted female regency from the Qara-Khitai.

as did his youngest son (ultimogeniture[75]), although these options were restricted to offspring of the senior wife, not those of junior wives or concubines.[76] But, partially offsetting these rules, a ruler might himself decide on some other son, grandson, or nephew (ruler's choice).[77] The participation of Chinggisids and commanders alike was also an important element of the decision making process.[78]

In the Mongol Empire, the story of succession became essentially one of systematic and exponentially increasing disenfranchisement, in which the role of women, although critical, is not always understood. Chinggis Khan's own decision on succession is well known: he chose Börte's third son, Ögedei, to rule the empire after him.[79] But the sources do not agree on how and when Chinggis Khan came to that decision, or whether he profited from advice in making it. The *Secret History* sets the decision in 1218 at a quriltai before a major campaign against the Khwarazm-Shah Empire (the Western Campaign). At it the senior Tatar wife, Yisüi, urged Chinggis Khan not to leave Mongolia without choosing an heir. He was amenable to this advice and asked the participants in the quriltai for their thoughts, among them Börte's sons. But the second son, Chaghatai, spoke out of turn and called his elder brother Jochi a Merkit bastard, which led first to a fistfight and thereafter to pages of poetic rebukes and grand statements before Ögedei was finally chosen.[80] (This passage does not appear in the *Altan Tobçı.*[81]) The passage also implies that Börte was alive and present at the quriltai of 1218.[82]

[75] De Nicola, *Khatuns*, 65, noting that ultimogeniture was not a strong claim; see also his footnote 8 with references and analysis.

[76] Juvaynī, *World-Conqueror*, 40; Polo, *Description*, §83. Also Holmgren, "Levirate," 148–9; De Nicola, *Khatuns*, 39.

[77] This was what Chinggis Khan and Ögedei did.

[78] Hope, *Ilkhanate*, Chapter 2.

[79] De Rachewiltz, Commentary, 937, with references, and Introduction, xxix–xxxiv.

[80] *Secret History*, §254–5.

[81] *Altan Tobçi*, §35, §37, §40–3.

[82] Börte was mentioned as if she were present in the poetic rebukes: "If you incur blame / from your mother who has borne you / from her heart, her affection / for you will grow cold" (etc.), and "Even now, does she not wish to see the happiness of you, her sons?" *Secret History*, §254. Her death date is unknown, but given the stellar health that allowed her to carry nine pregnancies to term and produce live children who lived to adulthood, it is possible that she survived at least until 1218. De Nicola, *Khatuns*, 65, and notes 5 (referring to Raverty's contention that she survived her husband and acted as regent until Ögedei took over) and 6. Other scholars believe that Börte predeceased her husband. De Rachewiltz, Commentary, 333–4.

By contrast, the Persian author Juvaynī placed a more sober account of the decision in 1226 during a campaign against the Tanguts (1226–7), when Chinggis Khan was struggling with ill health, and spoke to six of his sons privately (i.e., not during a quriltai). These were Börte's sons Chaghatai, Ögedei, and Tolui (Jochi had already died[83]), as well as Qulan's son Kölgen, and Jürchedei and Orchan, whose mothers were Naiman and Tatar concubines respectively.[84] Juvaynī did not mention Yisüi playing any advisorial role, but she was a candidate to have done so, since she accompanied Chinggis Khan on this campaign. In a third version of the succession story, Rashīd al-Dīn repeated Juvaynī's tale, also without Yisüi, but whittled the participants down to Ögedei, Tolui, and one of Jochi's sons, thus omitting the belligerent Chaghatai and all sons from mothers other than Börte.[85]

What to make of these divergent reports? Both Juvaynī and Rashīd al-Dīn worked for members of the Toluid house, and this observably affected what they included, or suppressed, in their work.[86] The most poetic but least credible is the *Secret History*, since this section is considered a later interpolation into the text for political reasons.[87] The fact that Chinggis Khan took Qulan with him on the Western Campaign instead of Yisüi also suggests that the succession decision took place undramatically in 1226, not in 1218 with fisticuffs and verbal fireworks.[88] Nevertheless, even the *Secret History* manages to provide valuable insight into Chinggisid history, since it illuminates the tension between Jochi and Chaghatai, to which other sources refer in less detail, and suggests that part of the reason for that hostility lay in the question of Jochi's contested parentage.[89] It also inadvertently demonstrates the long

83 Qu and Liu, "Jochi's Lifetime," 283–90.

84 Juvaynī, *World-Conqueror*, 180; also Bar Hebraeus, *Chronography*, 390.

85 Rashīd al-Dīn, *Jāmi'*, 538, 578–9, trans. Thackston, 262, 292. Boyle, *World-Conqueror*, 18 (in brief); also 181, and note 7, where Boyle says that Rashīd al-Dīn omitted Jürchedei and Orchan from the story, and elsewhere even claims that they both died young. As Boyle implies, this seems rather suspect given their presence with their father on campaign in 1226.

86 Peter Jackson, *The Mongols and the Islamic World: From Conquest to Conversion* (Yale University Press, 2017), 22–4, 26–8.

87 De Rachewiltz, Commentary, 922–3, 935–7, with references.

88 *Secret History*, §257 (Qulan) and de Rachewiltz, Commentary, 939–40.

89 This insight holds true given corroboration by other sources, despite Moses's contention that stories of quarrelling sons were a literary trope, not history. Moses, "Quarrelling Sons," 63–9.

range of the repercussions from the Merkit capture of Börte in 1180 or 1181.

Regardless of which story is closest to what actually happened, the effect was striking. By narrowing his options to Börte's sons, Chinggis Khan opposed the steppe principle of seniority. This excluded his uncles from consideration, although this was largely a moot point since they may have died already. More critically, Chinggis Khan cut out his last living full brother, Temüge; the male offspring of his other two full brothers, Jochi-Qasar and Qachi'un (deceased); and his half-brother, Belgütei.[90] If the decision on Ögedei took place in 1218, then Jochi, who could have tried to take over through primogeniture, was left out in the cold; if the decision was instead made in 1226–7, then Jochi was already dead.[91] Nevertheless the choice of Ögedei also shut out Tolui, who might otherwise have sought to inherit through ultimogeniture. Although Tolui did in fact take over the homeland appanage, as was customary, he did not acquire the position of Grand Khan along with it.[92]

Chinggis Khan's decision further disenfranchised his sons from wives other than Börte. The clearest example of this was Qulan's son Kölgen. Although Kölgen was treated like Börte's sons when it came to troop numbers, opportunities for military leadership and the right to participate in quriltais, his junior status showed clearly in inheritance.[93] Not only was Kölgen's appanage smaller than those of Börte's sons, but Chinggis Khan gave him no part of the empire to rule. Similarly Kölgen's descendants attended quriltais, but were never candidates for rule in any generation. In the words of the *Secret History*, and unlike all four of Börte's sons, Kölgen was not a prince "in charge of a domain."[94] This lesser

90 Jackson, "Dissolution," 197. Qachi'un is alleged to have died young (Rashīd al-Dīn, *Jāmi'*, 611, trans. Thackston, 281) and does not appear in references to the quriltais of 1206 or 1228 (*Secret History*, §202–34, §269; de Rachewiltz considers him deceased by 1218 in Commentary, 936). Jochi-Qasar lived long enough to fight in China in 1211–2 (Rashīd al-Dīn, *Jāmi'*, 447, trans. Thackston, 219; also Ratchnevsky, *Genghis Khan*, 112), and may have died on that campaign (de Rachewiltz, Commentary, 877). Belgütei was alive in 1206 (*Secret History*, §242), attended the quriltai of 1228 (Juvaynī, *World-Conqueror*, 184), and is said to have died in 1256 at a very old age. Rashīd al-Dīn, *Jāmi'*, 850, trans. Thackston, 414). Since Belgütei was not Hö'elün's son, he would not have been considered for succession.

91 He died in 1225. See Qu and Liu, "Jochi's Lifetime," 283–90.

92 Jackson, "Dissolution," 197.

93 Like Jochi, Chaghatai, or Ögedei, Kölgen commanded four thousand soldiers. Rashīd al-Dīn, *Jāmi'*, 609, trans. Thackston, 279–80.

94 *Secret History*, §270.

status must be attributed to Qulan's position as a junior wife, and the situation was surely the same for Chinggis Khan's other secondary sons.[95]

Börte's case therefore shows the influence that a wife's status and position had, not only on her children's careers and marriages, but also on their chances of inheriting rule. Furthermore, when candidacy was limited to Börte's male offspring, this led to the emergence of four new Chinggisid houses, all descended from one of these senior sons (including Jochi, who was considered a Chinggisid despite his uncertain parentage). This limitation of rule remained uncontested during Chinggis Khan's lifetime and immediately after his death, but soon enough the disenfranchised branches of the family made serious attempts to reverse Chinggis Khan's initial decision and reopen the field to a wider range of contenders.

As for Yisüi: at the least, we can deduce from the *Secret History* that she attended the quriltai to discuss the campaign against the Khwarazm-Shah, along with the other wives and Börte herself, who was mentioned clearly in the poetic rebukes.[96] This fits our understanding of women's active participation in public political ceremonies and major decision making. The *Secret History* also reinforces the idea that women could offer political advice – in this case, in the most public venue possible – and expect to have it heard and perhaps accepted. The report implies that Yisüi possessed high status among the wives and enjoyed Chinggis Khan's regard, since it describes him as taking her advice immediately.[97] Yisüi may indeed have advised Chinggis Khan on this matter for real (perhaps during the second Tangut campaign?). If so, he may have respected her opinion both because of her political acumen, and because she had no personal stake in the question of succession, having borne no known children – even her nephew Cha'ur (Yisügen's son) did not live to adulthood.[98] At the end of the Tangut campaign Yisüi was rewarded with large numbers of conquered Tanguts, which may have represented Chinggis Khan's (posthumous) appreciation for her support and, perhaps, her sound advice.[99]

[95] Kölgen and his junior half-brothers (i.e., the sons younger than Tolui) participated in campaigns and quriltais. Rashīd al-Dīn, *Jāmi'*, 665–9, trans. Thackston, 325–7; Juvaynī, *World-Conqueror*, 180, 184, 269, 568; also De Nicola, *Khatuns*, 38 (the significance of a mother's status).

[96] See footnote 82.

[97] This status and favor are also implied by her earlier intervention on behalf of the Tatars.

[98] Rashīd al-Dīn, *Jāmi'*, 302, trans. Thackston, 148, but see footnote 57 in Chapter 3.

[99] *Secret History*, §268.

CONCLUSION

No one disputes the political and symbolic impact of the quriltai of 1206, nor the importance of the adjoining years in which Chinggis Khan made such tremendous organizational changes to his military and thereafter embarked on his conquests. But the roles of Chinggisid women in the daily work of the imperial guard, the creation of the atomized army, and the inheritance of the empire have not been discussed adequately. And yet women were central to all of these processes. Chinggis Khan's wives, especially Börte, worked actively with the imperial guardsmen who watched their camps, cooked their meals, and interacted routinely with their staff. At the same time, Börte and her daughters, as well as the junior princesses, and even Hö'elün and Ibaqa, actively supported Chinggis Khan's career through strategic marriages with his political associates. These marriages then directly influenced the shape of Chinggis Khan's military reorganizations, and the course of the conquests. At the same time, two women contributed to the crucial questions of inheritance and succession: Börte as mother of the heirs, and Yisüi as a political advisor. It is thus clear that women played major roles in the formation of Chinggisid institutions, despite the paucity of the scholarship. Studying their contributions therefore not only adds depth to our understanding of Chinggis Khan's own narrative, but revises some of that narrative significantly.

5

Sons-in-Law, Daughters, and Conquests

After creating his highly efficient and disciplined war machine – and radically reorganizing steppe society as a result – Chinggis Khan needed something for it to do. Since his nomadic neighbors had largely come under his control during his rise to power or in the process of military reorganization, he found a new outlet for Mongol forces in his famous campaigns of conquest. The most important of these were four: one against the Tangut Kingdom of Xi-Xia in northwestern China in 1209–10, a second against the Jin Empire in northern China in 1211–15 (with continuations from 1217–23 and 1230–4), a third into the western Empire of the Khwarazm-Shah in the Islamic lands in 1219–23, and the fourth, a second advance against the Tanguts, in 1226–7.[1] Between these major expeditions Chinggis Khan also sent out secondary campaigns, which included an attack on the Naiman ruler Buiruq Khan in 1206,[2] preliminary raids on the Tanguts in 1205 and 1207,[3] defeats of his remaining Merkit enemies in 1209 and 1218,[4] a foray against the Qori-Tumat forest peoples to the west of Lake Baikal in

1 Ratchnevsky, *Genghis Khan*, 103–5, 105–16, 119–25, 128–34, 136–40; Martin, *North China*, 115–20, 131–219, 220–38, 239–82, 283–301; May, *War*, 13–17, 115–24; Dunnell, *Chinggis Khan*, 62–71, 73.

2 Ratchnevsky, *Genghis Khan*, 101–2; de Rachewiltz, Appendix 1 to the *Secret History*, 1047.

3 For details see Martin, "Mongol Wars," 197–9 and Dunnell, "Xia Empire," 164–5, 167–8; otherwise Ratchnevsky, *Genghis Khan*, 103–4; Martin, *North China*, 93–4, 102–3; May, *War*, 13; de Rachewiltz, Appendix 1 to the *Secret History*, 1046–7.

4 Buell, "Expansion," 9–16, 23–6; May, *War*, 15; de Rachewiltz, Appendix 1 to the *Secret History*, 1047–9.

1217–18, and an expedition against the Naiman Küchlüg, who had fled southwest to take over the faltering Qara-Khitai Empire, in 1218.[5]

Members of the Chinggisid confederation surfaced in most of the Mongol campaigns, but scholars have only partially acknowledged how many military leaders enjoyed marital relationships to the Chinggisid family. The goal of this chapter is therefore not to provide an exhaustive chronicle of the campaigns, but rather to reinsert warrior husbands and their imperial wives into the story of the conquests where they belong. Bringing sons-in-law on campaigns gave Chinggis Khan a chance to work with them, test their qualities, and reward them personally for services. Furthermore, the entrance of sons-in-law into the Chinggisid confederation allowed Chinggis Khan to incorporate into his empire (or "conquer") new lineages and their subjects without shedding Mongol blood. These rulers and their fighting men were then at his disposal as he looked farther afield, and in some cases allowed him to contemplate military campaigns that he could not have undertaken otherwise. At the same time, women regularly accompanied men on military campaigns, or were otherwise involved in military activities. Thus, whereas Chapter 4 examined the marriages of Chinggisid women structurally as they related to army reform, this chapter places those marriages in a chronological framework, and returns consort men and imperial women (where possible) to their rightful place in the Mongol campaigns of conquest.

THE MAJOR MONGOL MILITARY CAMPAIGNS

Although sons-in-laws appear as individuals in the historical sources and the scholarship, they are more usefully considered as members of a particular category, similar to other categories such as generals, commanders of a thousand, imperial guardsmen, Chinggis Khan's sons from Börte, or his sons from junior wives. Sons-in-law as a category were unique in that some were in the army, while others hailed from outside regular lines of command, as described in Chapter 4. Since Chinggis Khan regularly assigned at least two commanders to each campaign or maneuver, sons-in-law gave him an additional pool of men from which to draw officers, and he routinely chose them to lead armies alongside generals or Börte's sons. In addition, sons-in-law tended to control larger units than a thousand – especially the sizeable Uighur and Qarluq auxiliaries. This

[5] Buell, "Expansion," 17–19, 27–30; Ratchnevsky, *Genghis Khan*, 118–19; May, *War*, 15–16; de Rachewiltz, Appendix 1 to the *Secret History*, 1049–50.

could be especially useful when irregular forces were needed for a particular assignment.[6]

The princess wives of these men also contributed to Chinggis Khan's campaigns. The presence of women in general on Mongol military campaigns is attested in numerous places. Most dramatically the sources suggest that women attended battles, either as combatants or onlookers; one author claims that generals could oversee battles while watching with their families, who were mounted on extra horses to make an inflated show of numbers.[7] Another clarifies that even though women *with* children did go on campaigns, only those *without* children engaged in combat.[8] More prosaically, women appear to have functioned as support staff for military efforts. Wives of both commanders and ordinary soldiers accompanied the Mongol armies, tending (as usual) to managing logistics: packing and (some) supplies, food, clothing, and finance.[9] Particularly in the case of multiyear campaigns, men did not necessarily fight year-round, but rather engaged with enemies for one or two seasons (often but not exclusively winter into spring), and used other months to fatten horses, plan next steps, and hunt.[10] Imperial women were present during these long endeavors, and Chinggis Khan's wifely companions are particularly well known: the Merkit wife Qulan went on the Western Campaign, while the Tatar wife Yisüi accompanied the second Tanggut invasion.[11] We know that imperial wives managed the imperial traveling residence, probably in conjunction with a camp-commander, and we may further deduce that princess wives for sons-in-law could also have been present

[6] Such as the tamma army sent to China under Muqali in 1217 (see subsequent text in this chapter).

[7] Carpini, *History*, 36 (not in Rockhill); by contrast, de Bridia, *Tatar Relation*, §56–7, notes that women and families went on campaign, but stayed away from the action during battles. Note also that in 1260 the Mamluks at the Battle of 'Ayn Jālūt killed the general, Kitbuqa, then captured his wife and children. Connetable Smpad, "La Chronique Attribuée au Connétable Smbat," in *Documents relatifs à l'histoire des croisades*, trans. Gérard Dédéyan (Paris: l'Academie des inscriptions et belles-lettres, 1980), 108.

[8] Jean de Joinville (1865, 1965), *Histoire de Saint Louis*, ed. Natalis de Wailly (Paris: Jules Renouard), §324; Joinville, "Life," trans. Smith, §488.

[9] *Meng-ta pei-lu* [*Meng Da beilu*], trans. Olbricht and Pinks, 79; also Joinville, *Histoire*, §324; Joinville, "Life," trans. Smith, §488; de Bridia, *Tatar Relation*, §56. Note that men were at least partially responsible for their own weapons. May, *War*, 63–4.

[10] This pattern was particularly clear during the 1236–42 campaigns in Central Asia, Russia, and Europe.

[11] *Secret History*, §257 (Qulan), §265 (Yisüi).

on campaigns, although sources specify their presence only rarely.[12] Women can be assumed to have attended (and helped organize) feasts and celebrations after victories; they also received a share of spoils. The sources further reveal that imperial women who relocated outside the Mongol heartland after marriage hosted the leaders of Mongol armies that passed through their territory.[13] Finally, we may guess that women used their networks of informants to help further the war efforts conducted by men, but such information rarely appears in the sources.[14]

THE FIRST WAVE OF IN-LAWS (1190–1206)

The sons-in-law identified in Chapter 4 married into the Chinggisid family in two major waves, one from 1190 to 1206, and the second from 1208 to 1211. The earliest in-laws, that is, those in the first wave, either hailed from Chinggis Khan's own followers, or were leaders among nearby steppe peoples. Their marriages to Chinggisid women therefore created or strengthened connections between each man and Chinggis Khan, and brought the son-in-law's nomadic followers and subjects under Chinggis Khan's dominion. This group included men from Ikires, Olqunu'ut, Qonggirat, and Uru'ut lineages.

The very first in-law chronologically was Butu of the Ikires, one of Temüjin's nomadic supporters, who joined Temüjin after the latter's break with Jamuqa in about 1184.[15] Butu was posthumously remembered as heroic and martial in character, and he stood by Temüin during key events, including times of particular difficulty.[16] Butu's enduring loyalty allowed him to join the Chinggisid family first by marrying Temüjin's sister Temülün, then Börte's oldest daughter, Qojin. He later worked as a special commander in the Chinggisid confederation, which

[12] The junior princess wife of Toquchar went on the Western Campaign, while Princess Alaqa was involved in Jin campaigns because of her location in Öng'üt territory. See the subsequent discussion in this chapter for both.

[13] Orqīna, in company with Chaghatay's widows, hosted Hülegü and his wives in 1253 on their way to invade Iran. See Chapter 8.

[14] See subsequent text in this chapter, the hypothetical about Toquchar's junior princess wife.

[15] *Secret History*, §120, and de Rachewiltz, Commentary, 446–7, 597; Anonymous, *Campagnes*, trans. Pelliot and Hambis, 5, and Commentary, 49–50; Ratchnevsky, *Genghis Khan*, 40 (without Butu's name) and 281 (the date). Also Rashīd al-Dīn, *Jāmi'*, 328, 393, trans. Thackston, 160, 190.

[16] He was with Temüjin at Baljuna Lake, for example. Rashīd al-Dīn, *Jāmi'*, 164, 600, trans. Thackston, 88, 276; *Yuan shi* 9: 2921–3 (unpublished trans. Paul Buell).

brought his 2,000 Ikires soldiers under Chinggis Khan's control.[17] Similarly, it was some time during these early years that Hö'elün's Olqunu'ut family connected politically with Temüjin through the military appointments and imperial weddings of Hö'elün's father and then brother to a junior daughter of Chinggis Khan, as well as the marriage of Temüjin's youngest brother, Temüge, to an Olqunu'ut wife.[18]

Another set of early consorts were the Qonggirats, many of whom allied themselves with Temüjin in or after 1203–4.[19] As outlined in Chapter 4, the chief Qonggirat beneficiaries of new marital alliances and expanded military units were Börte's relatives, although other Qonggirats married lesser princesses and Chinggisid princes, and received respectable commands, as well.[20] During or after this wave of Qonggirats, another of Temüjin's followers, Jürchedei of the Uru'uts, similarly emerged. Jürchedei negotiated an agreement between one branch of the Qonggirats and Temüjin, then fought and executed Temüjin's former ally, the Kereyit lord Jaqa Gambu. For this service, and as mentioned in Chapter 3, Temüjin rewarded him by casting off his wife, Jaqa Gambu's daughter Ibaqa, and remarrying her to Jürchedei in 1206, which transformed Jürchedei into a unique sort of in-law, with command over 4,000 Uru'ut warriors.[21] Other sons-in-law are likely to have joined Chinggis Khan in these early years, among them Ashiq, whose lineage and people are unknown, and Buqa of the Baya'uts, both of whom married junior princesses.[22]

THE SECOND WAVE OF IN-LAWS (1207–1211)

After a certain point Chinggis Khan and his advisors stopped arranging marriages between the princesses and internal supporters or local nomadic allies, and instead contracted new marital alliances with men who lived farther from the Mongol heartland. The addition of these outsider sons-in-law to the confederation allowed Chinggis Khan to engage in a form of peaceful conquest of major peoples and regions. Such conquests began when potential sons-in-law indicated their willingness to submit to Chinggis Khan and provided him with useful information or military support, for which services they received the opportunity to

[17] See Chapter 4. [18] See Chapter 4.
[19] *Secret History*, §202, and de Rachewiltz, Commentary, 765, 914; also Atwood, "Chiku *küregen*," 16–23.
[20] See Chapter 4. [21] See Chapter 2. [22] See Chapter 4.

marry into the Golden Lineage. After marriage, these sons-in-law continued to support their new father-in-law militarily, and with their princess wives could contribute to the emerging administration of the growing empire (this was particularly true of the sophisticated Uighurs).[23] By making advantageous marital connections to the rising Mongol juggernaut, these sons-in-law facilitated the peaceful entrance of their considerable lands and peoples into the Empire, and also preserved (or improved) their own positions in the rapidly changing political world of the steppe.

The first of the politically, geographically, and militarily important outsider in-laws was Alaqush, lord of the Öng'üt Turks at Tenduc[24] (Tiande) who lived northwest of the Jin Empire.[25] The Öng'üts were mostly Nestorian Christian settled farmers who played the crucial role of guarding the frontier zone between the steppe and the Jin Empire on behalf of the Jin government; they were also strategically positioned to the northeast of the Tangut Kingdom of Xi-Xia.[26] The Öng'üts paid close attention to political and military developments in the steppe, and despite their responsibilities to the Jin, were able to form their own alliances with steppe powers if they so chose. This was the case with Alaqush, who first contacted Temüjin through a merchant deputy in 1203 when Temüjin was holed up at Baljuna Lake, recovering from a disastrous battle with the Kereyits.[27] Then, as outlined in Chapter 3, in 1204 the Naiman ruler Tayang Khan prepared to attack Temüjin and invited Alaqush to join him, since the two ruling families, both Turkic and both Nestorian Christians, were linked by marriage.[28] But Alaqush refused the invitation and instead warned Temüjin, which enabled him to prepare for and defeat Tayang Khan, who died (his son, Küchlüg, escaped to harass

[23] Cheng, "Career," 234; also Allsen, "Uighurs," 244–5, and "Appropriation," 8, and "Merchant Partners," 113–14.

[24] Tenduc is the name given by Polo, *Description*, §74.

[25] Buell, "Prolegomena," 45 (territory), 46–7 (the alliance); de Rachewiltz, Commentary, 656 (territory); also for the alliance Christopher P. Atwood, "Historiography and Transformation of Ethnic Identity in the Mongol Empire: The Öng'üt Case," *Asian Ethnicity* 15, no. 4 (2014): 522–5; Martin, *North China*, 128–9.

[26] Buell, "Prolegomena," 45; also Atwood, "Öng'üt Case," 515–16, 520–1.

[27] The battle was at Qalaqaljit Sands. *Secret History*, §170, §182 (Baljuna), de Rachewiltz, Commentary, 615–21, 657–68; Ratchnevsky, *Genghis Khan*, 70–3.

[28] *Secret History*, §190, and de Rachewiltz, Commentary, 685; Anonymous (2), *Campagnes*, trans. Pelliot and Hambis, §15 and Commentary, 319 (marriage), and *Kalmouke*, 62 (only Christianity, not marriage); Rashīd al-Dīn, *Jāmi'*, 366, trans. Thackston, 177.

Chinggis Khan later).[29] This gamble paid off for Alaqush, whose ruling lineage rose to consort status when Börte's third daughter Alaqa married into it, then later remarried within it several more times through the levirate.[30] As mentioned in Chapter 4, Alaqush appeared as a commander of a "thousand" in the *Secret History* with four thousand to five thousand troops.[31] Unfortunately the identity of Alaqa's first groom is not clear, nor is the date of the wedding. Her possible husbands included Alaqush himself; his older son, Buyan-Siban; his younger son Boyoqa, and perhaps his nephew, Jingüe, while the wedding(s) may have taken place in any (or all) of 1207, 1211, 1212, and 1225.[32]

[29] *Secret History*, §190; Rashīd al-Dīn, *Jāmi'*, 127, 131, trans. Thackston, 68, 71; Ratchnevsky, *Genghis Khan*, 83–6; de Rachewiltz, Appendix 1 to the *Secret History*, 1046; Biran, *Chinggis Khan*, 38–9; Dunnell, *Chinggis Khan*, 45–6; Atwood, "Öng'üt Case," 522.

[30] See footnote 32; also Holmgren, "Levirate," 165; Hope, *Ilkhanate*, 40.

[31] *Secret History*, §202 for 5,000; Rashīd al-Dīn, *Jāmi'*, 127, 131, trans. Thackston, 70, for 4,000.

[32] Alaqush: The *Secret History* implies that Alaqa married Alaqush, since he appears as a son-in-law in §202, although in the report of the wedding in 1207 the groom is not named. *Secret History*, §202, §239; de Rachewiltz, Commentary, 856–7. However in *Kalmouke*, 62, Pelliot argued that Alaqa's marriage to the Öng'üt ruler may not have happened in 1207 since it was tacked on to an unrelated campaign in §239 and thus placed inaccurately in the text. I suggest that the date is reasonable, since if Alaqa was born in about 1189 or 1190, she would have been 18 or 19 in 1207, a good age for marriage. §239 includes the weddings of Checheyigen and Qolui (Jochi's daughter) to the Oirats, while §238 mentions Al Altan's marriage to the Uighurs. Topically the cluster works, and it is also possible that in actuality Börte and Chinggis Khan held multiple festivities at the same time.

Jingüe: Some years ago Paul Buell used Rashīd al-Dīn and the *Da Jin guo zhi* to argue that the Jin government had Alaqush assassinated by a faction of his commanders in 1207 and instated his nephew, Bosibo (or Shengui [i.e., Jingüe], from the Chinese title *Chenguo*, "fortifier of the dynasty"), who had been living under Jin protection. But he refused to be their tool and turned to Chinggis Khan, who then married him to Alaqa. This was therefore her first wedding, not one to Alaqush. Paul Buell, "The Role of the Sino-Mongolian Frontier Zone in the Rise of Chinggis-qan," in *Studies on Mongolia: Proceedings of the First North American Conference on Mongolian Studies* (Bellingham, WA, 1979), 67–8; also Rashīd al-Dīn, *Jāmi'*, 131–2, 302, trans. Thackston, 71, 147, claiming that Alaqush described himself as too old for Alaqa and proposed her marriage to Jingüe, with whom she bore a son, Öngüdai. By contrast, Hambis, *Chapitre CVIII*, 25, and note 8 says she married Alaqush's younger son Boyoqa (see subsequent text in this footnote), also see 9, n. 2 and 94, n. 4, discussing Jingüe without suggesting he married Alaqa. For the most recent take on this see Atwood, arguing that Alaqa married Jingüe in 1211 in "Öng'üt Case," 522.

Buyan-Siban: Other Chinese sources suggest that Alaqa married Baisibu, whom scholars identify as Alaqush's older son Buyan-Siban: See the *Meng-Ta pei-lu* [*Meng Da beilu*], trans. Olbricht and Pinks, 24 and note 17 on 32; the *Hei-ta Shih-Lüeh (Hei Da shi lü)*, 193 and note 11 on 196. This happened not in 1207 but in 1211 (when Alaqa was about

Meanwhile, the second important outsider consort house emerged to historical view in 1207–8: this was the ruling lineage of the Oirats in the forested region west of Lake Baikal, whose leader, Qutuqa Beki, helped a Mongol force chase Merkit refugees through his territory. He also seized the moment to submit to Chinggis Khan.[33] Qutuqa Beki was rewarded for these two services with the opportunity to make his lineage a consort one.[34] As noted in Chapter 4, this resulted in a veritable marriage coup for Qutuqa Beki, who established what later became a long and illustrious line of Oirat consorts by wedding two sons and a daughter to Chinggisids.[35]

Next, to the southwest of Mongol territory, a series of disaffected Turks outside Mongol sway began to pay attention to the rising new star. These men were all vassals of the once powerful but now faltering Qara-Khitai Empire, ruled by the Gür Khan. It was in Qara-Khitai territory that the Naiman prince, Küchlüg, first took refuge, then married the daughter of the Gur Khan, then usurped rule from this father-in-law by 1211.[36] But not all of the Gür Khan's vassals supported their new lord, and several

21 or 22), according to the *Mengwuer shi ji*, 36, 1b–3a and 5b (the biography of Alaqush as cited by Martin, *North China*, 133, note 48, and Holmgren, "Levirate," 164–5).

Boyoqa: After Alaqush and Buyan-Siban were murdered in a Jin-sponsored uprising in 1211 or 1212, Alaqa was married again, either to Alaqush's younger son Boyoqa (*Yuan shi*, 13:2757–61, Table of Imperial Princesses [unpublished trans. Buell]; Hambis, *Chapitre CVIII*, 25 [table 4] and note 8), or first to Alaqush's nephew and temporary heir, Bosibo or Jingüe (Rashīd al-Dīn, *Jāmiʿ*, 131–2, 302, trans. Thackston, 71, 147), then later to Boyoqa (Holmgren, 165, citing the *Mengwuer shi ji*, 36, 1b–3a and 5b). Martin, *North China*, 149–50, 237 favors 1212 (and points out that Boyoqa was a child during the Western Campaign [1218–23], and therefore would have been very young in 1212). Pelliot, *Kalmouke*, 62–3 (favoring the Chinese sources over Rashīd al-Dīn for their geographical proximity to the Öng'üts), who notes the epitaph of the later Öng'üt prince George, who names Boyoqa and Alaqa as his grandparents (sic). Pelliot argues that Alaqa married Boyoqa in perhaps 1225, i.e., after the Western Campaign, but does not commit to any other marriages for her. I note that by then she was in her mid-thirties, so this was probably not her first marriage. The sources' confusion have, understandably, even misled de Rachewiltz, Commentary, in which Alaqa marries Boyoqa [first] (p. 656), or Alaqush first and Jingüe second (p. 765), or Alaqush first (p. 857). Cheng believes she married either Jingüe or Boyoqa, but not until after the Western Campaign. Cheng, "Career," 227.

I myself suspect that Alaqa married in 1207, at the age of 17 or 18, as a strategic match for her parents and at approximately the same time as several of her sisters. The groom was either Alaqush or Buyan-Siban. She then probably married Jingüe after the double assassination (whether in 1207 or 1212), and then undoubtedly Boyoqa in the 1220s, once he was old enough and had returned to the east.

33 Buell, "Early Mongol Expansion," 5–7 and note 12; Buell, "Sübötei," 15; Buell, "Bukhara," 127; Ratchnevsky, *Genghis Khan*, 102; Martin, *North China*, 103; Hope, *Ilkhanate*, 39–40.

34 Cheng, "Career," 232. 35 See Chapter 4. 36 Juvaynī, *World-Conqueror*, 61–5.

began to look for outside opportunities. The first to throw off his allegiance in favor of Chinggis Khan was Barchuk Art Tekin, the *iduqut* or ruler of the sophisticated, wealthy, sedentary (but formerly nomadic) Uighurs in the towns and oases of the Tarim River basin and Taklamakan desert.[37] Chinggis Khan first contacted Barchuk, who responded in 1209 with his own ambassadors. These not only informed Temüjin that Barchuk had refused to allow some of Temüjin's Merkit enemies into his realm, but went on helpfully to reveal the Merkits' whereabouts.[38] As if this were not enough, Barchuk further offered his submission to Chinggis Khan.[39] We may assume that Chinggis Khan and his advisors were quite interested in this favorable development, since Chinggis Khan responded with a new embassy that demanded extensive gifts of precious metals, pearls, gems, and cloth, in exchange for the reward of marriage between Barchuk and a Chinggisid princess, with all the responsibilities and privileges that that promised.[40] Barchuk thus began a two-year process of incorporation into the growing Mongol Empire.

THE FIRST CAMPAIGN AGAINST XI-XIA (1209–1210)

At the time of initial contact with Barchuk, Chinggis Khan was preparing to embark on his first major campaign against a sedentary power: the small but militarily powerful Tangut Kingdom of Xi-Xia on the south-eastern side of the Gobi Desert. Here his new alliances with in-laws are likely to have shaped his decision. Since the Uighurs lived west of the Tanguts, and enjoyed strong commercial, diplomatic, and cultural ties with them, Barchuk's decision to link himself to Chinggis Khan, rather than with the Tangut king, Weiming Anquan (r. 1206–11, Xianzong), probably encouraged Chinggis Khan as he contemplated his campaign.[41] At the same time, Chinggis Khan's other in-law relationship with Alaqush

[37] For *iduqut*, or rather *iduq qut*, meaning "holy fortune" or "luck," see Allsen, "Uighurs," 246 and note 15.

[38] Buell, "Early Mongol Expansion," 10–12 and "Sübōtei," 15.

[39] He offered to become a "fifth son," i.e., a vassal. *Secret History*, §238 and de Rachewiltz, Commentary, 845–9, 1047–8; Rashīd al-Dīn, *Jāmi'*, 97, 140–1, 423–5, trans. Thackston, 54, 76, 205–6; Juvaynī, *World-Conqueror*, 45–6; also Ratchnevsky, *Genghis Khan*, 102; Dunnell, *Chinggis Khan*, 61–2; Biran, *Chinggis Khan*, 49; Buell, "Early Mongol Expansion," 18–19 and "Bukhara," 128; Martin, *North China*, 109–11. For the Uighurs see Allsen, "Uighurs of Turfan," 245–7, and 248 on the question of the "fifth son;" also David O. Morgan, "Who Ran the Mongol Empire?" *The Journal of the Royal Asiatic Society of Great Britain and Ireland* 1 (1982): 128.

[40] *Secret History*, §238.

[41] Dunnell, *Chinggis Khan*, 63, also her "Xia Empire," 168–9.

of the Öng'üts, whose lands bordered Xi-Xia on the northeast, may also have influenced his plans by giving him hope of a quiet eastern front. Nevertheless the invasion of Xi-Xia was difficult – Mongol forces first had to travel 650 miles, including 200 in the inhospitable Gobi desert, then later besiege the Tangut capital, Zhongxing, even though sieges at that time were unfamiliar to the Mongol cavalry. Although at first the Mongols prevailed by building dams to divert the floodwaters of the Yellow River into the city, they were themselves later flooded when the dams broke (possibly sabotaged by the Tanguts).[42] Peace negotiations ensued in January 1210, during which Weiming Anquan agreed to become a vassal, send tremendous tribute, supply future military campaigns, and provide a daughter-hostage, Chaqa, to join the ranks of Chinggis Khan's wives (as described in Chapter 3).[43]

In addition to the strategic support implied by Chinggis Khan's developing alliances with the Uighur and Öng'üt rulers, it is most probable that imperial sons-in-law took part in this first Tangut invasion, especially given the evidence of their participation in later campaigns against the Jin and the Khwarazm-Shah Empires (see the subsequent discussion in this chapter). Unfortunately the particulars of son-in-law support in Xi-Xia are hard to discern, although possible participants included those sons-in-law appointed to the atomized army, like Princess Qojin's husband (Butu of the Ikires) and Princess Tümelün's husband (Chigü of the Qonggirats), as well as the sons-in-law married to junior princesses who were commanders of a thousand.[44]

After the conclusion of the Tangut campaign, two more Turkish vassals to the Qara-Khitai Empire appeared on the scene as aspiring sons-in-law. Both were neighbors to the *iduqut* Barchuk, and both offered Chinggis Khan a new opportunity to acquire allies to the west. The first was the Muslim Arslan Khan (lit. "Lion Khan," likely a title) of the Qarluq Turks whose territory centered on the trade entrepôt of

[42] For details see H. D. Martin, "The Mongol Wars with Hsi Hsia (1205–27)," *Journal of the Royal Asiatic Society*, parts 3–4 (1942): 195–228, and Martin, *North China*, 116–19. For brevity and a more recent interpretation see Dunnell, "Xia Empire" entire and *Chinggis Khan*, 62–5; Ratchnevsky, *Genghis Khan*, 103–5; Allsen, "North China," 349; Biran, *Chinggis Khan*, 49.

[43] Dunnell, *Chinggis Khan*, 64; for Chaqa see Chapter 3.

[44] Rashīd al-Dīn gives few details about the campaign, and mentions no in-laws in *Jāmiʿ*, 536–41, trans. Thackston, 261–3. Martin, relying on the *Yuan shi*, *Xi Xia ji shi ben mo* and *Xi Xia shu shi*, ignores the Mongol commanders in "Mongol Wars" 199–202 and *North China*, 115–20.

Qayaliq in the lower Ili river valley.[45] Arslan Khan's father had been on uneasy terms with the Gür Khan, and Arslan Khan himself ruled under the oversight of one of the Gür Khan's officers (*shahnah*).[46] It seems that Arslan Khan was seeking a new arrangement, because when a Mongol general advanced toward him in the late twelve-aughts, he immediately took the opportunity to surrender, and followed this with more formal submission directly to Chinggis Khan. Indeed, in March 1211, after the successful conclusion of the Xi-Xia campaign, both Arslan Khan and his neighbor Barchuk arrived separately in Mongolia to pay their respects.[47]

The next aspirant was another Qarluq Turk, the enterprising Ozar from the garden-ringed city of Almaliq, who had also been busy informing Chinggis Khan about Merkit and Naiman enemies, and who similarly traveled to Mongolia to demonstrate his new allegiance.[48] Chinggis Khan held a quriltai at which he honored all three petitioners, formally accepted their submission, and brought them into the Chinggisid confederation by arranging marriage alliances: Barchuk married Börte's fifth daughter, Al Altan; Arslan Khan married the junior princess Töre; and Ozar married a daughter of Jochi.[49]

Geographically this formed a cluster of sons-in-law and daughter-managers to the southwest of Mongolia, in addition to north of China (Alaqa and the Öng'üts) and west of Lake Baikal (Checheyigen, Qolui and the Oirats). (See Map 2.) Strategically, the addition of these western in-laws may have shaped Chinggis Khan's plans for his next major campaign against the Jin Empire in northern China. He appears to have been encouraged by his success against the Tanguts in 1210, and the activities of defectors from the Jin, who brought him important

[45] Rubruck, *Mission*, 148 (Qayaliq as a busy merchant town in the 1250s); also *Secret History*, §235, and de Rachewiltz, Commentary, 842–3.

[46] The father allegedly committed suicide out of fear of having displeased the Gür Khan. Juvaynī, *World-Conqueror*, 74–5.

[47] *Secret History*, §235; Juvaynī, *World-Conqueror*, 75–7, 82; Rashīd al-Dīn, *Jāmiʿ*, 144, 425, 440, trans. Thackston, 78, 206, 213; Abū al-Ghāzī, *Shajarah-yi Türk*, 38–9, trans. Desmaisons, 38; Dunnell, *Chinggis Khan*, 62; Biran, *Chinggis Khan*, 49; also Martin, *North China*, 111–12; Allsen, "North China," 350 and "Uighurs of Turfan," 247. Buell, "Early Mongol Expansion," 19, pointing out that an Arslan Khan had died in perhaps 1205, but his son took over thereafter; Buell, "Bukhara," 127.

[48] Juvaynī, *World-Conqueror*, 75–6; Buell, "Early Mongol Expansion," 19; Li, *Alchemist*, trans. Waley, 85, 120 (Almaliq's gardens).

[49] For Al Altan see Chapter 4, footnote 46. Rashīd al-Dīn, *Jāmiʿ*, 425, 573, trans. Thackston, 206, 290; Juvaynī, *World-Conqueror*, 45–6, 47, 75–7; also for Barchuk see Ratchnevsky, *Genghis Khan*, 102–3, 108; Martin, *North China*, 111–12.

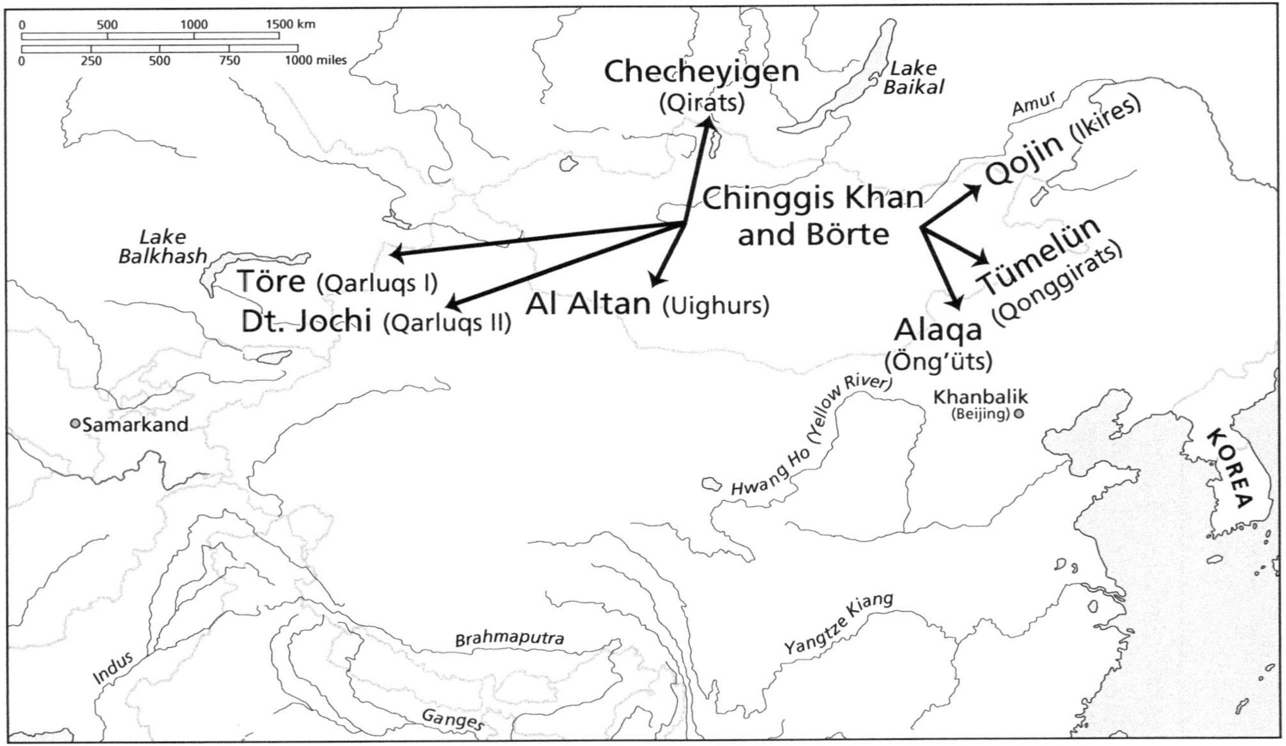

Map 2 Chinggis Khan with the territories of Börte's daughters.

information about that empire's weaknesses. At the same time, Chinggis Khan was challenged by new Jin construction on the Wusha Bao defensive line, which could not be allowed to continue.[50] In addition, Chinggis Khan's relationships with these outsider sons-in-law, especially the wealthy Uighur Barchuk and the powerful Öng'üt Alaqush, may have helped convince him that the campaign was possible.

THE JIN CAMPAIGN (1211–1215)

Unlike in the case of the first Tangut invasion, we know for certain that Chinggis Khan's sons-in-law participated in the campaign against the Jin. The Öng'üt in-laws, into whose leading family Princess Alaqa had married (or was about to), played an essential early role in facilitating the invasion. The Öng'üt case also provides a glimpse into the connections between one particular imperial woman – Princess Alaqa herself – and the military and political activities shaped by her marriage.

The Mongols set out in May 1211, and in June reached the outermost Jin defenses, which the Öng'üts held. There, their prince – either Alaqush or his nephew Jingüe[51] – not only let the invaders enter Öng'üt territory, but provided auxiliaries to the tune of 10,000 men, which can be understood as an immediate result of the Öng'üt-Chinggisid political and marital alliance.[52] At some point before or during the early days of the Jin campaign, Alaqa married, moved to Öng'üt territory, and settled into her new life there. Thus although we have no direct evidence that Alaqa met with her father as he crossed her husband's territory, she probably did. Öng'üt assistance allowed the Mongols to capture Jin fortifications, defeat Jin armies, and seize the strategic Juyong pass leading to the capital at Zhongdu (near modern Beijing), which the Mongols menaced but did not besiege. Rather they raided the

[50] Martin, *North China*, 101–2, 115; Ratchnevsky, *Genghis Khan*, 107; Buell, "Sübötei," 17 (the Wusha Bao line); Hsiao, *Establishment*, 12 (the defectors); Igor de Rachewiltz, "Personnel and Personalities in North China in the Early Mongol Period," *Journal of the Economic and Social History of the Orient* 9 (1966): 96–8.

[51] For the complexities of who was ruling see footnotes 32 and 54.

[52] Ratchnevsky, *Genghis Khan*, 108; Martin, *North China*, 128–9, 133, 138–9, (theorizing that Alaqush may have kept his men to reinforce his own territory, following the *Mengwuer shi ji*).

surrounding region until early 1212, then withdrew to Mongolia with considerable booty.[53]

But at some point the Öng'üt connection was threatened when Alaqush and his oldest son Buyan-Siban were assassinated by a faction of Öng'üt commanders backed by the Jin regime, and Alaqush was replaced by his nephew, Jingüe.[54] The date of the coup is not clear: some place it in 1205 or 1207 before Chinggis Khan had even entered China; others in 1211 just as the campaign began; still others in 1212 as Chinggis Khan was returning north after his first conquests in Jin territory.[55] Regardless of the date, Chinggis Khan's response to the murders was critical. Rather than condemning Jingüe he chose to support him (or if this occurred in 1207 even sheltered him as a refugee), and confirmed him as the next Öng'üt leader.[56] According to one source, Chinggis Khan went so far as

[53] Dunnell, *Chinggis Khan*, 65; Biran, *Chinggis Khan*, 50; Ratchnevsky, *Genghis Khan*, 109–10; for details see Martin, *North China*, 134–48.

[54] Buell, "Prolegomena," 53, and "Frontier Zone," 67–8; Martin, *North China*, 149. Some sources claim that Alaqa, Alaqush's second son Boyoqa, and his nephew, Jingüe, had to flee temporarily. Martin, *North China*, 149–50; Pelliot, *Kalmouke*, 62, albeit arguing that another widow of Alaqush – not Alaqa, who was not yet married into the family – fled with her son Boyoqa and nephew Jingüe (see next note on her).

[55] For the most recent take on this, see Atwood, "Öng'üt Case," 522–4, suggesting 1211 and providing a useful analysis of the sources for this report. Otherwise: Rashīd al-Dīn – whose work is analyzed by Atwood – mentions Alaqush's death, but omits that of his son, Buyan-Siban, and blames the officers bringing Jingüe back from exile. He hints that the murder was justified since Alaqush secretly meant to kill Jingüe after his return, and that Alaqush's own men were the ones to kill him – i.e., Jingüe was not himself a plotter. Rashīd al-Dīn, *Jāmi'*, 132, trans. Thackston, 71. Pelliot, relying on the *Yuan shi* and a funerary inscription of the Öng'üt prince, Körgüz (George or Girgis), argues that Alaqush met Chinggis Khan in 1204, but was murdered with Buyan-Siban after returning home (in about 1205?). His widow (Ariq not Alaqa; see Atwood, "Öng'üt Case," 522) fled with Boyoqa and Jingüe; then, during Chinggis Khan's invasion, met him at Yun-chong, and returned home with his help. See Pelliot, *Kalmouke*, 62–3. But it seems impossible that Chinggis Khan would attack the Jin without Öng'üt support; Ratchnevsky insists that the Jin campaign took place in part because of Chinggis Khan's ties to Alaqush, and concludes that the murder happened in 1211 (Ratchnevsky, *Genghis Khan*, 107, 109). By contrast, Martin suggests that Chinggis Khan entered Öng'üt territory with Alaqush's help, then headed south and left Alaqush guarding his own lands, meaning the murder happened after Chinggis Khan had entered China. Martin relies here less on the *Yuan shi* (suggesting that Alaqush was murdered before the Mongols entered China), and more on the *Mengwuer shi ji*. Martin, *North China*, 138–9 and note 65, also 149 and note 91. The *Secret History* ignores this incident.

[56] For 1207 see Buell, "Prolegomena," 53, and "Frontier," 68; Allsen, "North China," 349; for 1207 with Jingüe as a refugee see Pelliot, *Kalmouke*, 62; for 1211 see Rachnevsky, *Genghis Khan*, 109; for 1212 see Martin, *North China*, 149–50.

to personally oversee the execution of the murderer and the annihilation of the murderer's family. Otherwise, however, he did not punish any other conspirators, nor did he purge the Öng'üts themselves for disloyalty to Alaqush, both of which were atypically lenient.[57]

What was the cause of Chinggis Khan's close involvement in Öng'üt political affairs, and his relative restraint in these trying circumstances? One reason was surely his need for crucial Öng'üt support for his ambitious campaign, but another is likely to have been Alaqa and the custom of the levirate. After the coup, she became a widow (from either Alaqush or Buyan-Siban), and had to remarry within the Öng'üt ruling family, according to levirate practice. When Chinggis Khan favored Jingüe despite the fact that he had been the candidate elevated by the coup, the conqueror managed to retain his essential alliance with the Öng'üts, and assure the status and position of Börte's third daughter. Jingüe repaid Chinggis Khan by supporting him just as Alaqush had done, while some sources claim that Jingüe himself became one of Alaqa's husbands.[58] Chinggis Khan sought to further cement Öng'üt loyalty by taking Boyoqa, Jingüe's cousin and the younger son of the murdered Alaqush, with him as a hostage on the Western Campaign. After returning from that campaign, Boyoqa then became Alaqa's next husband.[59] One result was that Alaqa kept her position as her parents must have wanted. By 1221 a Song ambassador could describe her as ruling independently in Öng'üt territory, to the extent that she decided criminal cases and executions herself, and furthermore employed great numbers of women as religious devotees.[60] Elsewhere she was described as "intelligent and shrewd, and had knowledge and strategy."[61] She later acted as an independent regent for a son, and furthermore

[57] Rashīd al-Dīn, *Jāmi'*, 132, trans. Thackston, 71; Atwood, "Öng'üt Case," 523–4.

[58] For the coup see Rashīd al-Dīn, *Jāmi'*, 132, trans. Thackston, 71; also see Martin, *North China*, 128–9; Ratchnevsky, *Genghis Khan*, 109; Atwood, "Öng'üt Case," 522, and footnote 32 for Alaqa's various husbands.

[59] Martin, *North China*, 237; Pelliot, *Kalmouke*, 63.

[60] *Meng-ta Pei-lu* [*Meng Da beilu*], trans. Olbricht and Pinks, 3, 24. Alaqa's status appeared in her title of Princess Regent, which graced her seal (Adam T. Kessler, *Empires Beyond the Great Wall: The Heritage of Genghis Khan* [Natural History Museum of Los Angeles County, 1993], 156–9, fig. 99). Hambis, *Chapitre CVIII*, 25 and note 8, citing Alaqa's titles; Martin, *North China*, 235–6.

[61] *Yuan Shi*, 10:2923–4 (unpublished trans. Buell).

supported her father's general, Muqali, in his campaign against the Jin (1217–23).[62] But unlike princesses who accompanied men to war (see the subsequent discussion in this chapter), Alaqa instead remained in the strategically important Öng'üt territory to hold it whenever one of her husbands departed:

When he [one of her husbands] went out riding in chariots and attacked in four directions he constantly had her stay behind as a guard. When there were great government actions of the military and the dynasty, they consulted and petitioned, and later acted. When the army went forth there were no worries about internal concerns. The strength of the princess was great.[63]

But Alaqa and her several Öng'üt husbands were not the only princess and son(s)-in-law to contribute to the Jin campaign. The sources indicate that other members of the Chinggisid confederation played important military roles, but unfortunately and unlike in the case of Alaqa, they do not reveal whether their princess wives were also present. Among those other sons-in-law were four Qonggirat men. The first was Toquchar, husband of a junior princess, who did not go to attack the Jin, but rather remained in Mongolia to guard the western border while the armies were gone.[64] The other three Qonggirat in-laws traveled to northern China. These were Börte's brother, Alchi; Alchi's adopted son Chigü (Tümelün's husband);[65] and Qadai, a commander of a thousand in the atomized army and husband of a junior princess. Alchi began by making forays into Manchuria in spring 1212 with Chinggis Khan's brother Jochi-Qasar and two generals. Then, on a separate assignment, Alchi accompanied one of

62 For the son, Nieh-ku-te, see Holmgren, "Levirate," 164–5, citing the *Mengwuer shi ji* 36:1b–3a and 5b, and the *Yuan shi*, 116:2924, and implying that Jingüe was the father. For Muqali and the campaign see below.

63 *Yuan Shi*, 10:2923–4 (unpublished trans. Buell). This implies that she had troops at her command.

64 The number of Toquchar's men is unclear: 2,000 or 20,000? The latter makes more sense for the task. Ratchnevsky, *Genghis Khan*, 108, says 20,000 and cites the Russian translation of Rashīd al-Dīn (*Sbornik letopisei* [Collected Chronicles], trans. O. I. Smirnova [Moscow-Leningrad, 1952], 1:2, 163), but the English translation gives 2,000 (Rashīd al-Dīn, *Jāmi'*, 160, 573, trans. Thackston, 86, 290). Martin, *North China*, 130, says 2,000 and cites commentaries on the *Yuan Shengwu qinzheng lu*, then theorizes that Chinggis Khan must have left 20,000–25,000 as well, possibly with Temüge (as on the Western Campaign). Dunnell, *Chinggis Khan*, 65, gives 20,000; Allsen, "North China," 351, omits the matter; Biran, *Chinggis Khan*, 50, specifies no number.

65 For the adoption see Atwood, "Chikü *küregen*," 16–23.

Chinggis Khan's adopted sons as an envoy to the Khitans, who were considering a rebellion against the Jin.[66] As for Chigü: he was regularly paired with his brother-in-law, Tolui, in a position of joint leadership. This was particularly clear after the Mongols returned to China in fall 1212 and formed two armies, one led by Chinggis Khan himself, and the second by Tolui and Chigü.[67] The armies recaptured all the forts taken in earlier months – with Chigü demonstrating particular bravery[68] – and once again seized the Juyong pass. Tolui and Chigü then became instrumental in subduing the city of Dexing in summer 1213, and helped Chinggis Khan defeat a Jin army at Weiquan (modern Huailai) in September.[69] Finally, Qadai, a lesser Qonggirat son-in-law and commander of a thousand was also instrumental in this region, albeit in a less grand capacity, since he succeeded in holding first a valley and then a road so that Chinggis Khan could advance.[70]

Thereafter the two armies, one led by Tolui and Chigü and the other by Chinggis Khan, moved south into Jin territory, and blockaded Zhongdu in winter 1213–14.[71] During the months of blockade, Chinggis Khan reformed his forces into three smaller armies and sent them to subdue different nearby regions. The first army was led by Börte's three oldest sons (and no in-laws), and went to Hebei and Shanxi to the south and west. The second headed toward Shandong in the east, and was commanded by Chinggis Khan himself, with the help of his general, Muqali and his son Tolui, but it is unclear whether Chigü was also present. The third army, which also turned southeast toward the coast, had the clearest in-law contingent, and its leadership was definitely a family affair. It was

[66] The generals with Alchi in Manchuria were Jebe and Sübedei; his companion to the Khitans was Shigi Qutuqu. Martin, *North China*, 145, 150–1; Buell, "Subōtei," 17–18; also Zhao, "Conciliation," 8.

[67] Martin, *North China*, 155–6.

[68] This was during the capture of Dexingfu in perhaps fall 1212, for which see Atwood, "Chikü *küregen*," 10–12.

[69] Martin, *North China*, 158–9; also Rashīd al-Dīn, *Jāmiʿ*, 445–7, trans. Thackston, 217–18, trans. Boyle, 164–5. Martin does not specify Tolui and Chigü's presence at Dexing, but Rashīd al-Dīn – whom Martin did not cite here – does.

[70] Rashīd al-Dīn, *Jāmiʿ*, 446, trans. Thackston, 218. Another man, Bocha, was with Qadai at Huailai. Rashīd al-Dīn identifies him as a Qonggirat, but we know little about him. On Qadai see Pelliot, "Sur un passage," 924–5, note 4.

[71] Dunnell, *Chinggis Khan*, 66; Biran, *Chinggis Khan*, 50–51; Ratchnevsky, *Genghis Khan*, 110; Martin, *North China*, 155–65; also Pelliot, "Sur un passage," 914–15.

commanded by Börte's brother, Alchi, who had returned from his Khitan mission; Ibaqa's husband, Jürchedei of the Uru'ut; Chinggis Khan's brother, Jochi-Qasar; and Hö'elün's stepson, Tolun Cherbi of the Qongqotan.[72]

But the siege of Zhongdu was a challenge: the Mongols were still relatively unfamiliar with siege warfare, and they also faced illness within their army. Fortunately for them the Jin court was in disarray – in September 1213 the Jin emperor, Wanyan Yongji, a.k.a. Xingsheng, a.k.a. (posthumously) Wei Shao Wang (r. 1209–13),[73] had been seized and murdered by a general, and replaced by an imperial nephew, Xuanzong (r. 1213–23).[74] Eventually Emperor Xuanzong agreed to terms with the Mongols, and sent extensive tribute to Chinggis Khan, along with a dispossessed daughter of his deceased uncle as a hostage wife, as mentioned in Chapter 3.[75] The Mongols lifted the blockade on Zhongdu in spring 1214 and withdrew, but then in June heard that Emperor Xuanzong had fled for the southern capital of Bianlian (Kaifeng) on the Yellow River. The Mongols considered this a breach of terms, returned to resume the blockade, and finally took control of Zhongdu in grisly excess after it surrendered in May 1215.[76] Chinggis Khan returned to Mongolia in summer 1215.[77] Additional operations took place after his departure, including joint endeavors by Tolui and Chigü.[78]

MUQALI'S CAMPAIGN IN CHINA AND THE INVOLVEMENT OF IN-LAWS

Despite the Mongols' significant victories against the Jin, the overall campaign was hardly complete in 1215. Although Chinggis Khan did

[72] Martin, *North China*, 164; Rashīd al-Dīn, *Jāmi'*, 447, trans. Thackston, 219, misidentifies Jürchedei as Chinggis Khan's son of this name, and substitutes a Qonggirat commander named Bocha for Tolun Cherbi.

[73] I.e., "Prince Shao of Pei," a posthumous designation.

[74] Martin, *North China*, 161–2. [75] See Chapter 3.

[76] Dunnell, *Chinggis Khan*, 67; Biran, *Chinggis Khan*, 51; Ratchnevsky, *Genghis Khan*, 112–15; Martin, *North China*, 177–9.

[77] Martin, *North China*, 180.

[78] They cooperated to capture the T'ung-Kuan fort and pass in 1216. De Rachewiltz, Commentary, 913–14; Martin instead credits this to the general Samukha, *North China*, 187–8.

not himself return to China, in 1217 he appointed his talented and loyal general Muqali, a former hereditary servant and now commander-in-chief of the left wing, to be supreme commander in Northern China (*kuo-wang*, lit. prince of the realm[79]), and charged him with continuing military operations.[80] Chinggis Khan gave Muqali a special irregular force, known as a tamma army, which had been drawn from the larger Mongol armies and was meant to be stationed in the border region, from which it would extend control southward.[81] The composition of Muqali's force demonstrates the extent to which Chinggis Khan relied on the Chinggisid confederation of sons-in-law to provide both soldiers and the military leadership for them. The army included 2,000 Jalayirs (Muqali's own people), 10,000 Öng'üt (among whom Alaqa had married; these were led by Jingüe[82]), 2,000 Ikires with Butu (Qojin's husband), 3,000 Qonggirat under Börte's brother Alchi[83], 4,000 Uru'ut (probably under Jürchedei, Ibaqa's husband), as well as 1,000 Qoshqols, 1,000 Mangqut, and numerous local Kitan and Chinese auxiliaries.[84] This meant that 19,000 of the 23,000 soldiers in the nomadic units of Muqali's force (i.e., not the local auxiliaries) were led by officers with marital ties to Chinggis Khan. (See Table 4.) Thereafter princesses associated with these families received lands in northern China, and these same consort families dominated the military scene for decades into the Yuan period.[85]

[79] Allsen, "North China," 357.

[80] Igor de Rachewiltz, "Muqali (1170–1223), Bōl (1197–1220), Tas (1212–1239), An-T'ung (1245–1293)," in *In the Service of the Khans*, ed. Igor de Rachewiltz et al. (Wiesbaden, 1993), 5; Martin, "Mongol Wars," 207–10 and *North China*, 192–4, 239–41; Hope, *Ilkhanate*, 36.

[81] On Muqali's tamma force see Paul Buell, "Kalmyk Tanggaci People," 46–7; also May, *War*, 36–8.

[82] Martin, *North China*, 240.

[83] See Pelliot, "Sur un passage," 908–9.

[84] Rashīd al-Dīn, *Jāmi'*, 459, trans. Thackston, 227; also de Rachewiltz, "Muqali," 5–6, and "Personnel," 116–17; Martin, "Mongol Wars," 207–10, and *North China*, 192, 239–41; Buell, "Kalmyk Tanggaci People," 46; "Ratchnevsky, *Genghis Khan*, 116.

[85] Buell, "Kalmyk Tanggaci People," 49. Princess Qojin's territories were in northern China, as were those of Tümelün (at modern Shanxian in western Shandong). See *Yuan shi*, reign of Ögedei; trans. Abramowski, 132; Atwood, "Chikü *küregen*," 9–10; also Hsiao, *Establishment*, 16.

Table 4 *The Composition of Muqali's Army in 1217*

Unit	Number of men	Leader	Woman
Jalayirs	2,000	Muqali	–
Öng'üts	10,000	Jingüe	Alaqa
Ikires	2,000	Butu	Temülün, Qojin
Qonggirats	3,000	Alchi	Börte (Tümelün)
Uru'uts	4,000	Not specified[86]	Ibaqa the Kereyit
Qoshqols	1,000	–	–
Mangquts	1,000	–	–
Noqais (?)	?	–	–
Local auxiliaries			
Khitans from Manchuria	20,000?	Various[87]	–
Mixed	15,000?	Various	–
Chinese	10,000?	Various	–

Shading represents Chinggisid confederation (sons-in-law) units.[88]

Muqali's task was to lay the groundwork for Chinggis Khan's eventual return to China.[89] Although Muqali worked largely successfully until his death in 1223,[90] this campaign is less known than those in which Chinggis Khan took part. The contributions of specific in-laws are therefore difficult to discover, and the presence or absence of princesses simply cannot be discerned. At most we can say that Börte's brother Alchi appeared several times in important roles: he took command of the captured city Pingyang in 1218, from which he made a lightning attack

86 Martin, *North China*, 240, note 3 on Kita as a leader for the Uru'uts.

87 For the auxiliary unit commanders see Martin, *North China*, 240, notes 4–6; Buell, "Kalmyk Tanggaci People," 46 and notes 48–50, and "Bukhara," 126; for the Khitans also see Michal Biran, "The Mongols and Nomadic Identity: The Case of the Kitans in China," in *Mongols as Agents of Cultural Change: The Mongols and Their Eurasian Predecessors*, ed. Reuven Amitai and Michal Biran (Honolulu: University of Hawaii Press, 2015), 162.

88 Rashīd al-Dīn, *Jāmi'*, 459, trans. Thackston, 227, omitting the Noqai; Hsiao, *Establishment*, 16, also 96, including the Noqai but omitting the Ikires, Öng'üts, Qonggirats, and Qoshqols.

89 Martin, *North China*, 239.

90 Martin, *North China*, chapter 9, and "Mongol Wars," 207–10 for the Tanguts role; also de Rachewiltz, "Muqali," 7.

in 1222 to recover the city of Hezhong, which had been briefly occupied by an ambitious Jin commander. Later Alchi participated in a successful attack on Song forces in 1225.[91] Meanwhile one of his sons – possibly Chigü again? – commanded troops for a winter blockade in 1220–1.[92] It is also clear that the Öng'üts contributed significantly and repeatedly to Muqali's endeavors: Jingüe led a unit of ten thousand in Muqali's initial invasion in 1217.[93] In summer 1221, and in one of the few instances where we can pinpoint the participation of an imperial woman, Princess Alaqa hosted Muqali in Öng'üt lands as he prepared for a major new offensive.[94] Thereafter the Öng'üts provided warriors for a fresh invasion in 1222.[95] Alaqa may have been involved logistically at other moments as well, but if so, these have gone unrecorded by the sources.

SONS-IN-LAW ON THE WESTERN CAMPAIGN

Chinggis Khan's next major expedition was the Western Campaign against the Empire of the Khwarazm Shah and the eastern Islamic world (1219–23). As in China, several sons-in-law fought in this campaign. No single son-in-law or people made as dramatic an impact on the Western Campaign as the Öng'üts had during the Jin campaign, perhaps because no geographical and political parallel existed in Khwarazm-Shah territory. Nevertheless the contributions of sons-in-laws to the Western Campaign were significant, since these men provided large numbers of troops, and routinely helped lead major and minor campaigns. The contributions of their princess wives is a more difficult matter to discern.

By the late twelve-teens the Qara-Khitai Empire under the Gür Khan had crumbled into two main pieces. In the west reigned Muḥammad b. Tekish the Khwarzm-Shah (r. 1200–20), a former vassal of the Gür Khan, who had taken independent control of Transoxiana, Khwarazm, and Khurasan, as well as additional territories to the west that the Gür Khan had never held.[96] At the same time, the easternmost regions of Qara-Khitai territory had been ruled by the Naiman refugee Küchlüg covertly since 1211, and overtly since the Gür Khan's death in 1213. Küchlüg's realm included the fertile Fergana Valley and the trade center of Kashgar. Despite his new authority, however, Küchlüg was repeatedly occupied by hostilities with his own vassals, among them an ongoing struggle with the

[91] Martin, *North China*, 248 (for 1218), 272 (for 1222), and 279 (for 1225).
[92] Martin, *North China*, 259–60.
[93] Martin, *North China*, 240; also Rashīd al-Dīn, *Jāmiʿ*, 459, trans. Thackston, 227, for 1217.
[94] Martin, *North China*, 260. [95] Martin, *North China*, 264.
[96] Juvaynī, *World-Conqueror*, 63–5; Soucek, *Inner Asia*, 100–101.

Qarluq ruler, Ozar of Almaliq, who was a grandson-in-law to Chinggis Khan through his marriage to Jochi's daughter, and whom Küchlüg captured on a hunting trip and executed.[97] Sensibly enough, Ozar's son, Signag Tekin, immediately sought confirmation as Ozar's heir from Chinggis Khan, which he received and then sealed by marrying his stepmother, Ozar's princess wife (through the levirate).[98]

In 1218, therefore, in response to Küchlüg's enemy presence and new position of authority, and surely also in retribution for the murder of his grandson-in-law Ozar, Chinggis Khan dispatched his general Jebe southwest toward Kashgar to attack Küchlüg. He also ordered the most powerful of the western sons-in-law, the Uighur Barchuk (Princess Al Altan's husband), to join the mission; it is possible that the other Qarluq, Arslan Khan of Qayaliq (Princess Töre's husband), was there as well.[99] (We have no record of Signak Tekin's presence, but he most likely participated to avenge his father.) Küchlüg was captured and executed, which ended the Qara-Khitai state for good, and helped open the door to Mongol expansion westward.

Later that same year, the *casus belli* for a larger Western Campaign emerged when a governor for the Khwarazm-Shah Muḥammad b. Tekish executed a caravan of merchants at the important trade city of Otrar by the Jaxartes River and impounded all their wares. The governor may have believed that the merchants were spies (which some of them probably were); it is also possible that he felt one of them had insulted him during a conversation.[100] But the merchants had been sent by the Mongols, and a considerable portion of their funds and wares represented investments by members of the imperial family, who therefore lost their property, and any possible returns, all at once.[101] The governor at Otrar happened to be a relative of the Khwarazm-Shah Muḥammad and the powerful queen mother, Terken Khatun, and was not punished for his action. Meanwhile the Mongols had already been pressuring Khwarazmian territory as their own empire expanded westward and they subjugated enemies both old

97 Juvaynī, *World-Conqueror*, 65, 76; Soucek, *Inner Asia*, 100.

98 Juvaynī, *World-Conqueror*, 76–7; Soucek, *Inner Asia*, 100.

99 For Barchuk see Juvaynī, *World Conqueror*, 46; Rashīd al-Dīn, *Jāmiʿ*, 140, trans. Thackston, 76; and Allsen, "Uighurs of Turfan," 246–7. For a garbled report on Arslan Khan see Abū al-Ghāzī, *Shajarah-yi Türk*, 85–6, trans. Demaisons, 93. Also Ratchnevsky, *Genghis Khan*, 118–19; Buell, "Bukhara," 128.

100 Soucek, *Inner Asia*, 106.

101 May, *War*, 116; also Allsen, "North China," 355–6, and "Merchant Partners," 87–92; De Nicola, *Khatuns*, 145.

and new.[102] Despite posturing from both Chinggis Khan and the Khwarazm-Shah, no diplomatic resolution was reached, and the Mongols began their invasion in summer 1219. All of Börte's sons and those generals Chinggis Khan could spare from China participated in this attack. Chinggis Khan was accompanied by his Merkit wife, Qulan, and left behind his youngest brother, Temüge, defending the homeland; his loyal general, Muqali, continuing the campaign against the Jin, and his daughter, Alaqa, administering Öng'üt territory.[103]

The members of the Chinggisid confederation who participated in the dismantling of the Khwarazm-Shah Empire included all the western Turkic sons-in-law, whose proximity to the theatre of battle made participation de rigeuer. These were the Uighur Barchuk yet again, and this time definitely both Qarluqs: Arslan Khan of Qayaliq, and Signaq Tekin of Almaliq.[104] All three men contributed warriors and leadership: Barchuk brought 18,000 men and Arslan Khan 6,000; Signaq Tekin's men are described as "veteran warriors," but are unnumbered.[105] These sons-in-law may also have brought wives with them, and, given who they were fighting for, possibly the Chinggisid ones (Al Altan, Töre, and Jochi's daughter), but as usual the sources are silent on this topic.[106] Nor do they tell us that these daughters met with their father as he advanced through their husbands' lands, but it seems unimaginable that they would not have done so. The sources do tell us that at least one of Chinggis Khan's daughters went on the Western Campaign; she was the junior princess wife of the Qonggirat son-in-law, Toquchar, who traveled

102 Buell, "Early Expansion," 20–3.

103 Martin, *North China*, 236; May, *War*, 116; Paul Buell, 2010, "Some Royal Mongol Ladies: Alaqa-beki, Ergene-Qatun and Others." *World History Connected* vol. 7, issue 1. http://worldhistoryconnected.press.illinois.edu/7.1/buell.html. Accessed August 11, 2017.

104 His death must have been before or in 1218, the year that Küchlüg died. Küchlüg's men captured Ozar in his hunting grounds and attempted to seize Almaliq, but fled at news of an approaching Mongol force – the one sent against Küchlüg in 1218? They slew their prisoner on the road. See Juvaynī, *World-Conqueror*, 76.

105 Hambis, *Chapitre CVIII*, 133 and note 9, citing (Barchuk); Juzjānī, *Ṭabaqāt*, 2:112, trans. Raverty, 1004 (Arslan Khan); Juvaynī, *World-Conqueror*, 82 (Signak Tegin). Also Abū al-Ghāzī, *Shajarah-yi Türk*, 100, trans. Demaisons, 108; Ratchnevsky, *Genghis Khan*, 129.

106 Jochi's daughter was Ozar's widow, and married Ozar's son Signaq Tegin through the levirate. See Juvaynī, *World-Conqueror*, 75–6 (she marries Ozar) and 76 (Signaq Tegin receives his father's royal office and is "given one of Tushi's [Jochi's] daughters to wife"). This was presumably the same woman through the levirate, but the text is not completely clear.

with Chinggis Khan from Mongolia.[107] Another son-in-law, the mysterious Fiku (?), was also present, but little is known about him or his wife.

Since the Khwarazm-Shah governor who had killed the merchants was stationed at the city of Otrar, it became the Mongols' first target, which they attacked and captured in fall and winter 1219–20. At Chinggis Khan's command, all three western sons-in-law participated in this siege with their fighting men.[108] Next the Mongols conquered the wealthy and sophisticated Transoxanian cities of Bukhara and Samarqand, from the latter of which Muḥammad fled westward before them.[109]

Thereafter smaller armies went in different directions. The first chased the Khwarazm-Shah toward the west, and as it did so, accepted the submission of cities and towns across northern Iran. This army of pursuit was divided into three divisions led by three men: the generals Jebe and Sübedei, and the Qonggirat son-in-law Toquchar, who had guarded the homeland during the Jin campaign.[110] Although Toquchar had previously discharged his duties satisfactorily, perhaps leading to this new appointment, his conduct this time around was less becoming. Chinggis Khan had ordered all three generals to pass through the fertile region surrounding the city of Herat without violence because it had already submitted to the Mongols. But Toquchar disregarded those orders by plundering some of the villages, after which the region's leader reneged and turned against Chinggis Khan.[111] Early sources are silent about Toquchar's motivation, but a late one suggests that he breached discipline in this way because he doubted that the leader's submission was genuine.[112] Even if this was the case, Toquchar was not authorized to make such decisions on his own. Unsurprisingly, therefore, Chinggis Khan is said to have been so angry about the plundering and its political effect, not to mention the shocking insubordination, that he resolved initially to execute Toquchar. But then Chinggis Khan changed his mind and contented himself with demoting Toquchar from his position as a general and

[107] Juvaynī, *World Conqueror*, 177, in note 18 Boyle misidentifies her as Princess Tümelün. Also Saunders, *Conquests*, 60–1, following Abū al-Ghāzī. Note Rossabi, "Women," 154; also De Nicola, "Warfare," 101–2.

[108] Juvaynī, *World-Conqueror*, 46, 82; Rashīd al-Dīn, *Jāmi'*, 140–1, trans. Thackston, 76; Abū al-Ghāzī, *Shajarah-yi Türk*, 100, trans. Demaisons, 108.

[109] May, *War*, 1–4, 118–19, 120–1.

[110] Buell, "Sübötei," 19; *Secret History*, §257 (Jebe, Sübedei, and Toquchar); Juvaynī, *World-Conqueror*, 142–3; 150 (omitting Toquchar), similarly Juzjānī, *Ṭabaqāt*, 2:108, trans. Raverty, 987. Also May, *War*, 119.

[111] This was Qan Melik. *Secret History*, §257.

[112] Abu al-Ghazi, *Shajarah-yi Türk*, 115, 118, trans. Demaisons, 122, 126.

rebuking him severely, which was an unusually mild punishment for his transgression.[113]

What could have caused this uncharacteristic lenience? Although the meagerness of the sources forces us to hypothesize, one possibility is that someone interceded on Toquchar's behalf, and convinced Chinggis Khan to commute the sentence from death to punishment. Intercession was not unusual, and took place throughout Chinggis Khan's lifetime.[114] During the Western Campaign itself, Chinggis Khan lost his temper with three of Börte's sons, at which several of his close followers interceded successfully for them.[115] If intercession is the answer in Toquchar's situation, then a good candidate to make the plea was Toquchar's junior princess wife, who is known to have been present, and who was therefore in position to ask her father for the favor of her husband's life. Since once again not enough evidence is left to draw a clear picture, it is useful to ponder a hypothetical: the princess could have learned through report, messengers, or other agents of the trouble Toquchar had brought upon himself through his insubordinate behavior. If so, then she then surely pondered how most effectively to react. She might have consulted with other imperial women, of whom the most highly placed would have been Qulan, the seniormost of Chinggis Khan's wives present. Did the princess send a messenger to Qulan asking for an audience? Did the two women meet, perhaps with others whom we cannot make out, to discuss an intercession strategy? In addition to what we think might have been the princess's appeal for clemency, did Qulan herself offer intercession, or did men – perhaps officers – step in or advise?

Chinggis Khan's decision to let Toquchar live could thus reflect the role played by a daughter. If it did, then this situation had some precedent from the campaign against the Jin, during which Chinggis Khan had reacted with surprising lenience to the murder of the Öng'üt ruler Alaqush, in part because of the involvement of his daughter Alaqa.

113 *Secret History*, §257.

114 See commanders interceding with Temüjin for his uncle Daritai. *Secret History*, §242; also Hope, *Ilkhanate*, 39.

115 Jochi, Chaghatai, and Ögedei quarreled during their campaign against Urgench, failed to capture the city (and region) for months, then withheld spoils from their father. Chinggis Khan was furious. But several people interceded, including Bo'orchu, Shigi Qutuqu, and several quiverbearers (Muqali is named as an intercessor, but he was in China at the time). See *Secret History*, §260, and de Rachewiltz, Commentary, 950–7. Rashīd al-Dīn omits the withholding and intercessors but adds Tolui as a military power and family peacemaker in *Jāmi'*, 514–6, trans. Thackston, 254–5.

Certainly we do know that after being relieved of a death sentence, Toquchar was further rehabilitated and given a new assignment. This was at the city of Nishapur, which had originally submitted to the Mongols, but later chose to resist.[116] In 1221–2 Toquchar was sent across the Oxus to Nishapur in its wide, fertile plain, leading the vanguard for a larger army under Tolui, and in company with another son-in-law, Al Altan's husband Barchuk.[117] But Toquchar was shot and killed by a projectile during the siege, which forced Tolui to take a firmer stance as the commanding officer. After destroying the surrounding fields, gardens, and hamlets, he led an attack on the city and captured it. The population was annihilated, which was standard Mongol treatment after a rebellion; what was not was that Tolui permitted his half-sister, Chinggis Khan's daughter and Toquchar's widow, to personally oversee some of the executions in retribution for her husband's death.[118]

To return to the other sons-in-law: After the capture of Samarqand and the departure of the armies chasing the Khwarazm-Shah, a second force was sent southeast to the high mountains and cultivated valleys surrounding the two cities of Talaqan and Wakhsh, each located on a tributary of the Oxus River.[119] This force was led by a commander of a thousand: Alaq Noyan of the Ba'arin, and additional commander(s) whose names are unclear. They were assisted by the Uighur son-in-law, Barchuk, and his 18,000 men.[120] At the same time a third army began an eight-month siege of the fortress of Walkh. Both leaders of this force were linked to the imperial family, albeit in different ways: Tolun Cherbi of the Qongqotan was Hö'elün's stepson and led his own Qongqotan troops, while Arslan Khan of Qayaliq was the greater Qarluq son-in-law (Princess Töre's husband), and brought 6,000 Qarluq warriors.[121] Meanwhile Chinggis

[116] It submitted to Jebe and Sübedei as they chased Muḥammad.

[117] Hambis, *Chapitre CVIII,* 133 and note 9.

[118] See footnote 107; also Brack, "Mongol Princess," 337.

[119] Taloqan, in northeastern Afghanistan, was on the Taloqan (or Talaqan) River, and Wakhsh or Vakhsh, in Tajikistan, was on the Vakhsh River.

[120] The commanders Ghadaq and Yasa'ur appear with Barchuk in Juvaynī, *World-Conqueror*, 46–7 and note 15, 118; for Barchuk also see Rashīd al-Dīn, *Jāmi'*, 140–1, 488, trans. Thackston, 76, 241; also Ratchnevsky, *Genghis Khan*, 129. Ghadaq and Yasa'ur are not in the *Secret History*, Rashīd al-Dīn, or Juzjānī. Alaq Noyan was a Ba'arin commander of a thousand in 1206, but his brother Naya'a is better known as lieutenant of the Left Wing. *Secret History*, §149, §202, §220; Rashīd al-Dīn, *Jāmi'*, 601, trans. Thackston, 276. For this second army see May, *War*, 119.

[121] Juzjānī, *Ṭabaqāt*, 2:112 [118–19, pages missing], trans. Raverty, 1004, 1023; May, *War*, 122; Ratchnevsky, *Genghis Khan*, 129.

Khan led a fourth army to capture the oasis town of Nakhshab in central Transoxiana, where he summered, then headed south to seize Tirmidh (Termez) on the Oxus River, and wintered there in 1220–1.[122] Finally, a fifth army under Jochi, Chaghatai, and Ögedei – but no sons-in-law – invaded Muḥammad's home region of Khwarazm in 1221, where they captured the important city of Urgench and assumed control over the rest of the area, then subdued the Qangli Turk tribes to the north.[123]

But despite the Khwarazm-Shah's death in 1220 and the near-simultaneous capture of most of his family, one of his adult sons, prince Jalāl al-Dīn Mangubertī, fled south toward the regions of Khurasan and Ghazna, where he kept busy attacking Mongol forces near the Afghan cities of Qandahar and Parvan.[124] In response, Chinggis Khan sent several armies southward in 1221. One of these may have been led by Chinggis Khan's least-known son-in-law, Fiqu or Fitqu, who bore significant responsibilities: he was a joint commander over large forces (40,000–45,000 men) in the regions of Ghur and Khurasan, including at an attack on the centrally located fortress of Tulak.[125] But Jalāl al-Dīn eluded capture, and eventually Chinggis Khan himself took up pursuit of the Khwarazm-Shah prince, whom he chased as far as the Indus River without success.[126] There Chinggis Khan turned north in 1223, concerned about unfavorable omens and reports of trouble from the Tanguts at home.[127] Although he was joined by his other forces on the way or in Mongolia, it seems probable that the western sons-in-law returned to their own realms as the Mongol armies passed them.[128] If so, and if their Chinggisids wives had not already gone on the campaign with them, this may have provided another opportunity for these princesses to greet and host their father or grandfather.

122 Termez is in southern Uzbekistan.
123 May, *War*, 119–20.
124 May, *War*, 119, 122–3.
125 Juzjānī, *Ṭabaqāt*, 2:113 (Fiku, Ughlan / Uklan the Juzbi and "Sa'di the Juzbi," leading the large army in Ghur and Khurasan) [118–19, pages missing] (Fiku leading at Parvan but losing to Jalāl al-Dīn three times in Raverty), 133 (1221 attacking the fortress of Tulak between Ghur and Khurasan); trans. Raverty, 1006, 1017–23, 1058–9. But Juvaynī, *World-Conqueror*, 133, 405, claims the leaders at Parvan were Tekechük, Molghir, and a group of commanders. Was Fiku among them?
126 May, *War*, 123; also Juvaynī, *World-Conqueror*, 409–11.
127 May, *War*, 123–4; Martin, *North China*, 283 (the date).
128 Chaghatai and Ögedei joined him, but Jochi stayed away and died in 1225. Later Jebe and Sübedei arrived, having pursued Muḥammad to the Caspian Sea, then headed north through the Caucasus and east across Central Asia. Qu and Liu, "Jochi's Lifetime," 283–90; Ratchnevsky, *Genghis Khan*, 136–7; also Buell, "Sübötei," 19; May, *War*, 121 (Jebe and Sübedei's long trek).

TANGUTS II

Chinggis Khan's final campaign was a second attack on the Tangut Empire in 1226–7, undertaken for a host of reasons: the Tangut king Weiming Zunxu (r. 1211–23, Shenzong) had failed to send troops on the Western Campaign at Chinggis Khan's request in 1218 (despite providing men elsewhere in 1216 and 1221); the Tanguts developed an increasingly warm relationship with the beleaguered Jin in the 1220s and withdrew soldiers from Muqali's war in 1222; and they refused to send a royal male hostage to serve in Chinggis Khan's imperial guard, despite his adequate treatment of the Tangut wifely hostage, Chaqa.[129]

As in the case of the first Tangut campaign, it is difficult to determine which in-laws accompanied the Mongol armies, and how they contributed to Chinggis Khan's endeavors. But at least two sons-in-law were present: one was Barchuk, the Uighur *iduqut*, whom Chinggis Khan ordered to join him, although as usual we cannot discern whether Princess Al Altan was also present.[130] Barchuk's participation made sense geographically because his territory bordered the Tanguts; by contrast there is no evidence that the Turkic sons-in-law from points farther west attended. In addition to this geographical convenience, Chinggis Khan had responded favorably to Barchuk's request in 1224 or 1225 to send home many of the Uighurs working in Mongol dominions, and may have expected Barchuk to demonstrate his appreciation for this favor by fighting.[131] The other son-in-law known to have been present was Butu of the Ikires, although in this case as in that of Al Altan, it is impossible to tell whether Princess Qojin was also there. Other army officers who were sons-in-law may also have gone. We do know that Tolui participated in the fighting (but came late because his senior wife was pregnant), and it is worth wondering whether his partner from the Jin campaign, Tümelün's Qonggirat husband, Chigü, was there.[132]

Chinggis Khan headed for Xi-Xia in winter 1225–6, accompanied by his senior Tatar wife Yisüi.[133] The Mongol armies began to capture Tangut fortifications beginning in late winter, and took Lingzhou, south of Zhongxing, in December 1226. Thereafter Chinggis Khan left the

[129] Dunnell, *Chinggis Khan*, 64, 86–7, and "Xi-Xia," 174–5; Allsen, "North China," 364; Martin, *North China*, 270–1, 285–8 and "Hsi-Hsia," 209–13; Ratchnevsky, *Genghis Khan*, 140–1; Biran, *Chinggis Khan*, 61–2.

[130] Juvaynī, *World-Conqueror*, 46–7.

[131] Allsen, "Uighurs," 248.

[132] This was Sorqoqtani. Rashīd al-Dīn, *Jāmi'*, 537, trans. Thackston, 261; de Rachewiltz, Commentary, 913–14. Chigü also partnered with Ögedei's son, Köten, whose territories abutted his own. Atwood, "Chikü *küregen*," 7–9.

[133] *Secret History*, §265.

capital under siege and headed west to conquer the Gansu region, but he moved into the mountains in spring 1227 to avoid summer temperatures. It was during this second Tangut campaign that Chinggis Khan probably decided on Ögedei's succession to the empire, perhaps as advised by Yisüi, as discussed in Chapter 4. The last Tangut ruler, Weiming Xian (r. 1226–7), surrendered in summer 1227, but he, his family, and many of his subjects were nevertheless slaughtered, and his kingdom was annihilated.[134] Chinggis Khan himself died in August 1227, either of injuries from an earlier fall from his horse, or from an undiagnosed illness. A funeral cortege took him home for secret burial in Mongolia, and legends immediately began to proliferate.[135]

CONCLUSION

After taking over steppe society and drastically reorganizing it, Chinggis Khan spent the remainder of his career engaging in military action on a very grand scale. This gave his war machine and the society behind it a new purpose, and also stifled attempts at rebellion within the ranks. The inclusion of sons-in-law in the empire as it was forming permitted the peaceful incorporation of new territories and subjects without bloodshed, and in some cases freed Chinggis Khan to plan military conquests that would not have been within his grasp without these marital alliances. Sons-in-law also provided a pool of leaders from which to staff the Mongol armies, alongside generals, imperial guardsmen, commanders of a thousand, and Chinggis Khan's sons from various mothers. Sons-in-law frequently brought to the campaigns more men than the average commander of a thousand. In addition, each son-in-law had a princess wife who could act as an advisor, manager, and political informant. At least some princesses accompanied their husbands on military campaigns, or otherwise supported military efforts. Imperial women may therefore have interacted with their father, his wife or wives, and their brothers throughout these years-long endeavors, although the sources' treatment of this topic is patchy at best. In any case, the sons-in-law, their forces, and at times their Chinggisid wives made special contributions to the Mongol conquests, but the nature of these contributions has not been acknowledged fully until now.

134 Dunnell, *Chinggis Khan*, 86–8 and "Xi-Xia," 177–9; also Allsen, "North China," 365; for details but an older treatment see Martin, *North China*, 288–304 and "Hsi-Hsia," 216–25; also Ratchnevsky, *Genghis Khan*, 140–1; Biran, *Chinggis Khan*, 61–2.

135 Ratchnevsky, *Genghis Khan*, 141–4; Biran, *Chinggis Khan*, 61–2; Dunnell, *Chinggis Khan*, 88–9; Martin, *North China*, 304–6 and "Hsi-Hsia," 225–6.

6

Töregene

After Chinggis Khan's death in 1227, women remained as active as ever, even though these activities were scarcely recorded for several years. Chinggisid wives and daughters attended the quriltai that brought Ögedei formally to power in 1229.[1] They contributed to the military expansion of the empire: Ögedei ordered the princesses and their son-in-law husbands, along with the princes and the commanders of all ranks, to send their oldest sons on the Central Asia, Russia, and Eastern Europe campaign (1236–42).[2] When not participating in the martial side of empire building, women, especially the senior princesses and important widows, could be irregularly consulted on other matters, like empire-wide taxation.[3] Otherwise imperial women continued to manage their camps, maintain personal, political, and economic connections, and marry their children into other branches of the family, as they had been doing all along.

[1] The decision quriltai took place in 1228, but Ögedei was raised at a second gathering in September 1229. Hodong Kim, "A Reappraisal of Güyüg Khan," in *Mongols, Turks and Others: Eurasian Nomads and the Sedentary World*, ed. Reuven Amitai and Michal Biran (Leiden, 2005), 320 and note 49, on dual quriltais; otherwise *Secret History*, §269 and de Rachewiltz, Commentary, 984–8; Juvaynī, *World-Conqueror*, 183–9; Rashīd al-Dīn, *Jāmiʿ*, 635, trans. Thackston, 312, trans. Boyle, 30–1 (omitting women). For the 1229 quriltai, see Allsen, "North China," 367–8, and a new interpretation by Hope, *Ilkhanate*, 50–3, 55–7.

[2] *Secret History*, §270.

[3] Ögedei sought the approval of princesses, sons-in-law, princes, and highest commanders, when adjusting a tax on animals. *Secret History*, §280. Hope, *Ilkhanate*, 58 (Sorqoqtani as an advisor on policy).

But real details of women's involvement in the history of the empire do not emerge until the 1240s, an era dominated by troubles. These included financial stresses caused by imperial overspending and struggles over taxation, tension between the Grand Khan and the regional khans, and Ögedei's contested redistributions of people and territory.[4] Worse still was the specter of Chinggisid succession and the battles over the position of Grand Khan that captured the attention of the entire Imperial House. In those battles key women played central roles, first among them the famous imperial widow Töregene. This chapter examines the advantages that Töregene enjoyed as regent, the challenges she faced as a secondary wife and conquered woman, and the difficulty we have in extricating her history from the extreme biases of the historical sources. Meanwhile, other Chinggisids became lesser characters in the dramas of the decade, especially Börte's daughter, Princess Al Altan, Chinggis Khan's brother Temüge, and Ögedei's son Köten. As losers in the political battles of the age, however, these figures have either been partially obscured by the sources, or written out of the histories entirely. This chapter redresses those omissions by extricating these individuals from the obscurity to which they have been relegated, and realigning their stories with the better-known one of Töregene herself.

THE FIRST IMPERIAL WIDOW: TÖREGENE

The first powerful imperial widow was Töregene. The historical sources' largely posthumous descriptions of her character, habits, and accomplishments are mixed. Most agree that she was shrewd, capable, and determined (some say domineering).[5] In the *Yuan Shi*, compiled over a century after her reign, several anecdotes highlight Töregene's poor governance, tendencies toward oppression, and reliance on corrupt officials.[6] The disapproving Persian authors, writing within decades of Töregene's career

[4] Allsen, "Maḥmūd Yalavač (?–1254), Mas'ūd Beg (?–1289), 'Alī Beg (?–1280), Bujir (flo. 1206–60)," in *Service*," 124, and *Mongol Imperialism*, 46–7 for contestation over lands and administrative control. For his redistribution of people see the subsequent text in this chapter under Purges, also Rashīd al-Dīn, *Jāmi'*, 612–13, trans. Thackston, 282. For his need for cash see de Rachewiltz, "Yeh-Lü Ch'u-Ts'ai," 159–60.

[5] Rashīd al-Dīn says shrewd (*Jāmi'*, 799, trans. Thackston, 390, trans. Boyle, 176), domineering (or masterful) (*Jāmi'*, 620, trans. Thackston, 304, trans. Boyle, 20); Juvaynī says shrewd, shrewder (than the widow Möge), sagacious and capable in *World-Conqueror*, 240.

[6] *Yuan shi*, 7:3463–4 (unpublished trans. Buell).

for the Toluid usurpers who supplanted her family, similarly remarked that she possessed finesse and cunning,[7] was vengeful,[8] failed to consult with others,[9] and ultimately caused disturbances and chaos within the empire.[10] One author even records the petty detail that she was not particularly good-looking.[11] But since the Persian writers in particular had to situate Töregene on the losing side of history in order to whitewash the Toluids' usurpation, their assessments must be taken with reservation.[12] Tellingly, even these detractors acknowledged that Töregene was well capable of convincing people to support her.[13] She could certainly display an appealing charm of manner – one European source described her as friendly and courteous in person, while the Syrian Christian historian Bar Hebraeus claimed she was "exceedingly wise and discreet."[14] Despite the hostility of some authors, it makes more sense to recognize Töregene as a rare example of a conquered woman who achieved startling success: she overcame a weak political position, consolidated significant authority, and openly thwarted her husband's will in order to place their son Güyük on a throne he could not have held without her backing.

Her achievements can best be understood when measured against the challenges of her position. Töregene was a conquered woman: when the Mongols defeated a large force of Merkits in 1204–5, she was a wife to one of the Merkit leaders, and became part of the spoils.[15] (Unfortunately

[7] Juvaynī, *World-Conqueror*, 240.

[8] Juvaynī, *World-Conqueror*, 241; Rashīd al-Dīn, *Jāmi'*, 799, trans. Thackston, 390, trans. Boyle, 176.

[9] Rashīd al-Dīn, *Jāmi'*, 620–1, 799, trans. Thackston, 304, 390, trans. Boyle, 176.

[10] Rashīd al-Dīn, *Jāmi'*, 734, trans. Thackston, 360, trans. Boyle, 121.

[11] Rashīd al-Dīn, *Jāmi'*, 620, trans. Thackston, 304, trans. Boyle, 19.

[12] For an assessment of Rashīd al-Dīn's treatment of women see De Nicola, *Khatuns*, 42.

[13] "Töregene Khatun, through shrewd tricks and on her own, without consulting the *aqa-inis*, seized control of the kingdom and won over the hearts of her relatives and the commanders by giving various gifts and presents until all were inclined to her side and came under her control." Rashīd al-Dīn, *Jāmi'*, 799, trans. Thackston, 390, trans. Boyle, 176 (citation from Thackston). Juvaynī, *World-Conqueror*, 240–1, on which Rashīd al-Dīn probably relied: "by means of finesse and cunning she obtained control of all affairs of state and won over the hearts of her relatives by all kinds of favours and kindnesses and the sending of gifts and presents. And for the most part strangers and kindred, family and army inclined towards her, and submitted themselves obediently and gladly to her commands and prohibitions, and came under her sway."

[14] Bar Hebraeus, *Chronography*, 410; Benedict the Pole, *Narrative*, 82.

[15] The details vary: either Chinggis Khan simply gave her to Ögedei (*Secret History*, §198), or Ögedei boldly chose her for himself (Rashīd al-Dīn, *Jāmi'*, 620, trans. Thackston, 304, trans. Boyle, 19–20). The identity of her first husband is not clear: the sources name Qudu, a son of the Merkit leader Toqto'a, for whom she was the second of two wives

Töregene's own lineage is unclear.[16]) At the time of her capture Töregene had already assumed responsibilities and begun to acquire management experience, although her lack of children suggests she had not been married long when the Mongols gained possession of her. Her status meant that she immediately married again, also highly, to Ögedei, although she became a junior to his senior wife, Boraqchin.[17] In some ways Töregene resembled Chinggis Khan's captured wife Gürbesü, widow of the Naiman Tayang Khan, who had to content herself with the position of a lesser wife living in a senior wife's camp. The difference in Töregene's case was that she produced five sons with Ögedei: Güyük, the eldest; Köten, a later contender for the throne; Köchü, Ögedei's favorite and choice as heir; Qarachar; and Qashi.[18] This major wifely achievement gave Töregene the human capital of her offspring, and moral force as the mother of heirs. Better still, Ögedei's senior wife, Boraqchin, had no children who lived, while his two remaining sons, Qadan Oghul and Melik, were both from concubines.[19] This opened a door of opportunity for Töregene.

She also benefited from a number of lucky breaks. It is well known that the Mongols believed in good fortune, especially the particular kind (*suu*) held by the Chinggisid house and granted by the Enduring Blue Sky (*Gök Möngke Tenggeri*). As a member of that house through marriage, Töregene can be understood to have possessed some degree of the corporate *suu*.[20] Nevertheless, although we cannot discern whether her contemporaries would have seen the events of her career as fortunate in this particular sense, she was certainly fortunate by modern terms. First, Ögedei possessed a "steady and reliable" disposition, which may have

(*Secret History*, §198), or Dayir-Usun, chief of the Uhaz Merkits (whose daughter Qulan married Chinggis Khan; no evidence suggests that Töregene was her mother). Rashīd al-Dīn, *Jāmi'*, 620, trans. Thackston, 304, trans. Boyle, 19–20. Also De Nicola, *Khatuns*, 66.

16 Suggestions that she was a Naiman may be inaccurate; see de Rachewiltz, "Sixth Empress," 74, 76, although in his Commentary, 728, he leans toward the Naiman appellation, with reservations.

17 De Rachewiltz, "Sixth Empress," 72–4.

18 Rashīd al-Dīn, *Jāmi'*, 620–26, trans. Thackston, 304–06; trans. Boyle, 19–22; on Qashi see Kim, "Güyüg," 321–2.

19 On Boraqchin's lack of children see de Rachewiltz, "Sixth Empress," 75. Qadan Oghul was the son of one Erkene, and was raised in Chaghatai's ordo. Melik's mother was an (unnamed) concubine; he was brought up in the household of Danishmend Hajib in Ögedei's ordo. Rashīd al-Dīn, *Jāmi'*, 631–3, trans. Thackston, 310–11; trans. Boyle, 27–8.

20 Tom Allsen, email correspondence, August 2016.

made him easy to live with.[21] Second, Chinggis Khan chose Ögedei to succeed him as Grand Khan, which transformed not only Ögedei's position within the empire, but also Töregene's chances for advancement. An additional stroke of good fortune was Boraqchin's death in (perhaps) the 1230s, which allowed Töregene to become the senior wife.[22] This she accomplished despite Ögedei's favor for Möge Khatun, a widow of Chinggis Khan whom Ögedei had married through the levirate after 1227, but who did not have children (as far as we know).[23]

Another key to Töregene's success was Ögedei's addiction to alcohol, which caused him to withdraw from administration later in his reign.[24] This left Töregene to take over management of the empire with the help of select administrators.[25] One was the Central Asian Muslim merchant 'Abd al-Raḥmān, whom Ögedei appointed to collect taxes in Northern China in 1239, with an expansion of powers in 1240.[26] Then, however, 'Abd al-Raḥmān was demoted in fall 1241, although he remained at court.[27] In addition to his financial services, and even after being fired, 'Abd al-Raḥmān acted as a convivial participant in Ögedei's alcoholic binges. It was he who sent wine to the Grand Khan at a party on the night of December 10, 1241, after which Ögedei died at dawn on the 11th, most likely of alcohol poisoning or organ failure.[28]

Although 'Abd al-Raḥmān is noted as enabling Ögedei to drink, he was not implicated in causing the Grand Khan's death. But this does not mean that it was seen as a tragic natural event; rather, rumors of poison immediately began to circulate, and targeted two prominent women. First came the Kereit princess Ibaqa, Chinggis Khan's former wife who had remarried Jürchedei of the Uru'uts. She and her son had been in the ordo and had attended the party as cupbearers for Ögedei. Both were therefore

[21] *Secret History*, §255; also Rashīd al-Dīn, *Jāmi'*, 618, 619, trans. Thackston, 303, 304, trans. Boyle, 17–18.

[22] De Rachewiltz, "Sixth Empress," 75–6.

[23] Juvaynī, *World-Conqueror*, 218, 240; Rashīd al-Dīn, *Jāmi'*, 621, 799, trans. Thackston, 304, 390, trans. Boyle, 19 (omitting Möge), 176; also the illuminating discussion in de Rachewiltz, "Sixth Empress," 73–5.

[24] De Rachewiltz, "Edict," 42, and "Sixth Empress," 72.

[25] Thomas T. Allsen, "Ögedei and Alcohol," *Mongolian Studies* XXIX (2007), 3–7, and "North China," 382.

[26] Allsen, "North China," 381; de Rachewiltz, "Yeh-lü Ch'u-ts'ai," 160–1; Allsen, "Merchant Partners," 101–3, 124; De Nicola, *Khatuns*, 146.

[27] Allsen, "Maḥmūd Yalavač," 125, and "North China," 381, and "Merchant Partners," 103.

[28] *Yuan shi*, reign of Ögedei; trans. Abramowski, 135, also *Yuan Shi*, 7:3463–4 (unpublished trans. Buell); Allsen, "Ögedei and Alcohol," 5–6.

accused straightaway by the ladies and commanders of poisoning him. But a well-respected Jalayir general and Ögedeyid loyalist, Eljigidei, protested that they were innocent, on the grounds that Ögedei's alcoholism was too well-known for poison to be believable. The two were thus cleared of suspicion.[29] The other woman was not so fortunate. This was Börte's youngest daughter, Princess Al Altan and queen of the Uighurs, who also must have attended the party, since she appears to have been similarly accused of poisoning her brother, as later events demonstrated.[30] But neither Eljigidei nor anyone else seems to have rushed to her defense, and the alcohol excuse did not save her as it had the other two. Nevertheless the full inquiry, and her eventual execution for murdering Ögedei, were delayed until after Güyük's coronation in 1246.

Meanwhile, Töregene did not begin her widowhood easily, for she immediately found herself facing a rival in Möge Khatun. As someone who possessed the seniority of having married both Chinggis Khan and Ögedei, and whom Ögedei favored publicly, Möge's status surpassed Töregene's own.[31] This meant that all eyes turned to Möge Khatun for leadership after Ögedei's death: "therefore in accordance with precedent the dispatch of orders and the assembling of the people took place at the door of the *ordu* or palace of his wife, Möge Khatun."[32] But Töregene, pointedly described as "shrewder and more sagacious than Möge," quickly contained her rival by sending messages to her one remaining brother-in-law, Chaghatai, and his sons, as well as to her nephews in the Jochid and Toluid houses.[33] (We may surmise that she also sent word to the princesses and the families of Chinggis Khan's brothers, but the sources omit these details.) The messengers announced Ögedei's death, pointed out the need for interim leadership, raised the specter of an uncontrolled army under a leaderless court, and warned of the damage these could inflict on the Empire.[34] Töregene's timeliness, her appeal to the good of the empire, her warnings about the consequences of a

[29] Rashīd al-Dīn, *Jāmi'*, 673, trans. Thackston, 330, trans. Boyle, 65–6.

[30] Given the way Al Altan's death was covered up, we must deduce the accusation from statements by Friar Carpini and de Bridia's *Tatar Relation* that her execution was for poisoning Ögedei; see "purges" in the subsequent discussion in this chapter.

[31] Juvaynī, *World-Conqueror*, 211–12, 218; Rashīd al-Dīn, *Jāmi'*, 142–3, trans. Thackston, 77; also De Nicola, *Khatuns*, 68.

[32] Juvaynī, *World-Conqueror*, 240.

[33] Jochi died in 1225, and Tolui in 1233. Qu and Liu, "Jochi's Lifetime," 283–90. Citation from Juvaynī, *World-Conqueror*, 240; see Rashīd al-Dīn *Jāmi'*, 799, trans. Thackston, 390, trans. Boyle, 176.

[34] Juvaynī, *World-Conqueror*, 240.

headless state, and her position as mother of the important sons were convincing: Chaghatai declared that she herself should be regent and maintain the court with all existing ministers until a quriltai could be convened to discuss succession.[35] She was probably in her fifties. Töregene's position was further strengthened by another lucky break when the beloved Möge died shortly thereafter.[36]

An important question arises here about the source of Töregene's opportunities. Was she the beneficiary of genuine good fortune, or did she have a hand in creating her own luck? To put the matter in other words, were the deaths that led to Töregene's accession as regent simply convenient, perfectly timed, and fortuitous, or did Töregene herself play a role, whether directly or indirectly, in the fates of Ögedei and Möge? Certainly Töregene stood to benefit from both deaths. She was already the acting ruler at the end of Ögedei's life, and she, along with Güyük after her, rose to greater political power and increased control of resources as a result of Ögedei's demise. Similarly, although Töregene adeptly contained Möge's threat by rapidly winning confirmation of her own position as regent from the Chaghatayids, Möge's convenient death shortly thereafter permanently removed any continuing wifely challenge to Töregene's position. Although the two authors who mentioned Möge's end, Juvaynī and Rashīd al-Dīn, claim no mysterious causes, both situated their reports of her death within statements about Töregene's cunning, shrewdness, trickery, and refusal to consult with others.[37]

On the strength of these passages alone, we cannot necessarily surmise a veiled connection between Töregene's cunning and Möge's convenient death. But perhaps it is useful to look further, at Ögedei's situation and the accusations of poison that accompanied his demise. On the one hand, poison was known among the Mongols, who sometimes used it for matters of state when they needed to execute a person bloodlessly.[38] Furthermore, poison and medicine could appear as two sides of the same

[35] Juvaynī, *World-Conqueror*, 240; this contradicts Rashīd al-Dīn's assertion that Töregene "took it upon herself to rule," and "though shrewd tricks and on her own, without consulting the *aqa-inis*, seized control of the kingdom." Rashīd al-Dīn, *Jāmi'*, 793, 799, trans. Thackston, 387, 390, trans. Boyle, 170, 176. Also see De Nicola, *Khatuns*, 53–7, 66 (Töregene).

[36] Juvaynī, *World-Conqueror*, 240; Rashīd al-Dīn, *Jāmi'*, 799, trans. Thackston, 390, trans. Boyle, 176.

[37] Juvaynī, *World-Conqueror*, 240; Rashīd al-Dīn, *Jāmi'*, 799, trans. Thackston, 390, trans. Boyle, 176.

[38] Elizabeth Endicott, "The Role of Poison in Mongolian History," *Archivum Eurasiaii Medii Aevi* 21 (2014–15), 103–6.

coin: Ögedei had been ill shortly before that fateful night in December, and as we know, the charge of poison had indeed been leveled.[39] It is worth noting that Töregene's own protégé, 'Abd al-Raḥmān, had sent wine to the Grand Khan that fateful night, although he himself was not accused.[40] But was his intention merely to be convivial? Or something else? The belief that Ögedei had been murdered was still lingering several years later – Friar Carpini picked it up during his visit, and it was this poison charge that Töregene and Güyük's faction used to condemn and execute Princess Al Altan, as will be discussed subsequently in this chapter.[41]

It should be added that Töregene herself was indeed thought to have engaged in poisoning, quite independent from the deaths of Ögedei and Möge. Friar Carpini claimed that Töregene poisoned Grand Duke Yaroslav of Suzdal for cynical reasons: "He was invited by the Emperor's mother, who gave him to eat and drink with her own hand as if to show him honour. On his return to his lodging he was immediately taken ill and died seven days later and his whole body turned bluish-grey in a strange fashion. This made everybody think that he had been poisoned there, so that the Tartars could obtain free and full possession of his lands."[42] In the light of this belief in murder, it seems that some in the camp at the time of Friar Carpini's visit linked the regent to the general concept of death by poison, albeit for a person other than her late husband or deceased co-wife. Thus although the "crafty" Töregene cannot be proved to have plotted against those who stood in her way, like Ögedei and Möge, it is at least worth wondering whether she tried.

In any case, once the field was entirely clear, Töregene took power with the blessings of most, if not all, the Chinggisid family, as Juvaynī illustrates: "And for the most part strangers and kindred, family and army inclined towards her, and submitted themselves gladly and obediently to her commands and prohibitions, and came under her sway."[43] Even the

[39] Meaning the accusations against Ibaqa and then Princess Al Altan. For poison and medicine see Endicott, "Poison," 103; Juvaynī, *World-Conqueror*, does not mention illness on 200, but he includes a pointed reference to alcohol in "the drinking-place of Life [being] muddied by the dust of Death"; also 239–40. Rashīd al-Dīn mentions illness in *Jāmi'*, 673, trans. Thackston 330, trans. Boyle, 65–6; illness also appears in *Yuan Shi*, 7:3463–4 (unpublished trans. Buell).

[40] *Yuan Shi*, reign of Ögedei, trans. Abramowski, 135.

[41] Friar Carpini, *History*, 65, trans. Rockhill 25.

[42] Friar Carpini, *History*, 65, trans. Rockhill 25.

[43] Juvaynī, *World-Conqueror*, 240–1.

Figure 6.1 Museum Honoring Imperial Women, which is shaped like an imperial khatun's hat, Bayan Adraga, Mongolia, 2011
(photo courtesy of Karolina Zygmanowska).

begrudging Rashīd al-Dīn refers to this happy unity: she "... won over the hearts of her relatives and the commanders by giving various gifts and presents until all were inclined to her side and came under her control."[44] Thus initially Töregene seems to have emerged as an approved, able, and competent ruler, who had already managed the empire during her husband's alcoholic absences, and who was familiar with the ministers, commanders, and staff under her control. She also engaged in the established custom of providing presents to powerful figures to garner their support, a standard political tool that was employed by women and men as needed[45] (see Figure 6.1).

[44] Rashīd al-Dīn, *Jāmi'*, 799, trans. Thackston, 390, trans. Boyle, 176; citation from Thackston.
[45] I thank Tom Allsen for this observation.

HIGH FINANCE AND HIGH SPENDING

But before long, tension appeared between Ögedei's officials and Töregene, and soon she replaced several powerful figures in the administration. The reasons were partly financial. Early on, Ögedei had tried to revive the most important sedentary regions under Mongol control and use the flow of revenue from them to refill a treasury largely depleted by campaigns.[46] Several high officials supervised this rebuilding activity: the Öng'üt chief minister Chinqai; the Khwarazmian merchant Maḥmūd Yalavach, who first supervised East and West Turkestan and later moved to China; and Yelu Chucai, a Khitan and former advisor to Chinggis Khan, who was assigned to Northern China.[47] A similar but less prominent figure was the Qara-Khitayan commander Chin Temür in Khurasan and Mazandaran, who was helped, and succeeded, by the talented Uighur secretary Körgüz.[48] All of these men sought to repair the Mongols' destruction by implementing building programs, promoting agriculture, and, perhaps most importantly, regularizing the tax system to end the practice of extraordinary and irregular levies made on behalf of a wide array of Chinggisids.[49]

These men represented what can be seen as a progressive faction within the empire, meaning that they preferred to limit the demands the Mongols made on their subjects in favor of rebuilding long-term prosperity among settled peoples. It has also been argued that these financial reforms indicated an attempt to regularize and centralize the Grand Khan's control over the resources he needed to reward the empire's elite.[50] Because of their protective view of subjects, the progressives were at odds with traditionalists, who favored a more exploitative relationship to the

[46] P. D. Buell, "Chinqai (Ca. 1169–1252)," in *In the Service of the Khan: Eminent Personalities of the Early Mongol-Yüan Period*, ed. Igor de Rachewiltz et al. (Wiesbaden: Harrassowitz, 1993), 101.

[47] Buell, "Chinqai," 95–111; Allsen, "Maḥmūd Yalavač," 122–8; de Rachewiltz, "Yeh-lü Ch'u-ts'ai," 136–75, and "Personnel," 137–41; Allsen, "Merchant Partners," 100 (Yelu Chucai), 101 (noting that Chinqai sometimes supported rapacious policies).

[48] Körgüz took over after Chin Temür's death in 1235–6, albeit with challenges from his son, Edgu Temür. Juvaynī, *World-Conqueror*, 482, 488, 491–500; Rashīd al-Dīn, *Jāmi'*, 679–83, trans. Thackston, 332–4; also Buell, "Chinqai," 102–4; Boyle, "Introduction" to *World-Conqueror*, xvii–xviii; Kolbas, *Mongols in Iran*, 98–103; Jackson, "Dissolution," 214; Kim, "Güyüg," 326.

[49] Allsen, "Mahmud Yalavač," 123–4, and "North China," 372–81, and "Merchant Partners, 100, 101, and *Mongol Imperialism*, 100–13; de Rachewiltz, "Yeh-lü Ch'u-ts'ai," 155. Also De Nicola, *Khatuns*, 69. For Chin Temür and Körgüz see footnote 48.

[50] Hope, *Ilkhanate*, 59–60.

sedentary populace.[51] But the regularization of taxation may have been partially offset by Ögedei's decision to expand appanages granted to members of the ruling elite in 1235–6.[52] Furthermore, in the late 1230s Ögedei began to lean toward a more aggressive financial policy overall, promoted by Central Asian Muslim financiers and merchants who already monopolized money lending, and who offered to pay handsomely for the privilege of tax farming; that is, extracting money from the sedentary population without interference, and increasing the amounts collected by any means.[53] The sums offered were high enough to tempt Ögedei, who in 1239 allowed one such financier, Töregene's abovementioned protégé 'Abd al-Raḥmān, to take over tax farming in Northern China (to Yelu Chucai's horror), and then expand his duties in 1240.[54]

In the struggle between progressive and traditional approaches, Töregene sided with the traditionalists and their exploitative view of the sedentary populace. In fact, Töregene was hostile to most of the progressives her husband employed, although she seems to have concealed this while Ögedei was alive.[55] After his death, however, she moved quickly. Yelu Chucai's influence was on the wane, and perhaps as a result of this and of his reputation as an astrologer, he himself was spared, but Chinqai and Maḥmūd Yalavach had to run for their lives, while she permitted the Chaghatayids to execute Körgüz for a minor altercation with a member of their retinue.[56] This removal of progressives was encouraged by Töregene's advisors, especially her closest intimate, Fāṭimah, a Muslim from Tus in Khurasan and herself a merchant, who was connected to the

[51] Buell, "Chinqai," 104–5; Allsen, "Merchant Partners," 97–103.

[52] Hope, *Ilkhanate*, 58–9.

[53] De Rachewiltz, "Yeh-lü Ch'u-ts'ai," 159–60; Buell, "Chinqai," 105; Allsen, "Merchant Partners," 97–103; Endicott-West, "Merchant Associations," 132; De Nicola, *Khatuns*, 148.

[54] De Rachewiltz, "Yeh-lü Ch'u-ts'ai," 160–1; Allsen, "Mahmud Yalavač," 125; Buell, "Chinqai," 106.

[55] The exception was Yelu Chucai, whom she tolerated politely, perhaps because his influence at court had waned after his reforms of 1236, which protected subjects in China. De Rachewiltz, "Yeh-lü Ch'u-ts'ai," 159, 161; Allsen, "Merchant Partners," 103; also *Yuan shi*, 7:3463–4 (unpublished trans., Buell).

[56] These Chaghatayids included Qara-Hülegü and Orqīna, who only opposed the Ögedeyids later, after Güyük's ascension. See Chapters 7 and 8. Buell, "Chinqai," 103–4, 106; Allsen, "North China," 381, 383, and "Merchant Partners," 103; de Rachewiltz, "Yeh-lü Ch'u-ts'ai," 159, 161; Juvaynī, *World-Conqueror*, 504–5; Rashīd al-Dīn, *Jāmi'*, 133–4, 682–3, 813, trans. Thackston, 72, 334, 397; *Yuan shi*, 7:3463–4 (unpublished trans. Buell).

Central Asian financiers.[57] Two of Fāṭimah's protégés were the same 'Abd al-Raḥmān, and another Muslim, Sharaf al-Dīn, who collected taxes in Khurasan and Mazandaran. Both men were widely renowned for extreme "efficiency" (i.e., rapacity) in their work.[58]

But why did Töregene purge the progressives? Juvaynī and Rashīd al-Dīn described her attacks on officials as a result of her vengeful, hate-filled, grudgeholding character.[59] The *Yuan Shi* added that she venerated and trusted corrupt officials, engaged in poor decision making, and tried to oppress others.[60] Töregene's advisor Fāṭimah received similar treatment: one source described her as motivated by grudges, not policy, while another went so far as to describe her as a procurer of prostitutes, which reads like slander.[61] But were these accurate descriptions of real personalities, or simply misogynistic critiques of women in power? The non-Mongol authors of these disparate historical sources wrote in societies where sedentary women, at least, did not customarily wield authority in clear public view. Their characterizations of Töregene (and to a lesser degree, Fāṭimah), present both women's grudgeholding and oppressive tendencies as petty traits, with the underlying implication that women in general were unfit to rule.[62] It is useful to contrast Töregene with the later Toluid ruler Möngke (r. 1251–9), who indulged his own grudges by killing many more Chinggisids and their servants than Töregene ever did. But the Persian authors in particular lauded Möngke's retaliatory behavior, both because it came from the house of their patrons, for which unequivocal support was necessary and prudent, and, probably, because the executions were ordered by a man, whom they presumably viewed as more fit to rule by virtue of his "appropriate" gender. Although Töregene may have disliked the officials she sacked, it is probably that she sought first and foremost to neutralize their fiscal policies and

[57] Juvaynī, *World-Conqueror*, 243–5; Rashīd al-Dīn, *Jāmi'*, 799, trans. Thackston, 390, trans. Boyle, 176; Bar Hebraeus, 411–12; V. V. Bartol'd, *Turkestan down to the Mongol Invasion* (London: E. J. Gibb Memorial Trust, Philadelphia: Porcupine Press, 1977), 475; also De Nicola, *Khatuns*, 70–1.

[58] Juvaynī, *World-Conqueror*, 243, 525–46; for 'Abd al-Raḥmān see Allsen, "Mahmud Yalavač," 125; de Rachewiltz, "Yeh-lü Ch'u-ts'ai," 160.

[59] Juvaynī, *World-Conqueror*, 241; Rashīd al-Dīn, *Jāmi'*, 799, trans. Thackston, 390, trans. Boyle, 176.

[60] *Yuan shi*, 7:3463–4 (unpublished trans. Buell).

[61] Rashīd al-Dīn, *Jāmi'*, 800, trans. Thackston, 390, trans. Boyle, 177 (grudgeholding); Juvaynī, *World-Conqueror*, 244–5 (procuring).

[62] De Nicola argues instead that their opposition to both women lay in questions of policy, not gender. See *Khatuns*, 71, 72.

outlook, not just to take petty revenge for slights, as the Persian authors imply, or because she was simply corrupt herself, according to the *Yuan Shi* 's characterization.

Indeed, some scholars do credit Töregene with an active interest in the empire's finances, rather than a mindless attempt to destroy.[63] It has also been suggested that Töregene's recourse to Central Asians reflects her attempt to reduce the influence of Chinese-trained administrators, although this should not be confused with her personal patronage of Taoism.[64] Or, as another scholar argues, her financial shakeup allowed her to retain the financial status quo for those entrenched members of the elite whose positions under Chinggis Khan had been confirmed by Ögedei. Thereafter her administrative changes allowed her to grant them new financial rewards out of tax revenues.[65]

In addition to these possibilities, a more balanced view and further evidence suggest that Töregene's shakeup of the administration was motivated by particular political considerations alongside the financial ones. In the case of Körgüz, for example, Töregene may actually have been opposing the Jochid house. Jochi himself had first assigned Körgüz's predecessor and patron, Chin-Temür, to Khwarazm, and only later did Ögedei reassign Chin-Temür and his entourage, including Körgüz, to Khurasan and Mazandaran.[66] Although it was Ögedei, not Jochi's heir, Batu, who chose Körgüz as Chin-Temür's successor in 1239, Körgüz remained intimately tied to the Jochid house: immediately after his official appointment, for example, he chose to travel from Mongolia to Khurasan not directly through Uighur territory and Transoxiana, but by detouring a considerable distance through Central Asia and Khwarazm. He undertook this longer route for the sole purpose of paying his respects to the Jochid prince Tangut.[67] Later, after authorizing Körgüz's execution, Töregene replaced him with Amir Arghun, a loyal servant who owed his career to the Ögedeyid house, who actively worked to limit Jochid

[63] De Nicola, *Khatuns*, 70, 71.
[64] De Nicola, *Khatuns*, 71, 212. De Rachewiltz, "Edict," entire.
[65] Hope, *Ilkhanate*, 62, on these entrenched members of the elite (the *aqa-nar*).
[66] Juvaynī, *World-Conqueror*, 482; Rashīd al-Dīn, *Jāmi'*, 660–2, trans. Thackston, 322–3; see also Jackson, "Dissolution," 214–15; Buell, "Chinqai," 102–4; Boyle, "Introduction," xvii–xviii.
[67] Juvaynī, *World-Conqueror*, 500; Rashīd al-Dīn, *Jāmi'*, 682, 726, trans. Thackston, 333, 353, trans. Boyle, 74, 112–13; also Kolbas, *Mongols in Iran*, 101; also see Buell, "Chinqai," 102–4.

influence in Azerbaijan in 1243–4.[68] (Although Töregene did not replace Körgüz's Jochid subordinate, the tax-collector Sharaf al-Dīn, this is probably because he was Fāṭimah's protégé, and by 1243–4 had fallen into disfavor among the Jochids.[69])

Finally, at the heart of Töregene's administrative upheaval was her tremendous demand for money to achieve her own ends. She needed both to run the empire and to support the candidacy of her oldest son, Güyük, as Grand Khan. In the redistributive world of the Mongol Empire, rulers were expected to lavish wealth upon relatives, retainers, subordinates, and subjects, especially at key moments like the accession of a new sovereign.[70] This practice was observed by both men and women, and indicated to recipients that a candidate (or in Töregene's case, the chief sponsor of a candidate), was a genuine contender because she (or he) commanded "regular access to the desired products of the steppe and sown."[71] This meant that Töregene was obliged to hand out gifts upon gifts: robes, animals, furs, jewels, belts, cash, and more, sent with emissaries or, better still, presented at the lavish parties and feasts that were the cornerstone of Mongol political life. For the high level of Chinggisid politics-as-usual, an extraordinary flow of cash and goods was always necessary, but in this case Güyük was a contested candidate, which meant that Töregene probably had to spend even more than the staggering norm to woo the doubtful. Her financial demands, and the administrative upheaval she caused, must therefore be seen against the backdrop of the single issue that defined her regency: succession.

SUCCESSION: GÜYÜK

Throughout her regency Töregene was consumed by the thorny problem of succession. Chinggis Khan had already done tremendous violence to

68 Juvaynī, *World-Conqueror*, 243, 506–8 (his replacement of Körgüz and opposition to the Jochids); Rashīd al-Dīn, *Jāmi'*, 68–9, 103, 133, trans. Thackston, 39, 57, 72 (his relationship to the Ögedeyids); also Boyle, "Introduction," xviii–xxi; Hope, *Ilkhanate*, 64.

69 Juvaynī, *World-Conqueror*, 532 (forced to work for Chin Temür), 504 (as Fāṭimah's protégé), and 538 (summoned by Batu and accusations against him at Batu's court); Rashīd al-Dīn, *Jāmi'*, 660–2, 679–82, trans. Thackston 323 (his early work for Chin Temür), 332–3 (his work for Batu). Also Jackson, "Dissolution," 215–16.

70 Allsen, "Redistribution," esp. 11–15, 31, 33, 38; also Hope, *Ilkhanate*, 62–3, on the indispensability of currying the favor of "seniors" (*aqa-nar*) within the empire's ranks.

71 Tom Allsen, email correspondence, August 2016; also see his "Redistribution," 11–15, 31, 33, 38.

the Golden Lineage by restricting succession to Börte's four sons in general and to Ögedei in particular. Then Ögedei had imitated his father by choosing his own heir, who was Töregene's third son, Köchü.[72] In this way Ögedei had further disenfranchised the Jochids, Chaghatayids, and Toluids by confirming their status as collateral branches of the family with ever-waning access to the grand khanate, despite their direct control over portions of the empire. He had also bypassed Töregene's oldest son, Güyük (primogeniture), and youngest son, Qashi (ultimogeniture), and of course his two sons from concubines.

Unfortunately Köchü had inconveniently died before his father, which quite likely contributed to Ögedei's increasing drunkenness late in his reign, since the personal and political blows caused by the death of a favorite son and heir had to be staggering. But still an heir was needed, and so between (or even during[73]) bouts of alcoholic stupor Ögedei named Köchü's son Shiremün. As a junior member of the Ögedeyid house, Shiremün possessed none of the seniority that the Mongols held so dear.[74] After Ögedei's own death and Töregene's accession as regent, therefore, other competitors for the position of Grand Khan soon emerged. These included Töregene's two oldest sons, Güyük and Köten, who could claim seniority to Shiremün by virtue of being his uncles.[75] Another was Chinggis Khan's brother Temüge, who possessed even greater seniority within the Golden Lineage despite having already been dispossessed by Börte's sons in 1226.[76]

Töregene herself was a key player in this struggle, since she immediately thwarted her dead husband's wishes by supporting (and largely engineering) Güyük's candidacy. She appears to have used the time-honored tactic of giving lavish presents to key Chinggisids and commanders in hopes of garnering their backing.[77] Because she was working in the important role of a regent, Töregene avoided a levirate marriage, which would otherwise have been standard treatment of a widow, especially a

[72] Rashīd al-Dīn, *Jāmi'*, 624–5, trans. Thackston, 306, trans. Boyle, 21.

[73] I thank Tom Allsen for this observation.

[74] On seniority see Jackson, "Dissolution," 193.

[75] Töregene's two youngest sons, Qarachar and Qashi, were not contenders: the alcoholic Qashi had already died, as perhaps had Qarachar, of whom little is known. Rashīd al-Dīn, *Jāmi'*, 625, trans. Thackston, 306, trans. Boyle, 22.

[76] See Chapter 4.

[77] Rashīd al-Dīn, *Jāmi'*, 799, trans. Thackston, 390, trans. Boyle, 176; Tom Allsen, "Redistribution," esp. 11–15, 31, 33, 38; Hope, *Ilkhanate*, 62–4.

senior one with offspring who had substantial property to oversee.[78] This ability to maintain her own autonomy and cash flow as an essentially independent ruler was crucial to her achievements.

As outlined above, Töregene's need for gifts to promote Güyük's enthronement may have partly motivated her replacement of progressive financial officials with rapacious Central Asian financiers. But Töregene's financial policies and political ambitions bore unintended consequences. Among these was her contentious relationship to her second son, Köten, who also wanted to be Grand Khan. His claim rested on statements attributed to Chinggis Khan, in which the founder of the empire appeared to acknowledge Köten's abilities, although the nature and strength of those abilities are unclear. Juvaynī essentially dismissed this idea: "Köten aspired to this honour [of being Grand Khan] because his grandfather had once made a reference to him."[79] But Rashīd al-Dīn argued that, on the contrary, Chinggis Khan had actually chosen Köten as Ögedei's heir: "Köten, whom Chinggis Khan had appointed to be emperor after [Ögedei] Qa'an ..."[80] In a society that retained a significant oral tradition despite the adoption of Uighur script for administrative purposes, statements attributed to the great man himself could be found, created, or reinterpreted to cast any political narrative into a more favorable light.[81] Thus Rashīd al-Dīn's comment could have reflected an earlier understanding (or creation) of Köten's claim, or it could have been his embroidery on the truth, designed to demonstrate that Ögedei himself had contravened Chinggis Khan's will by passing over Köten in favor of his third son and heir, Köchü, which therefore implied that Ögedei's entire house deserved to be overthrown by Rashīd al-Dīn's Toluid employers. But even if this was Rashīd al-Dīn's aim, the testimony of the two authors together suggests that Köten, at least, claimed he possessed special favor from the conqueror that made him a legitimate candidate. On a more practical level, Köten was a grown man, unlike the youthful Shiremün, and had most recently distinguished himself by winning an important battle against the Kipchaks in 1242.[82]

The bad blood between Köten and his mother may have begun as a result of Töregene's emboldened position after Ögedei's death, or it may have had earlier roots, details of which are unknown to us now. But

[78] Holmgren, "Levirate," 152–4. [79] Juvaynī, *World-Conqueror*, 251.
[80] Rashīd al-Dīn, *Jāmi'*, 805, trans. Thackston, 393, trans. Boyle, 181.
[81] I thank Tom Allsen for this interpretation; email correspondence, August 2016.
[82] Rashīd al-Dīn, *Jāmi'*, 678–9, trans. Thackston, 332, trans. Boyle, 71.

certainly the hostility became clear once Töregene began to build the campaign to elect Güyük. In response, Köten openly opposed his mother's activities by sheltering the two most prominent purged financial officials: Maḥmūd Yalavach and Chinqai, who fled desperately to Köten's appanage in former Tangut territory in the early 1240s.[83] Köten's welcome of both men is no great surprise, since the presence of such able, experienced, and trustworthy ministers in his own camp could only strengthen Köten's position and fuel his ambitions in opposition to his mother and brother. Thus when Töregene demanded that Köten return the officials, he not only refused to comply, but threatened her with the collective authority of the Chinggisid family by asserting that he would only produce the officials once all the relatives assembled and were ready to judge the matter properly: "Tell my mother, 'The kite that takes refuge in a bramble patch from the talons of the hawk is safe from his enemy's might.' Since they have sought refuge with us, to send them back would be unchivalrous. In the near future a quriltai will be held, and I will bring them there with me. In the presence of my relatives and the amirs [commanders] an investigation into their crimes can be undertaken, and they can be punished accordingly."[84] This legalistic appeal to family seniority and the promise of an upcoming gathering may also have served as a delaying tactic, thereby giving Köten the opportunity to gather support for his own claim.[85]

Köten's insistence on thwarting her will was not Töregene's only problem. Another was the behavior of the seniormost man in the Golden Lineage, Chinggis Khan's youngest brother Temüge, now probably in his 70s. When both Chinggis Khan and Ögedei in turn had eliminated the principle of familial seniority from succession, Temüge became the most strongly dispossessed member of the family. After Ögedei's death, however, and perhaps as a result of Töregene's own disregard of Ögedei's wishes, Temüge saw an opportunity and moved to reopen succession to the claims of seniority within the family. To this end he mustered his

[83] Kim, "Güyüg," 326–7. Rashīd al-Dīn's contention that Möngke gave Köten this appanage is untenable if Köten died before Möngke's accession in 1251. (Rashīd al-Dīn, *Jāmi'*, 623–4, trans. Thackston, 305–6, trans. Boyle, 20–1.) Note that Juvaynī has Köten attending Güyük's coronation *from the east* in 1246 (Juvaynī, *World-Conqueror*, 249), which suggests that he already held these lands. Perhaps Ögedei gave them directly to his son in 1236 when he redistributed territories in Northern China, then Möngke reconfirmed the appanage for Köten's heirs in 1251. See de Rachewiltz, "Yeh-lü Ch'u-ts'ai," 155. On Köten's lands also see Atwood, "Chikü *küregen*," 7, 9.

[84] Rashīd al-Dīn, *Jāmi'*, 801, trans. Thackston, 390, trans. Boyle, 177; also Juvaynī, *World-Conqueror*, 241–2.

[85] I thank Tom Allsen for this idea; email correspondence, August 2016.

forces in the flat, marshy grasslands of his appanage near Lake Hulun, and led them, armed and ready, west toward Töregene's court.[86] This was before Güyük had returned from the far west, where he had been campaigning with his cousins.[87] On her own, therefore, Töregene swiftly sent multiple emissaries with their retinues and soldiers to stop Temüge: these included Temüge's son Orutai, who worked as an attendant at court, and Töregene's stepson, Mengli Oghul, one of Ögedei's sons from a concubine mother.[88] At least according to Rashīd al-Dīn, Töregene appealed to family unity: she reminded Temüge of her status as a Chinggisid daughter-in-law, asked why he was approaching with an army, and remarked that he was upsetting both the soldiers (*lashkar*) and state (*ulus*).[89] Although Juvaynī omitted Töregene's message and credited Mengli Oghul alone with convincing Temüge to retreat, certainly the combination of Töregene's ideas, Melik's diplomatic ability, and the presence of Temüge's son Orutai was persuasive. The final blow to Temüge's hopes appeared in the news that Güyük himself was fast approaching. Realizing his position was untenable, Temüge excused his aggression with the claim that he was in mourning (and thus not in his right mind), and withdrew.[90]

One final Chinggisid prince who gave Töregene trouble was the Jochid Batu. According to her duty as regent, Töregene tried to convene a quriltai at which to decide the question of succession, but Batu stymied her efforts by refusing to attend on vague medical grounds.[91] Given that Töregene was continuing Ögedei's attempts to limit Jochid territorial and financial control, and that Güyük and Batu had argued terribly during the Russian conquests, it is no surprise that Batu was unwilling to bring his person within Ögedeyid reach, or cooperate with them in any way. But his refusal meant that the quriltai did not convene, leaving Töregene to

[86] For his appanage see Juvaynī, *World-Conqueror*, 42; for the terrain see Li, *Alchemist*, trans. Waley, 64–5.

[87] This was the campaign into Central Asia, Russia, and Eastern Europe (1236–42).

[88] Juvaynī, *World-Conqueror*, 244, mentioning only Mengli Oghul as "a grandson [of Chingiz-Khan]" but see note 15 on the same page identifying him as Ögedei's son Malik; Rashīd al-Dīn, *Jāmi'*, 802, trans. Thackston, 391, trans. Boyle, 178, mentioning Temüge's son Orutai, then Mengli Oghul, identified as "the grandson of _____ (blank)."

[89] Rashīd al-Dīn, *Jāmi'*, 802 (*lashkar va ulūs*), trans. Thackston, 391 (Soldiery and ulus; ulus and army), trans. Boyle, 178 (whole army and ulus).

[90] Juvaynī, *World-Conqueror*, 244; Rashīd al-Dīn, *Jāmi'*, 802, trans. Thackston, 391, trans. Boyle, 178.

[91] "*Istirkhā'* " in Rashīd al-Dīn, *Jāmi'*, 734, "flaccidity" in Thackston, 360, "paralysis" in Boyle, 120 and note 92; but gout on 170, 200.

rule independently for several years while she tried to arrange another. Again Batu declined to attend, this time for even vaguer reasons.[92] Despite his refusal, however, this second time Töregene managed to convince (or compel) enough people to come.

THE QURILTAI OF 1246

The enthronement quriltai finally convened in summer 1246 in the traditional region near the Kerülen river.[93] Almost everyone who mattered attended, although the historians did not mention them equally. From the east came Chinggis Khan's brothers and nephews, chief among them Temüge, despite his previous attempt to become Grand Khan by force. Chinggis Khan's half-brother Belgütei must also have been there, but the historians disregarded him.[94] As for Börte's sons: by this point none of the four remained alive – the last, Chaghatai, had died in 1242,[95] and so their houses were represented by widows and offspring. Naturally the Ögedeyids appeared in force as the candidates and the ruling house under Töregene. They were joined by Tolui's chief widow, Sorqoqtani, who brought her four sons from Northern China; Chaghatai's sons, who came from the southwest; and the Jochids from the wide grasslands in the west, from which the wary Batu sent several brothers, but himself stayed away.[96] The most important of these brothers was Orda, the eldest of Jochi's sons and therefore a senior Chinggisid in this generation.[97] Juvaynī also recorded the presence of military commanders and state officials, especially officials he knew personally, along with vassals and ambassadors from the western end of the empire.[98] Rashīd al-Dīn largely

[92] Rashīd al-Dīn, *Jāmi'*, 734, 805, trans. Thackston, 360, 392, trans. Boyle, 120, 178.

[93] Kim, "Güyüg," 320, note 48. De Rachewiltz, Commentary, 728. Juvaynī and Rashīd al-Dīn mention spring (Juvaynī, *World-Conqueror*, 249; Rashīd al-Dīn, *Jāmi'*, 804, trans. Thackston 392, trans. Boyle, 180, mentioning the Kerülen River), but Friar Carpini dates the events to summer by specifying Christian festivals. Summer is also likely given the quantities of qumiz, a summer beverage, consumed. Friar Carpini, *History*, 60, 63, trans. Rockhill, 18, 21. The reference to the Kerülen contradicts de Bridia, *Tatar Relation*, 86, who suggested that the quriltai convened [close] outside Qara-qorum.

[94] He lived until the 1250s. See Chapter 4, footnote 90.

[95] De Rachewiltz, Commentary, 864.

[96] Juvaynī, *World-Conqueror*, 249, mentioning that "Batu did not come in person"; Rashīd al-Dīn allows that Batu was offended with the Ögedeyids and used medical excuses to avoid attending. See Rashīd al-Dīn, *Jāmi'*, 805, trans. Thackston, 392, trans. Boyle, 180.

[97] I thank Tom Allsen for this observation; email correspondence, August 2016.

[98] Juvaynī, *World-Conqueror*, 249–50.

copied these names, with a few changes.[99] According to a recent study, those present could be defined as senior persons within the empire (*aqa-nār*), who enjoyed authority and influence, and whose indispensable support Töregene had worked for so long to obtain.[100]

But despite their seemingly comprehensive lists of attendees, the Persian historians failed to mention the prominent women who came to the quriltai as members of the Golden Lineage, with the single exception of the influential and highly respected widow of Tolui, Sorqoqtani.[101] Because five years later some of Chinggis Khan's widowed sisters-in-law attended the quriltai of 1251, it is reasonable to assume that they also came to that of 1246, even though the Persian historians omitted them.[102] Similarly the historians ignored the senior princesses and the imperial sons-in-laws, even though these had participated in the quriltai of 1229, and surely attended this one as well.[103] Indeed, when relating the participation of women (other than Sorqoqtani), Juvaynī semi-cryptically mentioned only the "princesses" seated on Güyük's left hand, which could be Güyük's wives, but also could mean his own wives *and* women from other branches of the family.[104] The situation becomes only slightly clearer after Juvaynī referred to the largesse handed out first to "the princes and princesses that were present *of the race and lineage of Chingiz-Khan*," (emphasis added), indicating members of the Golden Lineage in general.[105] Friar Carpini corroborated that each day "a great crowd of women came," but he did not identify them.[106] Nevertheless we must assume that the fifth daughter, Al Altan, was in the great camp, given

[99] Rashīd al-Dīn, *Jāmi'*, 805, trans. Thackston, 392, trans. Boyle, 180–1. Rashīd al-Dīn mentions the Jochid Tangut ("Tangqut"), whom Juvaynī omits, but then omits the Chaghatayids Büri, Baidar, and Yesün-Toqa, whom Juvaynī includes. Rashīd al-Dīn also skips Güyük's brother Köten, but then mentions him in the next paragraph anyhow; he leaves out the Sultan of Takavor (i.e., the Armenian constable Smbat), whom Juvaynī includes (*World-Conqueror*, 250, note 6). See a partial list of vassal rulers and their ambassadors in Friar Carpini, *History*, 62, trans. Rockhill, 20.

[100] See Hope's thesis on the *aqa-nār* in *Ilkhanate*, 46–56.

[101] Juvaynī, *World-Conqueror*, 249; Rashīd al-Dīn, *Jāmi'*, 805, trans. Thackston, 392, trans. Boyle, 180.

[102] Möngke mentioned this to rebuke Oghul-Qaimish: "The wives of Jochi Qasar, [Temüge-] Otchigin and Belgütei Noyan, the brothers of Chinggis Khan, have attended the deliberations of the quriltai [of 1251], but Oghul Qaimish has not." Rashīd al-Dīn, *Jāmi'*, 839, trans. Thackston, 409, trans. Boyle, 215.

[103] For the quriltai of 1229 see *Secret History*, §269.

[104] Juvaynī, *World-Conqueror*, 252, 254.

[105] Juvaynī, *World-Conqueror*, 252, 254.

[106] Friar Carpini, *History*, 65 (as "*Every* day ..."), trans. Rockhill, 24 as "the *whole* day there came ..." (emphasis added).

what happened to her immediately after the ceremonies (see the subsequent discussion in this chapter), but she was probably under a cloud because of the accusation that she had poisoned Ögedei. If Al Altan was allowed to attend the festivities (as perhaps did Temüge, presumably under his own cloud), there is still no way to discover what her sisters knew – or thought – of the situation. We may also assume that the junior Chinggisids participated in the quriltai, among them lesser princesses, and those princes "not in charge of a domain," like the offspring of Chinggis Khan's junior son Kölgen (d. 1237).[107] But again, these were not deemed worthy of inclusion in the record.

The quriltai itself was a lengthy session, but preserved the appearance of an open convention because three different candidates emerged for the grand khanate: the brothers Güyük and Köten, and the grandson whom Ögedei had actually chosen to succeed him, Shiremün. The first assemblies convened over the course of several days in a very beautiful white velvet tent surrounded by a painted wooden palisade with two gates, one dedicated solely to the not-yet-selected new Grand Khan, the other used by the throng.[108] Although the tent was enormous – it allegedly held 2,000 people – it was reserved for the nomadic ruling class, members of which donned new matching robes on each successive day – first three days of velvet in the bright August sun (white velvet, then red, and finally blue), followed by a day in brocade.[109] Discussions seem to have taken place in the morning, while the afternoon was reserved for drinking qumiz, followed by eating in the evening.[110] Meanwhile, ambassadors and vassals cooled their heels outside the palisade, where refreshments were brought to them.[111] The tent, the thousands of robes, the drinks, and the food must have been no small part of Töregene's extraordinary expenditures for this singular event.[112]

Although attendees discussed the candidates in turn, the conclusion was probably never in doubt. Töregene's position as regent, her support for Güyük, and her years' worth of expensive lobbying and equally costly preparations for the quriltai allowed her to carry the majority of the assembled in favor of her eldest son. Köten was passed over on the

[107] For the term see *Secret History*, §270. Kölgen's mother was the Merkit Qulan; see Chapter 3.
[108] Friar Carpini, *History*, 61, trans. Rockhill, 19.
[109] Friar Carpini, *History*, 61, trans. Rockhill, 19.
[110] Friar Carpini, *History*, 62–3, trans. Rockhill, 22.
[111] Friar Carpini, *History*, 62, trans. Rockhill, 20.
[112] Allsen, "Redistribution," 22–3, 33 (entertainment expenses).

grounds of poor health, while Shiremün's candidacy was set aside because of his youth and consequent lack of seniority. Nevertheless, as was proper, Güyük refused the honor of the nomination multiple times before finally acquiescing to the will of the assembly.[113]

The rest of the festivities, including the enthronement and the reception of ambassadors, took place slightly later in two other expensive tents, one made of red velvet brought from China and positioned a few leagues away, and another of unknown outside color, the inside of which was lined entirely with gold brocade and supported by gold-plated posts nailed to the roof beams with golden nails.[114] Unfortunately the enthronement was delayed because of a killer hailstorm. Given the Mongols' fear of extreme weather as an evil portent from a disapproving spirit world, the storm and the lives it claimed must have seemed deeply ominous to the assembly, but nevertheless the events were not unduly derailed.[115] After the sky cleared and the omens looked favorable, Güyük was at last placed on the throne, a beautiful carved seat adorned with gold, silver, gems, and pearls, which had been stationed on a high wooden platform under a canopy.[116] According to Mongol custom, he was led by the hand to his seat by two senior men in the family. But although Temüge and Chaghatai had done this for Ögedei in 1229, this time Temüge was publicly passed over for Güyük's cousins: Orda, the most senior man of Güyük's generation, and Chaghatai's son, Yesü Möngke.[117] This event was followed by days of feasting and drinking, and by the ceremonial, personalized, and slow distribution of gifts to all major figures in the empire as a demonstration of Güyük's new status, a sign of his spiritual favor in the form of good fortune (*suu*), and a reaffirmation of the political hierarchy. These presentations seem to have taken place in the open air, in the brocade-lined tent,

[113] Juvaynī, *World-Conqueror*, 251; Rashīd al-Dīn, *Jāmi'*, 806, trans. Thackston, 393, trans. Boyle, 181. Friar Carpini, *History*, 61–2, trans. Rockhill, 21–2 (a general description). Note the useful discussion in Hope, *Ilkhanate*, 64–7.

[114] Friar Carpini, *History*, 63–5, trans. Rockhill, 22–4.

[115] Friar Carpini, *History*, 6, 63, trans. Rockhill, 22. More than 160 people were drowned, while quantities of gers and baggage washed away. Neither Juvaynī nor Rashīd al-Dīn mentions the storm.

[116] Friar Carpini, *History*, 64–5, trans. Rockhill, 24; Benedict the Pole, *Narrative*, 82.

[117] Juvaynī, *World-Conqueror*, 251–2; Rashīd al-Dīn omits the leading by the hand in *Jāmi'*, 806, trans. Thackston, 393, trans. Boyle, 182. For the *quriltai* of 1229 see Juvaynī, *World-Conqueror*, 187; *Secret History*, §269, mentioning Chaghatai only; Rashīd al-Dīn claims that Chaghatai took Ögedei's right hand, Tolui his left, and Temüge his belt, *Jāmi'*, 636, trans. Thackston, 312, trans. Boyle, 31. Also Hope, *Ilkhanate*, 66.

and in the third marvelous tent of red velvet.[118] For all of these necessary ceremonies, which sealed Güyük's accession in full public view, Töregene no doubt paid astronomical prices.

THE PURGES: TEMÜGE, AL ALTAN, AND FĀṬIMAH

After the festivities were over, the fabulous robes put away, and the hangovers medicated, the serious business of daily government began. Güyük started his reign with a brief but bloody series of executions, which eliminated Chinggisids and high officials alike. The first Chinggisid was Temüge, who was tried semi-secretly by Orda and Möngke, the senior male Jochid and Toluid respectively, whose status outside the reconfirmed Ögedeyid ruling house may have implied their relative disinterest.[119] But Belgütei, Chinggis Khan's still-living half-brother, seems to have been excluded, despite his seniority within the family.[120] Information about Temüge's trial was suppressed at the time and thereafter: the princes spoke to no one of their investigation, and the sources reveal little of what happened.[121] But we can make some deductions. Certainly the most obvious concern that Orda and Möngke addressed had to have been Temüge's attempt to seize control of the empire during Töregene's regency. Although he had invoked a legitimate claim to rule by virtue of the principle of family seniority, it was no longer possible to appeal to this principle among the Chinggisids, and Temüge's actions could now be viewed as treason. In addition, and although unmentioned by the sources, Ögedei's policies may have contributed to Temüge's death. During his reign Ögedei had made unpopular choices about land, men, and women,[122] one of which affected Temüge when Ögedei requisitioned girls

[118] Friar Carpini, *History*, 63–5, trans. Rockhill, 21–4; Juvaynī, *World-Conqueror*, 254–5; Rashīd al-Dīn, *Jāmi'*, 806, trans. Thackston, 393, trans. Boyle, 182. Allsen, "Redistribution," 21–2 (the gift-giving ceremonies); also Hope, *Ilkhanate*, 64–6.

[119] For Orda see Allsen, "Left Hand," 8–18.

[120] He lived until the 1250s. See Chapter 4, footnote 92.

[121] Juvaynī, *World-Conqueror*, 255; Rashīd al-Dīn, *Jāmi'*, 806, trans. Thackston, 393, trans. Boyle, 182; also Friar Carpini, *History*, 25 (not in Rockhill); de Bridia, *Tatar Relation*, §41, albeit referring to him as a nephew of Chinggis Khan.

[122] Ögedei had distributed appanages in Northern China in 1236 despite Yelu Chucai's opposition (de Rachewiltz, "Yeh-lü Ch'u-ts'ai," 155); he had appointed officials in Western territories with the goal of reclaiming lands from the Jochids (see above, "High Finance and High Spending"); he had reassigned troops from the Toluids to his son Köten (Rashīd al-Dīn, *Jāmi'*, 612–13, 793, trans. Thackston, 282, 387, trans. Boyle, 169, 170).

from Temüge's territories, probably in 1237, without Temüge's approval. (This incident is often confused with an infamous alleged mass rape of Oirat girls.[123]) Temüge may well have resented the requisitioning and the toll it took on his own subjects; perhaps this became a grievance he held against the Ögedeyid house, and contributed to his desire to replace them with himself. But with almost all evidence suppressed, this can only be a surmise. What we do know is that after their secret investigation Orda and Möngke found Temüge guilty of treason and had him executed, in unknown fashion, by a group of officers.[124] For once and for all this ended succession through general seniority in the Golden Lineage.

The second Chinggisid casualty of Güyük's accession was the princess Al Altan, then about fifty, whose trial and execution for "poisoning" Ögedei were kept even more secret than Temüge's death.[125] Only a slip by Rashīd al-Dīn tells us that her killer was the loyal commander Eljigidei, whose spirited defense of Ibaqa for the first charge of poison helped the

[123] See *Secret History*, §281, "As to my second fault ... to have the girls of my uncle Otchigin's domain brought to me was surely a mistake [Ögedei said]," and de Rachewiltz, Commentary, 1034–6, where he suggests that this incident corresponds with Juvaynī's infamous tale about the acquisition of girls from a particular group, and the ugly mass rape of some of them, during Ögedei's reign (Juvaynī, *World-Conqueror*, 235–6). It also corresponds with the *Yuan shi* report of a similar incident in 1237 (*Yuan shi* 2:35 as cited by de Rachewiltz). De Rachewiltz points out that Rashīd al-Dīn's identification of this group as the Oirats (Rashīd al-Dīn, *Jāmi'*, 705 (without using the word Oirat), trans. Thackston, 345 (using Oirat), trans. Boyle, 93–4, does not make sense. I agree, given the Oirats' cooperation with the Ögedeyids before Güyük. The *Yuan shi* and *Secret History* both specify peoples of the Left Hand (i.e., eastern territories controlled by Chinggis Khan's brothers and nephews, including Temüge), not the Oirats in the west.

[124] Juvaynī, *World-Conqueror*, 255; Rashīd al-Dīn, *Jāmi'*, 806, trans. Thackston, 393, trans. Boyle, 182; see also Friar Carpini, *History*, 25 (not in Rockhill); de Bridia, *Tatar Relation*, §41, identifying him as Chinggis Khan's nephew, not brother. Also Kim, "Güyüg," 328.

[125] The charge of poison, and the timing of the trial and execution after Güyük's coronation, appear in Friar Carpini, *History*, 45 (for poison), and 65 (for poison and the trial), although on 65 the translator incorrectly identifies Al Altan as Güyük's mistress by misreading *amita* (aunt) for *amica* ([female] friend). This is written correctly as his "paternal aunt" in the translation by Rockhill, 25 (who however does not translate the section that includes Dawson's p. 45). In *Tatar Relation*, §30, de Bridia describes Al Altan accurately as Ögedei's sister, although in note 2 on p. 83 of that text this situation is mistaken for Fāṭimah's trial. Rashīd al-Dīn argues that the Kereit Ibaqa was accused of poisoning Ögedei, along with her son, but she was immediately cleared and let go by Eljigidei (Rashīd al-Dīn, *Jāmi'*, 673, trans. Thackston, 330, trans. Boyle, 65–6). Rashīd al-Dīn and Juvaynī do not mention Al Altan in relation to Ögedei's demise at all, although Rashīd al-Dīn does mention the alcoholism in *Jāmi'*, 673, trans. Thackston, 330, trans. Boyle, 65; also Juvaynī, *World-Conqueror*, 200; Allsen, "Alcohol," 3–6.

second poison charge – leveled against Al Altan – proceed. The situation begs the question of whether Eljigidei knew of a plot against Al Altan. If he did, it would explain his speed in exonerating Ibaqa. Ultimately Eljigidei himself secretly executed Al Altan by an unknown method.[126] Eljigidei had been a follower of the Ögedeyids for years, and demonstrated it with his willingness to kill a Chinggisid, which put a mark on his head in the eyes of princes from other branches of the family. Thereafter Güyük gave Eljigidei a large army and appointed him as senior military commander in the western regions of Anatolia, Georgia, Diyarbakr, Aleppo, and Mosul.[127] This was a position of weighty responsibility, since Güyük needed Eljigidei to counter Jochid authority in the area and curb the commanders holding the Caucasus region.[128] It may also have allowed Güyük to reward Eljigidei for killing the princess while simultaneously removing him from the center of power and keeping the execution under wraps.[129]

But what was Al Altan's crime? Like the details of Temüge's trial, it has been suppressed. Here treason was surely not a factor, for as a princess Al Altan was not in line to inherit: all she could do was help a son to the Uighur throne, not the Chinggisid one. Rather, the problem seems to have concerned Al Altan's link to the Uighurs or residency among them, since the Persian historians went to extraordinary lengths to obscure her connections to them. They thus claimed variously that she never married the *iduqut* Barchuk despite promises made, or even that she wedded into Hö'elün's family among the distant Olqunu'uts, not the Uighurs at all.[130] But according to Chinese and Mongolian sources, Al Altan did marry Barchuk, who lived as an honored son-in-law and valuable contributor to the conquests from the time of their wedding in 1211 until his death

[126] Rashīd al-Dīn, *Jāmi'*, 69, 735, trans. Thackston, 39, 361, trans. Boyle, 121.

[127] Rashīd al-Dīn dutifully lies about Al Altan's marriage and death when discussing her directly (Rashīd al-Dīn, *Jāmi'*, 162, 274, 302, 597–8, trans. Thackston, 87, 134, 147–8, 275, trans. Boyle, 198). Then he lets the execution slip out when addressing other topics likes Eljigidei (Rashīd al-Dīn, *Jāmi'*, 69, trans. Thackston, 39), or when quoting Möngke (Rashīd al-Dīn, *Jāmi'*, 735, trans. Thackston, 361, trans. Boyle, 121).

[128] Jackson, "Dissolution," 200, 215–19; Jackson, *Friar William*, 18; Paul Pelliot, "Les Mongols et la papauté," *Revue de l'Orient Chrétien*, XXIII (1922–3), 3–30; XXIV (1924), 225–335; XXVIII (1932), 117, 172–5; Allsen, *Mongol Imperialism*, 21–2; Juvaynī, *World-Conqueror*, 257; al-'Umarī, *Masālik*, 15–16 and trans. Lech, 100–1. For the counter-argument that the local commander, Baiju, was actually inimical to the Jochids see Hope, *Ilkhanate*, 95–7.

[129] Rashīd al-Dīn, *Jāmi'*, 69, 735, trans. Thackston, 39, 361, trans. Boyle, 121.

[130] See Chapter 4, footnote 46.

during Ögedei's reign.[131] Thereafter Barchuk was succeeded by a son, Kesmes (or Kishmayin; i.e., one of Al Altan's sons or stepsons[132]). Kesmes dutifully visited the ordo, was officially confirmed as *iduqut* and, as befitted his status as the son of an in-law (and of a princess if he was Al Altan's son), became a son-in-law himself by marrying a new Chinggisid lady.[133] At first glance, therefore, nothing here seemed worthy of obfuscation by the Persian historians.

Could Al Altan's "crime" have related to Uighur territory? As Tom Allsen has argued in his important article on the Uighurs, during the years of Chinggis Khan's conquests, Uighuria seems to have answered directly to the Grand Khan through its own ruler.[134] The realm was independent both from the Ögedeyids, whose lands lay to the northwest by the Emil and Qobaq Rivers, and the Chagatayids to the southwest toward Ferghana and Transoxiana. With both appanages, the Uighurs simply shared borders.[135] Furthermore, unlike in other regions in the twelve-teens and 1220s, including the neighboring areas controlled by the imperial sons-in-law of the Qarluqs, Uighur lands seem to have remained under the exclusive control of members of Barchuk's own family and administration.[136] Although Mongol resident officers (*darugha*s) otherwise maintained order and collected taxes across Central Asia and in North China in the 1220s, none appear to have been assigned to Uighur lands.[137]

Under Ögedei, however, the status of Uighuria seems to have changed. After his accession in 1229, Ögedei established three regional secretariats. The one headed by the Khwarazmian Maḥmūd Yalavach in East and West Turkestan included Uighuria. Now Mongol resident officials began to appear in that region, and can be found collecting taxes from farmers who were subjects of the *iduqut*, as well as requisitioning animals for

[131] The marriage with Barchuk is clear in *Secret History*, §238; also Hambis, *Chapter CVIII*, Table 11, also 133 footnote 9, *Yuan shi*, 13:2757–61, Table of Imperial Princesses (unpublished trans. Buell).

[132] Kesmes or K-smay-n in Juvaynī, *World-Conqueror*, 47 and note 19; Kishmayīn in Rashīd al-Dīn, *Jāmi'*, 141, trans. Thackston, 76. He is Yügürülchi-digin in Hambis, *Chapter CVIII*, Table 11, also 133, footnote 10.

[133] Alajin Beki in Juvaynī, *World-Conqueror*, 47–8; Alajai Beki in Rashīd al-Dīn, *Jāmi'*, 141, trans. Thackston, 76.

[134] Allsen, "Uighurs of Turfan," 250.

[135] Allsen, "Uighurs of Turfan," 248–9, and notes 38 and 39, pointing out that Boyle twice left "borders" out of his translation of Juvaynī's *World-Conqueror*.

[136] Allsen, "Uighurs of Turfan," 251–2; Li, *Alchemist*, trans. Waley, 80–1, 83, 85–6 (the Mongol *darughachi* in Qarluq territory).

[137] Allsen, "Uighurs of Turfan," 251–2 and *Secret History*, §263, where Besh-Baliq is noteworthy for its absence, as Allsen points out.

Ögedei's armies.[138] We also know that at some point either Ögedei or Güyük (or both) appropriated territories for Köten in the Uighur capital itself, Besh-Baliq.[139] Thus, what appears to have been increasing imperial control over Uighur territory, taxes, and animals may well have adversely affected Al Altan and Barchuk's lands and heirs. Nor can it be an accident that the single paragraph in the *Secret History* enumerating the inheritance given to Chinggis Khan's daughters has been cut from the text, which scholars believe was a response to political events of the 1240s.[140] The appropriation of lands earmarked for Al Altan's descendants would make an excellent reason to excise information about all the princesses and their inheritance. This might also help explain the Persian historians' later failure to note the presence of princesses at the quriltai of 1246, and their heroic attempts to obscure Al Altan's marriage and connections to the Uighur ruling family.

From her presence at the fateful party we may deduce that Al Altan left her pleasant and fertile adopted realm in the Tarim river basin to return to the colder airs and waters of Mongolia while Ögedei was still alive. If it was Ögedei's closing grip on Uighur lands that was the trouble, Al Altan could have confronted him about it during her visit. Resisting Ögedei's will, and disputing a policy that strengthened the Ögedeyids at the expense of the Uighur consorts, might have been the criminal offense for which Al Altan suffered a hidden death. If Al Altan did speak to her brother, she probably could not have anticipated what followed, nor is it a given that Ögedei would necessarily have ordered her execution. But it was not Al Altan's mild-mannered sibling who trumped up the accusation of poison and engineered the secret execution, but rather her strong-willed sister-in-law and perhaps her stern nephew.

Despite the secrecy of the proceedings, Al Altan's death cast long shadows, and became a justification for the coup that overturned the Ögedeyid house during the next succession struggle (see Chapter 7). Nor did this purge necessarily end with Al Altan: Kesmes himself soon died of unknown causes, possibly while Al Altan was in custody, and it

[138] Allsen, "Uighurs of Turfan," 252 and notes 67–8, referring to Uighur administrative documents.

[139] Allsen, "Uighurs of Turfan," 249, and notes 42, 43.

[140] This was §215. De Rachewiltz, Commentary, 807; also xxix–xxxiv, suggesting that the section on Ögedei was probably written before 1246. If so, and if Ögedei had made inroads on Uighur territory, then this could support the possibility that Al Altan complained during his lifetime, which then resulted in the excision of the text to remove information about her territories, along with those of her sisters.

was Töregene who chose another son of Barchuk, Salindi, as the new *iduqut*.[141] Salindi consistently backed Ögedeyid policy, despite the family's treatment of Al Altan and their territorial encroachment. Later one of Güyük's daughters married into the Uighur ruling house.[142]

In addition to overseeing the executions of Chinggis Khan's youngest brother and favorite daughter, Güyük also rearranged the Chaghatayid house by deposing its ruler, a grandson, Qara-Hülegü, in favor of his own drinking companion and one of the two attendants who had led him to the throne, Chaghatai's son Yesü-Möngke, on the grounds that a son outranked a grandson.[143] He further moved quickly and mercilessly against two of his mother's officials, in what has been seen as an attempt to wrest control of both power and finance from her.[144] The first official was the central Asian financier 'Abd al-Raḥmān, who was executed, possibly in part to please the Jochids who opposed him and his policies.[145] The other was Fāṭimah, Töregene's chief advisor. This latter case brought Güyük into direct conflict with his mother.[146] Unlike the secret executions of Temüge and Al Altan, Fāṭimah's execution was prominent, public, and very ugly. Güyük was spurred on by the last wishes of his brother and former rival for the throne, Köten, who had been on such bad terms with Töregene. As previously mentioned and in direct contravention of Töregene's will, Köten had harbored the officials she had tried to kill, Chinqai and Maḥmūd Yalavach, both agents of regularized taxation plans, and both enemies of Fāṭimah's more extractive approach to finance. But Güyük took them into his own administration immediately upon assuming power, in an apparent return to his father's sometimes

141 Juvaynī, *World-Conqueror*, 48. In the *Yuan shi* he is Mamula [Tekin]; see Hambis, *Chapter CVIII*, Table 11, also 133, footnote 10.

142 This was Babagal (?), who married Barchuk's great-grandson, Quchar-[Tekin]. Another, Elmish or Yelmish, married Junbuqa or Kunbuqa from the Öng'üt consort family. *Yuan shi*, 13:2757–61 (unpublished trans., Buell); Hambis, *Chapter CVIII*, Table 11 and 133, footnote 10 (the Uighurs), also Table 3, 24–7 footnote 10 (the Öng'üts); also Zhao, *Marriage*, 156, 160.

143 Juvaynī, *World-Conqueror*, 251–2, 255, 273; Rashīd al-Dīn, *Jāmi'*, 760, trans. Thackston, 372, trans. Boyle, 143; also Bartol'd, *Turkestan*, 477, 480; Kim, "Güyüg," 328.

144 Hope, *Ilkhanate*, 66–8; De Nicola, email correspondence, June 2017.

145 Allsen, "Merchant Partners," 103; also Rashīd al-Dīn, *Jāmi'*, 807–8, trans. Thackston, 394.

146 Juvaynī, *World-Conqueror*, 244; also Rashīd al-Dīn, *Jāmi'*, 802, trans. Thackston, 391, trans. Boyle, 179.

progressive model of rule.[147] Then Köten, whose health had deteriorated enough that he was passed over at the quriltai, died mysteriously, believing he had been murdered by Fāṭimah's witchcraft. As a final request he urged Güyük to take vengeance. Chinqai pressed this point with Güyük until the Grand Khan acquiesced by demanding that Töregene surrender her advisor.[148] Although Töregene refused repeatedly, making up a new excuse each time, eventually Güyük sent a commander with orders not to leave without Fāṭimah, and at this point Töregene finally let her go.[149]

It must have been a dark time for both women, and rightly so: Fāṭimah was bound and starved, then questioned, tortured, and humiliated, after which her family and supporters were killed. She herself was executed with the distinctive method reserved for practitioners of witchcraft: her orifices were sewn up (perhaps to contain her spirit?), after which she was rolled in felt and cast into the cold running water of a river, most likely the Kerülen, to drown.[150] (See Figures 6.2 and 6.3.) This unusual method, in which water itself was defiled despite shamanistic taboos on such defilement, seems to have been used in order to contain the evil powers of a witch.[151]

As for Töregene: she had lost her intimate and closest advisor. The Persian historians' dismissals of Fāṭimah as corrupt and evil need not be taken entirely at face value. Although certainly Fāṭimah encouraged the rapacious Central Asian financiers more than the moderate forces within the empire, she must have worked very hard to help Töregene achieve her tremendous success in Güyük's coronation. Fāṭimah's death also showed Töregene that her own power had blown away like smoke, since she could not even protect her favorite from the displeasure of the son she had just spent five years striving to enthrone. Either that, or promoting Güyük had simply exhausted her. Töregene seems to have died only two or three months after the coronation,[152] on bad terms with her son,

[147] Kim, "Güyüg," 327. [148] Buell, "Chinqai," 108; Kim, "Güyüg," 327–8.

[149] Juvaynī, *World-Conqueror*, 245; Bar Hebraeus, *Chronography*, 411–12; also Rashīd al-Dīn, *Jāmi'*, 802–3, trans. Thackston, 391, trans. Boyle, 179.

[150] Allegedly her bodily orifices were sewn up and she was cast into a river [the Kelüren] to drown. Juvaynī, *World-Conqueror*, 245–6; Rashīd al-Dīn, *Jāmi'*, 802–3, trans. Thackston, 391, trans. Boyle, 179; Bar Hebraeus, *Chronography*, 411–12. Also De Nicola, *Khatuns*, 71, 187.

[151] I thank Tim May for his many useful email observations on this topic in October, 2016. May, discussing Oghul-Qaimish, "Commercial Queens," (unpublished article), 10–12.

[152] Juvaynī, *World-Conqueror*, 244; Rashīd al-Dīn, *Jāmi'*, 802, trans. Thackston, 391, trans. Boyle, 179; Bar Hebraeus, *Chronography*, 412. By contrast, Qu Yihao of Fudan University suggests that Töregene lived considerably longer than this in "Who Will Be

Figure 6.2 The Kerülen River (author's image).

probably broken-hearted about Fāṭimah and possibly afraid of the Grand Khan she had created.

CONCLUSION

After Chinggis Khan's death in 1227, imperial women continued to participate in the military expansion of the empire and in daily government, politics, and society, but the historical record of these contributions is often scanty. Only in the 1240s with the regency of Töregene did a real picture emerge showing the authority a woman might wield, and the power she could have to shape politics and rule. As this chapter has shown, Töregene's story was marked by long, patient struggle to overcome her initial disadvantages as a junior wife, very hard work – under wraps – as senior wife, and even harder but more public work as regent,

Remembered as a Princess? A Comparative Study on the Princesses of Chinggizid [sic] Recorded in the *Shu'āb-i Panjganah* and the 'Table of Princesses' of *Yuanshi*," at the Migrations in Mongol Eurasia Conference at The Hebrew University of Jerusalem, December 18–20, 2017.

Figure 6.3 The Onon River (author's image).

which culminated in her successful enthronement of Güyük and her subsequent rapid and bitter loss of power, influence, health, and life. Set in contrast to Töregene's largely successful story are those of the Chinggisids she helped destroy: possibly her alcoholic husband and his widow, Möge; her sister-in-law, Al Altan; her husband's uncle, Temüge; and perhaps even, indirectly, her second son, Köten. The historical record has not been kind to Töregene, but the gripings of the biased historians who wrote for her Toluid successors must not obscure her unquestionable talent, determination, clear sight and ambition. Her achievements must also be set against the troubles of the times: financial strain on the empire as a whole, political struggles between the Ögedeyids and the Jochids, and the ramifications of Ögedei's unpopular policies on taxes, territory, and people. Finally, it was during Töregene's regency that Chinggisid succession first showed its nightmarish potential for division and destruction, thus Töregene's victory in bending succession to her will, even at tremendous cost to the cohesion of the empire, must be remembered as an accomplishment.

7

Sorqoqtani and Oghul-Qaimish

As if the ugly succession struggle of the early 1240s had not been enough, another, worse such tangle emerged following Güyük's death in 1248, less than two years after his accession. The contest highlighted the activities of two more widows, Güyük's wife Oghul-Qaimish and Tolui's widow Sorqoqtani, who were set in opposition to one another. This chapter traces the reasons for the powers and weaknesses of each widow, and charts the intricacies of the struggle in which they starred. Both can be considered conquered women, with the limitations that that implies, even though this was largely obscured by the standing and wealth they achieved through marriage and, in Sorqoqtani's case, a long widowhood. During their contest, Oghul-Qaimish presided as regent over a tumultuous period marked by economic instability and political unrest, yet ultimately lost her position, family, and life. Unfortunately she has been so badly maligned by the historical sources that very little can be truly know about her, including her hideous fate. By contrast, her opponent, Sorqoqtani, was lauded by historians and contemporaries alike, yet was, ironically, by far the more destructive of the two. It was Sorqoqtani's plotting with her son Möngke and nephew Batu that led to the coup that set Möngke in power in 1251, followed by the political division of the empire and the ghastly purges of the Ögedeyid and Chaghatayid families. Thereafter Möngke revisited one of Güyük's own purges – the execution of Princess Al Altan – in an effort to correct an injustice. Although the coup and the purges are very well known, this chapter is the first to focus exclusively on the women involved, and to reveal the way their status, resources, and abilities critically shaped these important political events.

THE REGENT AND THE KHANMAKERS: OGHUL-QAIMISH VERSUS SORQOQTANI AND BATU

In spring 1248 Güyük was heading for his personal lands near the Emil River in Jungharia, allegedly to enjoy a pleasant tour of his patrimony, but according to some scholars, in reality to spring an invasion of the lands of his cousin, Batu.[1] Unbeknownst to Güyük's court, however, Tolui's widow Sorqoqtani had already engaged in treason by sending a messenger to Batu with news of the imperial armies' approach, which allowed him to muster his own men and come east toward the Grand Khan, rather than be caught unawares with his forces scattered.[2] But after Güyük's sudden, possibly alcohol-related death in spring 1248 before the two armies could meet, both Batu and Sorqoqtani hid their treachery a little longer and wrote to Güyük's senior widow, Oghul-Qaimish, with condolences, advice, gifts of clothing, and, from Sorqoqtani, a headdress, as well as the logical suggestion that Oghul-Qaimish take over the empire as regent for one of her sons, albeit with the help of the minister Chinqai, the arbitrator Qadaq, and the secretary, Bala, until the next quriltai could be called.[3]

But who was this regent, Oghul-Qaimish? She appeared in the histories largely after Güyük's death, and little is known of her before that. Unfortunately the scant ink spilled about Oghul-Qaimish has only discredited her in the extreme, making a clear understanding of her nigh impossible to achieve.[4] Certainly her regency was just as tumultuous as that of her mother-in-law, but far less successful: whereas Töregene achieved her goals, albeit at great personal cost, Oghul-Qaimish failed spectacularly to reach hers. Like Töregene, Oghul-Qaimish emerged from the ruined remnants of the Merkit people. Assuming that she married Güyük in the 1220s in her mid to late teens, she was likely born in the early twelve-aughts during the relentless persecution of all branches of the

1 For the complex personal, political, and geographical factors behind this campaign see Jackson, "Dissolution," 198–201; Allsen, *Mongol Imperialism*, 46. Hope, *Ilkhanate*, 70 does not believe Güyük meant to attack Batu; Kim, "Güyüg," 328–31, thinks that Güyüg planned to mount a general campaign to the west, and may have intended to attack Batu during that campaign.

2 Rashīd al-Dīn, *Jāmi'*, 809, trans. Thackston, 395, trans. Boyle, 185.

3 Juvaynī, *World-Conqueror*, 262–3; Rashīd al-Dīn, *Jāmi'*, 810, trans. Thackston, 395, trans. Boyle, 185–6; also Allsen, "North China," 389; Buell, "Čingai," in *Service*, 108; De Nicola, *Khatuns*, 54, 56, 74, noting that Töregene was the first female regent in Mongol society.

4 See the apt lament of De Nicola, *Khatuns*, 75.

Merkits, which lasted until its bloody conclusion in 1218.[5] Oghul-Qaimish therefore probably entered the Chinggisid family without some of the useful connections provided by a natal family, just as Töregene had. In other words, Oghul-Qaimish's mother or sisters may have been alive, but there is no evidence that she had brothers to appoint in her husband's armies, who could have eventually provided nieces and nephews for her to marry with her own offspring; furthermore, the Merkit subjects (those who remained alive) were dispersed among the Mongols. Unlike Töregene, Oghul-Qaimish did enjoy immediate status as senior wife, rather than working up to that position through childbearing and the convenient deaths of rivals as Töregene had done. As for fertility: Oghul-Qaimish produced two sons, Qucha and Naqu, but it is unknown whether she was also the mother of any of Güyük's three known daughters: Elmish, Babaqan (?), and an unnamed third.[6]

In the Toluid house, Oghul-Qaimish's rival, the Nestorian Christian Sorqoqtani and mother of four sons (and possibly a daughter), was also technically a conquered woman, but of a far different sort from the Ögedeyid wives.[7] True, like Töregene and Oghul-Qaimish, Sorqoqtani had first entered the Golden Lineage shortly after the conquest and dismemberment of the Kereit people and the death of its leader, her uncle Ong Qan. But unlike the Merkits, the Kereits were treated relatively leniently: although they were distributed among the Mongols, the families were allowed to remain intact, and most men stayed alive. Furthermore, Ong Khan's brother and Sorqoqtani's father, Jaqa Gambu, actually joined Chinggis Khan as a trusted ally in 1204, which allowed three of his daughters to make less violent marriages into the imperial family, complete with at least dowries and possibly bride prices, rather than enduring forced marriages as part of the spoils.[8] Sorqoqtani was one of these princesses, and became the senior wife of Tolui, who was then perhaps nine years old.[9] Sorqoqtani brought with her a full entourage of servants, wagons of goods, and livestock, as well

5 Buell, "Expansion," 9–16, 23–6; May, *War*, 15.

6 Or Babaqal? See *Yuan Shi*, 2757–61 (unpublished trans. Buell), for her and for Elmish; see Rashīd al-Dīn, *Jāmi'*, 101–2, trans. Thackston, 56 (the unnamed daughter); also footnote 35 of this chapter and footnote 142 of Chapter 6.

7 Rashīd al-Dīn, *Jāmi'*, 969, trans. Thackston, 471, albeit claiming five sons (sic).

8 *Secret History*, §208 (the dowry); Togan, *Flexibility and Limitation*, 100–6 (the alliance); also Atwood, "Ja'a Gambo," 164–70.

9 See Chapter 2 for his possible birth year of 1192 or 1193.

as the company of her cousin, Dokuz, who married Tolui as a junior wife.[10] At the same time Sorqoqtani's sisters Begtütmish and Ibaqa married Jochi and Chinggis Khan.[11] In addition, some Kereit princes were allowed to live, and later worked as military officers in the Chinggisid armies, which permitted the eventual rise of a Kereit consort clan throughout the empire and in the successor khanates.[12] Even after the death of Sorqoqtani's father Jaqa Gambu in 1204, the network of Kereit princesses and princes remained intact, despite the fact that their most senior princes were dead. This then accounts for Sorqoqtani's peculiar status: her marriage resembled those of Börte and the senior princesses, complete with negotiations, ceremonies, and gifts, but most of the Kereit people had themselves been conquered and were scattered among the Mongols, making Sorqoqtani into a kind of conquered woman, albeit one with advantages that neither Töregene or Oghul-Qaimish enjoyed.

Tolui's early death in 1233 opened many doors for his widow, even as it weakened his house overall. First, Sorqoqtani possessed the diplomatic skill to refuse Ögedei's proposal of a levirate marriage with Güyük without causing offence.[13] This was a critical victory for her, and an exception to the rule for widows. Had Sorqoqtani married again, she would have been thrown into regular contact with Oghul-Qaimish, and she would have lost the privacy she needed to plan and execute her treasons. Her sons would have been in an untenable position as well: Güyük's grown cousins (and, until his crowning, equals) suddenly living as his stepsons. Sorqoqtani's ability to remain single was an essential element in her ability to plot.

Financial stability further added to Sorqoqtani's powers. From 1236 on Sorqoqtani lived in Northern China, after gaining an appanage there from Ögedei.[14] Like other imperial wives, she had her hand in trade. She must have been among those imperial family members who invested in the disastrous merchant caravan that was wiped out at Otrar in 1218, and surely participated in other, more successful ventures as well.[15] She is

10 See Chapter 8. 11 See Chapter 3. 12 See Chapter 8.

13 Rashīd al-Dīn, *Jāmi'*, 792, trans. Thackston, 387 trans. Boyle, 169; also De Nicola, *Khatuns*, 73.

14 *Yuan Shi*, trans. Abramowski, "Ögödei und Güyük," 131–2; Rossabi, "Women," 161.

15 One such was in 1234, for which see Allsen, "Merchant Partners," 94, 117, also 87–92 (for Otrar).

known to have sent out commercial ventures on her own initiative.[16] Eventually she convinced Ögedei to grant her access to a particularly skilled merchant investor (*ortaq*) despite his initial hesitation.[17] As Tolui's senior widow she also maintained agents to help administer the empire, which included collecting the portion of tax revenue that was the right of Tolui's house.[18] This allowed Sorqoqtani to live quietly in her appanage, ably managing her property and people.[19] With the monies she gathered from her own subjects, from empirewide taxes and from trade, she was able to provide the gifts with which she achieved her political ends.[20] Later, after the accession of her son, she was equally lavish in donations to religious foundations.[21]

It was from this secure base that Sorqoqtani could call on a network of people whenever she wanted information, advice, or support. This network included Dokuz, possibly in the same camp, and Ibaqa, who also lived in Northern China.[22] At the same time and despite the distance, Sorqoqtani maintained strong ties with the Jochids, perhaps aided by her other sister, Begtütmish. However Begtütmish bore no children (or none who lived), and so Jochi's senior sons, Batu and Orda, came from two Qonggirat mothers (see Chapter 8). Therefore Sorqoqtani took care to forge a strong relationship with her nephew Batu, who became her chief co-conspirator.

16 See Rashīd al-Dīn, *Jāmiʿ*, 77, trans. Thackston, 43, for a failed expedition to exploit Tatar silver; also Abū al-Ghāzī, *Shajarah-yi Türk*, 44, trans. Desmaisons, 45; and De Nicola, *Khatuns*, 147.

17 Rashīd al-Dīn claimed that she did this by manipulating Ögedei's grief and guilt over Tolui's death. It is hard to discern whether this actually happened, or whether Rashīd al-Dīn was employing tropes of women as manipulative, even though he wrote positively about all her skills. Rashīd al-Dīn, *Jāmiʿ*, 791, trans. Thackston, 386, trans. Boyle, 168; Allsen, "Merchant Partners," 116; De Nicola, *Khatuns*, 147.

18 Allsen, "Guard and Government," 502–3 and note 15; for her representatives in Khurasan see Juvaynī, *World-Conqueror*, 483, 519; in Rashīd al-Dīn, *Jāmiʿ*, 856, trans. Thackston, 417, Sorqoqtani Beki has surprisingly been replaced by "Negübai," but Sorqoqtani appears as herself in trans. Boyle, 231.

19 It has been suggested that her mother could have been the Tangut princess whom Jaqa Gambu married, from whom Sorqoqtani could have learned how to administer settled peoples, but the paucity of evidence forces us to leave this as conjecture. Togan, *Flexibility and Limitation*, 77, note 108.

20 Juvaynī, *World-Conqueror*, 550–3; Rashīd al-Dīn, *Jāmiʿ*, 791–4, 823, trans. Thackston, 386–7, 401, trans. Boyle, 168–70, 199–200.

21 For her famous donation of cash to construct an Islamic complex in Bukhara see De Nicola, *Khatuns*, 211, with references. For the timing see Juvaynī, *World-Conqueror*, 552; Rashīd al-Dīn, *Jāmiʿ*, 823, trans. Thackston, 401, trans. Boyle, 200.

22 Rashīd al-Dīn, *Jāmiʿ*, 673, trans. Thackston, 330, trans. Boyle, 66.

Sorqoqtani is also known to have been on good terms with her four sons (and perhaps her daughter[23]), which must have helped as she contemplated raising the family from its status as a junior house within the Golden Lineage.[24] That said, the historical description of her single-minded, devoted motherhood should be taken with a grain of salt, since like her contemporaries, Sorqoqtani shared the education and training of her children with others, including wet nurses, tutors, and staff, and even other imperial ladies like Ögedei's wife Anghui, who fostered Möngke for some years.[25] But Sorqoqtani is likely to have arranged many of her children's marriages, which provided useful connections to important consort clans. Chief among them were the Oirats, from whom Tolui himself had gained a wife, who then married Möngke through the levirate.[26] The Toluids forged strong new ties with the Oirats when two of Princess Checheyigen's daughters, Elchiqmish and Güyük Khatun,[27] married Sorqoqtani's sons Arik Böke and Hülegü as senior wives. Checheyigen's third daughter, Orqīna, did the same for Qara-Hülegü of the Chaghatayids and became the Toluids' loyal ally after Güyük's demotion of her husband in 1246, and the fourth daughter married into the Jochids.[28] Other marriage ties connected the Toluids to the Qonggirats, especially Börte's descendants, and to the Ikires in-law lineage, whose matriarch was Börte's oldest daughter, Princess Qojin.[29] (See Family Tree 7.1.)

By contrast, Töregene and Oghul-Qaimish turned to networks of outsiders for advice and help. In Töregene's case as shown in Chapter 6, her chief advisors were Central Asian Muslim financiers, while Oghul-Qaimish

[23] Rashīd al-Dīn, *Jāmi'*, 969, trans. Thackston, 471.

[24] Rashīd al-Dīn, *Jāmi'*, 791–2, trans. Thackston, 386, trans. Boyle, 169; also Juvaynī, *World-Conqueror*, 551.

[25] Anghui or Alghui. *Yuan Shi*, 17:43 (unpublished trans. Buell); and *Yuan Shi*, trans. Abramowski, "Möngke," 16; also de Rachewiltz, "Sixth Empress," 73. For Sorqoqtani's proposed (Naiman) and actual (Tangut) wet nurses for Qubilai see De Nicola, "Domestic Sphere," 360. For tutors see Rossabi, "Women," 161.

[26] This was Oghul-Qaimish, a daughter of Qutuqa Beki and one of Tolui's widows. See Chapter 4; also Zhao, *Marriage*, 137–8.

[27] Not to be confused with the Ögedeyid man Güyük the Grand Khan.

[28] See Chapter 8. For Orqīna and Qara-Hülegü's politics see De Nicola, *Khatuns*, 77.

[29] Qubilai's favored wife Chabi was Börte's niece (see Chapter 8). Hülegü and Ariq Böke had Qonggirat wives (Qutui and Qutlu). Möngke's senior wife was the Ikires Qutuqtai. Rashīd al-Dīn, *Jāmi'*, 820, 865–8, 940, 1056, trans. Thackston, 399, 422–3, 460, 515, trans. Boyle, 197–8, 241–5, 310–11 (not Hülegü). By contrast, the *Yuan Shi* names Möngke's wife (implied senior) as Qoricha of the Qorlat. *Yuan* Shi, 17:43 (unpublished trans. Buell); *Yuan Shi*, trans. Abramowski, "Möngke," 16.

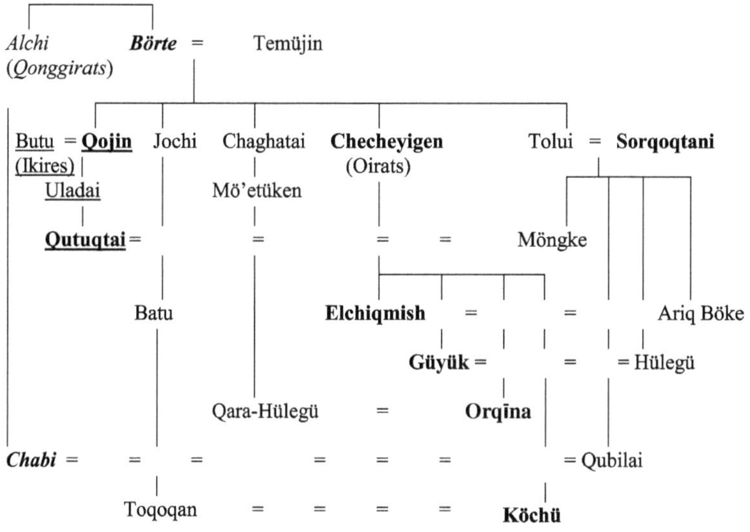

Family Tree 7.1 Toluid marital connections by the 1240s.
All women are in **bold.**
Qonggirats are in *italics.*
Ikires are underlined.

favored shamans.[30] Although this latter fell well within nomadic traditions – Möngke himself consulted shamans[31] – it is likely that Oghul-Qaimish's favoritism toward them played a role in Möngke's decision to execute her in 1251 as a witch, rather than as a mere traitor.[32]

But the Ögedeyid widows proved slightly more savvy in their choices of consorts than in their advisors. True, as a Merkit Oghul-Qaimish was a strategically poor choice for Güyük's senior wife, since the Merkit people and leadership had been so thoroughly dispersed in Chinggis Khan's campaigns of retribution. It is to be wondered whether Töregene chose Oghul-Qaimish because of her own former ties to the Merkits, and why she overlooked the many other consort families that could easily have provided more politically suitable young women to be the senior wife.

[30] Juvaynī, *World-Conqueror*, 265; Rashīd al-Dīn, *Jāmi'*, 810, trans. Thackston, 395, trans. Boyle, 186; Buell, "Činqai," 108.

[31] Igor de Rachewiltz, *Papal Envoys to the Great Khans* (London: Faber and Faber, 1971), 135.

[32] Juvaynī, *World-Conqueror*, 265; Rashīd al-Dīn, *Jāmi'*, 810, trans. Thackston, 395, trans. Boyle, 186. Möngke described her as a witch to Friar William. Rubruck, *Mission*, 249; also *Yuan Shi*, trans. Abramowski, "Möngke," 20.

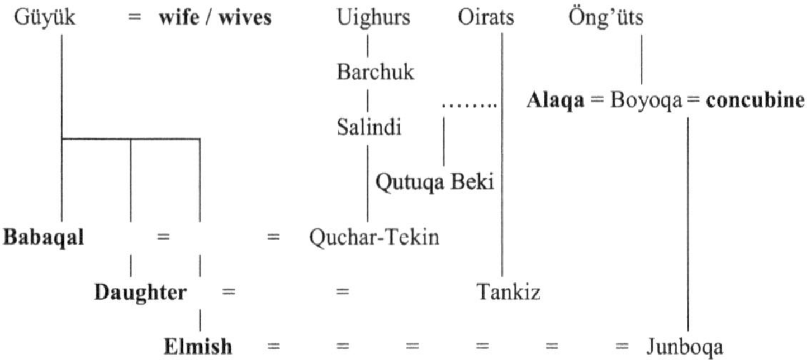

Family Tree 7.2 Marital connections of Güyük's daughters by the 1240s.
All women are in **bold.**
Dotted line indicates cousin or other relationship.

(As a point of contrast, the ever astute Sorqoqtani seems to have married only one of her sons to a Merkit woman, who may then actually have been demoted in rank in favor of a Qonggirat bride.)[33]

The marital connections of Güyük's children seem to have been stronger than those of Oghul-Qaimish. Although the histories tell us little about the strategic links that Qucha and Naqu made, we can at least be certain that Qucha in particular had several wives, probably from a variety of families.[34] But we do know that three of their sisters (or half-sisters) made useful strategic marriages: one into the Öng'üt offspring of Princess Alaqa, another into the Uighurs, and a third to a lesser man from the Oirat in-law family (i.e., not a son of Princess Checheyigen).[35] These marriages connected the Ögedeyids to three of the major consort clans descended from Börte's daughters (see Family Tree 7.2).

[33] This was Qoruqchin, niece of Toqtoa, who married Sorqoqtani's son Qubilai and bore a son, but was then demoted in favor of the Qonggirat Chabi, Börte's niece. Rashīd al-Dīn, *Jāmi'*, trans. Thackston, 422, trans. Boyle, 243.

[34] Rashīd al-Dīn, *Jāmi'*, 838, trans. Thackston, 408, trans. Boyle, 214.

[35] Güyük's daughter, Princess Elmish, married Boyoqa's son Junbuqa of the Öng'üts, while Princess Babagal (?) married the Uighur Barchuk's great-grandson, Quchar-Tekin. *Yuan Shi*, 10:2923–4, 13:2757–61 (unpublished trans., Buell); Hambis, *Chapter CVIII*, Table 11 and 133–4, note 10, albeit claiming that Babagal was Möngke's daughter (sic). The unnamed princess married Tankiz, a relative of the Oirat leader Qutuqa Beki but not a descendant of Checheyigen. Rashīd al-Dīn, *Jāmi'*, 101–2, trans. Thackston, 56; Zhao, *Marriages*, 134–5.

THE RUMP QURILTAI IN CENTRAL ASIA

After proposing Oghul-Qaimish as regent, Batu's next act was to call for a quriltai to discuss succession. Rather than set it in the region of the Kerülen and Onon rivers as tradition demanded, however, he summoned the Chinggisids to attend him two-thousand-odd miles (four thousand kilometers) away at Ala-Qamaq in Central Asia not far from Qayaliq, arguing variously that his gout, or the state of his horses, kept him from riding as far as the Mongol homeland.[36] Whatever they thought of the excuses or the location, some members of the Golden Lineage came or sent representatives. Other princes did not attend, among them Ögedei's overlooked heir, Shiremün, other Ögedeyids, and many Chaghatayids.[37] It is unrecorded whether the major princesses and their associated consort lineages were present, although they had the right to be.[38]

But certainly Sorqoqtani's sons attended. One historian suggested disingenuously that Sorqoqtani urged them to visit their cousin in his illness (the gout), and added moral force by commenting that the Chinggisids who failed to come at Batu's summons had in fact disrespected such a senior prince, so the Toluids, at least, did their duty by going.[39] This must be understood as retroactive whitewashing of what was actually a conspiracy, hatched among Sorqoqtani, Batu, and Möngke. There was no question that the Toluids had to travel to Central Asia, since they were there expressly to help usurp power from the Ögedeyids, and the whole purpose of the rump quriltai was to allow Batu to orchestrate a coup.

The question of whether or not Oghul-Qaimish and her sons attended the quriltai is surprisingly unclear. Some sources fail to mention their

[36] Juvaynī, *World-Conqueror*, 263 (Batu's horses were lean); Rashīd al-Dīn, *Jāmi'*, 824, trans. Thackston, 401 (gout).

[37] Jackson, "Dissolution," 203–4; Allsen, *Mongol Imperialism*, 23–5; Hope, *Ilkhanate*, 73–4; also Juvaynī, *World-Conqueror*, 263–4, 557–8; Rashīd al-Dīn, *Jāmi'*, 824–8, trans. Thackston, 401–3, trans. Boyle, 200–2; *Yuan Shi*, trans. Abramowski, "Möngke," 17.

[38] The list of those absent is those to whom Batu sent the results: Chinggis Khan's widows; the Ögedeyids, Sorqoqtani, and "other princes of the right and left hand." Rashīd al-Dīn, *Jāmi'*, 825, trans. Thackston, 402, trans. Boyle, 202. Neither Juvaynī nor Rashīd al-Dīn refers to the Chinggisid daughters and sons-in-law; the *Yuan Shi* is even less revealing. *Yuan Shi*, trans. Abramowski, "Möngke," 17.

[39] Rashīd al-Dīn, *Jāmi'*, 824, trans. Thackston, 401, trans. Boyle, 201. Allsen, *Mongol Imperialism*, 29, highlighting Sorqoqtani's influence.

whereabouts at all.[40] Rashīd al-Dīn claims that the sons merely sent a representative (i.e., rather than going in person), but this reads as an attempt to portray them as unsuitable for rule on the grounds that they had disrespected Batu (their elder) by failing to respond to his summons.[41] By contrast, Juvaynī allows that Qucha and Naqu did go to Batu, but stayed only briefly, then withdrew before the quriltai began with the excuse that the shamans had not authorized a longer sojourn, and left a representative, Temür Noyan, to speak for them.[42] Most sources also state or imply that Oghul-Qaimish did not attend the quriltai, except for the Syrian Christian author Bar Hebraeus, who specified that the regent did visit Batu with her sons, but only for the same brief period before departing prior to the actual quriltai.[43] She too was represented at it, albeit by her own man, the Uighur secretary, Bala.[44]

Additional questions surround the representatives and the instructions they received. Juvaynī claims that Temür Noyan was told to agree with the majority.[45] But was this true, or did Juvaynī assert this in order to criticize Qucha and Naqu in poetic detail for the inexperience of their youth when the majority chose something other than what they would have wanted? It cannot be doubted that Qucha and Naqu unwisely removed themselves from the critical decision-making arena of the assembled family and supporters at the precise moment when they might have advanced claims for themselves. Peter Jackson's theory that Naqu, at least, believed he had an assurance from Batu that his claim would prevail, seems probable.[46] Nevertheless it is likely that the sons would have instructed their representative more carefully;

[40] They do not appear in Kirakos of Ganjak, *Deux Historiens Arméniens: Kiracos de Gantzac, XIIIe S, Histoire d'Arménie; Oukhtanès D'Ourha, Xe siècle, Histoire En Trois Parties*, trans. M. Brosset (St. Petersburg, 1870), 172; Juzjānī, *Ṭabaqāt*, 2:176; *into Islam,* by trans. Raverty 1172.

[41] Rashīd al-Dīn, *Jāmi'*, 824, trans. Thackston, 401, trans. Boyle, 200.

[42] Juvaynī, *World-Conqueror*, 263–4, 558; also Jackson, "Dissolution," 203–4.

[43] Bar Hebraeus, *Chronography*, 416.

[44] *Yuan Shi*, trans. Abramowski, "Möngke," 17. For a translation and analysis see Allsen, *Mongol Imperialism*, 24. Elsewhere the *Yuan Shi* garbles a report about Oghul-Qaimish attending a gathering with Batu where succession was discussed, but she came too late because the matter had already been decided. *Yuan Shi*, 11:2979 (unpublished trans. Buell).

[45] Juvaynī, *World-Conqueror*, 558.

[46] Jackson, "Dissolution," 203–4.

Juvayni's claim reads as too facile a way of blaming Qucha and Naqu for their later reversals.[47]

By contrast, Oghul-Qaimish's representative Bala was under clearer instructions, and spoke up strongly in open assembly in favor of the Ögedeyids. But even here, too, mysteries abound. Bala is said to have proposed Shiremün as a candidate, not one of Oghul-Qaimish's sons.[48] If true, this would certainly explain Oghul-Qaimish's close relations with Shiremün's family, and the poor relations that later developed between her and her own sons. But another source claims that the candidate from the regent's court was Qucha, not Shiremün.[49] Which was it, really? In any case, it is an open question whether Oghul-Qaimish or her sons, or Shiremün, could have prevailed even if they had been there, since Batu, Sorqoqtani, and Möngke seem to have agreed beforehand to divide the Mongol Empire into two halves: Batu and the Jochids would command the west; Möngke and the Toluids would rule the east; and the cousins would agree to a partnership, with Möngke holding the title of Grand Khan.[50]

The arguments advanced at the quriltai to justify the political upheaval were numerous. Some argued that Batu's seniority among the princes gave him a strong claim to rule as Grand Khan.[51] But Batu countered this proposal by suggesting that the geographical spread of the empire mitigated against a single sovereign, in favor of two rulers working in cooperation.[52] The arguments attributed to Batu in favor of Möngke as co-ruler were numerous. On the milder end, Batu is said to have argued that Möngke was mature, intelligent, and brave, and had successfully led troops in the campaign to Central Asia and Russia in 1236–42.[53] A less clear argument was also advanced about Möngke being the son of Tolui, who had inherited Chinggis Khan's encampment according to tradition (which perhaps implied that Möngke therefore deserved Chinggis Khan's empire as well?).[54] In response, Oghul-Qaimish's deputy Bala spoke

47 Juvaynī, *World-Conqueror*, 265, 266; Rashīd al-Dīn, *Jāmi'*, 810, trans. Thackston, 395, trans. Boyle, 186.

48 *Yuan Shi*, trans. Abramowski, "Möngke," 17; Allsen, *Mongol Imperialism*, 24.

49 Kirakos, *Histoire*, trans. Brosset, 172.

50 Allsen, *Mongol Imperialism*, 54–61; Jackson, "Dissolution," 207–8.

51 Juzjānī, *Ṭabaqāt*, 2:179, trans. Raverty, 1177–81; Kirakos, *Histoire*, trans. Brosset, 172; al-'Umarī, *Masālik*, 10–13, trans. Lech, 101.

52 Juzjānī, *Ṭabaqāt*, 2:178–9, trans. Raverty, 1177–81.

53 Rashīd al-Dīn, *Jāmi'*, 824–5, trans. Thackston, 401–2, trans. Boyle, 201–2, and briefly, Juvaynī, *World-Conqueror*, 560.

54 Rashīd al-Dīn, *Jāmi'*, 825, trans. Thackston, 402, trans. Boyle, 202; Bartol'd, *Turkestan*, 479, saw this claim as illogical, since although Tolui inherited by virtue of being Chinggis

against Möngke and argued that Shiremün should be considered as Grand Khan since Ögedei had chosen him heir during his lifetime.[55] But a stern rebuke to Bala appeared either in Batu's mouth, or in the mouth of Möngke's half-brother Möge Oghul, and was far more inflammatory than any previous claims. This was the assertion that the Ögedeyids in general, or Töregene in particular, had already contravened Ögedei's will by passing over Shiremün in favor of Güyük, and therefore their house did not deserve to rule any longer.[56] Allegedly this silenced Bala at the quriltai.[57]

But the most incendiary accusation made against the Ögedeyids was that their house was unfit for rule because it had broken custom and law (*yasa* and *yosun*) by unjustly executing Chinggis Khan's favorite daughter, Al Altan, without consulting the rest of the family.[58] It is to be wondered whether Batu advanced the idea of unlawful execution in the public arena of the quriltai, or circulated it through private conversations. But this concept did emerge thereafter in justifications for the Toluid takeover.[59] Furthermore, the Toluids' own later behavior suggests that they accepted all of these ideas, including the injustice of Al Altan's death, as legitimate foundations for their actions (see the subsequent discussion).

Indeed, Möngke's legitimacy ultimately came to rest on four major pillars. First was that proper procedure, especially in consulting all family members, was being followed, unlike in the case of Töregene, who had ignored dissent over her promotion of Güyük. Second was that Möngke in particular and the Toluids in general had always upheld the laws (*yasa* and *yosun*) of Chinggis Khan, unlike both Töregene, who had contravened Ögedei's will by supplanting his chosen heir, and the Ögedeyid

Khan's youngest son, Möngke was the oldest and could not make the same claim. Bartol'd suggests that it makes more sense if it indicates that Möngke inherited because Tolui was the closest to his father during his lifetime. Michael Hope sees this as a Toluid attempt to highlight their family knowledge of Chinggis Khan's traditions and thereby counter the commanders who claimed similar knowledge of the founder in *Ilkhanate*, 83–4.

[55] *Yuan Shi*, trans. Abramowski, "Möngke," 17.

[56] For this point in Batu's mouth see Rashīd al-Dīn, *Jāmi'*, 825, trans. Thackston, 402, trans. Boyle, 201. For the same point but now from Möge see *Yuan Shi*, trans. Abramowski, "Möngke," 17. Allsen, *Mongol Imperialism*, 24, notes that Qubilai and Menggeser similarly advanced this argument at other moments; also Hope, *Ilkhanate*, 85–6.

[57] *Yuan Shi*, trans. Abramowski, "Möngke," 17; Allsen, *Mongol Imperialism*, 24.

[58] Rashīd al-Dīn, *Jāmi'*, 735, trans. Thackston, 361, trans. Boyle, 121. No similar argument has emerged about the other Chinggisid executed in Güyük's purges, Temüge.

[59] Rashīd al-Dīn, *Jāmi'*, 69, 735, trans. Thackston, 39, 361, trans. Boyle, 121.

family, which had killed Al Altan unlawfully. Third, Chinggis Khan had believed that rule could move outside the Ögedeyid house if need be, in contrast to Ögedeyid beliefs that rule was theirs alone. Fourth, like Chinggis Khan, Möngke had been favored by the Enduring Blue Sky in a series of fortunate events and lucky breaks during his campaigning days.[60]

As was only proper, Möngke modestly refused the nomination, and had to be persuaded to accept it for the good of the empire by the same half-brother, Möge.[61] Thereafter those assembled swore him allegiance as Grand Khan (and presumably acknowledged Batu's rule in the west), promised to hold another quriltai as soon as possible at Köde'ü Aral, situated in its vast plain extending to the Kerülen River in Mongolia, and departed for their homes to prepare for it. Batu himself sent out announcements that the rump quriltai had agreed on Möngke as Grand Khan, and provided fresh invitations to a new coronation quriltai in Mongolia. This must have shocked those who had stayed away, including Oghul-Qaimish and her sons in the royal encampment on the Emil.[62]

MANEUVERING

With this news Oghul-Qaimish found her regency on shaky ground, since no Ögedeyid would rule if Batu and Sorqoqtani had their way. Oghul-Qaimish's challenge was similar to what Töregene had faced: simultaneously to administer what she had inherited, and to promote an unpopular candidate for the grand khanate in competition with a recognized rival. But whereas Töregene had diverted the wealth of the empire toward pushing Güyük into Shiremün's place, Oghul-Qaimish was not nearly as successful. Neither of her sons emerged as a distinct candidate for Grand Khan, and, as mentioned, it is even unclear which of them Oghul-Qaimish herself favored, if she even did so in addition to her support of Shiremün. Family trouble further complicated matters, since at some point Qucha and Naqu each formed their own courts in competition with that of their mother.[63]

60 Allsen, *Mongol Imperialism*, 34–44; for a measured response to this passage see Hope, *Ilkhanate*, 81–90. Neither discusses Al Altan.

61 Juvaynī, *World-Conqueror*, 561; Rashīd al-Dīn, *Jāmi'*, 826, trans. Thackston, 402, trans. Boyle, 202.

62 Jackson, "Dissolution," 204.

63 Juvaynī, *World-Conqueror*, 265; Rashīd al-Dīn, *Jāmi'*, 810, trans. Thackston, 395, trans. Boyle, 186; also Allsen, "North China," 390; Hope, *Ilkhanate*, 72.

Nor does evidence suggest that Oghul-Qaimish managed to harness wealth to her own purposes, in marked contrast to the savvy, prudent, and financially able Sorqoqtani.[64] One source implies a lack of firm administration after Güyük's death, since "the court did not establish a lord for a long time."[65] Möngke's opinion of Oghul-Qaimish was extremely low, as he later told Friar William: "But as for knowing the business of war and the affairs of peace, subduing the wide world and discerning how to act for the best – what could that worthless woman, lower than a bitch, have known of this?"[66] Additional complaints about the regent's poor administration from the pro-Toluid historians were legion. Although their views must be taken with a grain of salt since they had to justify the Toluid takeover, these men were nevertheless professional bureaucrats, and thus knew precisely what running an empire should mean.

In theory the resources Oghul-Qaimish commanded were those of the entire empire, and thus should have been substantially greater than what her rivals enjoyed. They included the standard access to investment with merchant partners that all imperial figures enjoyed, additional access to merchants in her role as regent, and the empowering benefits of empire-wide tax revenue. But the challenges Oghul-Qaimish faced were also several, and she does not give any sign of having risen to them well. One problem was with the very same merchants: Güyük and his ministers had negotiated trade agreements during his reign, funded initially with drafts on various regions of the empire. After Güyük's sudden death, most of these drafts remained unpaid. When Oghul-Qaimish assumed the regency, she continued to conduct transactions with merchants on the basis of drafts, rather than actual payments, as did her sons, and other Ögedeyids like Shiremün.[67] Although these interactions suggested that Oghul-Qaimish was receiving supplies, the payment side of the transaction was a growing problem, and imperial debts reached monstrous proportions.[68] This contrasted sharply with Sorqoqtani's years' worth of experience dealing with her personal merchants.

[64] A comparison with Batu's style of administration would be useful, if the sources permitted.

[65] *Yuan Shi*, 17:43 (unpublished trans. Buell).

[66] Rubruck, *Mission*, 249.

[67] Juvaynī, *World-Conqueror*, 603; Rashīd al-Dīn, *Jāmi'*, 846, trans. Thackston, 412, trans. Boyle, 221; see also Allsen, "North China," 388 and "Merchant Partners," 103–5; De Nicola, *Khatuns*, 147–8.

[68] Allsen, "Merchant Partners," 108, 121.

Tax collection was a second headache, and another area in which Oghul-Qaimish compared unfavorably to Sorqoqtani. Oghul-Qaimish is said to have sent out increasing numbers of tax collectors during her regency, which implies that she was short on funds. She also is reported to have dispatched emergency distributions of money to regions within the empire on an irregular basis, which surely added to her demands for cash.[69] But the taxable populace, especially farmers, were becoming increasingly unable to pay with the crops they could produce in a single growing season.[70] Even nomads were pressured, as when in 1250 Oghul-Qaimish drastically raised taxes on horses, perhaps as an unsuccessful remedy for her shortfall.[71] Again in clear distinction to the regent's troubles, Sorqoqtani's record of tax collection was stellar (and lauded by the historians), although to be fair, much of this was in a much smaller, manageable appanage, not a gigantic, unwieldy empire.[72]

Oghul-Qaimish's cash flow problems were then exacerbated by the activities of others. Some were loyal to her house, like the general Eljigidei, whose requisitioning in Iran for the armies he intended to use against Jochid agents in Anatolia severely oppressed taxpayers.[73] The trouble was compounded by other members of the Golden Lineage, who everywhere became prone to demanding their own funds from the helpless populace. The final complaint of the pro-Toluid historians about Oghul-Qaimish was her method of solving her problems by turning to the shamans for help, and passing over the advice of her administrators, including the able and experienced minister Chinqai.[74]

In addition to struggling with finances, Oghul-Qaimish sought to bolster her shaky political position through diplomacy. To this end she received an embassy from the French King Louis IX (r. 1226–70), which had been sent to Güyük.[75] Oghul-Qaimish welcomed the ambassadors

[69] Juvaynī, *World-Conqueror*, 264–5, 512, 556.

[70] Juvaynī, *World-Conqueror*, 599; Rashīd al-Dīn, *Jāmi'*, 844, trans. Thackston, 411, trans. Boyle, 219.

[71] She raised it from one in a hundred horses to one in ten. Allsen, "North China," 390.

[72] Juvaynī, *World-Conqueror*, 551; Rashīd al-Dīn, *Jāmi'*, 822, trans. Thackston, 401, trans. Boyle, 219.

[73] Juvaynī, *World-Conqueror*, 512.

[74] Juvaynī, *World-Conqueror*, 265; Buell, "Činqai," 108. De Nicola points out that Rashīd al-Dīn may have been critiquing shamanism for purposes of supporting Gazan's conversion to Islam in the Ilkhanate. Email correspondence, June 2017.

[75] Denis Sinor, "The Mongols and Western Europe," in *A History of the Crusades, Vol. III: The Fourteenth and Fifteenth Centuries*, ed. Harry W. Hazard and Kenneth M. Setton (Madison: The University of Wisconsin Press), reprint, 1977 in *Inner Asia and Its*

at the court on the Emil, and accepted King Louis's gift of a sumptuous, highly decorated tent-chapel of scarlet cloth as an indication of the French king's submission to Mongol rule. Although this was not at all what he had intended, she took advantage of the occasion and the showy presents to assert herself as a sovereign, and sent the embassy back with her own envoys, a letter demanding that Louis confirm his submission to her, and gifts including brocade.[76]

But despite this and perhaps other such bold diplomatic shows, and despite her attempts to administer her territories or at least extract useful wealth from them through tax-collection, Oghul-Qaimish ultimately failed at the most important task of all: to summon a quriltai of her own. Because the rump assembly was not in the heartland, and furthermore had failed to attract a full complement of Chinggisids, Batu had closed it by calling for the second, coronation gathering in the proper location in Mongolia. This put Oghul-Qaimish in the unenviable position of scrambling to react to Batu's call rather than actively working to establish her own convention. Perhaps a more skilled tactician and strategist would have successfully organized a counterassembly, as was the case ten years later when competing quriltais were held in the same year in Mongolia and China, but Oghul-Qaimish did not manage any such thing.[77] Instead, she and those Chinggisids unhappy with the coup simply worked to delay the new quriltai as Batu had once delayed Töregene.[78] This set up a period of stalemate, which Batu and Sorqoqtani countered with tremendous outpourings of diplomacy, gifts, and threats.[79] This time the dawdling worked for well over a year.

Contacts with Medieval Europe (London: Variorum), 523–4. The embassy first passed through the court of Eljigidei, who had previously corresponded with Louis, but in the uncertain times after the rump quriltai he simply sent the diplomats on to the Emil. Pelliot, "Papauté," 150–77 and 188–211.

[76] For her show of strength at home see de Rachewiltz, *Papal Envoys*, 123; Jackson, Introduction (to Rubruck, *Mission*), 36; also Joinville, "Life", trans. Smith, 266–7 (paragraph 473); and Joinville, *Histoire* 1965), 175. For the return trip and her ambassadors and message see Joinville, "Life" trans. Smith, 178, 262, 266–7, and Joinville, *Histoire*, 47, 168, 175. Note that Joinville describes Oghul-Qaimish as a king (sic). Also de Rachewiltz, *Papal Envoys*, 119–23; Paul Pelliot, "Papauté," 3–84; Jackson, Introduction, 30, 35–6, and Rubruck, *Mission*, 249, citing Möngke's letter to Louis IX.

[77] These were the quriltais of the brothers Qubilai and Ariq Böke in May and June 1260.

[78] Allsen, "North China," 390.

[79] Rashīd al-Dīn, *Jāmi'*, 826–7, trans. Thackston, 402–3, trans. Boyle, 203–4; Juvaynī, *World-Conqueror*, 562–3; see also Hope, *Ilkhanate*, 73.

Figure 7.1 The long plain at Köde'ü Aral (author's image).

THE CORONATION QURILTAI IN THE HEARTLAND

Finally the next act in Batu and Sorqoqtani's joint coup, the coronation quriltai, took place at the hallowed grounds at Köde'ü Aral by the Kerülen River, where the long plain easily accommodated large numbers of people and animals[80] (see Figure 7.1). The event took place in high summer 1251, when the weather was warm enough for parties, and mares were being milked again after spring foaling season, which led to the production of the qumiz needed for a celebration. The attendance at the coronation quriltai clearly demonstrated the fault lines within the empire's ruling echelon. As half of the usurping party, the Jochids were amply represented by Batu's brothers Berke and Toqa-Temür, and were further accompanied by a substantial army in case of need.[81] Unsurprisingly the other plotters, the Toluids, were there in entirety since their man

[80] On this location see Allsen, *Mongol Imperialism*, 25 and n. 26.

[81] The Jochid attendees did not include Orda; Allsen, "Left Hand," 15. For the army and attendees see Allsen, *Mongol Imperialism*, 25; Juvaynī, *World-Conqueror*, 568; Rashīd al-Dīn, *Jāmi'*, 826, 828, trans. Thackston, 402, 403, trans. Boyle, 202, 204.

was to ascend the throne. Other Chinggisids also attended, especially those who had no claim to succession. These included senior members of the family who had already been barred from imperial rule or regency, namely Chinggis Khan's nephews, and their mothers and step-mothers, the widows of Chinggis Khan's brothers and half-brothers.[82] Also in this category were the heirs of Kölgen, Chinggis Khan's son by his Merkit wife Qulan. Although Kölgen had proved himself an able commander, he had never been a prince in charge of a domain like Börte's sons; his heirs were similarly junior in the Golden Lineage, and they showed up compliantly in 1251. Various commanders and officials also came.[83]

It is probable that some of the major princesses and consort lineages attended as was their right, although the Persian historians do not mention them. But these families would have included the Ikires under Princess Qojin, the Qonggirats of Börte's lineage with Princess Tümelün as matriarch, to both of which families the Toluids were linked by marriage, as well as the Oirats and Princess Checheyigen, who seems herself to have been a long-standing ally, and whose daughters had married into the Toluid, Jochid, and Chaghatayid houses.[84] It is less clear whether the Öng'üts, descended from Princess Alaqa, would have come, since they had made an alliance with one of Güyük's daughters; similarly the Uighur in-laws would certainly not have been present: the disgrace and death of their princess, Al Altan, the subsequent cooptation of their ruler by the Ögedeyids, and their marital connection with another of Güyük's daughters linked them too closely to the Ögedeyids for them to support the usurpers.[85]

Those Chinggisids who refused to attend included the regent, Oghul-Qaimish, and her two sons; the null-and-never-king Shiremün and his partisans; and the majority of the Chaghatayid family, including its khan,

[82] Juvaynī, *World-Conqueror*, 568, albeit omitting the Toluids (as too obvious?) and omitting widows; Rashīd al-Dīn, *Jāmi'*, 276 (widows were still alive), 828, 839 (widows at the quriltai), trans. Thackston, 135, 403, 409, trans. Boyle, 204, 215.

[83] Juvaynī, *World-Conqueror*, 568. Rashīd al-Dīn omits Kölgen's sons in *Jāmi'*, 828, trans. Thackston, 403, trans. Boyle, 204.

[84] See Family Trees 7.1, 7.2, and Chapter 8.

[85] This princess was (obviously) conceived while Güyük was alive, but since she married Quchar-Tekin, great-grandson of the Uighur iduqut, Barchuk, she may have been young at Güyük's death. If so, the connection may have begun as a long engagement. See footnote 35 for both marriages.

Yesü-Möngke.[86] In an ironic reversal from when Batu had dragged out Töregene's attempts to organize a quriltai, the boycotters' tactics appear to have driven the plotters to some desperation. Batu's brother Berke is said to have complained: "We have been wanting to place Möngke Qa'an on the throne for two years. Ögedei Qa'an's and Güyük Khan's sons and Chaghatai's son Yesü Mongke have not come." "Seat him on the throne!" replied Batu. "And any creature that disobeys the Yasa [law] will lose his head."[87] Finally deciding to proceed, the assembly gathered, Chinggisids together inside a large tent, with commanders and troops outside.[88] Men took off their hats and belts in the traditional gestures of submission to authority, then probably raised Möngke up (possibly on a carpet[89]), placed him on the throne, whether Güyük's splendid carved and bejeweled seat or another;[90] and finally knelt to him nine times.[91]

The next day was given over to celebration, which took place in a different, magnificent tent lined with gold brocade and floored with exquisite carpets, all of which had been provided by the administrator Maḥmūd Yalavach, surely at Sorqoqtani's orders.[92] It is reasonable to assume that Batu had taken on the expenses of the Central Asian quriltai, and that Sorqoqtani therefore paid for the Mongolian one, while both shared the burden of the gifts and bribes that smoothed the way between

[86] Juvaynī, *World-Conqueror*, 566–7; Rashīd al-Dīn, *Jāmi'*, 828, trans. Thackston, 403, trans. Boyle, 204; also Allsen, *Mongol Imperialism*, 26.

[87] Rashīd al-Dīn, *Jāmi'*, 828, trans. Thackston, 403, trans. Boyle, 204; citation from Thackston.

[88] Juvaynī, *World-Conqueror*, 568; Rashīd al-Dīn, *Jāmi'*, 828–9, trans. Thackston, 404, trans. Boyle, 205.

[89] Juvaynī only vaguely mentions raising Möngke. Juvaynī, *World-Conqueror*, 568. Also Ron Sela, *Ritual and Authority in Central Asia: The Khan's Inauguration Ceremony* (Bloomington, IN, 2003), entire.

[90] It is unknown whether this was still in Oghul-Qaimish's possession. Juvaynī, *World-Conqueror*, 568; Rashīd al-Dīn, *Jāmi'*, 829, trans. Thackston, 403–4, trans. Boyle, 205. Friar William mentions Möngke sitting on a couch, a golden couch, and an "elevated position" at a palace in Qara-qorum high enough to require stairs. Rubruck, *Mission*, 178, 190, 210; for the elevated seat see Juvaynī, *World-Conqueror*, 237. The throne at Qara-qorum seems to have been stationary and thus different from Güyük's beautiful and clearly portable throne.

[91] Juvaynī, *World-Conqueror*, 568 and footnote 50 (saying three in Boyle's translation, but nine in several manuscripts); Rashīd al-Dīn, *Jāmi'*, 829 (saying nine – the order of paragraphs is slightly different than in the translations), trans. Thackston, 404, trans. Boyle, 205; Bar Hebraeus, *Chronography*, 411 (nine for Güyük), 417 (no number for Möngke).

[92] Juvaynī, *World-Conqueror*, 570–1; Rashīd al-Dīn, *Jāmi'*, 830, trans. Thackston, 404, trans. Boyle, 206; also Allsen, "Maḥmūd Yalavač," 126.

the two. Crowning Möngke officially (and Batu unofficially) was an expensive undertaking. A tent of this sort would have taken an entire workshop of artisans about three years to make, and had to have been ordered in perhaps 1248.[93] Like the three tents that Töregene had provided for Güyük's coronation, therefore, Möngke's party pavilion represented a huge investment of money and time. It was used for a full week of feasting, which witnessed the daily consumption of two thousand carts of qumiz and wine, three hundred horses and oxen, and two thousand sheep by attendees who all donned gleaming new brocaded robes of a single color each morning.[94] Food, drinks, and clothes were provided by the new ruler (and presumably paid for by his mother).[95] Thus Möngke was established in name as Grand Khan, and in reality as Batu's co-ruler in the east.[96]

But what made the quriltai work, at least well enough for the plotters' purposes, was the presence of a few independent-minded men from the two boycotting houses: Qadan and Melik, junior sons of Ögedei, and Monggetü, a son of Töregene's son Köten, whom she had passed over in favor of Güyük. Also present was Chaghatai's grandson Qara-Hülegü, whose senior wife Orqīna was one of Princess Checheyigen's daughters and therefore a sister to the senior wives of the Toluids, Arik Böke and Hülegü.[97] Although these stray representatives of the missing houses arrived after Möngke had been elevated, their submission to him was seen as acknowledgement of his rule, and legitimation of it from the absent families. Qadan and Melik were the sons of concubines, and thus were junior men in their own families, and so had little to lose and perhaps much to gain from breaking away to join the usurpers.[98] As for Mönggetü: he must have known that his father had believed he had been bewitched by Töregene's advisor, Fāṭimah, which caused his fatal illness and inability to become Grand Khan. Although Güyük did execute Fātimah, it is worth wondering whether Köten's tragic story of Töregene's

93 Allsen, *Commodity and Exchange*, 15.

94 Allsen, *Commodity and Exchange*, 19–20, and "Robing in the Mongolian Empire," 305.

95 Juvaynī mentions robes and provisions; Rashīd al-Dīn lists only food and drink. Juvaynī, *World-Conqueror*, 573; Rashīd al-Dīn, *Jāmi'*, 830, trans. Thackston, 404–5, trans. Boyle, 207.

96 See footnote 50.

97 For Orqīna see Chapter 8. For the Chaghatayids and Ögedeyids see Jackson, "Dissolution," 204 and esp. note 73; Juvaynī, *World-Conqueror*, 573; Rashīd al-Dīn, *Jāmi'*, 828, trans. Thackston, 403, trans. Boyle, 204; Hope, *Ilkhanate*, 82.

98 Jackson, "Dissolution," 204 note 73; Allsen, *Mongol Imperialism*, 26; Hope, *Ilkhanate*, 82.

"betrayal" influenced Mönggetu's decision to break with his immediate kin in favor of his cousins.[99] He also may have hoped for advancement under the Toluids, which may not have seemed likely under Oghul-Qaimish. As for Qara-Hülegü: he had once ruled as Chaghatayid Khan and supported Töregene and her exacting financial policies. But Güyük had summarily deposed Qara-Hülegü in favor of his uncle, possibly in a reversal of his mother's economic measures.[100] Qara-Hülegü thus had every reason to support Möngke for his own sake, in addition to Orqīna's connections to her sisters.

TRIALS AND PURGES

Like Güyük, Möngke moved straight from the delights of his coronation to the bloodier business of killing Chinggisids; unlike Güyük, Möngke cast a far wider net. But what happened exactly is made murky by the pious obfuscation of the sources, who were either Toluid employees whitewashing with all their might, or outsiders hearing the story after it had been spoon-fed to them by the victors or their agents.[101]

Fortunately a few important details can be gleaned. Some of the dispossessed Ögedeyids and Chaghatayids, whether separately or in alliance, gathered their forces and set out to reclaim what had been wrested from them by the Jochid and Toluid usurpers. But these had taken all necessary precautions, and had surrounded their quriltai with the army that Batu had provided. At some point during the festivities, a servant of Möngke allegedly happened upon some of the approaching forces while innocently searching for a lost animal. He immediately alerted the new Grand Khan, who either sent out an army, or led one himself, to settle the matter militarily.[102] (The charming fiction that Möngke refused to believe that his relatives could bear him any ill will, and had to be convinced to

[99] De Nicola notes the presence also of Temüge-Otchigin's sons, who had rebelled with Köten against Töregene, then later switched to the Toluids. See *Khatuns*, note 74 on p. 87.

[100] De Nicola, *Khatuns*, 77; Hope, *Ilkhanate*, 70.

[101] Juvaynī, *World-Conqueror*, 574–89 (the whitewashers); and Rashīd al-Dīn, *Jāmi'*, 831–40, trans. Thackston, 405–9, trans. Boyle, 208–15; Rubruck, *Mission*, 168–9 (an outsider); also Juzjānī, whom Jackson thinks heard the story from Mongol ambassadors later: Jackson, "Dissolution," 205 note 76; Juzjānī, *Ṭabaqāt*, 2:179–80, trans. Raverty, 1179–81.

[102] Allsen, *Mongol Imperialism*, 26–7; also Hope, *Ilkhanate*, 74–5.

take action, must be dismissed out of hand.)[103] Some men seem to have died on the field.[104] Those of higher rank appear to have been brought in for questioning. The conclusions were foregone: effective torturers, using among their techniques the bastinado or burning brands,[105] wrung enough confessions from enough people to allow Möngke to stamp out the opposition quite ruthlessly. Thereafter agents and armies were sent out to conduct investigations and execute as many additional "conspirators" as required.[106]

Although the sources work hard to portray the purges as a necessary but near-spontaneous Toluid reaction to rebellious behavior on the part of the Ögedeyid and Chaghatayid families, in fact, the comprehensive pursuit and execution of so many Chinggisids and their adherents are better seen as a calculated and premeditated policy designed to seal the Toluid-Jochid ascension for good. The empire had already witnessed several cases of tension between the Grand Khan and certain regional khans during the reign of Ögedei, and it might have seen an actual war between the Grank Khan Güyük and the regional Khan Batu if Güyük had lived long enough to wage it.[107] Now as he took over as Grand Khan, Möngke risked facing the same kind of tensions with regional rulers, but greatly complicated by resentment from the families that he and his allies had just overthrown. Another danger was posed by the entrenched, privileged commanders who had supported what was now the losing side.[108] Nor can the shrewd, intelligent, and politically astute Sorqoqtani, her well-trained eldest son, and their experienced and sage ally, Batu, have overlooked the threat posed by living members of the dispossessed houses and their allies.[109] Their meticulous plotting took years to reach its maturity; during it, therefore, they must also have contemplated the possibility that the Ögedeyids, at least, might have to be largely wiped out in order to consolidate Toluid-Jochid gains, and perhaps the

[103] Juvaynī, *World-Conqueror*, 576–7; Rashīd al-Dīn, *Jāmiʿ*, 832, trans. Thackston, 405–6, trans. Boyle, 208–9.

[104] Juzjānī, *Ṭabaqāt*, 2:179–80, trans. Raverty, 1182–6.

[105] Rashīd al-Dīn, *Jāmiʿ*, 834, trans. Thackston, 406, trans. Boyle, 211 (the bastinado); Rubruck, *Mission*, 169 (burning brands).

[106] Allsen, *Mongol Imperialism*, 31; Hope, *Ilkhanate*, 75–6; Juvaynī, *World-Conqueror*, 585, 590; Rashīd al-Dīn, *Jāmiʿ*, 838, trans. Thackston, 408, 409, trans. Boyle, 214–15, 216.

[107] Allsen, *Mongol Imperialism*, 46–7; also Jackson, "Dissolution," 198–201.

[108] Hope, *Ilkhanate*, 75–6, 80–1.

[109] Allsen argues that Sorqoqtani laid the real foundations for Toluid political power, but does not mention her views of the "rebels" per se. Allsen, *Mongol Imperialism*, 59–60.

Chaghatayids as well, depending on whether or not they could be won over to the victorious side. This lends a new, ominous undertone to the urgency of the diplomatic flurry in which Sorqoqtani in particular engaged during the months between the Central Asian and Mongolian quriltais, and may explain why she worked so hard to persuade doubters to join them.[110] The only real question is how far in advance the plotters realized that purges on such a significant scale could be necessary, and then prepared for that day. Möngke's own policies thereafter, including a return to centralized regulation of finances, trade, and taxation, and new conquests in China and Iran under his brothers, demonstrate his active interest in bringing the empire firmly and permanently under his own control.[111]

Oghul-Qaimish was a key figure in the purges, and it is no surprise that Möngke soon claimed that she had allied herself with Shiremün and urged him to rebel.[112] Then, after the Grand Khan had rounded up and killed or imprisoned an initial wave of Chinggisids, commanders, and soldiers, including Shiremün, and Oghul-Qaimish's son Naqu, he summoned the regent and her other son Qucha to court. Oghul-Qaimish was with Qucha when the messenger arrived, and both at first refused the summons. Qucha was eventually convinced to go to the royal encampment by one of his wives, but Oghul-Qaimish sent the messenger back. Her refusal encapsulated the Ögedeyid and Chaghatayid view of the coup as illegitimate: "You princes pledged and gave *möchälgä*s [written pledges] that the rule would always remain among Ogödai Qa'an's offspring and that you would never rebel against his sons. Now you have broken your word."[113]

Möngke's threatening response took the form of a decree (*yarligh*), which ran thus: "The wives of Jochi Qasar, [Temüge]-Otchigin, and Belgütei Noyan, the brothers of Chinggis Khan, have attended the deliberations of the quriltai, but Oghul-Qaimish has not. If the shamans or Qadaq, Chinqai, or Bala (who were Güyük Khan's *amir-ordus*) call or proclaim anyone *padishah* or *khatun*, or anyone becomes a *padishah* or a *khatun* by their word, they shall see what they shall see!"[114] This can be

110 Allsen, *Mongol Imperialism*, 60; also Juvaynī, *World-Conqueror*, 562–3; Rashīd al-Dīn, *Jāmi'*, 827, trans. Thackston, 403, trans. Boyle, 203.

111 Allsen, *Mongol Imperialism*, 47; De Nicola, *Khatuns*, 146, 148–9; Hope, *Ilkhanate*, 75–8, 80–1.

112 Rubruck, *Mission*, 168.

113 Rashīd al-Dīn, *Jāmi'*, 838–9, trans. Thackston, 408–9 (and citation), trans. Boyle, 215.

114 Rashīd al-Dīn, *Jāmi'*, 839, trans. Thackston, 409 (and citation), trans. Boyle, 215.

understood first as condemnation of Oghul-Qaimish for not attending the quriltai properly like other widows, including senior ones from Chinggis Khan's generation, to whom Oghul-Qaimish was arguably still junior despite her status as regent. Möngke may have meant that the families of these widows had already been dispossessed from succession, and yet they had reconciled themselves and attend the quriltai peacefully. Surely, therefore, Oghul-Qaimish should follow their example. Möngke's second point about kingmakers among the shamans or powerful administrators is best understood in two ways. First, it was an ominous reference to Oghul-Qaimish's frequent interactions with shamans, which here suggested Möngke's belief that Oghul-Qaimish was a witch.[115] Second, it was a condemnation of the administrators working for her, especially Qadaq, who was thought to have encouraged the Ögedeyids in their rejection of Möngke, Batu, and Sorqoqtani, and who was himself on the list for execution.[116] (Chinqai was also put to death, but somewhat later.)[117]

Immediately after she refused his summons, Möngke had Oghul-Qaimish forcibly brought to the ordo as a dangerous prisoner, "with both hands stitched in rawhide."[118] She was sent to the camp of her now terminally ill rival, Sorqoqtani, along with Shiremün's mother, Qadagach. There they were allegedly beaten with burning brands.[119] Once the torture had made them confess, they were put on trial by Menggeser, the chief judge (*yarghuchi*). He is reported to have stripped Oghul-Qaimish naked for her trial, although it is unknown whether Qadagach suffered the same fate. The exposure served several purposes: In this society where clothing demonstrated status, Oghul-Qaimish's nakedness provided a visible expression of her downfall from the highest woman in the land to the lowest.[120] It is also possible that Menggeser believed he could weaken her reputed magical powers by taking her clothes from her. Her nakedness further sent a powerful warning about the perils of contravening Möngke's will, and finally, humiliated her. Oghul-Qaimish, who was probably close to 40 at this point, protested with some spirit: "How can anyone else look upon a body that only an

115 Rubruck, *Mission*, 249; *Yuan shi*, trans. Abramowski, "Möngke," 20. Also De Nicola, *Khatuns*, 187.
116 Juvaynī, *World-Conqueror*, 263–4; 583–5, 587–8; Rashīd al-Dīn, *Jāmi'*, 839, trans. Thackston, 408, trans. Boyle, 213.
117 Buell, "Činqai," 108–9; Hope, *Ilkhanate*, 76.
118 Rashīd al-Dīn, *Jāmi'*, 839, trans. Thackston, 409 (and citation), trans. Boyle, 215.
119 Rubruck, *Mission*, 169.
120 On the symbolism of removing clothing see Allsen, *Commodity and Exchange*, 49.

emperor has seen?"[121] But of course it was a foregone conclusion that she would be found guilty, since as a central figure in the Ögedeyid house, she needed to die in order to secure Jochid-Toluid rule.[122] What set Oghul-Qaimish and Qadagach apart was the fact that they alone among the Ögedeyids were condemned and executed specifically as witches. Like Fāṭimah only a few years earlier, they were wrapped in felt and cast into the chilly waters of the swift-flowing Kerülen River to drown, unable even to move their arms and legs as the water soaked through the felt. (That said, they at least did not have their orifices sewn.) The running water may have contained their magic even at the spiritual cost of being polluted itself.[123] (See Figure 7.2.) Although we have no hint of what sorcery Oghul-Qaimish might have performed, it is possible that Möngke thought she caused Sorqoqtani's final illness.[124] We do know that Möngke feared witches with good reason, since he believed they had killed one of his wives, and on another occasion, one of his infant sons.[125] He therefore may have thought that Oghul-Qaimish had magically attacked him or his family, which necessitated her watery death.

RIGHTING ÖGEDEYID WRONGS

After the main work of killing princes, princesses, and their supporters had been achieved, Möngke, Batu, and Sorqoqtani set themselves to righting Ögedeyid wrongs, and widened their scope to include the supporters of their enemies. One of these wrongs was the unlawful execution of Al Altan, to which the avengers turned immediately. They began by targeting the Ögedeyid general Eljigidei. One accusation, which was

[121] Rashīd al-Dīn, *Jāmi'*, 839, trans. Thackston, 409 (and citation), trans. Boyle, 215.

[122] Allsen, *Mongol Imperialism*, 32.

[123] See May, "Commercial Queens," 10–12; note also Fāṭimah in Chapter 6, and the similar execution of El-Qutlugh, widow of the Ilkhan Tegüder (r. 1282–4), for witchcraft in 1291. See Chapter 9. Juvaynī, *World-Conqueror*, 588 (saying that Oghul-Qaimish's crime was inciting conspiracy but omitting the execution); Bar Hebraeus, *Chronography*, 417 (mentioning execution without cause or method); Rashīd al-Dīn, *Jāmi'*, 839, trans. Thackston, 409, trans. Boyle, 215 (filling in witchcraft and drowning).

[124] Sorqoqtani died of her illness in February–March 1252. *Yuan Shi*, trans. Abramowski, "Möngke," 20; Juvaynī, *World-Conqueror*, 553; Rashīd al-Dīn, *Jāmi'*, 823, trans. Thackston, 401, trans. Boyle, 200.

[125] The wifely victim was the Oirat Oghul-Qaimish (not to be confused with the subject of this chapter), while the child was the son of Möngke's Ikires senior wife, Qutuqtai. Rubruck, *Mission*, 178 (Oghul-Qaimish, unnamed), 189 (Qutuqtai), 242–4 (the infant's death); also Rashīd al-Dīn, *Jāmi'*, 820, trans. Thackston, 399, trans. Boyle, 197–8. On Qutuqtai's Christianity and other religious leanings see De Nicola, *Khatuns*, 192, 213.

Figure 7.2 The Kerülen River (author's image).

addressed directly to Eljigedei, is attributed to Möngke's brother, Qubilai: "'Chinggis Khan commanded that if anyone from his family acted contrary to the Yasa [law], he and his elder and younger brothers were not to be molested unless a council was convened. Why did you kill Altalunqan [Al Altan]?"[126] Elsewhere a similar but more general statement was put in Batu's mouth: "They [the Ögedeyids] broke the ancient Yasa and Yosun, for, without consulting their brethren, they put to death Genghis Khan's guiltless daughter, the one he loved the most of all his children."[127] Retribution was now swift. First Eljigedei's sons were captured and put to death in horrible fashion.[128] Eljigidei himself was in Iraq when the

[126] Rashīd al-Dīn, *Jāmi'*, 69, trans. Thackston, 39. This is alleged to have happened at the coronation quriltai, but it is unlikely that Eljigedei would have attended, and he is said to have been in Iraq when the purges began. Perhaps this indicates the Central Asian quriltai? The timing is not clear.

[127] Rashīd al-Dīn, *Jāmi'*, 735, trans. Thackston, 361, trans. Boyle, 121.

[128] Their mouths were stuffed with stones until they died. Rashīd al-Dīn, *Jāmi'*, 837, trans. Thackston, 407, trans. Boyle, 212–3.

manhunt began,[129] but soon fled east with almost no attendants. His destination is unclear – did he hope to take refuge with those few Ögedeyids still alive? Before long he was captured in Badghis near Herat, and sent from there to Batu, who had him killed, terribly.[130] Although the rest of Eljigidei's family was allowed to live, they were demoted in status and found themselves entered onto the next census as ordinary taxpayers.[131]

With Eljigidei's death, Sorqoqtani, Batu, and Möngke eliminated one of the most militarily powerful Ögedeyid agents, removed his threat to Batu's lieutenants in Anatolia and the Caucasus region, and achieved part of their vengeance for the death of Princess Al Altan. Thereafter the new rulers turned against the Uighur *iduqut*, Salindi, whom Töregene had appointed in the 1240s.[132] Given his loyalty to the Ögedeyids and physical proximity to Oghul-Qaimish's camp on the Emil, not to mention the marriage connections between the Ögedeyid and Uighur houses,[133] Salindi cannot have abandoned his patrons to attend the coronation quriltai in support of Möngke. He is reported to have gathered an army outside Besh-Baliq, and may have meant to support the dispossessed with force.[134] But as in the case of all resistance to Möngke, events went otherwise. The details are similar to the other trials: Salindi and some of his commanders were arrested and brought to court. After torture, which this time involved beating with drumsticks, twisting of hands, and a wooden face press, those involved unsurprisingly confessed to a plot.[135] According to the story related by the Toluid historians, this was a devious plan to massacre all the Muslims living in Uighur territory. Although the truth of the matter is unknown, historians suggest a political motive.[136] In any case, the *iduqut* was sent back to Besh-Baliq for a public execution at the hands of his own brother, Ögünch, who became Möngke's loyal

129 Juvaynī, *World-Conqueror*, 590.

130 Al-'Umarī claims he was boiled in water. Al-'Umarī, *Masālik*, 15–16 and trans. Lech, 100–1; otherwise Juvaynī, *World-Conqueror*, 590; Rashīd al-Dīn, *Jāmi'*, 837 (no cause of death), trans. Thackston, 407, trans. Boyle, 212–13, Kirakos, *Histoire*, trans. Brosset, *Arméniens*, 172, noting that Eljigedei was singled out as the principal personage to punish.

131 This was in winter 1251–2. *Yūan Shi* trans. Abramowski, "Möngke," 20.

132 Allsen, *Mongol Imperialism*, 67–9.

133 I am referring both to the relationship through the princess wife of the now deceased Kesmes, and the later engagement of Güyük's daughter to Quchar-Tekin.

134 Juvaynī, *World-Conqueror*, 48–9.

135 Juvaynī, *World-Conqueror*, 50–1; also Rashīd al-Dīn, *Jāmi'*, 839–40, trans. Thackston, 409, trans. Boyle, 215.

136 Juvaynī, *World-Conqueror*, 48–9; Rashīd al-Dīn, *Jāmi'*, 839, trans. Thackston, 409, trans. Boyle, 215; Allsen, "Uighurs of Turfan," 250–1 and especially note 54.

vassal, later followed by his son.[137] With Salindi's death Möngke removed yet another of his enemies' agents, this one a member of a major consort lineage and ruler of an important people that provided well-educated and useful personnel to the empire.[138] He also completed the vengeance for Princess Al Altan. Thereafter a thousand Uighurs dutifully traveled to Iran to fight with an imperial army.[139] But if Princess Al Altan's death was caused by changes in imperial control of Uighur territories, the Uighurs do not seem to have regained what they lost, since thereafter we still find (at least one remaining) Ögedeyid holding appanages in the region: Qadan near Beshbaliq, the Uighur summer capital.[140]

OGHUL-QAIMISH VERSUS SORQOQTANI: A SUMMATION

Unlike all the other women we have met so far, even the other conquered ones, Oghul-Qaimish's story was one of failure, made more painful to read because of the opportunities, wealth, and power that she seems to have enjoyed. Although an accurate view of her is impossible to extract from the close-mouthed and unflattering sources, the results of her actions speak for themselves. She failed as a politician: she either misunderstood the significance of the rump quriltai, or simply miscalculated by sending Bala to represent her without also attending, or attending long enough, with her sons. If she did indeed ally herself with Shiremün and also support Qucha's claim to the grand khanate, perhaps at different moments, then this surely muddied the political waters in her own camp and weakened both men's chances. She never produced an effective counter to the coup that pushed Möngke to the position of Grand Khan, nor called her own quriltai to foil the plotters. Oghul-Qaimish also failed as a regent by continuing the rapacious financial policies her husband had started, although naturally Güyük deserves considerable blame for these. Finally, she failed to defend herself during the purges, with the result that her death was particularly ugly, both morally and physically. One wonders whether she became a cautionary tale for imperial women throughout thc cmpirc. Friar William's citation is particularly telling: "[Möngke] told me with his own lips that [Oghul-Qaimish] was the worst

137 Allsen, *Mongol Imperialism*, 68–9; Juvaynī, *World-Conqueror*, 52.
138 Thomas T. Allsen, "Ever Closer Encounters: The Appropriation of Culture and the Apportionment of Peoples in the Mongol Empire," *Journal of Early Modern History* 1 (1997), 7.
139 Allsen, "Encounters," 8.
140 *Yuan Shi*, trans. Abramowski, "Möngke," 20; Allsen, *Mongol Imperialism*, 53.

of witches, and that with her sorcery she had destroyed her entire family."[141] Although patently unfair – there would have been no destruction without the plot that Möngke himself hatched with his mother and cousin – the words are a chilling eulogy.

As for Sorqoqtani: hers was a story of triumph at last. But what precisely were her achievements? Born into a royal family among the Kereits, she had married into an imperial one, although she had faced the insecurity of watching her father-in-law destroy Kereit unity on the way to creating his empire. She had secured her future by bearing several children, then had seen her husband die conveniently young. Next she diplomatically staved off levirate marriage and remained in control of her own finances and children, on whose education and training she spent her attention. At some point, perhaps during the quiet years of the 1230s, she began to plan. She strengthened her own ties to certain members of the Chinggisid family, especially the Jochids among whom her sister Begtütmish lived. She also built new ties for her sons and daughter through strategic marriages, particularly to the senior Chinggisid princesses and their families, and to Börte's Qonggirat lineage. Sorqoqtani also watched the Ögedeyids, saw the short-lived but dangerous accusation against her sister Ibaqa in Ögedei's death, and surely learned about the deaths of Temüge and Al Altan despite the cover-up. Temüge's trial and execution were not entirely secret even though the details remained generally unknown, while if the visiting Friar Carpini picked up knowledge of the princess's death, then surely Sorqoqtani learned of it also. Nor can Sorqoqtani have missed the cooptation of the Uighurs. At some point she, Batu, and Möngke began to plan, perhaps with the advice of Begtütmish; at some point Sorqoqtani let in the other sons and her daughter.

By the end of her life Sorqoqtani had restored her family not just to the royalty from which she had begun, but to an even loftier station. She had furthermore achieved this even though Tolui's was a junior branch of the Golden Lineage, and arguably should have had no reason to contest Ögedeyid claims to rule. In the process, she, Möngke, and Batu managed to damage the empire severely: they gutted the Chinggisid family by purging the Ögedeyid and Chaghatayid houses, and they drastically curtailed Chinggis Khan's original division of his inheritance into four appanages ruled by the families of Börte's four sons. Like Hö'elün

141 Rubruck, *Mission*, 249.

and Töregene before her, Sorqoqtani did not live long past her own son's enthronement, and perished of a wasting illness. It should be mentioned that unlike her predecessors, Sorqoqtani died while still on excellent terms with her son.

CONCLUSION

In the competition between Oghul-Qaimish on the one hand and Sorqoqtani, Möngke, and Batu on the other, the empire, which had already begun to fracture under Töregene and Güyük, finally cracked irrevocably. Sorqoqtani won; Oghul-Qaimish lost; both died. Princess Al Altan was avenged, but this could not bring her back to life. Thereafter Möngke tightened the reins over his portion of Mongol territory in an attempt to centralize power and wealth in his own hands for his own purposes. Many scholars have charted the well-known and complex tale of the quriltais that raised Möngke and the purges that crushed his opponents, but this chapter is the first to focus on the women involved: the way their status as conquered women influenced their choices, the methods they used to handle money and the people who paid it, their abilities to build coalitions that worked (or not), and finally, the skewed portraits of both women in the historical sources, and the caution we must use as a result.

8

Consort Houses in the Successor Khanates

As we have seen, the succession struggles of the 1240s were shaped by the extraordinary efforts of three imperial widows from conquered backgrounds, and resulted both in Möngke's ascent to the throne, and his purges. These latter dismantled the Ögedeyid Khanate in Jungaria and greatly weakened the adjacent Chaghatayid Khanate. Thereafter and perhaps in part to draw attention away from this destruction, Möngke sent out two new major campaigns in the 1250s: one against the Song Dynasty in southern China, led by his brother Qubilai and later joined by Möngke himself, and the other into Khurasan, Iran, Iraq, and Anatolia under their brother Hülegü, which later formed the basis of a new Toluid realm, the Ilkhanate (1256–1335). Möngke's death in China in 1259 led directly to the Mongol Civil War of 1260–4, in which Qubilai and the fourth brother, Ariq Böke, vied for control of the grand khanate, which Qubilai won by 1264.

Thereafter the United Mongol Empire was transformed into four independent khanates. First of these chronologically was the Jochid realm in Central Asia and Russia, which had been established during a series of military campaigns in 1236–42. Second came the weak Chaghatayid realm, third the new Toluid territory of the Ilkhanids in Iran under the descendants of Hülegü, and fourth the grand khanate in China and Mongolia under Qubilai's offspring, the Yuan dynasty. These independent khanates were influenced by new political players who emerged from existing Chinggisid marital patterns, but were now connected to particular locales and regions. It is here that we find royal women from consort houses participating actively in the politics, economies, and daily lives of the khanates, and it is to these women and those houses that this chapter turns. The most influential consort houses remained those whose members descended from Börte's daughters or kin: the Qonggirats, Ikires, and Oirats, and to a lesser degree, the Öng'üts and Uighurs. These houses ensured their own continuation and vitality through vigorous policies of intermarriage with the Chinggisids in all the khanates: they provided senior wives for Chinggisid princes, then, if these women produced heirs, politicked energetically to place "their" heir on the throne, for which the clearest picture emerges in the Ilkhanate (see Chapter 9). Simultaneously consort families produced sons to marry royal princesses, and the children from both sets of unions ensured the continuation of the house for each subsequent generation. Wives from the major houses often managed the big camps, with junior wives and concubines living under their aegis.

Although minor consort families also existed, none came close to dominating in the same way, with the single exception of the Kereits, who provided the only real competition to the princesses' houses for decades. The Kereit house was anomalous since it was linked to none of Börte's daughters, but rather was peopled by descendants of the Kereit sisters and their brothers, despite the annexation of their ruling lineages and subjects under Chinggis Khan. This was part of Sorqoqtani's legacy, and it was her female kin who vigorously maintained the Kereit lineage, most clearly her cousin Dokuz in the Ilkhanate. To continue the investigation of women's roles in Chinggisid life, this chapter explores the establishment of major and minor consort houses in the khanates, demonstrates the prevailing yet hitherto understudied patterns of consort behavior, and highlights particular women about whom we know more (Chabi, Orqīna, Kelmish Aqa, etc.), and from whose examples we can theorize about others. Note that the chapter is deliberately organized by the consort families (i.e., matrilineally), not the more common rubric of the khanates (patrilineally), to maintain our focus on the women's kin. Thereafter Chapter 9 provides a case study of consort families in the Ilkhanate to demonstrate how they interacted with one another in a single polity.

CONSORT FAMILIES

By now we know that the Chinggisids favored exchange marriages during the formation period of the empire. They continued this preference in the successor khanates. When wives from consort lineages married

Chinggisid princes, they later wedded children back into their natal families to complete the exchange. During the establishment phases of the khanates, the best way to find relatives with whom to arrange these marriages was to have a brother of the royal wife work for her husband as a military commander, accompany the invading armies to the new khanate, then settle down with his own wives, who could provide the offspring to marry his sister's royal children. In some cases these men commanded soldiers who came from their own subject peoples. After the khanates had been established, and especially in the western territories, royal wives tended to arrange marriages with these convenient local branches of their families, rather than sending back to Mongolia for cousins.[1] In eastern terrain, by contrast, continued access to the original branches of the consort houses was guaranteed.

Although this system appears consanguineous to modern eyes as mentioned in Chapter 1, it was not deemed so by Mongol standards, since the fathers of the bride and groom were not related by blood. Furthermore, even though consanguinity may lead to increased risks of certain genetic disorders, historians should heed the cautions of some medical experts not to overestimate those risks, nor underestimate the value gained when both families knew each other well, and the consort family line with its access to the heart of Chinggisid authority could be maintained and continued.[2] These families then played roles in the complex politics of the khanates in which they were located, along with a constellation of Chinggisids, important commanders, members of the royal bodyguards, and many others.[3]

From their positions at the top of the social and political hierarchy, royal wives engaged in a long list of activities. They met with ambassadors from outside monarchs, usually in company with the ruler, but

[1] See Chapter 9.

[2] A. H. Bittles et al., "Consanguinity, Human Evolution, and Complex Diseases," *Proceedings of the National Academy of Sciences of the United States of America*, 107, supplement 1: Evolution in Health and Medicine (January 26, 2010): 1779–86; Emily Lyons et al., "Consanguinity and Susceptibility to Infectious Diseases in Humans," *Biology Letters* 5 (2009): 574–6; also Broadbridge, "Ilkhanid-Oirat Connection," 122. By contrast, Zhao sees consanguinity as a serious health problem. Zhao, *Marriage*, 18–22.

[3] A full investigation of interactions among these groups is beyond the scope of this book, yet would be very worthwhile. For the commander families see Michael Hope, "'The Pillars of State': Some Notes on the *Qarachu Begs* and the *Kešikten* in the Īl-Khānate (1256–1335)," https://anu-au.academia.edu/MichaelHope, and his book, *Ilkhanate*, entire.

sometimes by themselves.[4] They participated in and patronized a wide variety of religions, often extensively.[5] They invested capital with merchants, who engaged in long-distance trade on their behalf.[6] They corresponded within their khanate, or wrote to relatives or contacts in other khanates.[7] They interceded regularly with the ruler on matters of policy and personnel. They patronized artists, scholars, and holy figures.[8] And as usual, they ran their establishments (*ordos*) if they were fortunate enough to have them; managed the thousand details of their flocks, dependents, and possessions; enjoyed portions of any and all spoils from conquest; strategized about the marriages of their children; and, when the opportunity arose, worked to seat their sons on the throne in competition with rivals.[9]

THE QONGGIRATS

As scholars have rightly observed, the Qonggirat consort family was paramount to the Chinggisids, especially members of Börte's family: "There were – and still are – many imperial sons-in-law from them [i.e., Börte's kin] during Ögedei Qa'an, Möngke Qa'an, and Qubilai Qa'an's times, and they sat above the emperor's sons."[10] The Qonggirat consort house similarly dominated the khanates, especially in Jochid territory and in China, although the situation under the Chaghatayids is less clear,

4 In 1253 Friar William met Batu, then Sartaq, with all wives present. Rubruck, *Mission*, 114, 117, 132. In the 1330s Ibn Baṭūṭah met Özbek, his wives and his daughter. Ibn Baṭūṭah, *Travels*, 3:485–9. In 1357 Taidula, the wife of Janibek Khan (r. 1342–57), engaged in diplomacy on her own behalf, while in 1365 another wife sent her own envoy with her husband's man. Anonymous, *The Nikonian Chronicle*, trans. Serge A. and Betty Jean Zenkovsky (Princeton, The Kingston Press, Inc., 1984–6), 3:180, 195. Also Brack, "Mongol Princess," 341–6 (the Ilkhanid princess El-Qutlugh, who corresponded with the Mamluks); Zhao, "Concilation," 21 (Mongol princesses in Korea). See Chapter 6 for Töregene's meeting *with* Friar Carpini but *without* Güyük.

5 See the Christian Dokuz in Chapter 9; De Nicola, *Khatuns*, 193–8, 213–22, and "Domestic Sphere," 359, and "Ladies of Rum," 150 (Seljuk women); Brack, "Mongol Princess," especially 347–52 (the Muslim princess El-Qutlugh; see also his footnote 5).

6 Batu and Berke both engaged actively in trade. Allsen, "Merchant Partners," 111–2. Their wives surely did the same, which was commonplace. See Chapter 1.

7 See the subsequent text in this chapter under Qonggirats for Kelmish Aqa.

8 See the subsequent text in this chapter under Qonggirats for Chabi.

9 See the subsequent text in this chapter under Other Families for Batu's wife, Boraqchin; also Chapter 9 (Hülegü's wife Öljei and Prince Möngke-Temür); Hillenbrand, "Women," 115–16 (Seljuk examples).

10 Rashīd al-Dīn, *Jāmi'*, 600–1, trans. Thackston, 277; Zhao, *Marriage*, 207–12 (the family's importance).

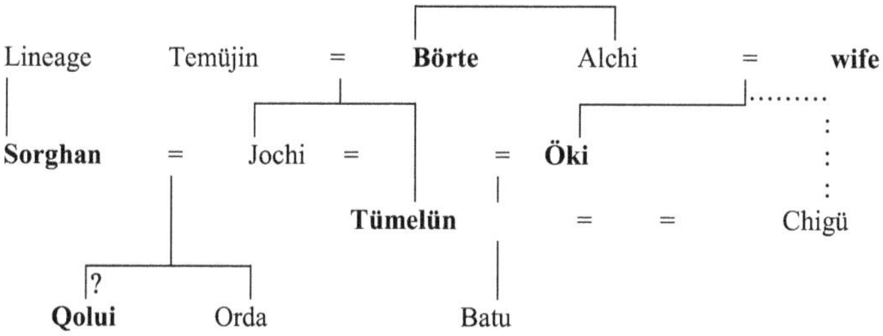

Family Tree 8.1 Jochi's Qonggirat wives and their children.
All women are in **bold**.
Dots indicate adoption.

while the house faced challenges from other consorts in the Ilkhanate. In all regions, the Qonggirat house contained multiple strands from different lineages. The senior lines descended from Börte's kin and from princess Tümelün, but junior lines coexisted along with them, and stemmed from other families within the Qonggirat people, especially Qonggirat military commanders who had proved themselves in service to the Chinggisids.

The Qonggirat ascendancy was especially marked among the Jochid rulers in their home region along the Volga River, where Jochi's two most noteworthy wives were Qonggirats. One was a Qonggirat but apparently not a relative of Börte, Sorghan, while the other was Jochi's first cousin Öki, a daughter of Börte's brother Alchi.[11] The marriage between Öki and Jochi also represented a sort of "sister-exchange," since Öki's adopted brother Chigü married Jochi's sister Tümelün.[12] Sorghan and Öki then solidified their respectable positions by bearing Jochi's two most important sons: Sorghan produced the eldest, Orda, while Öki gave birth to the second prince, Batu.[13] (See Family Tree 8.1.) But the scant record does not permit us to discern whether either wife had a brother who worked militarily for Jochi and produced his own children to marry to those of his sister, which was the preferred method of assuring the continuation of the family (see Chapter 9).

[11] Rashīd al-Dīn, *Jāmi'*, 710 (*khātūn-i buzurg-i ū* [Jochi]), 720, trans. Thackston, 348 ("great lady"), 351, trans. Boyle, 98 "chief wife"), 107; and in the Temürid-era *Mu'izz al-Anṣāb*, British Library OR 467, fol. 19a (*buzurgtarīn-i khavātīn-i jūchī khān*); Rashīd al-Dīn, *Shu'āb-i Panjgānah*, fol. 108a (*buzurgtarīn-i khātūnān-i jūchī khān*); also Zhao, *Marriage*, 109, 113. No evidence suggests that she was related to Börte.

[12] See Chapters 1 and 4. [13] See footnote 11 for Sorghan; Öki is on the same pages.

One particular challenge in the Jochid case is to determine the identity of Jochi's senior wife, about which the sources are curiously contradictory. Rashīd al-Dīn claims that she was neither Qonggirat lady, but rather the Kereit princess Begtütmish.[14] But later sources name Sorghan as the senior wife, Begtütmish as the second, and Öki farther down among the other wives.[15] Fortunately some clues emerge from a contemplation of the question of timing: When did Jochi marry his first wife? We can work backward from 1207 to 1208, when Jochi's daughter Qolui married into the Oirat ruling family in a double wedding with her aunt Checheyigen.[16] It is probable that Jochi himself had previously married in his teens in the mid to late 1190s (after Temüjin's return from China?), and it was most likely this first wife who produced Qolui, who herself must still have been young at her own wedding. If Qolui's mother was the senior wife, then this woman cannot have been Begtütmish, since the Kereits did not marry into the Chinggisid family until after Chinggis Khan conquered them in 1203.[17] Thus Rashīd al-Dīn's assertion that Begtütmish was the senior wife cannot be taken at face value, and should instead be understood as an attempt to elevate the Kereit royal house from which his patrons descended. With Begtütmish eliminated, we may turn to the idea that the Qonggirat lady Sorghan was the senior wife. We know that certain Qonggirat families had long enjoyed marital relations with the Borjigin Mongols.[18] If Sorghan's family was among them, this could have permitted a marriage in the 1190s, even though other Qonggirats only joined Temüjin in 1203.[19] If so, then Sorghan may have been the mother of Qolui (possibly) and Orda (definitely), and, of course, mistress of the most important camp, with the privilege of precedence in ceremonies of all kinds, and of situating her compound to the farthest western point of the wifely line of camps.[20] It is useful to note that after Jochi's death, "his" camp moved to Orda's territory: "The orda or court of his [Orda's] father [i.e., Jochi] is there and it is ruled by one of his [i.e., Jochi's] wives."[21] It is reasonable to think that the widow in question could have been Orda's mother (Sorghan), who may have sought to be closer to her son in widowhood. If so, then the designation of the camp as

[14] Rashīd al-Dīn, *Jāmi'*, 709 ("*khātūn-i buzurgtar-i jūchī* "), trans. Thackston, 348 ("chief wife"), trans. Boyle, 99 ("eldest wife").

[15] See footnote 11. [16] See Chapter 4, Table 4.2, and Chapter 5. [17] See Chapter 3.

[18] Cheng, "Career," 214–15.

[19] De Rachewiltz, Commentary 325–6 (on *Secret History*, §61), 634 (on §176), albeit without reference to Sorghan.

[20] See Chapter 1. [21] Carpini, *History*, 60, trans. Rockhill, 17.

Jochi's own implies that it was the chief one, and that its wifely manager was therefore the senior lady.

If we accept the premise that this high-ranking woman from the most important consort lineage, Sorghan, was Jochi's senior wife, a second question arises about her relationship to the other Qonggirat wife, Öki. Although seniority in order mattered greatly to the Mongols, rank also counted for status. We should wonder whether Öki challenged Sorghan's rank by virtue of being a member of Börte's own family, not just a high-born Qonggirat. It is likely that Öki enjoyed the privilege of her own camp, rather than residing in another woman's establishment, since she was not only Börte's niece, but also mother of one of the two most senior princes. Unfortunately the sources simply do not tell us enough about her. Nevertheless, Chinggis Khan's later decision to give Batu lordship over all of Jochid territory, and Orda merely a large appanage within that territory, is well known.[22] Was the difference in maternity a factor? That is, did the fact that Öki hailed from Börte's line of the Qonggirats outweigh the earlier birth of Sorghan's son, and contribute to Chinggis Khan's preference for Batu over Orda as Khan of the Jochid territories? With no clear evidence available we can only surmise, but maternal status could have been a factor in his decision.

In any case, although Jochi fathered many other sons (and surely other daughters as well), their mothers hailed from junior consort houses or vassal dynasties, and little is known about them.[23] The ill-recorded careers of these junior sons, none of whom ever ruled, reflected their mothers' lesser rank.[24] The exception was Jochi's third son, Berke (r. 1257–67), who usurped the khanate in 1257 after the deaths of Batu's heirs.[25] Scholars have not settled the question of Berke's mother's identity, nor the influence she had on her son, but we can at least say that she was neither one of the Qonggirat wives, nor the Kereit Begtütmish.[26]

[22] Allsen, "Left Hand," 8–10.

[23] In addition to Sorghan, Begtütmish, and Öki, the wives were Qutlugh Khatun, Sultan Khatun (of the Ushin, but see footnote 26), another Kereit named Nubqus (?), Shīr, Qarajin, and a Merkit named Kul, along with concubines. *Mu'izz al-Anṣāb*, fol. 19a (not in Rashīd al-Dīn, *Shu'āb-i Panjgānah*); Rashīd al-Dīn, *Jāmi'*, 710–30, trans. Thackson, 348–55.

[24] But decades later some descendants of these junior sons did rise up. See Jackson, *Conquest to Conversion*, 388–9.

[25] Vásáry, István, "The Jochid Realm," 75.

[26] Jean Richard argues that she was Khan-Sultan (Sultan-Khatun from footnote 23), not from the Ushin but rather the daughter of Muḥammad Khwarazm-Shāh, who married Jochi in 1220 and was therefore a high-status conquered woman. This would make

In any case, after this first, relatively well-recorded generation of Jochid consorts, the picture grows dimmer, although we can discern that a robust Qonggirat consort family flourished both in Batu's lands and in those of Orda: for at least five generations, almost every major Jochid prince had at least one Qonggirat wife, who was usually the senior lady.[27] Furthermore, with one exception, only Qonggirat women produced the heirs.[28]

Meanwhile, although the scant records make it difficult to identify Qonggirat consort men, one does emerge to provide a case study for all the unknowns. This was the commander Salji'udai (d. 1301–2). Salji'udai

Berke's birthdate no earlier than 1221. Richard uses Nasawī, Juvaynī, Juzjānī, and Mufaḍḍal to make a compelling yet ultimately inconclusive argument in "La conversion de Berke et les débuts de l'islamisation de la Horde d'Or," *Revue des études islamiques* 35 (1967): 173–84; also see Nasawī, *Mankubartī*, ed. Ḥamdī, 97:300–1, trans. Houdas, 70, 305. By contrast, István Vásáry cites Mufaḍḍal to set Berke's birth in 1208, but says nothing about his mother. Vásáry does not account for Richard's work, nor considers Nasawī, and he therefore cannot be said to have the final word on this topic. István Vásáry, "History and Legend in Berke Khan's Conversion to Islam," in *Aspects of Altaistic Civilizations III: Proceedings of the Permanent Meeting of the Permanent International Altaistic Conference, Indiana University, Bloomington, IN, June 19–25*, 1987 (1990), 238.

[27] All women here are Qonggirats, unless stated otherwise. Numbers denote generations. Jochi (1) married Sorghan and Öki. Jochi's son Orda (2, from Sorghan) married Jüke, Tobaqana, and a daughter of one Öge Khan. Orda's son Sartaghtai (3, from Jüke) married Hujan, a sister of Hülegü (ilkhan's) Qonggirat wife Qutui. Sartaghtai's son Qonchi (4, from Hujan) married Toquluqan and Chingtüm. Qonchi's son Nayan / Bayan (5, from a wife named ["*Tūqūluqān khātūn az qawm-i qunghirāt*")] in *Jāmi'*, 712, with brackets in original, or "_____ of the Qonggirat" in Thackston, 349, and "Buluqun Khatun of the Qonggirat" in Boyle, 101 married Chingtüm through the levirate, and Elgen.

Orda's second son Quli (3, from one of Orda's Qonggirat wives), who died in the Ilkhanate, married Nendiken. Orda's sixth son Hülegü (3, from one of Orda's Qonggirat wives), had a grandson, Temür Buqa (5), who married Kökachin and Yebelün, allegedly another sister of Hülegü (ilkhan's) Qonggirat wife Qutui.

As for Batu (2, from Öki): His only known wife was the Alchi Tatar lady Boraqchin, while only a few daughters-in-law – none Qonggirats – have been recorded. Thereafter, however, Batu's grandsons Möngke-Temür and Töde-Möngke (4), both sons of Toqoqan (3), and Köchü (an Oirat daughter of Princess Checheyigen), married Qonggirats: Öljei and Öljeitü for Möngke-Temür, and Arighach for Töde-Möngke. Then Möngke-Temür's son Toqta (5, from Öljeitü) married Bulughan and Tükünche. Rashīd al-Dīn, *Jāmi'*, 89 (Batu's wife Boraqchin), 710–30 (the rest), trans. Thackston, 50 (Boraqchin), 348–55, trans. Boyle, 99–116; *Mu'izz al-Ansāb*, fols. 19a–23b (wives not in Rashīd al-Dīn, *Shu'āb-i Panjgānah*).

[28] The exception were the brothers Mönggke Temür and Töde-Möngke, whose mother was Princess Checheyigen's fourth daughter. See previous footnote, and Family Trees 8.2 and 8.7. See also Ishayahu Landa, "Sons-in-Law" 170–2.

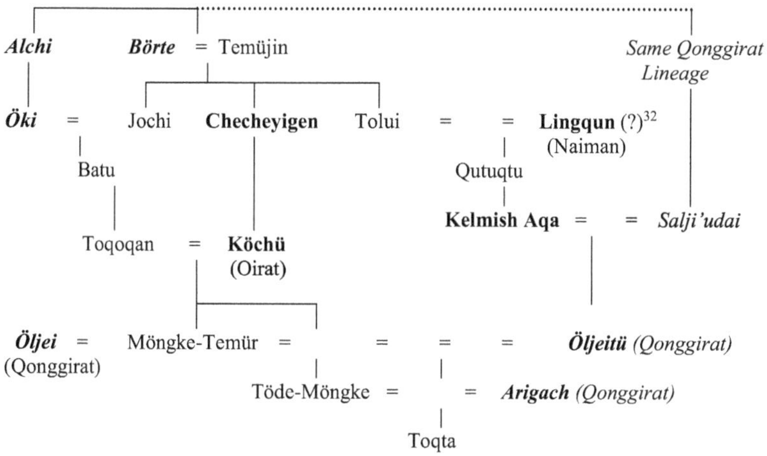

Family Tree 8.2 Oirat and Qonggirat consorts among the Jochids.[29]
All women are in **bold.**
Qonggirat consort family members are in *italics.*
Dots indicate unclear cousinly relationship.[30]

worked in the Jochid military for years, held grazing lands in the steppe near Khwarazm,[31] and became an imperial son-in-law by wedding Princess Kelmish Aqa, a lively and competent granddaughter of Tolui.[32] (See Family Tree 8.2.)

The relationship of these two members of the Qonggirat consort family to the ruling Jochids then becomes clear in the activities of their daughter, Öljeitü, who married the khan Möngke-Temür (r. 1267–80) as a junior

[29] For references on the Oirats see the subsequent text in the chapter, and footnote 61.

[30] Lingqun (garbled; possibly a Chinese honorific title, *ling-gong*), was possibly a daughter of the Naiman prince Küchlüg and her status is not entirely clear. Kai-Lung Ho, "The Office and the Noble Titles of the Mongols from the 14th to the 16th Centuries, and the Study of the 'White History' Čayan Teüke," *Central Asiatic Journal* 59, no. 1 (2016): 139 (for the title); otherwise Rashīd al-Dīn *Jāmi'*, 128, 779, 940, trans. Thackston, 69 (she is a slave), 382 (she is a wife aka *khatun*), 461 (She is a wife, *khatun*, with a camp), trans. Boyle, 160; George Lane (2006), *Daily Life in the Mongol Empire* (London: Greenwood Press), 244–5.

[31] Rashīd al-Dīn, *Jāmi'*, 741, 780, trans. Thackston, 363, 382, trans. Boyle, 124, 160. See also Landa, "Sons-in-Law," 170–2.

[32] She was the daughter of Tolui's son Qutuqtu and his wife Lingqun, for whom see footnote 30. Rashīd al-Dīn *Jāmi'*, 160, 173, 940, trans. Thackston, 86, 93, 461, trans. Boyle, 160; Lane, *Daily Life* 244–5.

wife.[33] In her capacity as royal childbearer, Öljeitü elevated herself by producing a son, Toqta, who later ruled (r. 1290–1312).[34] As a result of Öljetei's motherly achievement, her own parents found new opportunities: Salji'udai became intimately involved in his grandson's struggles with a cousin and rival, Noqai, in the 1290s,[35] while Kelmish Aqa demonstrated the kinds of activities that were typical for a wife in an important consort family. She followed Jochid affairs closely, corresponded regularly with her Ilkhanid cousins in Iran, and intervened in imperial matters by helping to arrange the release of a son of Grand Khan Qubilai (r. 1260–94) who had been imprisoned in Jochid territory.[36]

QONGGIRATS IN CHAGHATAYID AND ILKHANID LANDS

Meanwhile to the east of the Jochids in the Chaghatai Khanate, Qonggirats similarly figured as prominent consorts: Chaghatai's senior wife Yesülün was the daughter of Börte's first cousin, Qata, and bore most of Chaghatai's children. When Yesülün died, she was succeeded as senior wife by her sister, Tögen.[37] (See Family Tree 8.3.)

Unfortunately Chaghatai's other wives have not been recorded. Furthermore, after their initially strong showing, the Qonggirat family gave way to the Oirat consort house under Checheyigen's daughter Orqīna, who married the heir to the khanate, Qara-Hülegü (see Family Tree 8.3 and the following text). But after Orqīna's noteworthy tenure ended in the 1260s, the picture of all Chaghatayid consorts becomes murky.

The situation is clearer among the Ilkhanids, where Qonggirats formed one of three major consort families at the royal court as it

[33] The senior wife was another Qonggirat, Öljei. Rashīd al-Dīn, *Jāmi'*, 722, trans. Thackston, 352, trans. Boyle, 109.

[34] Rashīd al-Dīn, *Jāmi'*, 160, 173, 601, 722, 741, 940, trans. Thackston, 86, 93, 277, 352, 363, 461, trans. Boyle, 109, 160.

[35] Noqai married his daughter to Salji'udai's son, but it went badly. Rashīd al-Dīn, *Jāmi'*, 744, 779–80, trans. Thackston, 364, 382, trans. Boyle, 126, 160. On Noqai see Uli Schamiloglu, "The Golden Horde," in *The Turks II: Middle Ages*, ed. Hasan Celac Güzel et al. (Ankara, 2002), 822–5; DeWeese, *Islamization*, 88–9; Spuler, *Goldene Horde*, 64–77; Vernadsky, *Russia*, 162–5, 174–89; Rashīd al-Dīn, *Jāmi'*, 741–8, trans. Thackston, 363–6, trans. Boyle, 124–30.

[36] This was Qubilai and Chabi's son Nomoghan, who was captured by cousins in 1276 and imprisoned with the Jochids until 1284. Rashīd al-Dīn, *Jāmi'*, 779–80, trans. Thackston, 382, trans. Boyle, 160; Rossabi, *Khubilai*, 107–10 and esp. 109; de Rachewiltz, "Muqali," 10.

[37] Rashīd al-Dīn, *Jāmi'*, 751–61, trans. Thackston, 367–72, trans. Boyle, 135–44; *Mu'izz al-Anṣāb*, fols. 29a, 30a (not in Rashīd al-Dīn, *Shu'āb-i Panjgānah*).

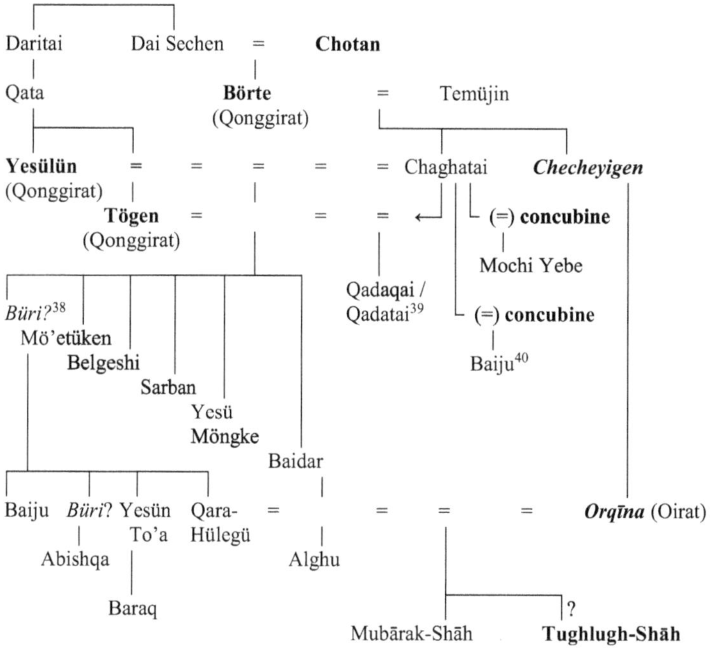

Family Tree 8.3 Many Chaghatayids, some Qonggirats, a few Oirats.
All women are in **bold**.
(=) denotes concubinage.
|? Denotes unclear maternal lineage.
Oirats are in *italics*.[38,39,40]

moved within the Caucasus region. Foremost among Qonggirat consorts in Ikhanid territory was the matriarch Qutui, wife of Hülegü, who was descended from relatives of Börte. Qutui was not Hülegü's senior wife, but after that lady died, Hülegü gave the senior camp, and the opportunity to be a manager, to Qutui.[41] This large establishment

[38] Jackson, "Dissolution," 199 and note 49 on the way Rashīd al-Dīn obscured Büri by making him into Chaghatai's grandson, rather than his eldest son; also *Secret History*, §270 (he is Chaghatai's *son*); Carpini, *Mission*, 26.

[39] This son is omitted from Rashīd al-Dīn, *Jāmi'*, 761, but included as "Qadatai" in Thackston, 372–3 and "Qadaqai" in Boyle, 144. Jackson, "Dissolution," 199, note 49, theorizes that here again Rashīd al-Dīn perhaps tampered with genealogy.

[40] This son is omitted from Rashīd al-Dīn, *Jāmi'*, 761, but included in Thackston, 372–3 and Boyle, 144.

[41] See Chapter 9.

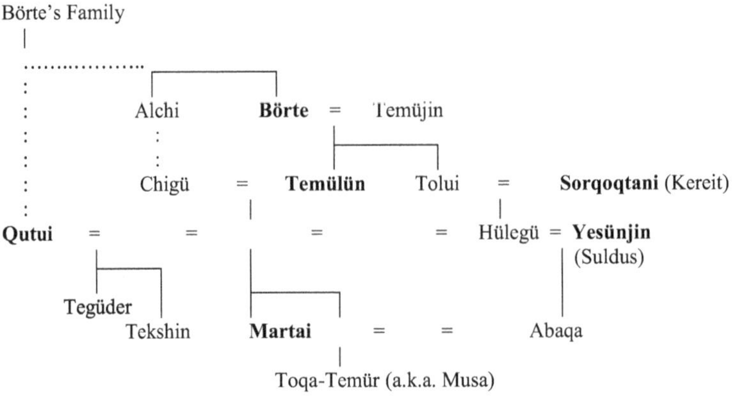

Family Tree 8.4 Qonggirat senior line in the Ilkhanate.
All women are in **bold**.
Dotted line indicates unclear relationship *or* adoption.
Börte's Family.

contained several of Hülegü's lesser wives and concubines, as well as most of his children. Qutui could also hold her own head high as the mother of two of Hülegü's sons, one of whom later ruled (Tegüder [r. 1282–4]).[42] In addition to Qutui, a related Qonggirat consort line in the Ilkhanate stemmed from her cousins, who were the offspring of Princess Tümelün and her husband Chigü (see Chapter 9).[43] (See Family Tree 8.4.)

Slightly later a third Qonggirat consort line sprang from a commander in the Ilkhanid armies of invasion, Abatai, whose sons fathered several daughters who married Toluid princes.[44] (See Family Tree 8.5.) A full discussion of the ups and downs of Qonggirat consorts in the Ilkhanate appears in Chapter 9.

[42] The second son was Prince Tekshin. See Chapter 9.

[43] Rashīd al-Dīn, *Jāmiʿ*, 161, 971, 1056, 1163, trans. Thackston, 86, 476, 515, 566.

[44] Rashīd al-Dīn, *Jāmiʿ*, 160 (Bulughan and Keremün), 1055 and 1189 (Eltüzmish), 1215 (Bulughan and Keremün), 1321–2 (Eltüzmish), trans. Thackston, 86, 515, 580, 593–4, 660; Fakhr al-Dīn Dawud Banākatī, *Taʾrīkh-i Banākatī* or *Rawḍat al-albāb fī maʿrifat al-tawārīkh va al-akābir va al-ansāb*, ed. Jaʿfar Shiʿār (Tehran: Anjuman-i Āthār-i Millī, 1969), 451; De Nicola, *Khatuns*, 158 (Eltüzmish).

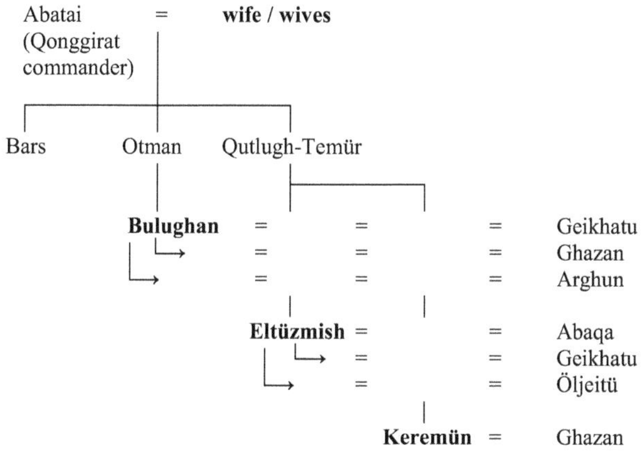

Family Tree 8.5 Qonggirat junior lines in the Ilkhanate.
All women are in **bold**.

QONGGIRATS IN CHINA: CHABI

It comes as no surprise that the Qonggirat consort star shone as brightly in China as it did everywhere else. The origin of the family dominance can be traced to the singular personality of Chabi, a niece of Börte, who married Sorqoqtani's son Qubilai (r. 1260–94), and became head of a wifely camp.[45] (See Figure 8.1.) Since we know more about Chabi than other imperial women, we can use her example as a window into the ways that imperial wives shaped events.

Chabi was not Qubilai's first wife, whose identity is unclear. She was either a woman of unknown family named Tegülün, or a Merkit named Qoruqchin. Significantly, Tegülün / Qoruqchin is said to have lost her status later during her marriage, despite having born a son, which should have cemented her authority and position.[46] This fits Chabi's story: she

[45] Zhao, *Marriage*, 19, and 239–41 for his translation of *Yuan Shi*, Biographies of Empresses; F. W. Cleaves, "The Biography of Empress Čabi in the Yuan Shih," *Harvard Ukrainian Studies* 3/4, no. 1 (1979–80): 138–50; *Yuan Shi*, 14:2693–6, 2698, 2701, Table of Empresses (unpublished trans. Buell); Rashīd al-Dīn, *Jāmi'*, 160, 865, trans. Thackston, 86, 422, trans. Boyle, 241–2; Hambis, *Chapter CVIII*, Table 2.

[46] For Tegülün see *Yuan shi*, Table of Empresses, 14:2693–6, 2698, 2701 (unpublished trans. Buell); Rossabi, *Khubilai*, 16, 225; Zhao states she was another Qonggirat from among Börte's relatives in *Marriage*, 20. For Qoruqchin see Rashīd al-Dīn, *Jāmi'*, 94–5, 866–7, trans. Thackston, 53 (claiming she had no children), 422 (claiming she had a son, "Qoridai").

Figure 8.1: Portrait of Qubilai. National Palace Museum, Taipei. Portrait of Empress Chabi. National Palace Museum, Taipei.

became Qubilai's most beloved and favored wife, so if a senior woman did lose status, it would have been to her. Chabi married Qubilai before 1240, in which year their first son, Dorji, was born.[47] This suggests that Chabi's own birth was perhaps in the mid-1220s, which would make her fifteen or sixteen by 1240, and which would accord with preferred marriage ages. Chabi successfully proved her worth as a royal mother by giving birth to four princes with Qubilai (including the one later imprisoned in Jochid lands).[48] One historical source claims that Chabi also had five daughters for a total of nine children, but the daughters' names are unrecorded, and their number cannot be verified elsewhere.[49]

[47] Rossabi, *Khubilai*, 16.

[48] See Kelmish Aqa previously in this chapter; Rashīd al-Dīn, *Jāmi'*, 865–8, trans. Thackston, 422–3, trans. Boyle, 421–3.

[49] Rashīd al-Dīn, *Jāmi'*, 160, trans. Thackston, 86. Qubilai's daughters include Miao-Yen, Yeli, Nanjiajin, Qutlugh Kelmish (aka Khudula), and an unnamed Orjin imperial princess. The scant evidence prevents us from determining whether any were Chabi's offspring. Rossabi, *Khubilai*, 226–7 (Miao-Yen and Qutlugh Kelmish); Zhao, *Marriage*, 20 (Nanjiaqin), 197 (Qutlugh Kelmish), also his "Conciliation," 4–5, 13–14; *Yuan Shi*, Table of Princesses (the Orjin princess, Yeli, Nanjiajin, and Qutlugh Kelmish, but not Miao-Yeh), *Yuan Shi*, Table of Princesses 13:2757–61 (unpublished trans. Buell); Hambis, *Chapitre CVIII*, table 2 (Nanjiajin), also 17–18 and note 2; also Robinson, *Empire's Twilight*, 100–1.

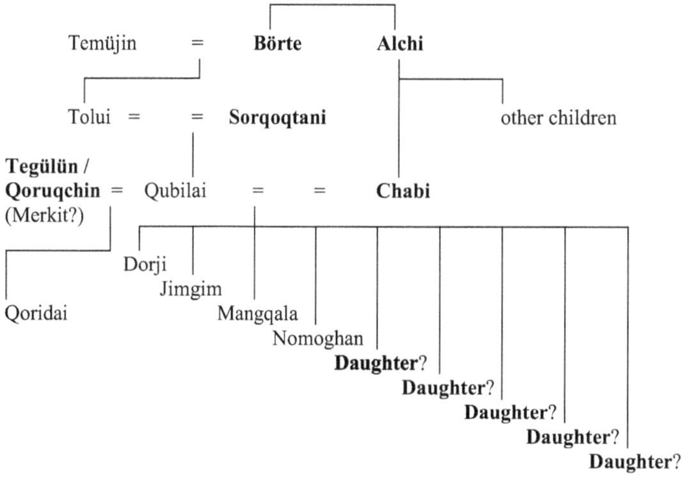

Family Tree 8.6 Qubilai and Chabi.
All women are in **bold**.
*The birth order of Chabi's (possible) daughters in relation to her (definite) sons is unknown.

To seal Chabi's success and maintain the supremacy of the Qonggirat consorts, only her sons became contenders for succession. (See Family Tree 8.6.)

As for Chabi's many activities and the light they shine on the position of a royal wife: she was credited with possessing political savoir faire, since it was she who sent Qubilai timely warnings as he and his brother Ariq Böke descended into civil war.[50] She made her mark on religion: she was devoted to Tibetan Buddhism, enjoyed a close relationship with the influential Phags-pa Lama, and is likely to have helped shape Qubilai's own favor for that form of worship.[51] Chabi lobbied on questions of government policy, whether by opposing the exploitation of farmers in Northern China, or promoting gentle treatment of the Song royal women after their capture in 1279, a responsibility that she oversaw personally after intervening successfully on their behalf.[52] Her influence extended to

[50] Rossabi, *Khubilai*, 51; also Rashīd al-Dīn, *Jāmi'*, 857, trans. Thackston, 416, trans. Boyle, 248.
[51] Rossabi, *Khubilai*, 16, 41, 138; De Nicola, *Khatuns*, 49, 188–9, 200, 210.
[52] Rossabi, *Khubilai*, 67, 91; also Cleaves, "Čabi," 142–5; Zhao, *Marriage*, 239–41 (biography of Chabi).

culture, where she patronized important artists like the Nepalese A-ni-ko, and to material culture, whether fashion, the design of uniforms and war materiel, or the frugal reuse of fabrics at court.[53] Before her demise in 1281 when she was in perhaps her fifties, she chose her own successor for Qubilai, a Qonggirat relative named Nambi.[54] But Chabi's death struck a crushing blow to the Grand Khan, as did that of her second son, Crown Prince Jingim, who died four years later in 1285.[55] Qubilai failed to recover from these devastating personal and dynastic losses, and tried to escape into drink, much like his uncle Grand Khan Ögedei, whose alcoholism worsened significantly after the untimely death of his own heir.[56] After Chabi it was Nambi who maintained Qonggirat prominence by acting as an intermediary between the bereaved and besotted Qubilai and his ministers.[57] Then, following Qubilai's death in 1294, wifely authority moved into the hands of yet another Qonggirat lady, Kökechin, the senior widow of the deceased crown prince, who became regent briefly until her son was enthroned as Grand Khan Temür (r. 1294–1307).[58] Thereafter the Chinggisids made a long series of additional marriages with this most favored lineage. At least seventeen imperial wives hailed from the Qonggirat lineages during the Yuan period (1260–1368), most of whom were senior wives, while Chinggisid princesses married Qonggirat men on an equally regular basis, and thereby solidified the principle of exchange marriage.[59]

THE OIRATS I: KÖCHÜ, ELCHIQMISH, GÜYÜK, AND ÖLJEI

The second major consorts after the influential Qonggirats were the Oirats, descendants of Börte's second daughter, Checheyigen. As established in Chapter 4, Checheyigen, Tolui, and their niece Qolui all married

[53] Robinson, *Empire's Twilight*, 102–3 (Chinggisid artistic influences on the Korean court). Rossabi, *Khubilai*, 67–9 (material culture), 171 (A-ni-ko); Cleaves, "Čabi," 143–4, 145; Zhao, *Marriage*, 239–41 (biography of Chabi).

[54] If she bore a child in 1240, she herself could not have been born later than the mid-1220s, and she was thus in her 50s at her death in 1281. For Nambi see Rossabi, *Khubilai*, 225; Zhao's translation of her *Yuan Shi* biography in *Marriage*, 239–41; *Yuan Shi*, Table of Empresses, 14:2693–6, 2698, 2701 (unpublished trans. Buell).

[55] Rossabi, *Khubilai*, 206, 226. [56] See Chapter 6.

[57] Zhao, translation of Nambi's *Yuan Shi* biography, *Marriage*, 241.

[58] Rashīd al-Dīn, *Jāmi'*, 947, trans. Thackston, 464, trans. Boyle, 320.

[59] Zhao notes perhaps 13–14 Qonggirats wives from one lineage, and four more from unknown parentage, in addition to the Yuan princess brides in *Marriage*, 106–11, 112–18.

into the Oirat ruling family in 1207–8.[60] Checheyigen went on to strengthen her position in the Oirat and imperial Chinggisid families by bearing seven children (more than any of her sisters). Three were sons: Buqa-Temür, Börtö'e, and Bars-Buqa, while the other four were daughters: Elchiqmish, Güyük, Köchü (?), and Orqīna.[61] As mentioned in Chapter 7, Checheyigen made brilliant matches for all of her girls with the Chinggisid houses of her brothers in accordance with exchange marriage patterns. In addition, two of her three sons married Chinggisid princesses.[62] (See Family Tree 8.7.) The Oirat consort house's story after Möngke's enthronement was one of considerable strength, stemming from Princess Checheyigen's dominance and political savvy, as shown in the excellent placement of all her offspring. Indeed, initially the Oirats stood to rival even the Qonggirats as consorts. But after this strong start, the fortunes of this house wavered in more than one khanate, caused by an unpredictable combination of bad luck, political upheaval, and early death. Only in the Ilkhanate did the Oirats maintain their position, albeit even there at some cost.

Oirat consorts among the Jochids:

Although it was the Qonggirat consorts who dominated marriage politics in the Jochid realm, the Oirats nevertheless kept the Qonggirats from taking their success for granted. When Checheyigen's daughter Köchü married Batu's son Toqoqan, Checheyigen's own status made Köchü the senior wife, not some Qonggirat lady. Köchü then sealed her position by bearing two sons. Although Toqoqan himself never ruled, both sons did: Möngke-Temür (r. 1267–80), then Töde-Möngke (r. 1280–7).[63] But neither man married into an Oirat consort lineage as might be expected; rather, both had Qonggirat wives: One for Töde-Möngke (Arigach), and

[60] See Chapter 4, Table 4.2. [61] Rashīd al-Dīn, *Jāmi'*, 100–1, trans. Thackston, 55–6.

[62] Rashīd al-Dīn, *Jāmi'*, 100–1 (all children; Börtö'e's marriage), 722 (Köchü and see footnote 63), 758 (Orqīna), 939–40 (Elchiqmish), 941 (Bars-Buqa), 968 (Güyük), trans. Thackston, 55–6 (all), 371 (Orqīna), 460 (Elchiqmish), 461 (Bars-Buqa), 352 (Köchü), 472 (Güyük), trans. Boyle, 109–10 (Köchü), 142 (Orqīna), 311 (Elchiqmish), 312 (Bars-Buqa).

[63] Rashīd al-Dīn, *Jāmi'*, 100–1, 722, trans. Thackston, 55–6, 352 (calling her Buqa-Temür's daughter (sic) and claiming that Checheyigen had two daughters (sic), then correcting himself to four), trans. Boyle, 109–10; Zhao, *Marriage*, 130–1, 137–41; also Pfeiffer, *Conversion to Islam*, 218–19, without distinguishing between half- and full siblings.

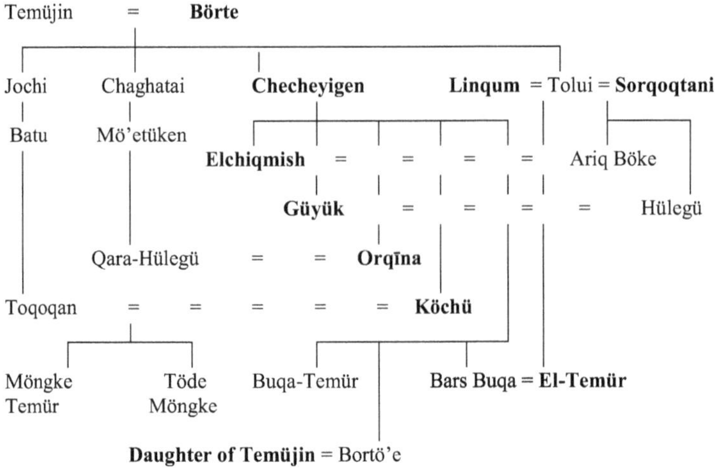

Family Tree 8.7 Checheyigen's children.
All women are in **bold**.

two for Möngke-Temür (Öljei, the senior wife, and Öljeitü).[64] (See Family Tree 8.2.)

The other wives of Köchü's sons hailed either from the Ushin family, or from the Alchi Tatars.[65] This raises an immediate question: Since, in an ideal circumstance, a royal wife's brother would accompany her to Jochid territory, work there as a commander, and provide nieces and nephews for a consort house, did any of Köchü's three brothers do this? The eldest, Buqa-Temür, did not; rather, he traveled to Iran with Hülegü and headed the Oirat consort house there (see Chapter 9). Meanwhile, the other two

[64] Öljei and Öljeitu should not be confused with one another. Rashīd al-Dīn, *Jāmi'*, 722, trans. Thackston, 352, trans. Boyle, 109–10; Aḥmad al-Nuwayrī, *Nihāyat al-Arab fī Funūn al-Adab*, ed. Sa'īd Āshūr (Cairo: al-Mu'assasah al-Miṣrīyah al-'Āmmah lil-Ta'līf wa al-Ṭibā'ah wa al-Nashr, 1985–98), 27:365.

[65] They may be descended from Batu's senior wife, Boraqchin. Juvaynī, *World-Conqueror*, 268; Vassāf, *Taḥrīr-i Ta'rīkh-i Vaṣṣāf*, ed. and condensed 'Abd al-Muḥammad Āyātī ([Tehran]: Bunyād-i Farhang-i Īrān, 1346 / 1967), 332; Rashīd al-Dīn, *Jāmi'*, 89, trans. Thackston, 50, although not mentioning her (or any others!) in the proper place for Batu's wives, which is *Jāmi'*, 710, trans. Thackston, 352. Note Ḥamd Allah Mustawfī Qazvīnī, *Ta'rīkh-i Gūzideh*, ed. 'Abd al-Ḥusayn Navā'ī (Tehran: Amīr Kabīr, 1983–4), 585 (making Boraqchin into Sartaq's wife, not mother); Nuwayri, *Nihāyah*, 27:357–8 (Boraqchin's failed attempts to keep her descendants in power); Jackson, "Dissolution," 223 and note 160; M. Brosset, trans., *Histoire de la Géorgie: depuis l'antiquité jusqu'au xix siècle* (St. Petersburg: l'Academie imperial des science, 1849), 569, text 377.

brothers, Börtö'e and Bars Buqa, stayed in the east. One of them must have ruled in Oirat territory, while both men married lesser daughters of Chinggis Khan or Tolui, and their sons served Qubilai in China.[66] Only later did Oirat men enter Jochid armies, but these were descendants of Jochi's daughter Qolui and her Oirat husband, and served Orda's offspring.[67] Thus if Köchü's brothers did not accompany her to the far west with the invading armies, she may not have been supported by an Oirat consort lineage into which to marry her sons. This might explain the way that Qonggirat women immediately resumed their ascendancy as senior wives after her.

Oirat consorts among the Toluids:

While Köchü was maintaining – but not expanding – the Oirat presence among the Jochids, her sister Elchiqmish was rising among the Toluids in Mongolia as the beloved senior wife of Ariq Böke. But this was an ephemeral golden moment: Elchiqmish was the only one of the four sisters not to bear children, while Ariq Böke's own career ended in death in the mid-1260s.[68] Meanwhile the third sister, Güyük, married Ariq Böke's brother Hülegü. Her wifely career began auspiciously: like all her sisters, she became the senior wife and received the largest wifely camp. She also produced the necessary children. Her position was further strengthened by the presence of her brother Buqa-Temür, commanding Oirat soldiers in Hülegü's armies, and her half-sister, Öljei – not Checheyigen's daughter – as one of Hülegü's junior wives.[69] And yet Güyük remains an almost unknown figure: she died early in Mongolia; her great camp was reassigned to a Qonggirat wife;[70] and her position was taken by the formidable Kereit princess Dokuz, Hülegü's second senior wife, whose

[66] Rashīd al-Dīn, *Jāmi'*, 100–1, 940, 893, trans. Thackston, 55–6, 461 (Bars-Buqa's marriage to a daughter of Tolui and Linqum Khatun, and his grandson Tuq-Temür's marriage to Princess Emegen, a descendant of Arik Böke); 436 (a commander named Beglemish, possibly Bars-Buqa's son). See also Landa, "Sons-in-Law," 180.

[67] This may mean that Qolui and Orda were full siblings, i.e., Sorghan was both their mother. Qolui's descendants served Orda's grandson Qonchi (or Qonichi) Khan (fl. 1290s). Rashīd al-Dīn, *Jāmi'*, 101, 710–16, trans. Thackston, 56, 348–50.

[68] Rashīd al-Dīn, *Jāmi'*, 100, 939–40, trans. Thackston, 55–6, 460, trans. Boyle, 311. This family remained unnoticed until Arik Böke's descendant Arpa became a contender in Iran in the 1330s. Charles Melville, *The Fall of Amir Chupan and the Decline of the Ikhanate: A Decade of Discord in Iran*, Papers on Inner Asia, no. 30 (Bloomington, IN: Research Center for Inner Asian Studies, 1999), 44–6, 48–50.

[69] See Chapter 9. [70] Rashīd al-Dīn, *Jāmi'*, 964, 965, trans. Thackston, 472, 473.

tenure relegated Güyük to complete obscurity.[71] To make matters worse, Güyük's name is quite unusual, is not used for any other women in the historical sources, and can be easily mistaken for the (in)famous Grand Khan. It took the remaining members of the Oirat consort house in the Ilkhanate no small effort to regain lost ground, as seen in Chapter 9. Nevertheless they did so, in part because of the presence of junior lines of Oirat consorts, one stemming from descendants of Töregene's administrator, Arghun Aqa, in Khurasan, and the other from Tankiz, a relative of the Oirat ruler Qutuqa Begi, who married both Ögedeyid and Toluid wives.[72]

THE OIRATS II: ORQĪNA

The last of Checheyigen's daughters to make a brilliant marriage was Orqīna, who wedded Qara-Hülegü, Chaghatai's grandson and heir to the Chaghatayid throne.[73] Like her sisters, Orqīna became a senior wife by virtue of her status as Checheyigen's daughter. Orqīna also produced the necessary son, Mubārak-Shāh, and possibly a daughter, Tughlugh-Shāh, who later married into the Ilkhanid nobility.[74] (See Family Tree 8.3.) Orqīna's own career as wife, mother, widow and independent regent was the most dramatic of the Oirat sisters, and bears a close investigation to demonstrate the opportunities she enjoyed and the challenges she faced.

Although Orqīna's husband Qara-Hülegü eventually rose to the position of Chaghatayid Khan, he did not become his grandfather's heir easily. His father Mö'etüken, a son of the Qonggirat senior wife, Yesülün, had been Chaghatai's beloved successor.[75] But after Mö'etuken's tragic demise during the Western Campaign, Chaghatai chose another son, Belgeshi, as the next heir, then was foiled by the boy's death at the age

71 She was the first cousin of his mother, Sorqoqtani. Rashīd al-Dīn, *Jāmi'*, 963, 967, trans. Thackston, 471, 479; Banākatī, *Ta'rīkh*, 411. Also De Nicola, *Khatuns*, 91.

72 See Chapter 9.

73 Juvayni, *World-Conqueror*, 274; Rashīd al-Dīn, *Jāmi'*, 758, 767, trans. Thackston, 371, 376–7, trans. Boyle, 142, 149; also De Nicola, *Khatuns*, 76–7.

74 The resemblance in names – Mubārakshāh, Tughluqshāh – could indicate that they were uterine siblings. Note the five children of Örüg, wife of the *ilkhan* Arghun (r. 1284–91), who were named Yesü-Temür and Öljeitü (the boys), and Öljetei, Ölji-Temür, and Qutlugh-Temür (the girls); similarly the *ilkhan* Geikhatu's senior wife, Aisha, had daughters named Ula-Qutlugh, El-Qutlugh, and Ara-Qutlugh.

75 Rashīd al-Dīn, *Jāmi'*, 752, 758–9, trans. Thackston, 368, 371, trans. Boyle, 137, 143; Juvaynī, *World-Conqueror*, 273.

of thirteen.[76] Only thereafter did Chaghatai select his grandson Qara-Hülegü to succeed him, seconded by his senior wife and the highly-respected vizier.[77] After Chaghatai's death in 1242, Qara-Hülegü took up the position of khan as expected, and cooperated with Töregene in matters of financial policy and personnel.[78]

But although Qara-Hülegü was the third of Chaghatai's hand-picked successors, he was also a grandson whose uncles were alive at the time that he was serving as khan. This pitted his relatively junior claim to the Chaghatayid throne against the weightier ones of his seniors, and was not lost on others, among them Grand Khan Güyük. Upon his own succession, Güyük overruled Chaghatai's last wishes and immediately appointed a new Chaghatayid Khan in the person of Yesü-Möngke, another of Chaghatai's sons and also Qara-Hülegü's uncle (see Chapter 6). Güyük argued that Yesü-Möngke enjoyed greater seniority than his nephew, Qara-Hülegü, which mirrored the precedent that Güyük and his mother had just set by wresting rule from Güyük's own nephew Shiremün. Güyük may have intended to favor Yesü-Möngke, who is said to have been a personal friend, and with whom Güyük shared a deep fondness for heavy drinking.[79] Scholars also suggest that Güyük was opposing his mother's removal of financial officials, which Qara-Hülegü and Orqīna had supported.[80] It is worth noting that the pro-Toluid Persian historian Juvaynī shored up Qara-Hülegü's claim and thereby subtly critiqued Güyük's decision by writing Belgeshi out of the chain of heirs.[81] Although Rashīd al-Dīn kept Belgeshi, he did state falsely that Qara-Hülegü was Mö'etüken's oldest son, not the youngest, in an attempt to elevate him.[82]

In any case, Güyük's decision and the bleakness of their prospects must have helped drive Qara-Hülegü and Orqīna to join Princess Checheyigen

[76] Rashīd al-Dīn, *Jāmi'*, 760, trans. Thackston, 371, trans. Boyle, 143.

[77] These were Yesülün and Ḥabash-Amīd. Juvaynī, *World-Conqueror*, 273.

[78] Qara-Hülegü helped purge the administrator Körgüz at Töregene's request. See Chapter 6; also Allsen, *Mongol Imperialism*, 52; De Nicola, "Orghīna," 114, and *Khatuns*, 77; Hope, *Ilkhanate*, 70.

[79] The claim that Güyük favored Yesü Möngke because the latter opposed Möngke reads like hindsight. Rashīd al-Dīn, *Jāmi'*, 761, 767–70, trans. Thackston, 372, 376–7, trans. Boyle, 149. Also De Nicola, "Orghīna," 114, and *Khatuns*, 77; Juvaynī, *World-Conqueror*, 274.

[80] De Nicola, *Khatuns*, 77; Hope, *Ilkhanate*, 70.

[81] Juvaynī, *World-Conqueror*, 273.

[82] Rashīd al-Dīn, *Jāmi'*, 758–60, trans. Thackston, 376, although he states accurately that Qara-Hülegü was the fourth son on 371, trans. Boyle, 149 and 142.

and other members of the Oirat consort family and ally themselves with the treasonous Toluid-Jochid alliance, even though this flew in the face of opinions among the Chaghatayid relatives. After his enthronement Möngke rewarded their courage and loyalty by reinstating Qara-Hülegü as Chaghatayid Khan,[83] while the reigning khan, Yesü-Möngke, was captured and sent to Batu.[84] This formed part of Möngke's program of undoing Ögedeyid wrongs.

Qara-Hülegü, Orqīna, and their troops promptly headed southwest from the quriltai to return to Chaghatayid lands, but Qara-Hülegü died in 1252 on the way. The stalwart Orqīna traveled on to Almaliq, to which Yesü Möngke soon returned.[85] With commanders and troops at her disposal, Orqīna had him executed and thus purged one more Chaghatayid for the Toluids. Then she assumed rule at Almaliq, officially on behalf of her young son Mubārak-Shāh, and in reality quite independently, all approved by Möngke himself.[86] In addition to whatever revenue accrued to her from taxes on the Silk Road trade that ran through her cities, Orqīna surely also invested with her own merchants.[87] Thus as the monarch of the Chaghatayids, Orqīna was in a position to welcome her brother-in-law Hülegü with his new senior wife, Dokuz, his secondary wife, Öljei (Orqīna's half sister), and her brother Buqa-Temür as one of Hülegü's commanders when they all arrived with the invading armies of the Iran campaign in 1253.[88] (See Family Tree 8.8.)

As was demanded of her position, and in conjunction with Chaghatai's widows, Orqīna treated her guests to a series of banquets and lavished gifts on them, which demonstrates the role that all imperial women – not just Orqīna as regent – played in hospitality. Next the guests departed for Transoxiana, where the governor repeated the procedure to the tune of

[83] Allsen, *Mongol Imperialism*, 52–3; De Nicola, "Orghīna," 114–15.

[84] He went with Büri. Batu tried both men and put Büri to death, but returned Yesü-Möngke alive to Chaghatayid lands. Juvaynī, *World-Conqueror*, 274, 588; Rashīd al-Dīn, *Jāmiʿ*, 837 (only Büri was sent west), trans. Thackston, 408, Boyle, 213. On Büri see Jackson, "Dissolution," 199 and note 49.

[85] Juvaynī, *World-Conqueror*, 274; Rashīd al-Dīn, *Jāmiʿ*, 761, 767–0, trans. Thackston, 372, 376–7, trans. Boyle, 143, 149.

[86] Allsen, *Mongol Imperialism*, 52–3; De Nicola, "Orghīna," 116–17 and *Khatuns*, 77–9, 106; Juvaynī, *World-Conqueror*, 274; Rashīd al-Dīn, *Jāmiʿ*, 761, 767–70, trans. Thackston, 372, 376–7, trans. Boyle, 143, 149.

[87] See Chapter 1.

[88] De Nicola, "Orghīna," 117, and *Khatuns*, 79; Juvaynī, *World-Conqueror*, 612; Rashīd al-Dīn, *Jāmiʿ*, 978, trans. Thackston, 479–80.

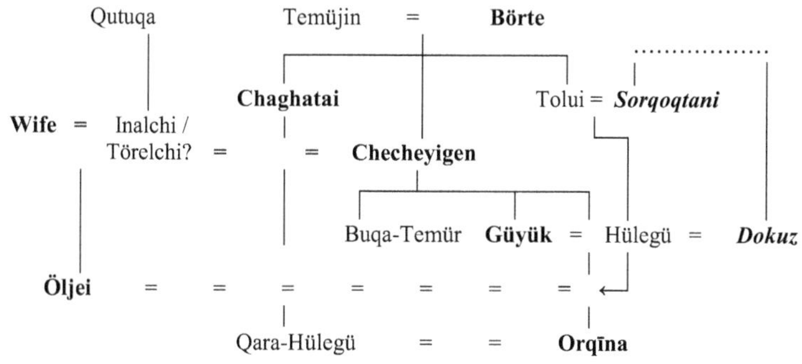

Family Tree 8.8 Hülegü, his Oirat in-laws and a few Kereits.[89]
All women are in **bold**.
Dotted line represents cousins.
Italics represents Kereits.

forty days of parties in a pavilion of gold brocade.[90] Thereafter Orqīna ruled in her own territories without known incident, and well enough that she was financially positioned to patronize religion (in this case, Islam[91]) until Möngke's death in 1259.[92]

In the civil war over the grand khanate between Ariq Böke and Qubilai that followed, Orqīna opposed Qubilai and sided with her sister Elchiqmish's husband, Ariq Böke, who was already supported by a contingent of Oirat troops.[93] First Orqīna exercised her rights as a member of both the Golden Lineage (by marriage and birth) and a consort family (by birth) and attended the quriltai in Mongolia in which

[89] For Checheyigen see Chapter 4, Family Trees 4.2, and 4.8 for the Kereits. For Checheyigen's children's marriages see footnote 62. For Öljei see Rashīd al-Dīn, *Jāmi'*, 101, 964, trans. Thackston, 56, 472.

[90] Mas'ūd Beg governed the region directly for Möngke. His working relationship to Orqīna is unclear. Juvaynī, *World-Conqueror*, 612; Rashīd al-Dīn, *Jāmi'*, 978, trans. Thackston, 479–80; also Allsen, "Mas'ūd Beg," in *Service*, 128.

[91] De Nicola, *Khatuns*, 218, and "Orghīna," entire.

[92] On Friar William's controversial reference by to a geographical region named Organum in today's Kazakhstan, which some see as a reference to Orqīna, see De Nicola, *Khatuns*, 79–80.

[93] Their number is unknown. Rashīd al-Dīn, *Jāmi'*, 880–1, trans. Thackston, 430; Junko Miyakawi, "The Birth of the Oyirad Khanship," *Central Asiatic Journal* 41, no. 1 (1997): 39–40; Hope, *Ilkhanate*, 108 and note 110, suggests that the Oirats turned Arik Böke over to Qubilai, citing the fifteenth-century author Hāfiz Abrū. See also Landa, "Sons-in-Law," 187–90 on geography and marital links together.

Ariq Böke was elected in 1260, not Qubilai's competing quriltai in China.[94] By this point Orqīna had ruled her realm for nearly a decade as capably as Töregene or Sorqoqtani. The suggestion of one Persian historian that she chose Ariq Böke only because she was misled by the flawed advice of her commanders is therefore insupportable, and should be read as an attempt to whitewash her favor for the "wrong" candidate by deflecting the blame to her subordinates.[95] Qubilai surely also shaped Orqīna's decision when he opposed her independence by sending Abishqa, a Chaghatayid cousin of her husband, to take her khanate from her through force or marriage (see Family Tree 8.3).[96] Fortunately for Orqīna, Ariq Böke rewarded her loyalty by arresting Abishqa on the way.[97]

After the quriltai Orqīna returned to Almaliq, but her plans were soon upset when Ariq Böke found his supplies cut off by Qubilai, and designated another Chaghatayid, Alghu, to become Chaghatayid Khan, perhaps needing a man to actually lead troops.[98] Alghu arrived and began collecting an army, but Orqīna immediately left for Ariq Böke's court with a slew of complaints, and made a lengthy stay.[99] Meanwhile the relationship between Ariq Böke and Alghu deteriorated until Ariq Böke sent Orqīna back to Alghu to broker an agreement.[100] Here we see Orqīna both as a negotiator, and as a political link between two men.

[94] Rashīd al-Dīn, *Jāmi'*, 875, trans. Thackston, 427, trans. Boyle, 251.

[95] Rashīd al-Dīn here was trying to emphasize the incorrectness of Arik Böke's claim, and denigrate the commanders; see previous note. For the latter see Hope, "Qarachu," 17–20.

[96] Rashīd al-Din claims that Abishqa was the son of Qara-Hülegü's brother, Büri, which would make him senior to Qara-Hülegü's son. But note Jackson's suggestion that Büri might have been Qara-Hülegü's uncle in "Dissolution," 199, footnote 49, which would make Abishqa even more senior to Mubarak-Shāh. See Family Tree 8.3. Rashīd al-Dīn, *Jāmi'*, 761 (Alghu), 875 (the quriltai), trans. Thackston, 372, 427, trans. Boyle, 143–4, 251. Also De Nicola, *Khatuns*, 81.

[97] Abishqa's orders toward Orqīna are unclear: "*bi-satānad* " in Rashīd al-Dīn, *Jāmi'*, 753 (take her as a wife), with varied translations: "arrest her" in Thackston, 369, but "marry her" in Boyle, 138. Also Rossabi, *Khubilai*, 53–62 (the civil war), 58 (Abishqa, albeit without Orqīna).

[98] Rashīd al-Dīn, *Jāmi'*, 878, trans. Thackston, 428, trans. Boyle, 253–4; De Nicola, *Khatuns*, 81. Although women could sometimes participate in battle or lead troops, male leadership was the standard, especially in wartime. Bruno De Nicola, "Warfare," 95–112.

[99] Rashīd al-Dīn, *Jāmi'*, 882, trans. Thackston, 430, trans. Boyle, 256; De Nicola, "Orghīna," 119, and *Khatuns*, 81–2.

[100] Alghu confiscated supplies that Arik Böke wanted (Rashīd al-Dīn, *Jāmi'*, 768, trans. Thackston, 376–7, trans. Boyle, 150), then realigned with Qubilai. Jackson, "Dissolution," 234; De Nicola, "Orghīna," 119, and *Khatuns*, 82.

But when she arrived, Alghu seized her (and the opportunity) and married her, possibly against her will.[101] This illustrates a weakness particular to women in this society, no matter how powerful: vulnerability to forced marriage, which men did not have to contemplate. Since by this point Alghu had switched his allegiance to Qubilai, Orqīna was not purged for her former support of Ariq Böke.[102] But about a year into the marriage in 1265–6 Alghu died after an illness, and Orqīna and her commanders then made her son Mubārak-Shāh into khan without, it seems, Qubilai's approval.[103] This was perhaps Orqīna's last act as independent ruler. In response Qubilai opposed her yet again, this time by dispatching yet another Chaghatayid, Baraq, to overthrow Mubārak-Shāh (see Family Tree 8.3). Baraq soon prevailed and demoted his cousin humiliatingly to a position as keeper of the hunting cats.[104] But after Baraq met his own end while fighting a rebel uprising, Mubārak-Shāh plundered Baraq's possessions down to his wife's jewelry and fled to the Ilkhan Abaqa (r. 1265–82) in Iran, who gave him command over troops stationed near Ghazna.[105]

Did Mubārak-Shāh take his mother with him? We do not know, especially since the date of Orqīna's death is contested. The Persian historian Vaṣṣāf suggests that she died before Alghu, perhaps in 1264 or so as a result of a pregnancy gone terribly wrong.[106] By contrast, Rashīd al-Dīn credits her with outliving Alghu and enthroning her son thereafter (as suggested previously), and gives no date for her demise.[107] Regardless,

[101] Alghu positioned the minister Mas'ūd Beg in Transoxiana to make Orqīna happier. Rashīd al-Dīn, *Jāmi'*, 885, trans. Thackston, 432, trans. Boyle, 260–1.

[102] De Nicola, "Orghīna," 119, and *Khatuns*, 82.

[103] The illness is unknown. Rashīd al-Dīn, *Jāmi'*, 769, 885, 891, trans. Thackston, 377, 432, 435, trans. Boyle, 151, 261, 265, in brief, Banākatī, *Ta'rīkh*, 398. Also De Nicola, "Orghīna," 119.

[104] Rashīd al-Dīn, *Jāmi'*, 759, 769–70, 891, trans. Thackston, 371, 377, 435, trans. Boyle, 142, 151, 265; Banākatī, *Ta'rīkh*, 398.

[105] The rebel was the Ögedeyid, Qaidu. The troops were those remaining from the Jochid general Negüder. Rashīd al-Dīn, *Jāmi'*, 722, 1096, trans. Thackston, 378, 535 (the plunder), trans. Boyle, *Successors*, 153–4. Also Jackson, "Dissolution," 239–44 (Negüderis), and *Conquest to Conversion*, 195, for Mubārak-Shāh's death in 1275–6.

[106] Vaṣṣāf / Āyatī, *Taḥrīr*, 4; Vaṣṣāf / Von Hammer-Purgstahl, *Geschichte's Vaṣṣāfs*, text 29, trans. 30; also Bartol'd, *Turkestan*, 491. De Nicola suggests death in 1266 in "Orghīna," 119.

[107] Bartol'd notes these differing readings in *Turkestan*, 491; also Rashīd al-Dīn, *Jāmi'*, 769, 885, trans. Thackston, 377, 432, trans. Boyle, 151, 261; Banākatī, *Ta'rīkh*, 398, echoing Rashīd al-Dīn. Also Monique Kervran, "Un monument baroque dans les steppes du Kazakhstan: Le tombeau d'Örkina Khatun, princess Chagatay?" *Arts Asiatiques* 57 (2002): 5–32, suggesting that Orqīna built the Ayesha Bibi tomb in Taraz for herself.

after Mubarak-Shāh's accession Orqīna disappeared from the historical sources.[108] When Mubārak-Shāh fled to Ilkhanid territory he seems at least to have taken his sister Tughlugh-Shāh, since there she married a Sulduz commander and bore a daughter.[109] If Orqīna was still alive, then Mubārak-Shāh surely would have taken her, too. In any case, Orqīna's story ended after the mid-1260s in either death or exile. After the Oirat consorts abandoned the Chaghatayid realm, this family was left weakened in all realms but the Ilkhanate, where they survived a little longer.

THE KEREITS

After the Qonggirats and Oirats, the third important consort family was the Kereits, despite their anomalous position as a captured ruling lineage whose subjects had been scattered. They managed this through two lucky breaks: first, Chinggis Khan married the Kereit princesses into his own family, and second, he allowed some of the junior Kereit princes to live. As a result, enough princes survived to produce the offspring necessary for intermarriage with the children that their sisters and cousins bore with Chinggisid husbands. This permitted the reconstitution of the lineage, although it was likely never as large as its competition.

The Kereits were first represented among the Jochids by the childless Begtütmish and a second Kereit wife, who bore one of Jochi's lesser sons.[110] Unfortunately the scant records preclude discovery of any further Kereit consort house in western Jochid lands. But in eastern Jochid terrain we may discern traces of a modest consort family: a Kereit imperial son-in-law served as a general in the Toluid armies in 1251, while later two of Orda's great-grandsons married Kereit senior wives.[111] Another Kereit man worked as a high-level financial officer for Qubilai, but it is unknown

[108] De Nicola, "Orghīna," 119, and *Khatuns*, 82.

[109] The daughter, Yedi Qurtuqa, married the Ilkhan Ghazan (r. 1295–1304). Rashīd al-Dīn, *Jāmi'*, 1215, trans. Thackston, 593. Rashīd al-Dīn, *Shu'āb-i Panjgānah*, fol. 149a (not in *Mu'izz*).

[110] Her name is unclear: N-b-q-sh? See *Mu'izz al-Anṣāb*, fol. 19a (not in Rashīd al-Dīn, *Shu'āb-i Panjgānah*). The son was Shaltut.

[111] The son-in-law was Choqbal Küregen, who fought under Möngke's half-brother Möge in 1251. His wife is unknown. Orda's great-grandsons were Bachqirtai, who married the Kereit Kökelün, and Chagan Buqa, whose Kereit wife was Sartish (or Sürmish), daughter of Qosh Temür. Rashīd al-Dīn, *Jāmi'*, 715, 833, trans. Thackston, 350, 406, trans. Boyle, 103–4.

whether he was also a son-in-law.[112] No record of Kereits among the Chaghatayids has been found, but the information on them is scant in any case.

The situation is clearer in the Ilkhanate, where the task of reconstructing a consort house fell to the Kereit princess Dokuz, Hülegü's influential second senior wife. Dokuz managed this with the help of her brother, Saricha, who accompanied Hülegü to Iran as a commander, and whose children were essential to forming the Kereit consort family since Dokuz bore no offspring at all (see Chapter 9). Saricha's descendants became the senior line of Kereit consorts, and were later supported by junior lines descended from Kereit commanders who had found work in Chinggis Khan's armies, and whose offspring traveled to Iran with Hülegü.[113] The Kereits therefore existed as a third consort house alongside the Qonggirats and Oirats, but their presence seems to have been limited in most khanates. Only in the Ilkhanate did they create a consort family to rival the others, as will be seen in Chapter 9. Their relative weakness should be traced to the damage done to the Kereit ruling lineage at the time of Chinggis Khan's conquest in 1203, despite the mildness with which it was treated in comparison with enemies like the Tatars.

OTHER FAMILIES

If the families related to Börte and her daughters – other than the Kereits – were the most prominent among the consort lineages, we should expect to see the Chinggisids intermarry not only with the Qonggirats and Oirats, but also with the Ikires, Öng'üts, and Uighurs. And so we do: in the Ikires case, the pattern was one of reciprocity for generations. At least two sons of Princess Qojin's husband, Butu, wedded Chinggisid women, thereby completing the exchange for her and for her aunt Temülün, while an Ikires granddaughter became the senior wife for Grand Khan Möngke.[114]

[112] Endicott-West, "Merchant Associations," 135.

[113] Kereit branches included the Jirqin and Tongqayit. Members of the Tongqayit descended from one Yesil / Nosal and intermarried with the Chinggisids beginning with the commander Alinaq (see Chapter 9). Whether the Jirqin were also sons-in-law is not clear. Juvayni, *World-Conqueror* (Nosal), footnote 1 (calling the lineage Tübe'üt), 488–9; Rashīd al-Dīn, *Jāmi'*, 114, 132, trans. Thackston, 62, 71 (Yesil).

[114] This was Qutuqtai, whose son died in infancy and thus heightened Möngke's fear of sorcery. See Chapter 7. Butu's son Tejingen (?) married Princesses Ikires (??) and Chalun, while his other son Sorqa married Ögedei's granddaughter (through Köchü), Princess Antu; *Yuan Shi*, 2921–3 and Table of Princesses, 13:2757–61 (unpublished trans. Buell). Butu's granddaughter, Qutuqtai, daughter of Huludai and an unknown wife, married

Later marriages followed.[115] The Chinggisid-Ikires relationship was particularly strong in Yuan territory: Princess Qojin's lands were in northern China, and her male descendants played important roles in the Yüan military.[116] By contrast, neither Ikires wives nor Ikires consort lineages figure among the Jochids, Ilkhanids, or Chaghatayids (as far as the incomplete evidence can show), and it is unclear whether this house's activities extended to the western regions.[117]

Similarly the Nestorian Christian Öng'üt descendants of Princess Alaqa formed ties with the Chinggisids, or, "from that time on [Alaqa's reign] it became customary for members of Chinggis Khan's family to intermarry with the Öng'üt."[118] Descendants of Alaqa's husbands and their secondary wives may have formed a junior consort line.[119] It has been suggested that the Öng'üt-Chinggisid marriage pattern was "one-way" and not a full exchange, meaning that Öng'üt men married Chinggisid women, but Chinggisid men only took Öng'üt concubines, not wives.[120] This was perhaps true in the east, where Öng'üt men regularly wedded Toluid princesses or descendants of Chinggis Khan's junior son, Kölgen: "the Great Khan[s] ... have always given of their daughters and others of their kindred to the kings who reign in that region [i.e., the Öng'üt rulers]," yet Öng'üt women do not seem to have married Chinggisid men.[121] Among the Jochids, by contrast, the pattern may have been reciprocal: "They [Öng'üts] are numerous in Khwarazm, and they have given their daughters [implied, as wives] to rulers."[122] In Ilkhanid and Chaghatayid realms we see little trace of Öng'üts, other than individual officers and the single female exception

Möngke. Rashīd al-Dīn, *Jāmi'*, 161–2, 820, trans. Thackston, 87, 399 (a family tree), trans. Boyle, 197; also Zhao, *Marriage*, 122–6 for commentary, charts, and lists covering these and later marriages.

115 Zhao, *Marriage*, 122–6.

116 *Yuan Shi*, trans. Abramowski, "Ögedei and Guyük," 132 (Qojin's appanage), and see Chapter 5, footnote 85, for the inheritance of military position among consort families.

117 For later Ikires-Chinggisid marriages in eastern lands see Zhao, *Marriages*, 122–6.

118 Rashīd al-Dīn, *Jāmi'*, 132, trans. Thackston, 71; also De Nicola, *Khatuns*, 201–2 on their Christianity, especially a Christian princess descended from Alaqa.

119 Not all mothers of Öng'üt imperial sons-in-law are known.

120 Zhao, *Marriage*, 156–62 and esp. 160.

121 In later generations, marriage resumed with the Ögedeyids and Chghatayids as well. See Hambis, *CVIII*, table 3 and 24–7; Polo, *Description*, §74 (the quote); Zhao, *Marriage*, 156–62 and esp. 160.

122 This passage refers to descendants of the administrator Chin Temür in particular. Rashīd al-Dīn, *Jāmi'*, 132, trans. Thackston, 71.

of a concubine named Qaitmish, mother of the ilkhan Arghun (r. 1284–91).[123] Meanwhile, the Uighur lineages descended from Al Altan and Barchuk functioned as a consort family to a limited degree – they made a handful of marriages with the eastern Toluids and the Chaghatayids, while in the west we see no Uighur wives at all, and only occasional Uighur officers.[124]

Then came the many lesser consort families, whose stories are even more elusive than those of the major houses. Among the Jochids, lesser consorts hailed from Jajirat, Ushin, Oghuz, Qipchak, Alchi Tatar, Suldus, and Togolas lineages.[125] Jochid men also occasionally married princesses from outside states like the Byzantines, although such wives never achieved senior status despite the honor with which they were treated.[126] By contrast, when Jochid princesses married Seljuk or Russian princelings or, on one memorable occasion, the Mamluk sultan of Egypt and Syria, they could expect to be either the only wife (in Christian marriages), or the senior one (in polygynous households).[127]

[123] A commander named Maqur worked for the Jochid Toqta, and a son of one Quru Buqa worked in the Ilkhanate; both were descended from the administrator Chin Temür, sent to Iran under Ögedei, who has been identified as either a Qara-Khitai, or an Önggüt. Rashīd al-Dīn, *Jāmi'*, 132 (an Önggüt), 660 (a Qara-Khitai), trans. Thackston, 71, 322; Juvayni, *World-Conqueror*, 482 (a Qara-Khitai); note Buell, "Činqai," 102 on this matter.

[124] Hambis, *CVIII*, table 11 and 130–3, lists seven marriages in over one hundred years, one of which was between the Uighur lady Aliqmish-Begi and the Chaghatayid prince Du'a; also Zhao, *Marriage*, 171–7; *Yuan Shi*, Table of Princesses, 13:2757–61 (unpublished trans. Buell) for the marriage of Güyük's daughter princess Babaqal to Quchar-Tekin. Uighur officers in the Ilkhanate included the brothers Ögrünch and Sevinch, Esen-Qutlugh and his son Maḥmūd, and Eretna. Melville, *Decline*, 45, 69; Broadbridge, *Kingship and Ideology*, 143.

[125] Rashīd al-Dīn, *Jāmi'* 710–30, trans. Thackston, 348–55, trans. Boyle, 99–116; also *Mu'izz al-Anṣāb*, fols. 19a–b to 28a–b (not Rashīd al-Dīn, *Shu'āb-i Panjgānah*).

[126] Özbek Khan's third wife was a Byzantine princess. Ibn Baṭūṭah, *Travels*, 488, 497–506.

[127] Examples include a princess who married Prince Gleb Vasilkovich of Rostov and Belozero in 1257; Konchaka, christened Agatha, who married Grand Prince Yuri Danilovich of Moscow in 1317. Anonymous, *Nikonian Chronicle*, 3:34, 101. Berke's daughter Urbai married the Seljuk prince 'Izz al-Dīn Kay Kāūs, then his son Mas'ūd. Baybars al-Manṣūrī al-Dawādār, *Zubdat al-Fikrah fī ta'rīkh al-hijrah*, ed. D. S. Richard (Beirut: Bibliotheka Islamica, with Deutschen Morganländischen Gesellschaft, 1998), 42, 126, 168; De Nicola, *Khatuns*, 115, 116. Princess Tulunbay married al-Nāṣir Muḥammad in Egypt (third r. 1311–41) in 1320, but the union was a personal and diplomatic failure. Broadbridge, *Kingship and Ideology*, 132–7.

Among the Chaghatayids, trends are difficult to discern. Other than the initial strength of the Qonggirats and the Oirats, the Chaghatayids intermarried with other branches of the Chinggisid tree, as well as major consort houses like the Uighurs, and families of their own commanders, such as the Dörbens, Jalayirs, and Baya'uts, among others.[128] Other known consorts included the Qipchaks of the Central Asian steppe, and the Dughlat and Saghrichi lineages.[129] The Chaghatayids also took wives from established Muslim Turkic lineages like the Qutlugh-Khanids of Kirman, and later formed links with rising dynasties like the Temürids in Transoxiana, or the rulers of Badakhshan.[130]

In the Ilkhanate, the domination of the Qonggirats, Oirats, and Kereits made it difficult for other lineages to compete, although they did exist. Among these were the Alchi Tatars, remnants of the people whom Chinggis Khan had destroyed in 1202. Other consort lineages included the Jedei Baya'ut, Suldus, and Jalayirs, all of which were former hereditary servants or allies of the Mongols. The Ilkhanids also intermarried with local aristocracies, especially those Muslim Turkic dynasties that predated their own arrival in Iran, like the Artuqids of Mardin in Eastern Anatolia, the Seljuks in Central and Western Anatolia, the Salghurids of Fars, and the Qutlugh-Khanids of Kirman. (See Map 3.) Like their Jochid cousins to the north, Ilkhanid rulers occasionally wedded Byzantine or Georgian princesses. (See Chapter 9.) It should be noted that women from local dynasties almost never bore children.[131]

But other than a proliferation of family names, the information on minor consort families is so scant that we cannot know much about them.

128 First noted by Sholeh Quinn, "*The Mu'izz al-Ansāb* and *Shu'āb-i Panjgānah* as Sources for the Chaghatayid Period of History: A Comparative Analysis," *Central Asiatic Journal* 33 (1989): 238. See Rashīd al-Dīn, *Shu'āb-i Panjgānah*, fols. 120a, 122b; *Mu'izz al-Ansāb*, fols. 32a, 38a. For the Uighur Aliqmish-Begi marrying the Chaghatayid prince Du'a see Hambis, *CVIII*, table 11 and 130–3.

129 Babur, *The Baburnama: Memoirs of Babur, Prince and Emperor*, trans. Wheeler M. Thackston (New York: Oxford University Press, 1996), 45, 46.

130 *Mu'izz al-Ansāb*, fols. 29a–32b (not in Rashīd al-Dīn, *Shu'āb-i Panjgānah*). Babur, *Baburnama*, trans. Thackston, 54, 62.

131 Pfeiffer points out that all Ilkhanids heirs were children of nomadic women from known lineages, and that women from local dynasties did not have children. Pfeiffer, *Conversion to Islam*, 133. One exception was Prince Möngke-Temür, whose second wife, the Salghurid Abish, bore Princess Kürdüchin. See Chapter 9.

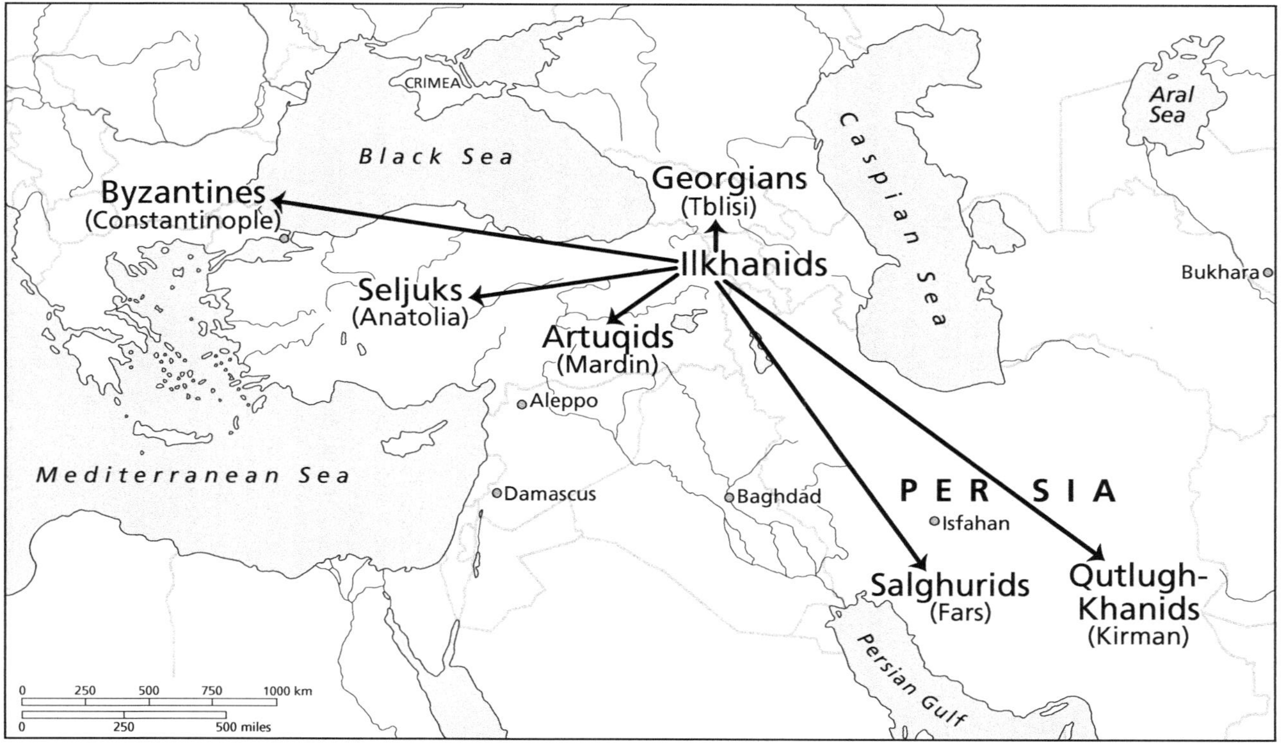

Map 3 The Ilkhanids and their vassal consorts.

Occasionally, however, we find just enough to catch a glimpse. To take the case of the Alchi Tatars: as mentioned above, Chinggis Khan had suppressed them brutally in 1202, but the conquered sister wives, Yisüi and Yisügen, thereafter worked behind the scenes to rehabilitate their people (see Chapter 3). They appear to have had modest success, since traces of what might be a skeleton lineage emerged among both the Jochids and the Ilkhanids. In the Jochid case, Batu's senior wife and (probably) the mother of the Christian heir, Sartaq, was the Alchi Tatar lady Boraqchin.[132] The traces about her in the historical sources demonstrate her clear involvement in Jochid political life. It was she who joined Batu to receive both Franciscans, Friar Carpini in 1246 and Friar William in 1253, from the elevated golden throne inside the beautiful linen tents that Batu had plundered from King Béla IV of Hungary.[133] After Sartaq's accession to the throne in 1257 and death soon thereafter, Boraqchin briefly served as regent for Sartaq's son Ulaghchi (probably her grandson) until his untimely death.[134] The Arabic historians even credit her with trying to flee to the Ilkhanids for help, for which she was hunted down and killed, but modern historians contest this admittedly garbled event.[135] Meanwhile an Alchi Tatar commander named Et-Qara worked in Batu's armies, and it would fit with Chinggisid preference that Et-Qara could have been Boraqchin's brother. Other Tatars appeared during the reigns of the brothers Möngke-Temür and Töde-Möngke: a commander named Beg Temür served the first, while a woman named Töre-Qutlugh reigned as senior wife for the second.[136] (One more Tatar wife cropped up for a later, lesser Chinggisid.[137]) It is likely that the wives Boraqchin and

[132] Rashīd al-Dīn, *Jāmi'*, 89, trans. Thackston, 50.

[133] Carpini, *History*, 57, trans. Rockhill, 10; Rubruck, *Mission*, 132, "completely overlaid with gold" – metal or brocade?

[134] Juvaynī, *World-Conqueror*, 268; Rashīd al-Dīn, *Jāmi'*, 738 (Batu's heirs without Boraqchin), trans. Thackston, 361; Vaṣṣāf / Āyatī, *Taḥrīr*, 332. De Nicola, *Khatuns*, 80–1, 106, noting that Boraqchin was regent for the Jochids while Orqīna ruled the Chaghatayids and the Qutlugh-Khanid princess Terkan Khatun ruled Kirman – see him also on Sartaq's Christianity, 202.

[135] She allegedly corresponded with Hülegü on behalf of Ulaghchi, then tried to flee to him but was captured and killed. This garbled story appears in Arabic and Georgian sources: Baybars al-Manṣūrī, *Zubdah*, 14, 16–17; al-Nuwayrī, *Nihāyah*, 27:357–8; Brosset, *Géorgie*, 569, text 377. However scholars contest it, for which see De Nicola, *Khatuns*, 80–1; Pelliot, *Horde d'Or*, 43–4; Spuler, *Goldene Horde*, 382.

[136] Rashīd al-Dīn, *Jāmi'*, 89, 721, trans. Thackston, 50, 352, trans. Boyle, 110.

[137] This was Bora'ujin, wife of Shiremün, son of Shingqur, son of Jochi. See Rashīd al-Dīn, *Jāmi'*, 727, trans. Thackston, 354, trans. Boyle, 114.

Töre-Qutlugh were related, and that the commanders Et-Qara and Beg-Temür were also connected to them (especially since so few Tatars lived in Mongol domains at all), but the sources themselves do not know for sure. (See Family Tree 8.9.) At the same time, the Nira'ut Tatars were relatively numerous among the Jochids, but few of them seem to have risen high enough for the historical sources to notice them.[138]

Meanwhile among the Ilkhanids, Abaqa had a senior wife named Nuqdan, who was an Alchi Tatar and mother of the Ilkhan Geikhatu (r. 1291–5).[139] In proper consort fashion, her brother Joma worked for Hülegü, and married two of his daughters in succession.[140] (See Family Tree 8.10.) Otherwise the Tatars were not well represented in the Ilkhanate even during the reign of Geikhatu, except for thirty families descended from those rescued by Yisüi.[141]

Thus despite the many lesser consort families in Chinggisid political life, they were hardly equal in status or influence to the major ones, their stories are more difficult to find, and their traces now appear merely as shadows across the historical page.

CONCLUSION

After the age of the three widows, women's influence shifted into the hands of the consort houses. This chapter has therefore continued the investigation of women's roles in Chinggisid life by charting the establishment of major and minor consort houses across the khanates, describing patterns of consort behavior, and focusing on specific individuals in order to suggest the actions of others. Members of the senior princess lineages, that is, the Qonggirat and Oirat families in all khanates, the Ikires and Öng'üts in some regions, and the Uighurs to a limited degree, positioned themselves to shape events, control property and people, patronize religions, make important political and social connections, inherit military

[138] Rashīd al-Dīn, *Jāmi'*, 89, trans. Thackston, 50.

[139] On her see Chapter 9. Rashīd al-Dīn, *Jāmi'*, 1055, trans. Thackston, 515; De Nicola, *Khatuns*, 158 (her camp).

[140] Rashīd al-Dīn, *Jāmi'*, 88, 600 (as "Jurma"), 971–2, trans. Thackston, 49, 276 ("Joma"), 476–7.

[141] "Of the Alchi Tatar there is no one in this land [the Ilkhanate] known to be of enough consequence to write about." Rashīd al-Dīn, *Jāmi'*, 89, trans. Thackston, 50.

[142] Rashīd al-Dīn claims in garbled fashion that Nuqdan and Joma were related to Yisüi and Yisügen (i.e., Alchi Tatars) through a brother, Shigi Qutuqtu (*sic*), but labels them as "Tatars." See footnote 140. Rashīd al-Dīn, *Jāmi'*, 88, trans. Thackston, 49.

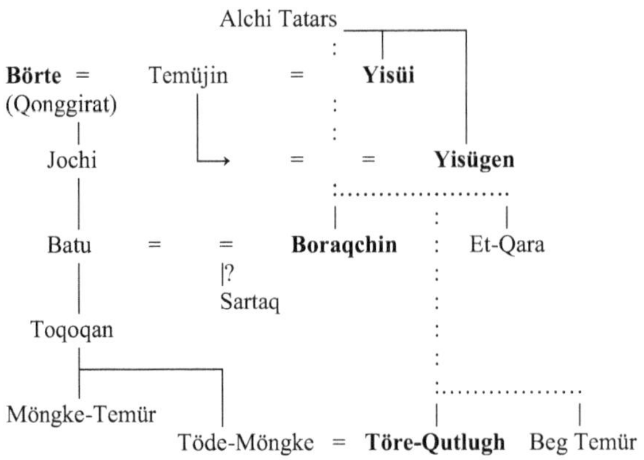

Family Tree 8.9 The Hypothetical Alchi Tatar skeleton "lineage" among the Jochids.
All women are in **bold**.
Dotted lines indicate unclear relationship (if any).

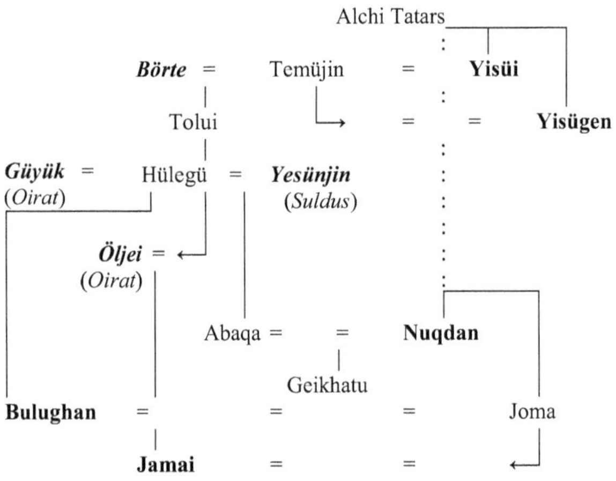

Family Tree 8.10 The [Alchi][142] Tatar skeleton "lineage" in the Ilkhanate.
All women are in **bold**.
Dotted lines indicate unclear relationship.
Other lineages marked with *italics*.

assignments, and generally dominate the highest echelon of their society by virtue of their descent from one of Börte's daughters, and the Chinggisid preference for intermarriage with them. The single addition to this handful of elite families was the Kereits – the only ones who lacked a connection to a senior princess. But determined Kereit women worked with a few Kereit princes and commanders to re-create this house out of almost whole cloth, and rose to compete with the others. Nor were any of the royal or consort families deterred by the medical challenges posed by the intermarriage of first cousins over decades, which passed by them unnoticed since it did not fit their definitions of consanguinity. In the next and final chapter, we will see these houses in action in the Ilkhanate.

9

Consort Houses in the Ilkhanate

In 1253 Hülegü's armies left Mongolia for Iran. By 1256 they were subduing the fortresses of the Nizari Shiite Assassins in the Caucasus. In winter 1258 they famously sacked the city of Baghdad and executed the Abbasid caliph, then drove west toward the Mediterranean Sea. But in 1260 after a surprise defeat by the Mamluk sultans of Egypt and Syria (1250–1517), and in response to news of Möngke's death, Hülegü withdrew to the Caucasus. Although the Iran campaign had been intended as a mission from which Hülegü would return to Mongolia, after the Mongol Civil War (1260–4) Hülegü and his descendants settled down to rule Khurasan, Iran, Iraq, and Anatolia.[1] Their power centered on the west of their realm, in royal camps in the fertile pasturelands of Mughan and Arran in the Caucasus region, with occasional trips south to the pleasant climes near Baghdad.[2] They ruled a largely settled, majority Muslim population, and were attended by a staff composed partly of Muslim scholars and bureaucrats. Some of these administrators produced extensive histories detailing the exploits of the Chinggisid family, especially the Ilkhanid branch.

As a result of the erudition and literary achievements of these scholars, information about the Ilkhanate is relatively plentiful and detailed. This permits us in this chapter to conduct a case study of Ilkhanid consort families, with which we can not only illustrate patterns of marriage and political engagement in the Ilkhanate, but also suggest possibilities for those regions about which we know less. This is not to imply that

[1] Bruno de Nicola, email correspondence, June 2017.
[2] Charles Melville, "The Itineraries of Sultan Öljeitü, 1304–16," *Iran* 28 (1990): 55–70.

marriage politics were exactly the same everywhere, but rather to provide a model for conjecture. Although this is not the place for a full study of Ikhanid political factions, we can use the behavior of individuals to hypothesize about the intentions of consort families as groups connected by the common interests of their members. In the Ilkhanate, marriage politics were first dominated by the Qonggirat, Oirat, and Kereit families, who were later challenged by two newcomers: the Jalayirs and Chobanids.[3] At stake were access to the ruling Toluid branch of the Chinggisid family, the chance to place a prince on the throne or position a daughter as a royal wife, a voice in quriltais and other politics, opportunities for military advancement, and last but certainly not least, control of the big wifely camps with their inhabitants, resources, and revenue. Roles particular to women included the royal childbearer, with the ability to become pregnant and give birth to live children who survived to adulthood;[4] the royal mother with influence over a child's training, opportunities, and strategic marriages; the royal wife or widow with a say in politics and patronage, and the ability to intercede with the ilkhan; and the royal manager, who controlled property and resources (both moveable camps and territories), managed finances, and engaged in a host of other economic and logistical activities.

ESTABLISHMENT OF THE SENIOR FAMILIES

The Oirats

Despite the Qonggirat preeminence throughout Mongol territory, it was the Oirat consort lineage that first dominated marriage politics within the Ilkhanate, largely because Hülegü's senior wife was Güyük, daughter of Princess Checheyigen. As established in Chapter 8, Güyük controlled the premier wifely camp. She enjoyed plenty of support from members of the Oirat ruling lineage: an Oirat cousin, Arighan, lived in her camp as Hülegü's concubine, while Güyük's half sister Öljei lived in a different camp as a wife.[5] Güyük's eldest brother (and Öljei's half brother), Buqa-Temür, commanded the Oirat troops sent with Hülegü's

[3] "Jalayirids" indicates the dynasty that ruled in the mid-fourteenth century; Jalayirs indicates the people before that dynasty's rise.

[4] De Nicola, *Khatuns*, 52, on this concept among the Ayyubids in Syria and Egypt.

[5] Arighan's son was Prince Ajai. Öljei's camp is not specified, but she did employ a camp commander. Rashīd al-Dīn, *Jāmi'*, 964 (Öljei), 977 (Arighan), 1017, 1063, 1110, 1113, trans. Thackston, 472 (Öljei), 474 (Arighan), 541 (grant of territory), 543 (intercession).

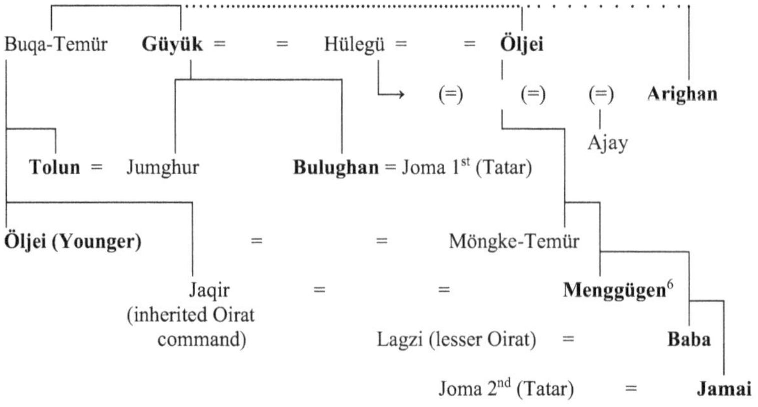

Family Tree 9.1 Oirat Senior Line, a.k.a Güyük, Hülegü, Öljei, and Buqa-Temür.
All women are in **bold.**
Close dotted line represents half-siblings.
Wide dotted line represents cousins.
(=) represents concubinage.

invasion army, and worked for Hülegü in Iran for years as a senior commander.[7] In the great camp Güyük did her wifely duty and produced two children: the first Tolui-Oirat prince, Jumghur, and a princess, Bulughan.[8] When it was time for the children to wed, Güyük and Buqa-Temür acted in proper consort family fashion by marrying them to one another: that is, Prince Jumghur wedded his cousin, Buqa-Temür's daughter Tolun. Later Buqa-Temür's other children married the progeny of the half sister and junior wife, Öljei, and Buqa-Temür's son inherited command of the Oirat troops.[9] (See Family Tree 9.1.) Buqa-Temür reliably supported Hülegü both during the Iran campaign

6 Rashīd al-Dīn has her marrying both Jaqir and his son, Taraqai. Perhaps the levirate was at play? Rashīd al-Dīn, *Jāmi'*, 102 (Taraqai), 971 (Jaqir), trans. Thackston, 56–7, 971.
7 Broadbridge, "Toluid-Oirat Connection," 126, note 24; Hope, *Ilkhanate*, 98–9.
8 Broadbridge, "Ilkhanid-Oirat Connection," 125 and table 2, 128; Rashīd al-Dīn, *Jāmi'*, 966, 971–2, trans. Thackston, 473, 476; Banākatī, *Ta'rīkh*, 412, 413 (garbled).
9 Broadbridge, "Toluid-Oirat Connection," 125, table 2, 127, table 3 on 129; Rashīd al-Dīn, *Jāmi'*, 966, 971–2, trans. Thackston, 473, 476; Banākatī, *Ta'rīkh*, 413 (garbled). Jonathan (Yoni) Brack comes to a similar conclusion about patterns of intermarriage in "Mediating Sacred Kingship: Conversion and Sovereignty in Mongol Iran" (PhD. diss., University of Michigan, 2016), 46–8. See also Landa, "Sons-in-law," 180–1.

and after his elevation to ilkhan; the Oirat family probably also enjoyed grants of grazing lands.[10]

Güyük was thus a prime example of a royal mother, royal wife, and royal manager of property. Her advantages of the best camp, the presence of so many relatives, and her production of children should have cemented Güyük's wifely power and position. But instead events conspired to relegate her to obscurity. First, she died early in Mongolia, and Hülegü remarried and gave her camp to his new wife, a Qonggirat, Qutui.[11] Second, Hülegü's next senior wife was the elderly Kereit princess Dokuz, a widow of Tolui and cousin of Sorqoqtani.[12] It is Dokuz who is remembered and lauded in histories, especially for her active patronage of Nestorian Christianity, while Güyük is virtually unknown.[13] Nor did Hülegü select Güyük's son, Prince Jumghur, to go on the Iran campaign, from which he himself expected to return.[14] Instead, he left him in Mongolia in a position of authority in Güyük's camp (now managed by Qutui), and instead took two sons born of lower-ranking women who lived in the great camp: Abaqa, from a Suldus wife,[15] and

[10] Hope, *Ilkhanate*, 108, suggesting that Buqa-Temür was following orders from another Oirat son-in-law, Tankiz, but I note that Buqa-Temür had stronger connections to Hülegü through Güyük and Öljei than Tankiz did. For the Oirat lands see Hope, *Ilkhanate*, 108 (suggesting southern Iraq), and Landa, "Sons-in-Law," 181 (suggesting Diyarbakr and northern Iraq).

[11] Broadbridge, "Toluid-Oirat Connection," 125; also Rashīd al-Dīn, *Jāmi'*, 964, trans. Thackston, 472; De Nicola, *Khatuns*, 155.

[12] Rashīd al-Dīn, *Jāmi'*, 963, 967, trans. Thackston, 471, 479; Banākatī, *Ta'rīkh*, 411. Also De Nicola, *Khatuns*, 91; Shai Shir, "Chief Wife," 54–63, 119–61, as discussed in Brack, "Sacred Kingship," 44–5 (I have not been able to examine Shir's work myself).

[13] Charles Melville, "Dokuz (Doquz) Kātūn," *Encyclopedia Iranica*, 7:475–6; De Nicola, *Khatuns*, 91–4, 115, 193, 213–14 and De Nicola, "Patrons or Murids? Mongol Women and Shaykhs in Ilkhanid Iran and Anatolia," *Iran Studies* 52 (2014): 147; also Bar Hebraeus, *Chronography*, 419, 444, albeit more fulsome about her Christianity than in his *Mukhtaṣar*, 263, 285; Grigor of Akner, *Archers*, 341, 351; Vardan Areweltz, "The Historical Compilation of Vardan Arewelc'i," ed. and trans. Robert W. Thompson, *Dumbarton Oaks Papers* 43 (1989): 217; Hetoum, *A Lytell Cronycle*, ed. Glenn Burger, Toronto Medieval Texts and Translations 6, from Richard Pynson's c. 1520 translation of *La Fleur des histoires de la terre d'Orient* (1307) (Toronto, 1988), 40; Stephannos Orbelian, *Historie de la Siounie*, trans. M. Brosset (Saint-Petersburg: Académie impériale des sciences, 1864), 234–5; Kirakos, *Histoire*, trans. Brosset, 185–6, 191, 194; James D. Ryan, "Christian Wives of Mongol Khans: Tartar Queens and Missionary Expectations in Asia," *Journal of the Royal Asiatic Society*, Series 3, 8, no. 3 (November 1998): 416.

[14] Hope, *Ilkhanate*, 94, 103–5.

[15] This was Yesünjin, who later managed a camp until her death in 1272, after which Pādishāh, the Qutlugh-Khanid wife from Kirman, took over. Rashīd al-Dīn, *Jāmi'*, 964, 1055, 1064, 1098, trans. Thackston, 472, 515, 519, 536; De Nicola, *Khatuns*, 94.

Yoshmut, from a concubine.[16] There is some confusion over the identity of Hülegü's eldest son: Rashīd al-Dīn claimed that Abaqa was the senior prince, but this may have been in order to legitimize the later succession of Abaqa's line in the Ilkhanate. In fact, Jumghur may actually have been the oldest.[17] He was certainly the senior prince by virtue of Güyük's rank. Jumghur remained in Mongolia until the later 1260s and played an active role in the Mongol Civil War.[18] When the dust of that war had settled, Hülegü had decided to remain where he was and rule the Ilkhanate, to which Qutui then brought the entire great camp in the 1260s. Unfortunately for the senior Oirat lineage, Jumghur perished en route, while his sister, Princess Bulughan, also seems to have died young.[19] Thus Güyük's immediate family was extinguished at the very beginning of the Ilkhanate, although descendants of her children did live on. Fortunately Güyük had been seconded by the other Oirat wife, Öljei, who went to Iran with Hülegü and Dokuz, and made her own contributions to the Oirat consort family. She did this first as a royal childbearer: she produced three princesses and the second Toluid-Oirat prince, Möngke-Temür, who was born in 1256 in Iran.[20]

In 1265 Hülegü died, followed shortly thereafter by his senior wife, Dokuz. Hülegü was succeeded by his junior son, Abaqa (r. 1265–82), who was conveniently present in the Ilkhanate and also supported by many influential commanders, despite the stronger claims of his senior half-brother Jumghur in Mongolia.[21] Meanwhile, although Prince Möngke-Temür was still a child, he remained Hülegü's son from a wife with

[16] Juvaynī, *World-Conqueror*, 611–2; Rashīd al-Dīn, *Jāmi'*, 966, 978, trans. Thackston, 474, 480; Bar Hebraeus, *Chronography*, 419, and *Mukhtaṣar*, 263; Banākatī, *Ta'rīkh*, 412. Yoshmut's mother was a concubine in Qutui's establishment, but Hülegü took him, perhaps because he was older than others. Another son, Taraghai, may have gone, but died on the way.

[17] Brack, "Sacred Kingship," 48, 51; Rashīd al-Dīn, *Jāmi'*, 102 (Jumghur was oldest), 1055, and 1145 (Abaqa was oldest), trans. Thackston, 57, 515, 558; Juvaynī, *World-Conqueror*, 611, describing Jumghur as senior in rank without addressing age.

[18] For details see Hope, *Ilkhanate*, 104.

[19] Bulughan's widower, Joma, remarried her half sister Jamai, daughter of Hülegü and Oljei. If this was Jamai's first marriage, and since Öljei and Güyük both married Hülegü in Mongolia and likely bore children reasonably close to one another, then Bulughan probably died young. Rashīd al-Dīn, *Jāmi'*, 88, 600, 970–1, trans. Thackston, 49, 276 (here as "Joha"), 476–7; Banākatī, *Ta'rīkh*, 413 (garbled). Also Pfeiffer, *Conversion to Islam*, 168–9.

[20] Broadbridge, "Toluid-Oirat Connection," 127–8 and table 3; Rashīd al-Dīn, *Jāmi'*, 968–9, trans. Thackston, 475; Banākatī, *Ta'rīkh*, 412–13.

[21] Hope, *Ilkhanate*, 113–17 (the critical role of commanders in this accession); De Nicola, *Khatuns*, 94 (proximity).

(by now) her own camp (Öljei), who represented an important consort family, and he could still be considered eligible for the throne one day. Öljei thus groomed him for a bright future, which provides a window onto the way a royal mother could mold the formation, training, and social position of her offspring. She accomplished this through marriages for all her children: Princess Meggügen and Prince Möngke-Temür married children of her (half) brother, Buqa-Temür, and produced a new generation of Toluid-Oirat children. Öljei's other daughters also made respectable matches, one into a junior Oirat line in Khurasan, and one outside the Oirat consort house.[22] (See Family Trees 9.1 and 9.4.) Then in 1272 Möngke-Temür married a second wife, Abish, heiress to the Muslim Turkic Salghurid family of Shiraz in Fars.[23]

Although the sources do not specify that Öljei arranged all these marriages, it is unimaginable that she would not have been involved in those with her own brother's children, or others from the Oirat consort house. In the case of Abish, we know at least that Abish moved into Öljei's camp after the nuptials and lived with her there.[24] Politically Möngke-Temür's marriage to his cousin formed the necessary connection to the Oirat consorts, while the union with Abish connected him to an important vassal family, and resembled a similar union between Abaqa and the Muslim Qutlugh-Khanid princess Pādishāh of Kirman.[25] Öljei's attention to her son's upbringing extended to military training: when Abaqa assigned Möngke-Temür to command a new defensive line in the Caucasus against the Jochids, Öljei moved there with him, and partnered with a military officer to tutor the prince in his duties.[26] Later Möngke-Temür was reassigned to the southeastern realm of Fars, inheritance of his

[22] Rashīd al-Dīn, *Jāmi'*, 969, 970–2, trans. Thackston, 475, 476; Banākatī, *Ta'rīkh*, 412–13.

[23] Lambton, *Continuity*, 273; De Nicola, *Khatuns*, 112; Bertold Spuler, "Abesh Khatun," *Encyclopedia Iranica*, ed. Ehsan Yarshater (Routledge and Kegan Paul, 1985), 210; C. E. Bosworth, "Salghurids," *EI2*, 8:979.

[24] Lambton, *Continuity*, 273; De Nicola, *Khatuns*, 109, 110–14, 220; also Vaṣṣāf / Āyatī, *Taḥrīr*, 114–15; Rashīd al-Dīn, *Jāmi'*, 936–7, 969, trans. Thackston, 459, 475; Qazvīnī, *Gūzīdah*, 507; Mirkhwand, Muḥammad b. Khwāndamīr b. Maḥmūd, *Rawzat al-Ṣafā fī Sīrat al-Anbiya' wa al-mulūk wa al-khulafa'*, ed. Jamshīd Kayānfar (Tehran: Aṣāṭīr, 2001–2), 7:3622.

[25] De Nicola, *Khatuns*, 104–10 and esp. 106, 216, 219–21; Vaṣṣāf / Āyātī, *Taḥrīr*, 177; Rashīd al-Dīn, *Jāmi'*, 934–5, 1055, trans. Thackston, 458, 515, Banākatī, *Ta'rīkh*, 426; Mirkhwand, *Rawzat*, 7:3391–3 (on Pādishāh in general, not her marriage).

[26] Abaqa gave him this position. Banākatī, *Ta'rīkh*, 428; Rashīd al-Dīn, *Jāmi'*, 1063, trans. Thackston, 519; Broadbridge, "Toluid-Oirat Connection," 127–8. Samaghar was the officer, functioning perhaps as a tutor (*atabek*), for which see Hope, *Ilkhanate*, 48.

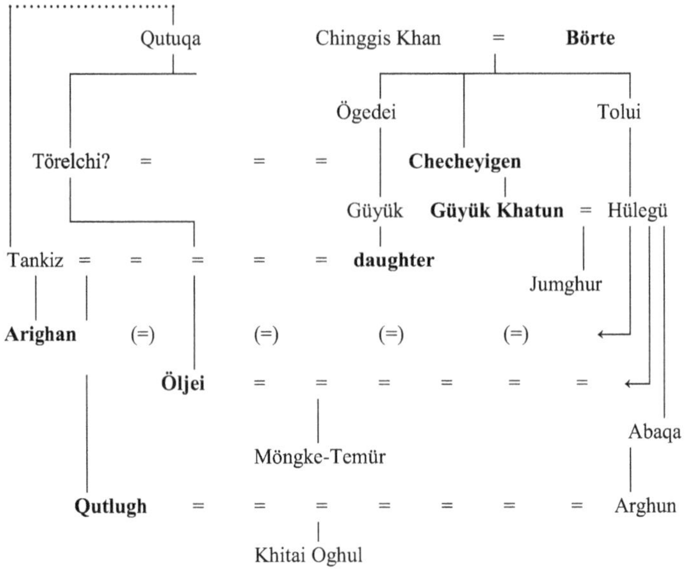

Family Tree 9.2 Oirat Junior Line a.k.a. Tankiz Küregen and Chinggisids.
All women are in **bold.**
Dotted line indicates unclear relationship.

Salghurid wife, Abish, but this time Öljei and Abish seem to have remained in Öljei's camp together.[27]

Meanwhile two additional lines of Oirat consorts emerged in the Ilkhanate. The first was descended from the Oirat Arghun Aqa, the Ögedeyid official whom Töregene had tasked with containing Jochid influence in the 1240s. This family was located in Khurasan, and became in-laws first when Arghun's son Lagzi married one of Öljei's daughters, then again when another of his sons married a junior daughter of Abaqa.[28] The other junior lineage was composed of descendants of a secondary Oirat commander, Tankiz, who was related to Checheyigen's husband, and who had previously married an Ögedeyid princess.[29] It was Tankiz's daughter, the abovementioned Arighan, who became Hülegü's

[27] Lambton, *Continuity*, 273.

[28] For Arghun Aqa or Amir Arghun see Chapter 6. Öljei's daughter was Baba, while Abaqa's junior daughter was Toghanchuk, whose mother Kawkabi was a concubine. Rashīd al-Dīn, *Jāmi'*, 971, 1057, trans. Thackston, 476, 516. Also see Landa, "Sons-in-law," 182–3 and "Oirats," 151–2, 154–5 with notes.

[29] This was Grand Khan Güyük's daughter. Rashīd al-Dīn, *Jāmi'*, 100, 970–1, trans. Thackston, 56, 476. See Chapter 7, Family Tree 7.2.

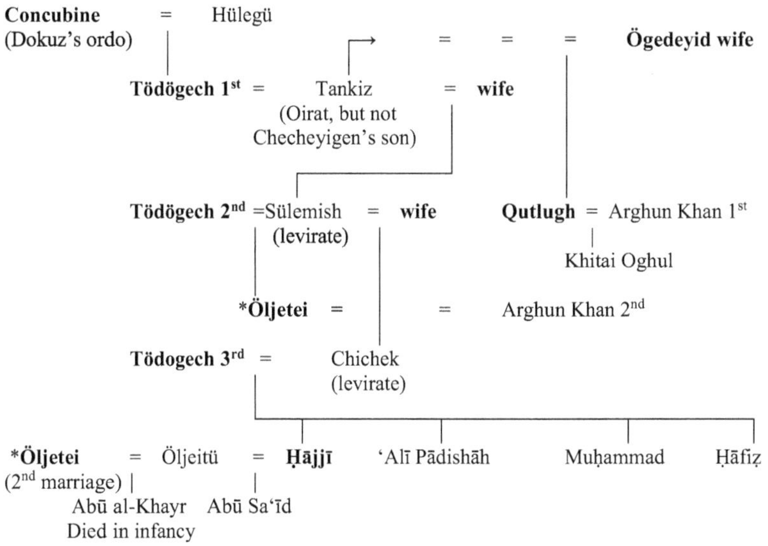

Family Tree 9.3 Tödögech and her children.[30]
All women are in **bold.**
* Note that Öljetei appears twice, once married to Arghun, once to Öljeitü. Öljetei's parentage is not entirely clear.[31]

concubine and mother of a prince.[32] Then Tankiz married one of Hülegü's daughters, Todogech, whose mother was a concubine in Dokuz's camp. Later Todogech remarried Tankiz's son, Sülemish, then grandson, Chichek, through the levirate.[33] Tankiz's children with the Ögedeyid princess, and the children from Todogech and her three Oirat husbands, all contributed to this junior line of the Oirat consort house, whose members surpassed the senior line in preeminence in later decades.[34] (See Family Trees 9.2 and 9.3.)

[30] This table is modified from the excellent work of Charles Melville in *Decline*, 17. Also see Rashīd al-Dīn, *Jāmi'*, 102, 971, trans. Thackston, 56, 476, and footnote 31.

[31] Rashīd al-Dīn claims she was Sülemish's daughter (as represented in Family Tree 9.3), but Qāshānī presents her as Ḥajjī's full sister and Chichek's daughter. Rashīd al-Dīn, *Jāmi'*, 1152, trans. Thackston, 561; Qāshānī, *Uljaytū*, 7–8.

[32] See footnote 5.

[33] Todogech's mother is unknown. Rashīd al-Dīn, *Jāmi'*, 102, 971, trans. Thackston, 56, 476; Banākatī, *Ta'rīkh*, 413. Hope uses Hāfiẓ Abrū to place Tankiz in Mongolia in the 1260s, but this conflicts with his marriage to Todogech and her life in the Ilkhanate. Hope, *Ilkhanate*, 108.

[34] Rashīd al-Dīn, *Jāmi'*, 102 (Qutlugh's Ögedeyid mother), 1152 (Qutlugh, Todogech's daughter Öljetei), trans. Thackston, 56, 561; Qāshānī, *Uljaytū*, 7–8 (Öljetei, Todogech's daughter Ḥajjī).

The Qonggirats

But despite the Oirat families' initial strength, the Qonggirat consorts soon emerged powerfully into the scene when Hülegü's Qonggirat wife, Qutui, arrived in Iran in the late 1260s with the large camp.[35] Like Öljei, Qutui exemplified a royal woman with property and wealth, the human capital of children, and the ability to shape politics. To examine the particulars: although Qutui reached the Caucasus after Hülegü's death, she finished her journey in a site in which her share of spoils from Hülegü's conquests were waiting under the care of a concubine she had previously dispatched.[36] Her stepson Abaqa further honored her with a grant of territory and its income north of Mosul near Mayyafariqin, and thereafter periodically threw parties in her honor, which reflected both her status as Hülegü's widow, and his as monarch.[37] Qutui's camp was a major establishment: in addition to Qutui it contained her two sons, Tekshin and Tegüder; the children of the deceased Toluid-Oirat prince Jumghur; Abaqa's mother, Yesünjin; the mother and younger brother of Hülegü's son Prince Yoshmut, who had participated in the Iran campaign; and three more of Hülegü's sons and their concubine mothers.[38] Furthermore, Qutui enjoyed the advantage of having relatives in the Ilkhanate to form a consort family: her cousin Martai was a wife of

[35] De Nicola, *Khatuns*, 94–5, 155; Hope, *Ilkhanate*, 99. Rashīd al-Dīn, *Jāmi'*, 1064–5, trans. Thackston, 519–20; Banākatī, *Ta'rīkh*, 429. The timing of her arrival in Iran is unclear, although De Nicola hypothesizes 1268 (p. 94). She crossed the Oxus before or in February 1268. See also Landa, "Sons-in-Law," 172–3.

[36] This was Arighan, the Oirat concubine. Rashīd al-Dīn, *Jāmi'*, 967, 1064–5, trans. Thackston, 474, 520; De Nicola, *Khatuns*, 150.

[37] The territory's annual income was 100,000 gold coins. Rashīd al-Dīn, *Jāmi'*, 1065, 1110, trans. Thackston, 520, 541; also De Nicola, *Khatuns*, 150, 152.

[38] These were Prince Tubshin (Yoshmut's brother) and his mother Noqachin; Prince Yesüder and his Kurlu'ut mother, Yesichin; Prince Ajai, whose Oirat mother Arighan had already arrived (see footnote 34); Prince Taraghai, whose mother was Boraqchin; and Prince Toghai Temür, whose mother's name is unknown. Two of Hülegü's daughters from concubines, Princesses Taraqai (daughter of Irqan), and Qutluqqan (daughter of Mengligech), have not been linked to wifely camps; there may have been others. Rashīd al-Dīn, *Jāmi'*, 966–70, trans. Thackston, 474–6; also Banākatī, *Ta'rīkh*, 429. Note the table in Charles Melville, "The End of the Ilkhanate and After: Observations on the Collapse of the Mongol World Empire," in *The Mongols' Middle East: Continuity and Transformation in Ilkhanid Iran*, ed. Bruno de Nicola and Charles Melville (Leiden, Boston: Brill, 2016), 318.

Abaqa, and Martai's brother, Toqa-Temür, was a commander; both were the offspring of Princess Tümelün.[39] (See Family Tree 8.4 in Chapter 8.) In addition, a junior line of Qonggirat consorts emerged in the Ilkhanate from the commander Abatai who accompanied Hülegü to Iran, became commander of the center, escorted Qutui from Mongolia,[40] and also fought against Berke of the Jochids. Scholars argue that Abatai was a major figure among Hülegü's commanders, and his influence continued into the reign of Abaqa.[41] Abatai also had three sons, who produced several daughters to marry princes, as did the descendants of a Qonggirat commander who had worked for Chinggis Khan, one Uqbai Noyan.[42] See Family Tree 8.5 in Chapter 8.

The Kereits

The Nestorian Christian princess Dokuz's power and authority as senior wife were unassailable: she held a large camp, intervened with Hülegü on politics, and patronized Christians as actively as she wished.[43] But the situation of the Kereit consort family was a different story because of a scarcity of offspring. This reflected the challenges that a royal wife faced if she was not also a royal childbearer. Dokuz was at least in her fifties when

[39] Qutui was a Qonggirat cousin to Martai and Taghai Temür (aka Mūsa), children of Princess Tümelün and Chigü. Qutui's exact parentage is unclear, although in one place Rashīd al-Dīn claims that she was also princess Temülün's daughter (!). Rashīd al-Dīn, *Jāmi'*, 160, 964, 1056 (the garbled claim), trans. Thackston, 86, 472, 515 and Shu'āb-i Panjgānah, fol. 139 (only that she was a Qonggirat); also *Mu'izz al-Anṣāb*, fol. 61a in brief. Brack suggests that Qutui was Princess Temulün's daughter, "Sacred Kingship," 46–7.

[40] He was temporarily disgraced for unbecoming conduct during this assignment. Rashīd al-Dīn, *Jāmi'*, 1064–5, trans. Thackston, 519–20; also Banākatī, *Ta'rīkh*, 429.

[41] Hope, *Ilkhanate*, 99, 107; also Rashīd al-Dī, *Jāmi'*, 160, 1064, 1070, 1086, 1110, trans. Thackston, 86, 519, 522, 530, 541; Banākatī, *Ta'rīkh*, 424, 429, 451; Vaṣṣāf / Āyātī, *Taḥrīr*, 42.

[42] Rashīd al-Dīn, *Jāmi'*, 160–1, trans. Thackston, 86.

[43] On her camp see Rashīd al-Dīn, *Jāmi'*, 963, 1055, 1215, trans. Thackston, 472, 515, 593; on politics see 1023, trans. Thackston, 501; also Baybars al-Manṣūrī, *Zubdah*, 52–3; Ibn Aybak al-Dawādārī, *Kanz al-durar fī jāmi' al-ghurar*, ed. Ulrich Haarmann (Wiesbaden: Franz Steiner, 1971), 8:53–4; on patronage of Christians see Grigor of Akner, "Archers," 341; Kirakos, *Histoire*, trans. Brosset, 185–6, 190–1 (patronage and politics), 194 (likewise). Also see Ibn 'Abd al-Ẓāhir, *al-Rawḍ al-Zāhir fī sīrat al-Malik al-Ẓāhir*, ed. 'Abd al-'Azīz Khuwayṭir (Riyadh: [n.p.], 1976), 89, on how she made Hülegü into a Christian (*sic*); Bar Hebraeus, *Chronography*, 444, and *Mukhtaṣar*, 285; De Nicola, *Khatuns*, 91–4, 115, 156–7, 193, 213–14; and J. M. Fiey, "Iconographie Syriac: Hulegu, Dokuz Khatun et … six ambons?" *Le Muséon. Review d'etudes orientales* 88 (1975): 59–68.

she married Hülegü, and therefore could not produce the progeny so essential for the consort line.[44] Hülegü may have had a second Kereit wife, but she had no offspring either.[45] Fortunately Dokuz could resort to the children of her brother, the commander Saricha. One niece, Tuqitani (or Toqiyatai, or Toqtai), lived in Dokuz's camp and became Hülegu's concubine.[46] Inconveniently for the Kereits, however, Tuqitani was also childless. Nevertheless a solution appeared in her fertile siblings because her brother, Irinjin, and sister, Örüg, engendered enough offspring to create a meaningful Kereit lineage. Both must have been children of Saricha's older years, given that their careers began in the 1280s (see the subsequent discussion in this chapter). The situation was further ameliorated by the presence of a Kereit junior line like those of the Oirats and Qonggirats. This stemmed from a Kereit officer, Tügür, who traveled with Hülegü to Iran as a commander of 100 and a secretary.[47] Tügür's son, Alinaq, worked as a commander for Abaqa and Aḥmad Tegüder (r. 1282–4), while Alinaq's son, Qurumishi, inherited his father's position under Gaikhatu (r. 1290–5), Ghazan (r. 1295–304), Öljeitü (r. 1304–16) and Abū Sa'īd (r. 1317–35). Both became royal sons-in-law during the 1280s.[48] (See Family Tree 9.5.)

Under Abaqa the general situation among royal wives was less dominated by individuals than had been the case under Hülegü with Güyük, Dokuz, Öljei, and Qutui. This was in part because Abaqa did not marry

[44] She was the granddaughter of Ong Qan through his son, Abaqu, who does not appear in the *Secret History*, nor does Rashīd al-Din say much about him. Assuming that Abaqu's absence from the sources implies that he died in 1203 when Chinggis Khan dismantled the Kereyits, then Dokuz must have been alive then or born shortly thereafter. If so, she would have been in her fifties by the 1250s. Shir suggests that she and Hülegü remained chaste, but I have not been able to examine this argument closely. In any case, Dokuz's age would have precluded childbearing. Shir, "Chief Wife," 54–63, cited in Brack, "Sacred Kingship," 44, note 98.

[45] *Mu'izz al-Ansāb*, fol. 61b (not in Rashīd al-Dīn, *Shu'āb-i Panjgānah*). She was called Dokuz's sister (?), but the name is unclear. She does not appear elsewhere.

[46] She was the daughter of Dokuz's brother Saricha, probably his older years, as she was young enough to be a concubine in the 1250s. Elsewhere Rashīd al-Dīn makes her Ong Qan's sister's daughter in an improbable garbled lineage. Rashīd al-Dīn, *Jāmi'*, 119, 963, trans. Thackston, 65, 472. Also Banākatī, *Ta'rīkh*, 411; Pfeiffer, *Conversion to Islam*, 275 and table A.

[47] This was Quyidu. See Hope, "*Qarachu Begs*," 5–6; also Rashīd al-Dīn, *Jāmi'*, 123, trans. Thackston, 66–7.

[48] Hope, "*Qarachu Begs*," 5–6. For marriages see Family Tree 9.5 and also footnote 89. Rashīd al-Dīn, *Jāmi'*, 123–4, 547, 553 (Alinaq's marriage), trans. Thackston, 66–7; 1122, 1134, and *Shu'āb-i Panjgānah*, fol. 142a; *Mu'izz al-Ansāb*, fol. 66b.

into his mother's Suldus family, which may reflect her (and his) junior status.[49] Instead he wedded three different senior wives, none of whom became overly influential. First was Dorji, of unknown lineage, who died young and childless. Second was the Alchi Tatar lady Nuqdan, a Christian and the mother of Gaikhatu. Nuqdan's brother was a commander and son-in-law in typical consort family fashion. The third senior wife was a Qonggirat from the junior line, Eltüzmish.[50] (See Family Tree 8.5 in Chapter 8.) Otherwise the status quo improved for the three principle consort houses during Abaqa's reign. The Oirats advanced their position when Abaqa married Hülegü's Oirat widow, Öljei, through the levirate, and granted her lands in Northern Iraq. Later she successfully intervened with him on personnel decisions.[51] The Qonggirats similarly improved theirs, since in addition to his third senior wife, Eltüzmish, Abaqa married a Qonggirat junior wife (Martai) who produced one of his seven daughters.[52] Finally the Kereits also raised their status when Abaqa married Hülegü's concubine, Tuqitani, and gave her Dokuz's camp, in which Tuqitani lived and maintained her aunt's customs and habits until her own death in 1292.[53]

THE BATTLE OF ḤOMS (1281) AND THE REIGN OF AḤMAD TEGÜDER (1282–1284)

In 1281 Abaqa sent a military campaign to Syria against the Mamluks. For the Oirat consort house the situation was promising, as it was the

[49] This was Yesünjin from Güyük's / Qutui's camp. On the theory see Brack, "Sacred Kingship," 48.

[50] Rashīd al-Dīn, *Jāmiʿ*, 88 (Joma and Nuqdan), 971 (Joma and Nuqdan), 1055 (all three wives), trans. Thackston, 49, 476, 515; Banākatī, *Ta'rīkh*, 398 (garbled), 426 (Dorji is "Orduchin"), 447. For Eltüzmish see Family Tree 8.5 in Chapter 8. Also De Nicola, *Khatuns*, 158, and "Domestic Sphere," 359 (Nuqdan's religion); Ryan, "Christian Wives," 417.

[51] Rashīd al-Dīn, *Jāmiʿ*, 1055 (marriage), 1110 (lands), and 1113 (intercession for the Juvaynī brothers), trans. Thackston, 515, 541, 543; also De Nicola, *Khatuns*, 152, 156 (lands and her *ordo*); Landa, "Sons-in-Law," 172.

[52] Eltüzmish had no children with Abaqa; Martai had one daughter, Nujin; the Qonggirat concubine Tödai had two daughters: Yol-Qutlugh and Tadai. Abaqa's sons were Gaikhatu (from the Tatar wife, Nuqdan) and Arghun (from a concubine, Qaitmish). Rashīd al-Dīn, *Jāmiʿ*, 1055–6, trans. Thackston, 515–6; Banākatī, *Ta'rīkh*, 426; Landa, "Sons-in-Law," 172.

[53] On the camp, see Rashīd al-Dīn, *Jāmiʿ*, 963, 1055, trans. Thackston, 472, 515; Banākatī, *Ta'rīkh*, 411, 426 (albeit omitting Tuqitani from Abaqa's women); also Pfeiffer, *Conversion to Islam*, 271–4, 275, and "Second Letter," 180–1; De Nicola, *Khatuns*, 97, 156.

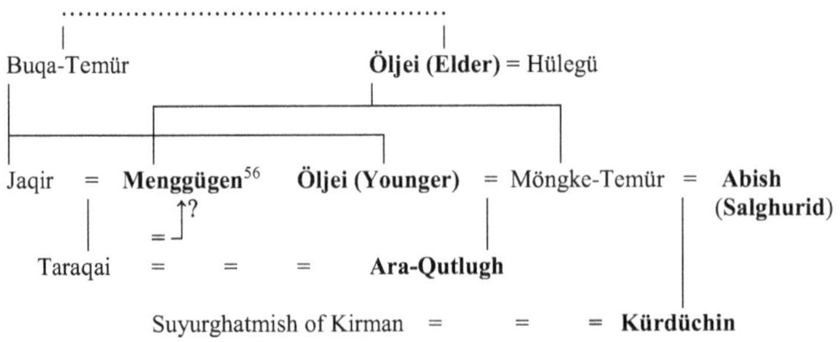

Family Tree 9.4 Möngke-Temür, his Oirat cousins, and some of his children.
All women are in **bold.**
Tiny dotted line represents half siblings.
Möngke-Temür's children from additional women omitted.[54,55]

second Toluid-Oirat prince and governor of Fars, Öljei's son, Möngke-Temür, whom Abaqa appointed to lead the vanguard. Also representing the Oirat consorts were two of Möngke-Temür's cousins, Jaqir and Taraqai, who were married to Möngke-Temür's female kin (see Family Tree 9.4), and together led the Oirat troops in the right wing.[56]

Unfortunately for the Ilkhanids, nothing went as planned. It is unclear whether Möngke-Temür was able to take command, or whether some of the commanders usurped his position.[57] But certainly when the Ilkhanid armies met the Mamluks at the battle of Homs on 29 October 1281, it went badly: Möngke-Temür was wounded, and the Ilkhanid forces were defeated and forced to retreat.[58] After their return from Syria, the prince went to recover in his mother's territory in Northern Iraq, while Abaqa raged at the news.[59]

So the matter stood six months later when in April 1282 Abaqa suddenly died after a session of alcoholic excess.[60] This changed the picture

[54] Princess Buyan Agha was from an unknown mother; princes Anbarchi, Taichu, and Gerei from a concubine named Alinaq. Rashīd al-Dīn, *Jāmi'*, 969, trans. Thackston, 475.

[55] See footnote 6 for confusion about Menggügen's marriage(s).

[56] Rashīd al-Dīn, *Jāmi'*, 102, 969, 971, trans. Thackston, 56–7, 475, 476. For Möngke Temür's marriages see footnotes 22–23.

[57] Broadbridge, "Toluid-Oirat Connection," 128, note 45.

[58] For the battle see Reuven Amitai-Preiss, *Mongols and Mamluks: The Mamluk-Ilkhānid War, 1260–1281* (Cambridge: Cambridge University Press, 1995), 187–201; otherwise Broadbridge, "Toluid-Oirat Connection," 128, note 46.

[59] Broadbridge, "Toluid-Oirat Connection," 128; also Rashīd al-Dīn, *Jāmi'*, 1117, trans. Thackston, 544–5; Banākatī, *Ta'rīkh*, 435.

[60] Boyle, "Il-Khans," 364.

completely as princes, princesses, widows, and commanders gathered at a quriltai in the Jaghatu river valley to discuss the weighty question of succession.[61] There, in a culmination of her years of tutelage, the Oirat matriarch Öljei proposed her son Möngke-Temür as the new ilkhan, even though he was not actually present, and regardless of his recent humiliation in Syria.[62] Öljei's case demonstrates one of the more visible moments of a woman's involvement in politics. It also represented the Oirat consort house's best chance at seeing their prince take the throne. Benefits for the consorts would include direct family ties and access to an ilkhan, not just a prince; likely promotions to governorships for Möngke-Temür's male cousins, control of the best camp for Möngke-Temür's Oirat wife, along with the future hope of placing additional Oirat women as royal wives or elevating a son of Möngke-Temür to the throne, with attendant benefits to be expected at that time. But other commanders, Chinggisids, and consorts stood in opposition to Möngke-Temür's party and promoted his half-brother Tegüder, Hülegü's son from Qutui and the senior prince from the Qonggirat consort house.[63] A third party represented the interests of Abaqa's son Arghun, but his claim was comparatively weak since he was junior to his uncles, and was also the son of a concubine, not a wife.[64] Then at this critical juncture the quriltai was stunned with the news that Möngke-Temür had died suddenly on his mother's properties in Northern Iraq of mysterious and possibly unsavory causes.[65] Öljei's reaction is unrecorded, but certainly the Oirat camp had to withdraw after this unexpected reversal. Since Arghun's party still could not prevail, in due course Tegüder was raised to the throne at Ala-Tagh in June 1282.[66]

61 Boyle, "Il-Khans," 365; Hope, "Pillars," 11, and *Ilkhanate*, 125–8; Pfeiffer, *Conversions to Islam*, 185–92; also De Nicola, *Khatuns*, 95. For the valley see H. C. Rawlinson, "Notes on a Journey from Tabriz, through Persian Kurdistan, to the Ruins of Takhti-Soleiman, and from thence by Zenjan and Tarom to Gilan, in October and November, 1838, with a memoir on the site of the Atropatenian Ecbatana," *Journal of the Royal Geographical Society* 10 (1841): 40, 42.

62 Rashīd al-Dīn, *Jāmiʿ*, 1125, trans. Thackston, 548; Pfeiffer, *Conversion to Islam*, 187.

63 De Nicola, *Khatuns*, 95; Hope, *Ilkhanate*, 127–34.

64 Arghun's mother was named Qaitmish. Rashīd al-Dīn's statement that Tegüder's mother Qutui supported Arghun, not her son, must be dismissed as another rewriting of history. Hope, *Ilkhanate*, 127–8. Rashīd al-Dīn, *Jāmiʿ*, 1056, 1125, trans. Thackston, 516, 548; also Pfeiffer, *Conversion to Islam*, 188–9, 276.

65 Broadbridge, "Toluid-Oirat Connection," 128, and note 49; Pfeiffer, *Conversion to Islam*, 191.

66 He was elected in Maragha in May, and enthroned in Ala-Tagh in June. Pfeiffer, *Conversion to Islam*, 192–4, 199, 203; Hope, "Transmission of Authority," 23–4, and "Pillars," 11; De Nicola, *Khatuns*, 95, noting only the May date.

The Qonggirat Moment

Tegüder's reign marked the pinnacle of Qonggirat consort influence. Although the sources do not reveal the negotiations that brought Tegüder his wives, his Qonggirat mother probably had a hand in their selection, since four out of six were Qonggirats: the senior wife, Töküz; the second wife, Armini; Tödegü (a granddaughter of Princess Tumelün and therefore Qutui's relative); and, late in Tegüder's reign, Abaqa's widow Tödei.[67] Unfortunately the lineage of these women is omitted from the sources: the only Qonggirat family of which we can be sure is the one descending from Princess Tümelün (i.e., Tödegü), while the junior Qonggirat lineage stemming from the commander, Abatai, does not seem to be represented at all. But nevertheless all four wives are identified as Qonggirats, and three of them produced seven of Tegüder's nine children, with the second Qonggirat wife, Armini, bearing an impressive five offspring.[68] (Tegüder's other two wives were the Toluid-Oirat princess El-Qutlugh, and a woman named Baytekin, possibly a Jalayir).[69] But Tegüder married none of his father's wives through the levirate, perhaps for religious reasons, even though some – including the experienced and savvy Oirat widow, Öljei – were still alive. As one historian has noted, this decision was politically unwise.[70] (See Family Tree 9.5.)

The Qonggirat wives provide examples of royal managers, since both Töküz and Armini controlled camps: Töküz as senior wife, with Armini as the second wife in rank. Armini further demonstrates the importance of royal childbearing through her production of those five children. This achievement in fertility is especially noteworthy since by the 1280s the Ilkhanids were having trouble producing offspring. The birth of live royal children who made it to adulthood was thus in no way taken for granted, or even common.[71] Furthermore, although no direct causal link can be posited between fertility and influence, Armini did possess plenty of the

[67] Rashīd al-Dīn, *Jāmi'*, 1122, trans. Thackston, 547 and *Shu'āb-i Panjgānah*, fol. 141a; *Mu'izz al-Ansāb*, fol. 65a; Banākatī, *Ta'rīkh*, 437–8; no further lineage appears for Töküz and Armini.

[68] Rashīd al-Dīn, *Jāmi'*, 1122–3, trans. Thackston, 547–8; Banākatī, *Ta'rīkh*, 438. Also Pfeiffer, *Conversion to Islam*, 130–1.

[69] El-Qutlugh was a granddaughter of Hülegü's Oirat wife Güyük. Broadbridge, "Tolui-Oirat Connection," 130 and table 4. Baytekin's father was probably the Jalayir Ḥusayn Agha. Rashīd al-Dīn, *Jāmi'*, 68, 1122, trans. Thackston, 39, 547; Banākatī, *Ta'rīkh*, 438.

[70] But he married one of Abaqa's concubines, Tödei. Pfeiffer, *Conversion to Islam*, 277.

[71] Melville, "End of the Ilkhanate," 318; Masson-Smith, "Dietary Decadence," 35–6; De Nicola, *Khatuns*, 136.

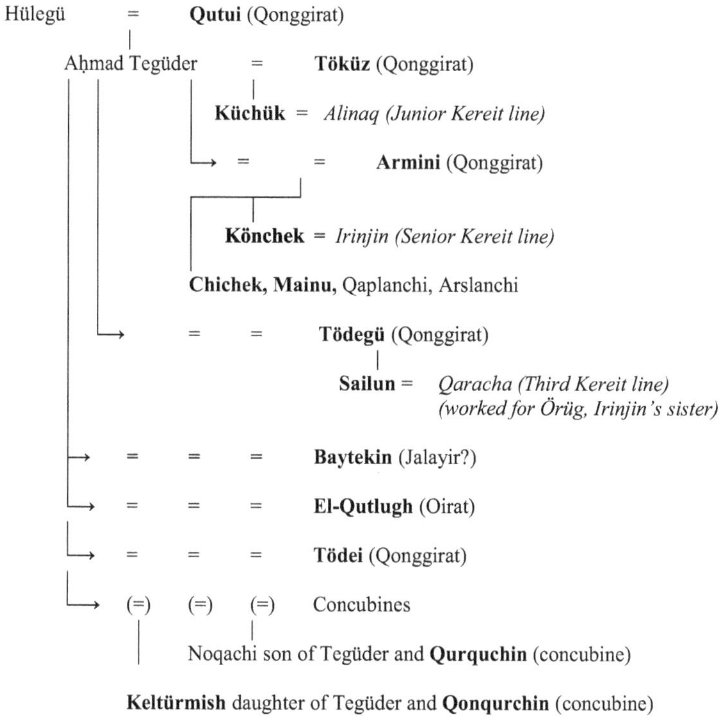

Family Tree 9.5 Aḥmad Tegüder, his wives and children, his Kereit in-laws.
All women are in **bold**.
Kereits are in *italics*.

latter: when a coalition of bureaucrats and commanders framed the minister brothers Alā' al-Dīn and Shams al-Dīn Juvaynī in an effort to target their wealth, it was she who thwarted the conspirators by intervening successfully with Tegüder in summer 1282.[72]

Surprisingly, however, the marriages arranged for the offspring of the Qonggirat wives were not with the Qonggirat consort lineages, which departs from the habits of other houses.[73] Instead, Tegüder and his wives

[72] Hülegü's widow, Öljei, had previously interceded for the Juvaynīs with Abaqa. Rashīd al-Dīn, *Jāmi'*, 1113 (Öljei), 1127 (Armini), trans. Thackston, 543, 549; also Hope, *Ilkhanate*, 123–5 and 131.

[73] Did Tegüder's short career play a role? I find no record of marriages for Armini's sons, Princes Qaplanchi or Arslanchi. For Armini's other daughters, Princess Chichek and Princess Mainu, see footnote 77.

proved themselves to be new friends to the Kereits by contracting marriages between three Kereit commanders on the one hand, and three Toluid-Qonggirat princesses on the other. The first son-in-law was the commander Alinaq, who had fought well at Ḥoms (despite the end result), and whom Tegüder rewarded with marriage to Küchük, his daughter with the senior wife, Tökuz.[74] This marked the transformation of Alinaq's family from a simple commander lineage into a consort one, and its members thereafter formed the junior Kereit line. Second, Tegüder linked himself with what became the senior Kereit consort lineage by marrying Könchek, a daughter of Armini, to the commander Irinjin, who was nephew of Dokuz and brother to Abaqa's widow Tuqitani (mistress of the great Kereit camp).[75] A third marriage was arranged between Sailun, a daughter of the third Qonggirat wife, Tödegü, and the Kereit commander Qaracha, who later worked for Irinjin and Tuqitani's other sister, Örüg.[76] (See Family Tree 9.5.) These new connections to royalty strengthened all of the Kereit house, and provided a useful foundation for the influence it wielded in later decades. Tegüder's other daughters married variously the governor of Diyarbakr (family unknown), the Tatar son of a bodyguardsman, and a Jalayir commander.[77]

But Teguder's reign was not so pleasing to others. He was the first Muslim ilkhan, having converted in his youth and whence he took his secondary name Aḥmad, which did not ingratiate him with the commanders.[78] He is alleged to have been so distracted from his duties by religious

[74] Rashīd al-Dīn, *Jāmiʿ*, 1122, 1126, trans. Thackston, 547, 553 and *Shuʿāb-i Panjgānah*, fol. 142a; Banākatī, *Taʾrīkh*, 435, 438 and *Shuʿāb-i Panjgānah*, fol. 142a; Vaṣṣāf / Āyatī, *Taḥrīr*, 55, 71; *Muʿizz al-Ansāb*, fol. 66b; Pfeiffer, *Conversion to Islam*, 190 (Alinaq's lesser status before becoming a son-in-law). For Homs see Hetum, http://rbedrosian.com/hetum4.htm (accessed August 1, 2017), Chapter 36 and Hetoum, *A Lytell Chronicle*, 47–8.

[75] Rashīd al-Dīn, *Jāmiʿ*, 1123, trans. Thackston, 547 and *Shuʿāb-i Panjgānah*, fol. 142a; Banākatī, *Taʾrīkh*, 438; Vaṣṣāf / Āyatī, *Taḥrīr*, 369–70; *Muʿizz al-Ansāb*, fol. 66b; De Nicola, *Khatuns*, 97, 156.

[76] He was an ev-oghlan in her camp. Rashīd al-Dīn, *Jāmiʿ*, 1123, trans. Thackston, 547 and *Shuʿāb-i Panjgānah*, fol. 142a; Banākatī, *Taʾrīkh*, 438; *Muʿizz al-Ansāb*, fol. 66b.

[77] Armini's daughter Princess Chechek married the governor of Diyarbakr, Princess Borachu son of Durabai, while her other daughter, Princess Mainu, married the Tatar Jandan son of Gerei *baʾurchi*, whom I have assumed to be a guardsman from his title of cook (*baʾurchi*); the last daughter, Princess Keltürmish, from a concubine, perhaps married the Jalayir Shadai son of Bughu (*sic*, Buqa?), then his son Toghan, but the source is unclear. See Rashīd al-Dīn, *Jāmiʿ*, 89, 1123, 1171, trans. Thackston, 49, 547, 570

[78] Pfeiffer, *Conversion*, entire; De Nicola, *Khatuns*, 95.

rituals that sometimes his mother Qutui attended to the Ilkhanate's finances for him in a useful application of her experience as royal manager.[79] (She is also credited with making major policy decisions, and patronizing religion actively.[80]) Contradictorily, however, Tegüder himself pursued a series of financial and administrative reforms, the extent and popularity of which are unclear.[81] He also failed to reward the commanders as they had hoped, which turned them violently against him.[82] The situation was not helped by members of earlier bodyguards, especially Hülegü's own, who had become powerful enough to manipulate politics for their own ends.[83] Furthermore Tegüder's nephew Princess Arghun continued to oppose him, and was reinforced not only by the disgruntled commanders, but also perhaps by his own uncle, Prince Qonqurtai, governor of Anatolia, and eventually by the influential Oirat matriarch, Öljei, and the Oirat commander Tankiz, head of one of the junior Oirat consort lines and father of Arghun's senior wife.[84] Tegüder's diplomatic interactions with the hated Mamluk sultans in Egypt also damaged his position, as did his decision to execute Prince Qonqurtai.[85] The end result was rebellion, led by several commanders who had been powerful under Abaqa, and, disappointed by Tegüder and afraid of retribution, sought to replace him with Arghun.[86] Tegüder was overthrown in July 1284 and executed in August in retribution for his murder of Qonqurtai (in part at the urging of that prince's bereaved mother).[87] Thereafter Arghun took his place, although not with unanimous backing.[88] During these violent days

[79] Qutui worked with her camp commander, Asiq. Rashīd al-Dīn, *Jāmi'*, 1126, 1130, trans. Thackston, 549, 551; also De Nicola, *Khatuns*, 95–7.

[80] De Nicola, *Khatuns*, 107–8 (Qutui's policies in Kirman), 193, 215 (patronage of Christians); also George Lane, "An Account of Gregory Bar Hebraeus Abu al-Farah and His Relations with the Mongols of Persia," *Hugoye Journal of Syriac Studies* 2, no. 2 (July 1999): 226–7; Budge, *The Monks of Kublai Khan, Emperor of China*, 161.

[81] Pfeiffer, *Conversion to Islam*, 204–11, 259–64.

[82] Hope, "Transmission," 24, and *Ilkhanate*, 127–34.

[83] Hope, "Pillars of State," 12.

[84] See footnote 96 for Arghun's wives; also Boyle, "Il-Khans," 365; De Nicola, *Khatuns*, 97, 112–13 (Öljei's importance); Brack, "Sacred Kingship," 52.

[85] Hope, "Transmission," 24, and *Ilkhanate*, 131 (Qonqortai); also Pfeiffer, "Second Letter," 180–1 and *Conversion to Islam*, 271–4; also Broadbridge, *Kingship and Ideology*, 38–44 (interactions with Mamluks).

[86] Hope, *Ilkhanate*, 133–4 and "Pillars of State," 12; Pfeiffer, *Conversion to Islam*, 283–4, 302–4, 312–13.

[87] Boyle, "Il-Khans," 367; Pfeiffer, "Second Letter," 181, and esp. 182, and *Conversion to Islam*, 284. The mother was a Khitan or Chinese concubine, Ajuja, from Dokuz's camp. Rashīd al-Dīn, *Jāmi'*, 968, 1148; trans. Thackston, 474, 559; also Banākatī, *Ta'rīkh*, 412.

[88] Hope, *Ilkhanate*, 135; also Brack, "Sacred Kingship," 55–6.

Tegüder's Kereit son-in-law Alinaq was also killed, but Alinaq's son Qurumshi inherited his wealth, and apparently his Chinggisid widow, Princess Küchük, as well. (He may later have married a second princess.)[89] The other Kereit in-laws escaped the upheaval intact.[90] As for the Qonggirats: Tegüder's murder signaled a decrease in their consort family power. Qutui and Tegüder's Qonggirat wives suffered the indignity of having their camps plundered during the coup.[91] After Tegüder's death, only one wife remarried.[92] Although later ilkhans wedded other Qonggirat women, and Qonggirat men continued to work as commanders, few of the later Qonggirat wives bore children who lived, and so this house was never again in a position to see one of its princes take the throne.[93]

THE OIRATS VERSUS THE KEREITS

Although Arghun had been raised by commanders, widows, and Chinggisids to take over after Tegüder, his short reign (r. 1284–91) was characterized by serious struggles. His greatest challenge was the Jalayir commander Buqa, who assumed power as both senior commander and head of the civilian administration – a novel combination – soon after Tegüder's death.[94] Buqa presided over a patchwork of regions controlled by commanders functioning as semi-independent governors, and himself reigned almost uncontested. Arghun thus spent several years preparing to oppose Buqa, assert a new, centralized authority as ilkhan, and take control of revenues.[95]

[89] Hope, *Ilkhanate*, 132–3 and "Transmission," 6; De Nicola, *Khatuns*, 98. Qurumishi's (unnamed) princess wife could have been Princess Küchük through the levirate. But elsewhere he is said to have married one of Gaikhatu's daughters: Rashīd al-Dīn, *Shu'āb-i Panjgānah*, fol. 146a (Princess El-Qutlugh), or *Mu'izz al-Ansāb*, fol. 71b (Princess Qutlugh-Temür).

[90] Irinjin's career lasted until his death in 1319; Qaracha was active through 1295. Rashīd al-Dīn, *Jāmi'*, 1201, trans. Thackston, 586.

[91] De Nicola, *Khatuns*, 98–9, also 158. These were Tödai (his newest Qonggirat bride, married just before the coup) and Armini, which raises a question: Where was the senior wife, Töküz, and her ordo? It is unclear. Rashīd al-Dīn, *Jāmi'*, 1147, trans. Thackston, 559.

[92] The exception was Tödai, see the subsequent discussion in this chapter and also De Nicola, *Khatuns*, 158.

[93] The exception was Eltüzmish, widow of Abaqa and Ghazan. With Öljeitü she bore three princes who died young, and Princess Sati Beg, who lived for decades. See footnotes 50, 164. Also see Landa, "Sons-in-Law," 173.

[94] Hope, *Ilkhanate*, 135–7.

[95] Note the extensive analysis in Hope, *Ilkhanate*, 138–47.

Although on a lesser scale, marriage politics were also fraught during Arghun's reign. Like his predecessors, Arghun married into the three main families, along with a Jedei Baya'ut woman, and another from the Muslim Turkic vassal house of the Seljuks of Anatolia.[96] But after the Qonggirat reversals caused by Tegüder's execution, a competition emerged between the Oirats and the Kereits. Initially Arghun's rule gave the Oirats an opportunity to regain lost ground: he was on good terms with the senior widow, Öljei, who had supported his efforts to become and remain ilkhan.[97] Arghun's senior wife was the Oirat lady Qutlugh from the junior line, whose father, the commander Tankiz, also supported her husband politically.[98] Qutlugh then did her duty by bearing a son, Khitai Oghul. (See Family Trees 9.2 and 9.3.) So far so good. Although Qutlugh died relatively young in 1288, Arghun then married her niece, Öljetei. However, this match was less advantageous for the Oirat consorts, since Öljetei was too young to bear children.[99] The relationship between Arghun and the Oirat consort family may also have been complicated by the ilkhan's surreptitious executions in 1289 of two Toluid-Oirat princes, Jüshkab and Kingshü, sons of the deceased Prince Jumghur, probably for political reasons. The secrecy of the executions meant that this shocking truth was not revealed immediately.[100]

But all of Arghun's wives found themselves left in the dust by the startling achievements of the fertile Kereit wife, Örüg, sister to Irinjin and Tuqitani, who provides another example of a successful royal child-bearer: whereas Arghun's other six wives and three concubines bore only three children among them (i.e., three children from nine women),[101] Örüg crushed her competition by producing five children: two princes

[96] The wives were the Oirats Qutlugh and Öljetei; the Qonggirats Tödei and Bulughan jr.; the Jedei Baya'ut Bulughan sr., the Seljuk princess, and the Kereyit Örüg. He also had three concubines. Rashīd al-Dīn, *Jāmi'*, 1152, 1206, trans. Thackston, 561–2, 589; Qāshānī, *Uljaytu*, 7 for Örüg; Banākatī, *Ta'rīkh*, 440–1. Also Pfeiffer, *Conversion to Islam*, 131–2.

[97] Rashīd al-Dīn, *Jāmi'*, 1146, 1168, trans. Thackston, 558, 570; also De Nicola, *Khatuns*, 97–8.

[98] Qutlugh's mother was the Ögedeyid princess, not Tanggiz's other wife, Hülegü's Christian daughter Todogech. Rashīd al-Dīn, *Jāmi'*, 102, trans. Thackston, 56; Banākatī, *Ta'rīkh*, 413 (on Todogech); Brack, "Sacred Kingship," 52 (Tankiz's political support as presented by Rashīd al-Dīn); De Nicola, *Khatuns*, 214 (religion).

[99] Broadbridge, "Toluid-Oirat Connection," 132.

[100] Brack, "Sacred Kingship," 55–8.

[101] Qutlugh bore Prince Khitai Oghul a.k.a. Selengge, Bulughan (the Qonggirat) bore Princess Dolanji, and the concubine Qultaq bore Prince Ghazan. Rashīd al-Dīn, *Jāmi'*, 1153, trans. Thackston, 562; Banākatī, *Ta'rīkh*, 441.

(Yesü-Temür and the future ilkhan Öljeitü), and three princesses (Öljetei, Öljei-Temür, and Qutlugh-Temür).[102] Örüg's childbearing surely improved her status: at some point she gained control of a camp, and she was wealthy enough to act as a patron, particularly of religion, in which realm her influence inspired the Latin Pope Nicolas IV (1288–92) to write to her.[103] All her children gave her the human capital on whose behalf to make strategic marriages, while her sons provided her with a reason to try and position one as ilkhan. Örüg thus became the center of a strengthened Kereit consort network clustered around her five children and including her brother Irinjin (a son-in-law via Tegüder's daughter), her sister Tuqitani with Dokuz's camp, and the junior Kereit son-in-law, Qaracha, who worked in Örüg's camp. Further support may have come from the junior Kereit line, headed now by the commander Qurumishi, whose wife may have been a half sister to Irinjin's and Saricha's wives, and with whom Irinjin later cooperated in military endeavors (see the subsequent discussion).[104]

As if Örüg's successful childbearing were not challenging enough to the Oirat consort family, further trouble emerged from two of their own women, and showed that position and connections could not always prevail. First was Prince Möngke-Temür's second widow, Abish of Fars and mother of Princess Kürdüchin.[105] In 1283–4 Tegüder had appointed Abish as governor in her homeland, where she embarked on a course of financial mismanagement, which was exacerbated by a multiyear drought. While Arghun was struggling to find a way to oppose the overly powerful commander Buqa, the latter recalled Abish and dispatched a replacement, but she refused to obey the summons.[106] Thereafter Abish's adherents murdered her replacement and she was compelled to go to Tabriz, where she was tried, found guilty, and fined. She then remained in one of the wifely camps,[107] and died in 1286–7, allegedly of illness but possibly of foul play.[108] Since Abish had married into the Oirat consort

[102] Rashīd al-Dīn, *Jāmi'*, 1153, trans. Thackston, 562; also Broadbridge, "Toluid-Oirat Connection," 132, note 62; De Nicola, *Khatuns*, 99.

[103] She had a camp by Ghazan's reign. Rashīd al-Dīn, *Jāmi'*, 1249, trans. Thackston, 615. Also De Nicola, *Khatuns*, 215–16; Ryan, "Christian Wives," 418.

[104] See footnote 89.

[105] For Abish as the princess' mother see Rashīd al-Dīn, *Jāmi'*, 937, trans. Thackston, 475; Vaṣṣāf / Āyatī, *Taḥrīr*, 130; Muḥammad b. 'Alī b. Shabankarā'ī, *Majma' al-Ansāb*, ed. Mīr Ḥāshim Muḥaddith (Tehran: Amīr Kabīr), 200; also De Nicola, *Khatuns*, 110–14.

[106] Hope, *Ilkhanate*, 137, 141.

[107] She probably stayed with Öljei again. See Lambton, *Continuity*, 273.

[108] Lambton, *Continuity*, 272–5, calling Möngke-Temür "Tash Möngke," as in Vaṣṣāf / Āyātī, *Taḥrīr*, 130; also De Nicola, *Khatuns*, 110–14; Hope, *Ilkhanate*, 137, 141; Rashīd

house, her disgrace surely did the family no good in the eyes of other consorts, Chinggisids, commanders, or bureaucrats.

Arghun's own royal demise in 1291 caused further trouble for the Oirat family. Because Arghun had been ill, and because some of the commanders had violently opposed his policies, foul play was suspected.[109] Accusations emerged first of poison, then witchcraft.[110] These targeted the Toluid-Oirat princess El-Qutlugh, a descendant of Prince Jumghur and a widow of Tegüder, who was accused of sorcery and tortured until she confessed. Like other accused witches before her she was cast into the frigid waters of a river, this time the Kura in the Caucasus, in January 1291, probably tightly wrapped in a felt blanket, to suffer cold shock and death by drowning.[111] Since, as we have seen, charges of sorcery usually covered up some other problem, it is to be wondered what she really did. Unfortunately the obfuscation in the sources does not reveal her true "crime." But regardless, El-Qutlugh's trial and execution may have tainted the Oirat house in the eyes of others, just like Abish's disgrace. Worse yet, at some point during these years the matriarch Öljei probably also died,[112] while other blows included the secret executions of another Toluid-Oirat prince, Möngke-Temür's son Prince Anbarchi, in 1294, followed by the death of Arghun's own son, the Toluid-Oirat prince Khitai-Oghul in 1298, of unknown causes.[113]

Arghun's death unleashed a new political struggle in the Ilkhanate between the offspring of Abaqa on the one hand, and descendants of Hülegü on the other, all backed by different commanders.[114] Contenders included Arghun's half brother Gaikhatu (r. 1291–5), who was supported by a contingent from Anatolia, and Baidu, a grandson of Hülegü

al-Dīn, *Jāmi'*, 936–7, 1161, trans. Thackston, 458, 565–6 (the trial), trans. Boyle, 305–6; Qazvīnī, *Gūzīdah*, 507; Mirkhwand, *Rawzat*, 7:3622–5.

109 Hope, *Ilkhanate*, 147.

110 Boyle, "Il-Khans," 371–2; De Nicola, *Khatuns*, 187.

111 Her lineage and death have been obscured. She may have been Jumghur's granddaughter. Some say her daughter, Toquchar, was killed; others claim that Qutlugh was a concubine, not a wife. Broadbridge, "Toluid-Oirat Connection," 130, table 5. Also Rashīd al-Dīn, *Jāmi'*, 966, 1122, 1180, trans. Thackston, 473, 547, 575; Orbelian, *Siounie*, trans. Brosset, 259; Boyle, "Il-Khans," 372. Hope, *Ilkhanate*, 147.

112 Öljei vanishes from the sources after Arghun's early reign.

113 Rashīd al-Dīn, *Jāmi'*, 1282–3, trans. Thackston, 641 (Khitai Oghul); Brack, "Sacred Kingship," 57–9, 62–3 (Prince Anbarchi's near rebellion against Gaikhatu as filtered through Rashīd al-Dīn).

114 De Nicola, *Khatuns*, 99, and citing Stephen Kamola, "The Making of History in Mongol Iran" (PhD diss., University of Washington, 2013), 88; Brack, "Sacred Kingship," chapter 1.

(r. 1295), whose adherents formed a coalition based in Iraq.[115] As usual the royal women were as partisan as anyone, and here again we catch glimpses of their involvement in politics. The resourceful Kereit widow and matriarch Örüg emerged as a political actor who worked directly with the commanders by contributing ideas to the plotting that resulted in Gaikhatu's enthronement.[116] She then became a new royal wife and intercessor: Gaikhatu married her, and she is known to have influenced his actions thereafter.[117]

It was at this time that a new family with many lineages emerged in the arena of marriage politics: the Jalayirs, some of them Muslims, who had previously been largely absent.[118] The kingmaker, Buqa, whom Arghun had executed, was from one of the Jalayir lineages.[119] But a different lineage rose dramatically under Gaikhatu, thanks to the Jalayir governor of Anatolia, Aq-Buqa, whose father, Elgei, had led Toluid troops in Hülegü's invasion, and was camp commander for Hülegü's wives.[120] Gaikhatu married two cousins from this lineage in succession as senior wives: first was 'Ā'ishah, Aq-Buqa's niece; then, after her death, he married Aq-Buqa's daughter Dondi.[121] (Gaikhatu's four other wives came through the levirate from Arghun or Abaqa.[122]) Both Jalayir senior

115 Hope, *Ilkhanate*, 148; Pfeiffer, *Conversion to Islam*, 180–2. Geikhatu was the son of Abaqa's second senior wife, the Tatar Nuqdan. Baidu's father was Taraghai, son of Hülegü and a concubine named Boraqchin from Qutui's camp. Taraghai was killed by lightning en route to Iran. Rashīd al-Dīn, *Jāmi'*, 967, trans. Thackston, 474; Banākatī, *Ta'rikh*, 412.

116 Örüg contributed ideas to a plan to move the women's ordus toward Gaikhatu in Anatolia, then block Baidu in the Caucasus with troops. Rashīd al-Dīn, *Jāmi'*, 1184, trans. Thackston, 576; also De Nicola, *Khatuns*, 99, 109.

117 She convinced him to execute the commander Toghan. Rashīd al-Dīn, *Jāmi'*, 1192, trans. Thackston, 581; De Nicola, *Khatuns*, 100.

118 De Nicola, *Khatuns*, 206 (religion). The first Jalayir was Tegüder's wife Baytekin. *Mu'izz al-Ansāb*, fol. 65a; Rashīd al-Dīn, *Jāmi'*, 68 (for Husayn, her father), 1122, trans. Thackston 38, 547 and *Shu'āb-i Panjgānah*, fol. 141a.

119 He and his brother Aruq were in Abaqa's guard. Rashīd al-Dīn, *Jāmi'*, 70, trans. Thackston, 40.

120 On Elgei see Hope, *Ilkhanate*, 100, 110, 117.

121 `Ā'ishah was a daughter of Elgei's son Toghu (Tüqü). See Hope, *Ilkhanate*, 121 (on Tüqü). Dondi was the daughter of Toghu's brother Aq-Buqa. Rashīd al-Dīn, *Jāmi'*, 1189, 1215, trans. Thackston, 579–80 and note 2, 593 (Dondi's levirate marriage to Ghazan); Banākatī, *Ta'rīkh*, 447, 451. De Nicola, "Domestic Sphere," 363 (`Ā'ishah as a Muslim).

122 The Kereyit Örüg, two Qonggirats (Bulughan (i.e., junior), Eltüzmish), and Pādishāh of Kirman. Rashīd al-Dīn, *Jāmi'*, 1055, 1152, 1189, trans. Thackston, 515, 561, 580 and *Shu'āb-i Panjgānah*, fol. 145a; Banākatī, *Ta'rikh*, 426, 440–1, 447; *Mu'izz al-Ansāb*, fol. 70a–b. Also De Nicola, *Khatuns*, 109, 116 (Pādishāh).

wives emerged as competent royal childbearers by producing six of Gaikhatu's seven children (four daughters and two sons), which indicates that he spent considerable time with them both. We may assume that both women held the senior wife's camp in succession.[123] Gaikhatu's marital connections to this new consort family must be linked directly to the strong support for his candidacy that was provided by his in-law Aq-Buqa with his troops and allies.[124] However Gaikhatu's children did not marry among the Jalayir consorts, possibly because at least one of these unions was arranged years after his death.[125] But Princess Öljetei (Arghun's oldest daughter with Örüg) did marry Aq-Buqa then his son Ḥusayn, which strengthened this Jalayir lineage in later years.[126]

Nevertheless, Gaikhatu soon proved to be yet another undesirable ruler. From early in his reign he was forced to contend fiercely with the commanders for control of the Ilkhanate.[127] This combined explosively with an ongoing economic crisis caused by drought, a pestilence among horses, and reduced trade with India, to say nothing of Gaikhatu's unsuccessful flirtation with paper money.[128] All of this ignited rebellion among the commanders in favor of the passive and easily controlled Baidu.[129] Gaikhatu was overthrown and executed in 1295, and Baidu ruled for a few months (1295) until he, too, was replaced, this time by Arghun's son Ghazan (r. 1295–1304), whose party emerged out of Khurasan and Mazandaran.[130] Ghazan's status as the son of a concubine renders him anomalous, yet comparable to Abaqa and Arghun, both

[123] They bore all four of his daughters, and two of three sons. Dondi bore princes Alafrang and Iranshah (the Qonggirat Bulughan bore Prince Ching Pulad). The princesses were Ula-Qutlugh, El-Qutlugh, and Ara-Qutlugh from `Ā'ishah, and Qutlugh-Malik from Dondi. Rashīd al-Dīn, *Jāmi'*, 1189, trans. Thackston, 580 and note 2; Banākatī, *Ta'rikh*, 447.

[124] Pfeiffer, *Conversion to Islam*, 132.

[125] Princess Ula-Qutlugh married the Hushin commander Ghurbatai (loyal to Arghun and Gaikhatu). In 1301 Princess El-Qutlugh married Ghazan's commander Qutlugh-Shah. Rashīd al-Dīn, *Jāmi'*, 1189, 1200, 1300; trans. Thackston, 580, 585, 650.

[126] Princess Öljetei was first engaged to the Qonggirat commander Qonchaqbal, then instead wedded Aq-Buqa and thereafter Amir Ḥusayn through the levirate. Rashīd al-Dīn, *Jāmi'*, 1153, trans. Thackston, 562; Abū Bakr al-Qutbī al-Ahrī, *Ta'rīkh-i Shaikh Uwais (History of Shaikh Uways): An Important Source for the History of Ādharbaijān in the Fourteenth Century*, trans. J. B. van Loon (The Hague: Mouton, 1954), 146 (text, omitting Aq-Buqa), trans. 48. Also Hope, *Ilkhanate*, 164 (Qonchaqbal).

[127] Hope, "Pillars of State," 14–15. [128] Hope, *Ilkhanate*, 149.

[129] Hope, *Ilkhanate*, 152–3.

[130] Hope, "Pillars of State," 14–15 and *Ilkhanate*, 151–2; Boyle, "Il-Khans," 372–9.

junior sons who nevertheless ruled. This puzzle certainly requires attention.[131]

Ghazan began his reign with a series of brutal yet successful purges among commanders and Chinggisids.[132] He also made considerable efforts to return to the centralized state and unquestioned authority that his father, Arghun, had sought.[133] After the purges Ghazan worked with Rashīd al-Dīn to reform the bureaucratic and financial structures of the empire, bring it under greater control, and reduce the power of the remaining commanders.[134] Simultaneously he reduced the financial independence of royal women.[135]

The story of the Kereit and Oirat consort families during Ghazan's reign was one of vicissitudes. First, marriage politics witnessed a continued widening of the consort field. Ghazan married into only two of the three major consort houses – the Oirats and Qonggirats, but not the Kereits – and his ladies otherwise came from junior consort families like the Jedei Baya'uts, the Eljigin, and the newly emerging Jalayirs. (He may also have wedded a granddaughter of the Chinggisid-Oirat lady Orqīna of the Chaghatayids, but this was a unique situation).[136]

More significantly, Ghazan's reign marked new setbacks for both the Oirat and Kereit consorts. In the Oirat case, this meant trouble for their military men. At this time, the leader of the Oirat troops was a veteran of the Battle of Homs named Taraqai, while Ghazan's senior wife was the Toluid-Oirat princess Günjüshkab, Taraqai's cousin.[137] (See Family Tree 9.6.)

Taraqai had previously opposed Ghazan's uncle, Geikhatu, in favor of the weaker Baidu, which put him in an untenable position as Ghazan

[131] Ghazan was Arghun's fourth son in rank. The first was Khitai-Oghul from the Oirat senior wife, Qutlugh; the second and third were Yesü-Temür and Öljeitü, a.k.a. Kharbanda, from the Kereit wife Örüg. I thank Bruno De Nicola for first mentioning this anomaly.

[132] Hope, *Ilkhanate*, 163–9. [133] Hope, *Ilkhanate*, 174.

[134] De Nicola, *Khatuns*, 161–5, esp. 164; Hope, *Ilkhanate*, 161, 169–72, 173–4.

[135] De Nicola, *Khatuns*, 161–5, esp. 164.

[136] Two Jedei Baya'ut wives (Eshil, Kökechin), two levirate wives (the Qonggirat Bulughan, the Jalayir Dondi), and the Suldus lady Yedi Qurtuqa, daughter of Princess Tughluqshāh, who was sister to the ousted Chaghatayid khan Mubārak-Shāh. Rashīd al-Dīn, *Jāmi'*, 758–9, 1215, trans. Thackston, 371, 593; Banākatī, *Ta'rikh*, 450–1.

[137] Melville, "Decline," 14–15, note 30 and table 1. She is omitted from Rashīd al-Dīn's list of Ghazan's wives, but is identified as his first wife elsewhere. Rashīd al-Dīn, *Jāmi'*, 102, 966, trans. Thackston, 57, 473. See also Qāshānī,*Uljaytu*, 7, Banākatī, *Ta'rīkh*, 473 (Günjüshkāb).

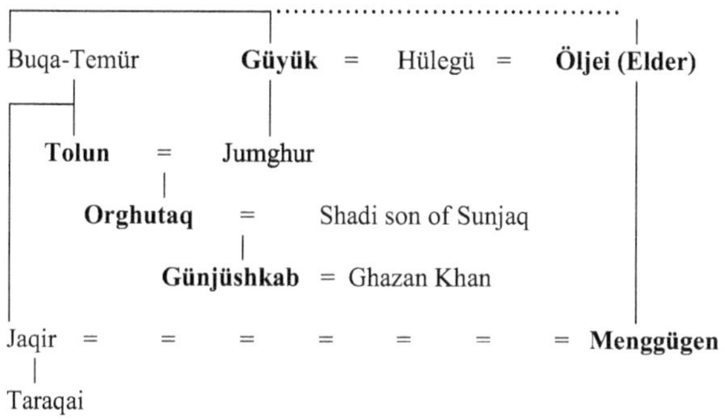

Family Tree 9.6 The Oirat cousins, Günjüshkab and Taraqai.[138]
All women are in **bold.**

began the purges. One solution would have been for Günjüshkab to intercede with her husband on Taraqai's behalf, a role that other royal wives had played successfully before her. But we have no hint either that she intervened, or that she refrained. This leads to two possibilities: perhaps Günjüshkab tried to speak for Taraqai but failed, which implies that she lacked the influence of a senior wife, and raises the question of why not. Or Günjüshkab did not try at all, which suggests a consort house whose branches were not working together for unseen reasons. Ultimately Taraqai fled to the Mamluk Sultanate with his family and numerous troops, never to return. This left the Oirat lineages somewhat depleted of members, and removed many of their inherited soldiers.[139] Thereafter the Oirat junior consort line from Khurasan, composed of descendants of Arghun Aqa, reached a brief pinnacle of authority under the Muslim commander Nawruz, whose influence on Ghazan, and Ghazan's decision to convert to Islam, was profound. But very soon Ghazan turned against his subordinate, executed him, and purged much of the rest of this family by 1297, which essentially eliminated them from further political considerations.[140]

[138] Rashīd al-Dīn, *Jāmi'*, 102, 966, 969, 971, trans. Thackston, 57, 473, 475, 476; Landa, "Son-in-Law," 181–2 and "Oirats," 157–63.

[139] In 695 / 1295–6; the number is given as 10,000–18,000. Broadbridge, "Toluid-Oirat Connection," 132–3; Hope, *Ilkhanate*, 164.

[140] See the excellent work of Ishayahu Landa, "New Light on Early Mongol Islamisation: The Case of Arghun Aqa's Family," *Journal of the Royal Asiatic Society*, Series 3, 28, no. 1 (January 2018): 1–24; also his "Oirats," 156 and his "Sons-in-Law," 183. Also see George Lane, Arghun Aqa: Mongol Bureaucrat," *Iranian Studies* 32, no. 4 (Autumn 1999): 459–82.

Meanwhile the Kereits had also suffered their own loss when the Kereit lady Tuqitani, mistress of Dokuz's camp, died in 1292. Contrary to precedent her camp was not handed over to her sister Örüg, the senior lady in the Kereit family, who already possessed one. Rather, Ghazan (then a prince) gave it to a Baya'ut wife, Kökechin, who had just arrived from China.[141] This demonstrates the authority that Ilkhanid princes retained over royal women's establishments, even though the women administered them.[142] It has also been argued that control over both the camp and Kökechin reflected Ghazan's attempt to bolster his claims on the throne in opposition to his uncle, Geikhatu.[143] In any case the decision was a departure from protocol, since the camp had been managed exclusively by Kereit women since the invasion of Iran. After Kökechin died in July 1299, Ghazan transferred the camp to a Qonggirat wife, Keremün.[144] Could this favorable placement of Keremün have allowed a revitalization of the Qonggirat house? Alas for them, no, since she herself died tragically young in January, 1304.[145]

But after Ghazan's own death a few months later in 1304, the accession of the Toluid-Kereit prince Öljeitü (r. 1304–16) marked the beginning of the Kereit consort family's own moment, and also resolved the situation of the Kereit camp. Öljeitu's mother was Dokuz's capable and intelligent niece Örüg, who had thrived with Arghun through her proliferation of children, helped maneuver Gaikhatu's takeover, and then survived a marriage to him. With her son on the throne, Örüg must have enjoyed the honors due to the queen mother, and the tangible and intangible benefits of her position, ranging from her existing camp and its economy – despite Ghazan's reforms – to political and religious patronage and proximity to the ruler. One of Örüg's daughters, Princess Öljetei, was not only married into the up-and-coming Jalayir family, but is also said to

141 Rashīd al-Dīn, *Jāmi'*, 963, 1215, 1237, trans. Thackston, 472, 593, 660; Banākatī, *Ta'rīkh*, 411, 451; Polo, *Description*, §18–19; De Nicola, *Khatuns*, 99, 136, 156–7, 162–3.

142 De Nicola, *Khatuns*, 155.

143 Kökechin was a Jedei Baya'ut, related to Arghun's widow, Bulughan (senior), whom Ghazan wanted to marry. Instead Gaikhatu married her and took her opulent camp. See De Nicola, *Khatuns*, 162–3.

144 See Family Tree 8.5 in Chapter 8. Rashīd al-Dīn, *Jāmi'*, 964, 1215, trans. Thackston, 472, 593; also Banākatī, *Ta'rīkh*, 411, 451; De Nicola, *Khatuns*, 157.

145 Rashīd al-Dīn, *Jāmi'*, 964, 1215, 1237, trans. Thackston, 472, 593–4, 660; Banākatī, *Ta'rīkh*, 411, 451; De Nicola, *Khatuns*, 136, 156–7, 162–3.

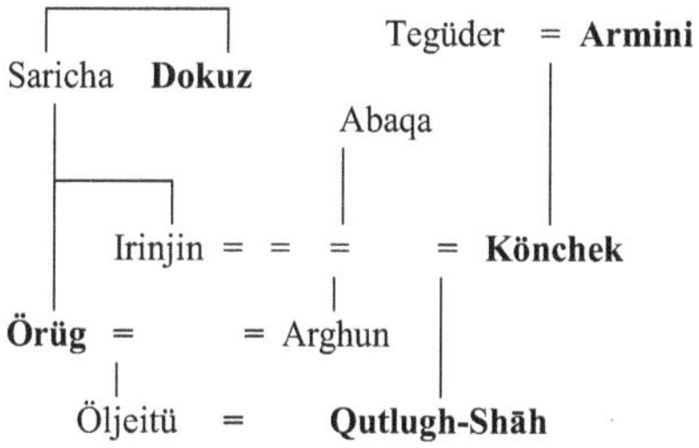

Family Tree 9.7 The Kereit-Toluid exchange at Örüg and Qutlugh-Shāh.

have influenced her royal brother greatly.[146] Örüg's brother Irinjin and his wife, Princess Könchek, accrued new advantages from their nephew's accession. Soon Irinjin was appointed governor of Anatolia, a post he held (and exploited)[147] for years; he also accompanied Öljeitü on campaigns to Gilan in 1306 and Syria in 1312.[148] Irinjin and Könchek acted as patrons to Christians despite Öljeitü's embrace of Islam.[149] Irinjin's children fared equally well: his son Shaykh ʿAlī worked for Öljeitü, then in 1316 gained a position with the heir, Prince Abū Saʿīd, whom he accompanied to Khurasan.[150] Meanwhile, Irinjin's daughter from Princess Könchek, Qutlugh-Shāh, married Öljeitü early in his reign in an exchange for Örüg.[151] (See Family Tree 9.7.) Furthermore, Öljeitü himself then returned Dokuz's camp to Kereit hands for the first time in thirteen years by bestowing it on Qutlugh-Shāh.[152] Although Qutlugh-

146 Al-Ahrī, *Uwais*, 148, trans. Van Loon, 50, "Sultan Uljaytu and Uljatay-Sultan, brother and sister, reigned, as it were, in condominium, for the sultan knew no command higher than her wish ... " As for the other sisters: Öljei-Temür married the commanders Tukel, then Qutlughshah; Qutlugh-Temür remained unwed. Rashīd al-Dīn, *Jāmiʿ*, 1153, trans. Thackston, 562.

147 Hope, *Ilkhanate*, 189 and note 42.

148 Qāshānī, *Uljaytu*, 44 (Anatolia); Ḥāfiẓ Abrū, *Dhayl-i Jāmiʿ al-Tawārīkh-i Rāshidī*, ed. Khānbābā Bāyānī (Tehran: Āsār-i Millī, 1972), 73, 104–5.

149 De Nicola, *Khatuns*, 157 (on the Kereyit ordo and Christians), 217; also Budge, *Monks of Kublai*, 257, 304–5.

150 Vaṣṣāf / Āyatī, *Taḥrīr*, 354; this was as *Qushghā Atakhchi*, likely a falconer position; also see Ḥāfiẓ Abrū, *Dhayl*, 112.

151 Their wedding was on 21 Shaʿbān 704 / March 27, 1305. Qāshānī, *Uljaytu*, 42; also Rashīd al-Dīn, *Jāmiʿ*, 472, 561 (for Orüg). For Qutlugh-Shāh's mother see Banākatī, *Ta'rikh*, 473; Budge, *Monks of Kublai*, 304–5. De Nicola, *Khatuns*, 137, 157; also 238, note 237, noting that later historians named her mother as Sarijah, not the princess.

152 Qāshānī, *Uljaytu*, 42; Banākatī, *Ta'rīkh*, 411; also Rashīd al-Dīn, *Jāmiʿ*, 472.

Shāh was not the senior of Öljeitü's twelve (!) wives, he reportedly loved her more than the others.[153] But despite her position as a royal wife and a royal manager of a camp, Qutlugh-Shāh had trouble as a royal childbearer: her only daughter died young, which kept her from engaging in marriage politics for her own offspring.[154]

The junior branch of the Kereit consort family also prospered under the rule of the Toluid-Kereit ilkhan. Its head, Qurumishi, who had worked loyally as a commander for Ghazan, maintained his command under Öljeitü and Abū Sa'īd, and was eventually appointed governor of Georgia.[155]

But even as Öljeitü's reign marked a moment of Kereit consort success, the Oirat consorts began to manage a comeback. This was because four of Öljeitü's wives hailed from Oirat lineages: the senior wife, Günjüshkab (Ghazan's widow), a descendant of Güyük and Hülegü; Büchigen, a descendant of Öljei and Hülegü; and two sisters (or cousins), Ḥajjī and Öljetei, who were descendants of Tankiz and Todogech (i.e., the junior line), and both of whom gave birth to boys.[156] Ḥajjī's son, Abū Sa'īd, survived to adulthood and became the final Ilkhanid ruler (r. 1317–35),[157] while two of Ḥajjī's brothers, 'Alī-Pādishāh and Muḥammad Beg, commanded the Oirat troops, which had been relocated

[153] Banākatī, *Ta'rīkh*, 41; Qāshānī, *Uljaytu*, 7–8, 43, 44. Öljeitü's wives were (1) the Toluid-Oirat Günjushkab, a descendant of Güyük; (2) the Toluid-Oirat Büchigen, descendant of Öljei and mother of Princess Dolandi; (3) the Qonggirat Eltüzmish, widow of Abaqa and Gaikhatu, mother of three princes (who died young) and princess Sati Beg; (4) the Oirat Ḥajjī, mother of Abū Sa'īd; (5) 'Ādilshāh, daughter of Commander Sutay; (6) the Oirat Öljetei, Ḥajjī's sister or half sister and mother of Abū al-Khayr; (7) the Eljigin Bulughan (3rd, aka Khurasani); (8) the Kereyit Qutlugh-Shah; (9) the Jalayirs Surghatmish and (10) Qutuqtai; (11) Dani, an Artuqid princess from Mardin; and (12) Tespine, the Byzantine widow of Abaqa (aka Maria Palaiologina, for whom see J. Herrin, *Unrivalled Influence: Women and Empire in Byzantium* [Princeton, 2013], 313–14). Also Banākatī, *Ta'rikh*, 473, switching the first two and misplacing Adilshah; corroborating details scattered in Rashīd al-Dīn, *Jāmi'*, 68, 102, 966, 1056, 1189, 1316, trans. Thackston, 39, 57, 473, 515, 580, 658; Qazvīnī, *Gūzīdah*, 607 for Eltüzmish's death in 1308.

[154] Qāshānī, *Uljaytu*, 8; Banākatī, *Ta'rīkh*, 473.

[155] Vaṣṣāf / Āyatī, *Taḥrir*, 196, 223, 226; Melville, "1319," 101 and note 69 (his later career).

[156] For Günjüshkab see Qāshānī, *Uljaytu*, 7, Melville, "Decline," 14–15 and note 30; Broadbridge, "Toluid-Oirat Connection," 133. For Büchigen et al. see Broadbridge, "Toluid-Oirat Connection, 133 and footnotes 74–6, also tables 6 and 7. Note also Brack, "Sacred Kingship," 79–81.

[157] Öljetei's son, Abū al-Khayr, died young. Broadbridge, "Toluid-Oirat Connection," 133, and tables 6, 7; also De Nicola, *Khatuns*, 101 (Ḥajjī).

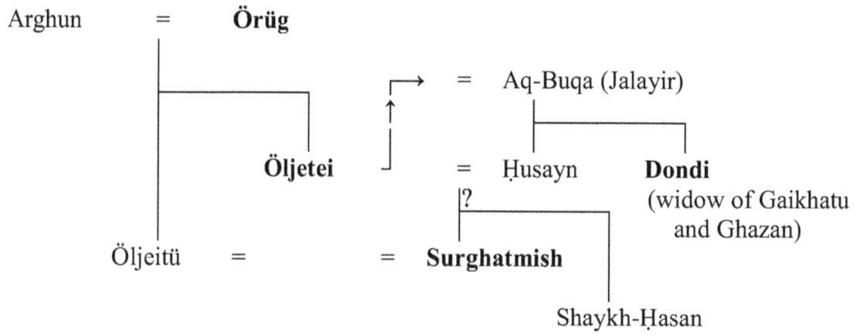

Family Tree 9.8 The Ilkhanid-Jalayir exchange.
All women are in **bold.**
|? Denotes that it is unclear whether Öljeteï was Surghatmish's mother. If so, then Öljeitü was marrying his sister's child, which was unprecedented.[158]

to the left wing of the Ilkhanid army. (The composition of the Oirat forces is unclear given the 1295 Oirat exodus to Egypt.)[159] But although Ḥajjī became the queen mother, she did not seem to exercise the same authority as had Qutui or Örüg; rather, considerable power rested with the senior commander, Choban.[160]

THE NEW CONSORTS: JALAYIRS AND CHOBANIDS

It was early in the reign of Abū Saʿīd that the balance shifted between the Kereit and Oirat families, complicated by the presence of two new consort lineages: the Suldus Chobanids and the Jalayirs. After emerging in the 1290s with marriages to Geikhatū on the one hand and the Toluid-Kereit princess Öljetei[161] on the other, the Jalayir lineage had retained its appeal, and Ghazan had married Gaikhatu's Jalayir widow.[162] Thereafter Öljeitü engaged in a variation on sister-exchange marriage with the Jalayirs: since his sister, Princess Öljetei, was the wife of the Jalayir commander Amir Ḥusayn, Öljeitü completed the exchange by marrying his niece, Ḥusayn's daughter Surghatmish. (See Family Tree 9.8.) Princess Öljetei's effect on

158 Qāshānī, *Uljaytu*, 8, claiming that Öljetei was her mother, but this would be a surprising uncle-niece marriage, rather than a usual one between first cousins. Banākatī, *Ta'rīkh*, 473. Also Melville, "Decline," table 2 on p. 17.

159 This was their position in 1319. Melville, "1319," 104.

160 De Nicola, *Khatuns*, 101.

161 This was the ilkhan Öljeitü's sister, and should not be confused with the Oirat lady Öljetei, Ḥajjī's sister or niece.

162 This was Aq-Buqa's daughter, Dondi. Rashīd al-Dīn, *Jāmiʿ*, 1215, trans. Thackston, 593; Banākatī, *Ta'rīkh*, 447, 451.

the fortunes of the later dynasty known as the Jalayirids emerged in the career of her son, Shaykh-Ḥasan (see the subsequent discussion).

By contrast, the emergence of a Suldus lineage in the form of the Chobanid family caused nothing but trouble to the established consort lineages. In 1307 Choban became senior commander under Öljeitü, and was reconfirmed by Abū Sa'īd.[163] In a series of distinctive marital coups, Choban managed to wed two of Öljeitü's daughters – princesses Dolandi in 1304 and Sati Beg in 1321[164] – and Princess Kürdüchin, a daughter of the deceased Toluid-Oirat prince Möngke-Temür and his Salghurid wife, Abish of Fars. Kürdüchin was heiress to that region.[165] (See Family Tree 9.9.)

THE DOWNFALL OF THE KEREIT CONSORTS

In 1319 an ugly struggle erupted between the Kereit consorts and their allies on the one hand, and the Chobanids and the sultan on the other, and led to the almost complete dismemberment of the Kereit families. Even before that point, the Kereit consorts had been disgruntled with the Chobanids. First, after Choban became senior commander of the Ilkhanate in 1307, he replaced Irinjin as governor of Anatolia with one of his own sons.[166] (Irinjin was later reassigned as governor of Diyarbakr.)[167] Second, Öljeitü overrode the engagement of Irinjin's daughter Dura'in, who was made to wed another of Choban's sons instead of the son of a commander for whom she had been intended. Although this was a happy

[163] Charles Melville and 'Abbās Zaryāb, "Chobanids," *Encyclopedia Iranica*, vol. 5, ed. Ehsan Yarshater (Costa Mesa, CA: Mazda, 1992), 496–502; also see De Nicola, *Khatuns*, 101; Hope, *Ikhanate*, 189.

[164] Dolandi's mother was Büchigen, a daughter of Öljei's daughter Bābā and the Oirat commander, Lagzi (Rashīd al-Dīn, *Jāmi'*, 103, 972, trans. Thackston, 57, 476; Qāshānī, *Uljaytu*, 7). Dolandi married Choban in Sha'bān 704 / March–April 1304 (Qāshānī, *Uljaytu*, 7, 43 [marriage consummated in 1307]); also Melville and Zaryāb, "Chobanids," 496–502. Sati Beg was daughter of the Qonggirat Eltüzmish, full sister of three princes, half sister to Ghazan, and married Choban in 1321 ('Abd al-Razzāq Samarqandī, *Maṭla' al-Sa'dayn va majma'-yi baḥrayn*, ed. 'Abd al-Ḥusayn Navā'ī [Tehran: Pazūhishgāh-i 'Ulūm-i Insānī va Muṭāla'āt-i Farhangī], 1993, 86–7); Rashīd al-Dīn, *Jāmi'*, 1189 (Eltüzmish), 1316 (Eltüzmish), trans. Thackston, 580, 658; Qāshānī, *Uljaytu*, 7; Banākatī, *Ta'rīkh*, 473 (only Sati Beg); Ḥāfiẓ Abrū, *Dhayl*, 120. Also De Nicola, *Khatuns*, 101 and note 73.

[165] See footnote 105; also Melville and Zaryāb, "Chobanids," 498; De Nicola, *Khatuns*, 102, and 197, 220 (her patronage of Muslim figures and architecture); see also footnote 183 for her as Choban's widow.

[166] This was Temürtash. Melville, "1319," 101 and notes 67 and 68.

[167] Melville, "1319," 101; Ḥāfiẓ Abrū, *Dhayl*, 123; Hope, *Ilkhanate*, 189.

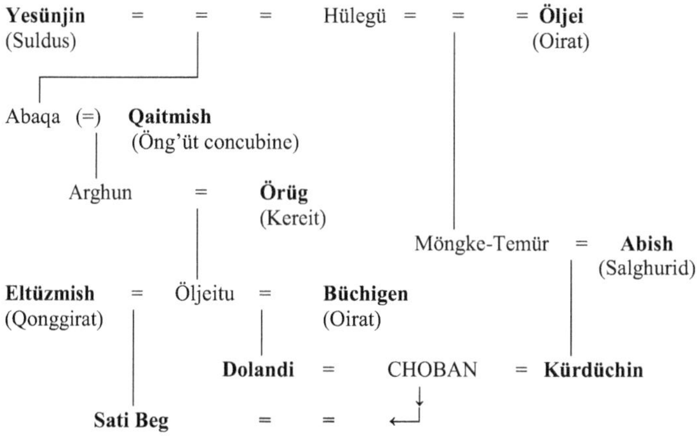

Family Tree 9.9 Choban and his many royal wives.
All women are in **bold**.

union, the forced substitution of a Chobanid bridegroom did not please her family.[168] Next came trouble for Irinjin's other daughter, Öljeitü's wife Qutlugh-Shāh, whom her husband accused of enjoying a liaison with a commander. Fortunately for the alleged lovers, Öljeitü was unable to punish them because of his final illness.[169] But after Abū Sa'īd's youthful (and powerless) accession, Choban had the commander arrested and fined heavily before releasing him.[170]

Next the junior Kereit line became involved in hostilities with Choban, which led to the final, ugly confrontation. This began in the winter of 1318–19, when the Jochid khan, Özbek, invaded the frozen Caucasus from the north, but Qurumishi, governor of Georgia and also a son-in-law, failed to join in the fighting that repelled him. In retribution Choban had Qurumishi humiliatingly punished.[171] Thereafter Qurumishi led an army against Choban, who was wounded and fled to Abū Sa'īd's court.[172] Historians wonder whether perhaps Abū Sa'īd secretly wished to espouse the "rebel" cause against this overly powerful commander, but ultimately he

[168] The son was Dimashq Khwaja. The commander Toqmaq had wanted her to marry one of his sons. See Melville, "1319," 98 and note 55, 101.

[169] This was Toqmaq (see footnote 168); also Melville, "1319," 93.

[170] He was 12. Melville, "1319," 92–3; also Qazvīnī, *Gūzīdah*, 611–12; and Hend Gilli-Elewy, "On Women, Power and Politics during the Last Phase of the Ilkhanate," *Arabica* 59 (2012): 713.

[171] Melville, "1319," 96–7, and footnotes 39, 40, 43; also see footnote 89.

[172] Melville, "1319," 97–9.

responded to Choban's need by mustering royal forces.[173] The senior Kereit consorts and their allies came to support Qurumishi in the form of Irinjin with his wife, family, and troops; Qutlugh-Shāh's reputed lover; and others.[174] Irinjin's children at court, Qutlugh-Shāh and Shaykh-'Alī, worked desperately to intervene between the two sides, but here the powers of intercession available to royal women (and in this case, their siblings) failed: the "rebels" and the royal forces met in battle in July 1319, and the royal forces won.[175] Thereafter the Kereit consort house was brutally crushed: Qurumishi, Irinjin, Princess Könchek, their son Shaykh-'Alī, and other members of their families were executed hideously, as were their allies.[176] Only one of Qurumishi's sons escaped north to the Jochid Khanate, while Qutlugh-Shāh, who now found herself accused of poisoning Öljeitü, avoided conviction and death, but was hastily remarried to a commander.[177] We do not know whether she kept the great Kereit camp. Although a few individual Kereits did live on, this consort house never recovered.

THE OIRATS' LAST GASP AND THE JALAYIRS' RISE

In contrast to the Kereits, the Oirat consorts sided with Abū Sa'īd in 1319, when his Oirat maternal uncles, 'Ali-Pādishāh and Muḥammad Beg, led their troops in the left wing of the royal forces.[178] Despite this public demonstration of loyalty, the queen mother, Ḥajjī, is said to have been just as hostile to Choban as the Kereits had been.[179] Her sentiments appear to have been shared by Öljeitü's seniormost widow, the Oirat lady Günjüshkab. Some years later in 1327, an opportunity arrived when one of Choban's sons engaged in an intrigue with a lady from Öljeitü's harem. In an example of how certain women possessed both insider political information and the contacts with which to use it to advantage, it was Günjüshkab who reported the transgression, which precipitated the son's capture and summary execution.[180] In an apparent show of Oirat

173 Melville, "1319," 104–5, 107–8; also Hope, *Ilkhanate*, 190–1.

174 Such as the commander Toqmaq; see footnotes 168 and 169; Melville, "1319," 93, 104.

175 Melville, "1319," 105–7.

176 They were hung on butcher hooks, skewered through the head, nailed, trampled by horses, shot and or beheaded. Melville, "1319," 109–10.

177 Melville, "1319," 109–10.

178 Melville, "1319," 104; Melville, *Decline*, table 2 on p. 17.

179 Melville, *Decline*, 15.

180 Meville, *Decline*, 12–18 and esp. 14, note 30; also Hope, *Ilkhanate*, 193, instead crediting two commanders with breaking the news to Abū Sa'īd. The Mamluk suggestion that the affair was with Ḥajjī seems untenable. Ibn al-Dawādārī, *Kanz*, 345.

family cooperation, Ḥajjī's brother 'Ali-Pādishāh sent word to indicate his approval, even though he did not take part in the arrest.[181]

Choban's reaction allowed the Oirat commanders to demonstrate further loyalty to their nephew. Choban received the evil news in Khurasan, then headed west with a large army. Abū Sa'īd gathered his own force, with his uncle 'Alī-Pādishāh among them. Although the other Oirat uncle, Muḥammad Beg, was serving under Choban, he took the first opportunity to defect to his nephew, along with other commanders.[182] This left Choban to flee to the ruler of Herat, who executed him in return for Abū Sa'īd's promise of marriage with Choban's widow, Princess Kürdüchin, the heiress to Fars.[183] The Jalayir Shaykh-Ḥasan replaced Choban as senior commander, although Abū Sa'īd made him divorce his beautiful and fascinating wife, Choban's daughter Baghdad Khatun, so that he could marry her himself.[184] Thereafter, some of Choban's family was purged, but other members of it survived: Baghdad Khatun intervened on behalf of her relatives, and was perhaps the greatest single reason why the Chobanids were able to rise as independent rulers after Abū Sa'īd's death.[185] Further influence may have come from Baghdad's niece, Dilshād, whom Abu Sa'īd married some years later.[186] However, the queen mother, Ḥajjī, maintained the same hostility to Baghdad (and Dilshad?) as she had to the rest of the Chobanids.[187]

As for the Oirats: Abū Sa'īd rewarded his uncles by appointing 'Ali-Pādishāh governor of Baghdad, and Muḥammad Beg governor of Anatolia, both high-level posts.[188] But their success did not last. In spring 1328, both men were sent east to curb the excesses of the new governor of Khurasan.[189] On the way 'Alī-Pādishāh began to question the mission, and, despite strongly worded letters from his sister Ḥajjī urging him to keep going, he returned west against orders in July. He was intercepted by

[181] Mevlille, *Decline*, 16. [182] Hope, *Ilkhanate*, 194.

[183] Melville, *Decline*, 19–28, esp. 22 and note 55; 23–4 and notes 62, 63. Choban's daughter Baghdad prevented this marriage from happening. Ḥāfiẓ Abru, *Dhayl*, 179 (Baghdad Khatun kept Kürdüchin in the ordo); Samarqandi, *Maṭla'* 108; Mirkhwānd, *Rawzah*, 4378 (both authors noting that Kürdüchin and Fars were promised); Nuwayrī, *Nihāyah*, 33:253 (Baghdad's power in general). See De Nicola, *Khatuns*, 113 (Kürdüchin's claim was restricted to Shiraz in the 1320s).

[184] See the useful discussion in Gilli-Elewy, "Last Phase," 713–17; also De Nicola, *Khatuns*, 101; Hope, *Ilkhanate*, 192.

[185] De Nicola, *Khatuns*, 101 (her influence). [186] Gilly-Elewy, "Last Phase," 713–17.

[187] Melville, *Decline*, 35. [188] Melville, *Decline*, 31.

[189] The ostensible reason was to respond to a Chaghatayid invasion. Melville, *Decline*, 30–2.

a royal army, to which several of his junior officers changed sides, and the result was a court-martial for him and his brother. It is unknown whether Abu Sa'īd's Chobanid wife Baghdad had a hand in the Oirats' downfall, but fortunately for them Ḥajjī intervened to secure sentences of exile, not death: 'Ali-Pādishāh near Baghdad, and Muḥammad in Khurasan.[190] The Oirat brothers remained out of circulation until their nephew's death without heir in November 1335. This left their sister to pursue her own intrigues and plots against rivals like Baghdad, largely unsuccessfully.[191]

Abū Sa'īd was the last Toluid-Oirat prince in the Ilkhanate, and the only one to rule. After his death his uncles and mother continued to engage in politics, but without the useful trump card of their sovereign. In the protracted struggles over succession that followed, the queen mother and her brothers favored different Chinggisid princes.[192] But neither side could prevail against the Jalayirs, whose moment had arrived. They were led by Shaykh-Ḥasan, the abovementioned senior commander and son of Princess Öljetei (ilkhan Öljeitü's sister) and her Jalayir husband Amir Ḥusayn. This marked the real ascendance of this family, the seeds of which had been sown decades earlier. Princess Öljetei's prestige shaped how others viewed her son. In a departure from the norm, some historical sources identified him as Shaykh-Ḥasan "Öljetei'i" (Shaykh-Ḥasan from Öljetei) in a nod to his royal mother, rather than as Shaykh-Ḥasan Jalayir after his father's family.[193] Shaykh-Ḥasan emerged with his own Chinggisid puppet to vie with the Oirats and the Chobanids, and established the Jalayirid dynasty. By 1337 both Oirat brothers were dead, while the fate of their sister, her camp, and the

[190] Melville, *Decline*, 32; Hope suggests that the brothers were rebelling against their nephew in *Ilkhanate*, 195.

[191] These included a plot against Baghdad Khatun in 1332, and one against the commander Maḥmūd-Shāh Injū in 1334–5. Melville, *Decline*, 35–6, 36–40, esp. 38; Hope, *Ilkhanate*, 195, suggesting that she also plotted against her son.

[192] Ḥajjī favored Arpa, a descendant of Hülegü's brother Ariq Böke, who executed her rival, Baghdad. Ḥajjī's brothers favored Musa, a descendant of prince Baidu (r. 1295). Melville, *Decline*, 44–6, and "End of the Ilkhanate," 323–4; Jackson, "Arpa Khan," 518–19; De Nicola, *Khatuns*, 102–3; also Khalīl b. Aybak al-Ṣafadī, *A'yān al-'Aṣr wa A'wān al-naṣr*, ed. 'Alī Abū Zayd (Beirut and Damascus: Dār al-Fikr al-Mu'āṣir, 1998), 3:293; Ibn Ḥajar al-'Asqalānī, *Al-Durar al-kāminah fī akhbār al-mi'ah wa al-thāminah*, 4 vols. (Beirut, 1993), 4:376–7.

[193] Ḥāfiẓ Abru, *Dhayl*, 232; Qazvīnī, Zayn al-Dīn b. Ḥamd Allah Mustawfī, *Zayl-i Ta'rīkh-i Gūzidah*, ed. Irāj Afshār, Mawqufāt-i Dr. Maḥmūd Afshār Yazdī 46, (Tehran, 1372/ 1993–4), 27, 35, 57, esp. 67.

remaining Oirat consort family is unknown.[194] We do know that the Jalayirs and Chobanids both carved independent states out of Ilkhanid domains: the Chobanids lasted until the 1350s,[195] and the Jalayirids until 1410.[196] But the role of marriage politics in those states remains a topic for another day.

CONCLUSION

The relatively abundant information from the Ilkhanate allows us to conduct this case study of Ilkhanid politics by viewing them through the lens of the consort families, which emerged as one kind of faction of the Ilkhanid period. These families had collective interests in maintaining ties of kinship to the ruling family, bearing likely children, engaging in politics, angling for prestigious promotions as governors, and controlling royal wifely camps whenever possible. Among consort houses, three stood out: the Oirats, the Qonggirats, and the Kereits. Two of three families, the Oirats and the Qonggirats, managed to place daughters as senior wives to the Chinggisids, while the Kereyits placed junior wives who then rose in status through a combination of childbearing, political savvy, and luck. All three families saw one of their princes ascend the throne: Aḥmad Tegüder for the Qonggirats, Öljeitü for the Kereits, Abū Saʿīd for the Oirats. All three families watched their men enjoy career advancement, to which their ties of kinship with the Chinggisids helped gain them access. And all three families ultimately lost their advantages at different times, whether because of the vagaries of fate, the inability to produce heirs, and the rise of the competing lineages of the Jalayirs and Suldus Chobanids. Although consort houses were far from being the only political factions within the Ilkhanate, their contributions to political events, and their shared interests as family groups, make them deserve more attention than they have yet received.

194 Shaykh-Ḥasan first defeated the Oirats on July 24, 1336, where ʿAli-Pādishāh was killed, then again on June 14, 1337, after which the puppet Musa was captured and executed, and Muḥammad-Beg was murdered by Kurds. Melville, *Decline*, 48 and note 139.

195 This included the brief reign of Choban's widow, Princess Sātī Beg in 1339, before she was made to marry a commander. De Nicola, *Khatuns*, 103; Gilli-Elewy, "Last Phase," 717; Melville, "End of the Ilkhanate," 319–20.

196 Melville, "End of the Ilkhanate," 324–5.

Conclusion

As this book has shown, the impact of women on the rise and expansion of the Mongol Empire was profound and varied. When we ask where women were in Chinggis Khan's life, empire, and conquests, the answer is: everywhere. One way that the magnitude of women's involvement can be understood is through a brief set of before-and-after descriptions. Before, we believed that the Mongol conquests were largely the achievement of men. After we look at women's activities, we grasp that women provided active logistical support by running non-combatant camps efficiently and effectively year round, and they managed traveling camps during campaigns, which was a critical element in freeing so many nomadic men to specialize in the warfare we know so well.

Before, Chinggis Khan's formation of a coalition of allies around 1206 could be seen primarily as the interactions of men who shared military goals and political ambitions. Now we understand that much of this coalition was created and sealed by women through marriage. For Chinggis Khan, these marriages created ties to the Olqunu'uts, which he inherited from Hö'elün, ties with the Qonggirats when he married Börte, or ties that he and Börte together forged with the Oirats, Uighurs, Öng'üts, and Ikires by choosing husbands for their own daughters, and with the Qarluqs for Chinggis Khan's granddaughters, or daughters with lesser wives. Another, anomalous tie was with the Uru'uts through Ibaqa's second marriage. All these women influenced Chinggis Khan's strategic decisions about army reform, and they facilitated the creation of a new group of commanders and men within the overall Chinggisid military forces – the Chinggisid confederation – which acted as a check and balance on other branches, brought needed support to particular battles and campaigns, and requires us to rethink our vision of Chinggis Khan's army reform. The presence of sons-in-law and the activities of their princess wives also shaped Chinggis Khan's famous conquests, while we know that the benefits accrued by the Chinggisid confederation were passed on to later generations as well.

Before, the names of Qojin, Checheyigen, Alaqa, Tümelün, and Al Altan, and even of Börte herself, were routinely excluded from family trees of the conqueror. Who knew them? Who imagined that their activities could matter? Now we see the integration of these women and the consort families that descended from them in every level of Chinggisid politics over decades. In particular we have seen Börte's central importance: as the mother of the four senior sons *and* the five senior daughters; as the person by whom access to succession to Chinggis Khan was defined; and as the link to the single most powerful and important consort house.

Before, we viewed Töregene, Oghul-Qaimish, and Sorqoqtani as interesting (or tragic, or pathetic) individuals. After, we see them as representatives of particular phenomena of war and empire: the conquered wife, and the regent (or kingmaker) widow. We have learned that their activities, and their relationship to the empire, were far more complex than has been imagined, and we now know better than to take the biased sources' assessments of them for granted. We have witnessed the destruction that all three women wreaked on the Chinggisid family, whether intentionally or not. We also know to include Orqina among the regents, rather than overlooking her years of independent rule, as has so often been the case.

This book has also focused on the challenges that were particular to many women: irregular marriage by kidnap and the potential weaknesses in family connection, wealth, and stability, as was true for Hö'elün, and briefly for Börte and even Orqina; or the significant limitations placed on conquered wives, who often lost family, people, possessions, power, influence, and opportunities to bear and raise children, even when they married into the highest ranks of Chinggisid men. It has shown the many ways – seen and unseen, loyal and disloyal – that conquered women responded to this plight. Among these conquered women, those from the Alchi Tatars and Kereits stood out for their singular impact on the empire, whether by saving an otherwise lost people (Yisüi and Yisügen), by gutting the Golden Lineage (Sorqaqtani), or reestablishing a consort family within it (Dokuz).

This book makes clear that the politics of the successor khanates must now be rethought with an eye to the interests and clout of the consort families, major and minor, who formed one more kind of faction, along with those that have been better studied. It has also highlighted the way women's behavior and activities could be sharply contained, most ominously through accusations of crime. The worst charge was witchcraft, which was leveled against Toregene's advisor Fāṭimah, the regent Oghul-Qaimish, and the Toluid-Oirat wife of Tegüder, El-Qutlugh, all of whom were hideously drowned, and probably for something other than sorcery. But even the lesser charge of poison sufficed to end a woman's life, as in the case of Princess Al Altan, or career, as for ilkhan Öljeitü's Kereyit wife, Qutlugh-Shah.

Ultimately the study of imperial women among the Mongols is still in its infancy. Thus, although this book should answer many of its readers' questions, it will have failed unless it also leads them to ask more. Only cooperation among scholars will help us uncover further information about the impact of women on the making of the Mongol Empire. I hope, then, that this book has suggested how much more we have to learn.

Bibliography

Primary Sources

Abū al-Fidā', Ismā'īl. 1983. *The Memoirs of a Syrian Prince: Abū'l-Fid'', Sultan of Ḥamāh (672–732/1273–1331)*. Translated and edited by P. M. Holt. Wiesbaden: Franz Steiner.

Abū al-Ghāzī Bahādur Khan. 1871–74. *Shajarah-yi Türk*. Edited and translated by Baron Petr I. Desmaisons as *Histoire des Mongols et des Tatars par Aboul-Ghazi Behadour Khan, Souverein de Kharezm et Historien Djaghatai, 1603–1664 A. D.*, St. Petersburg. Reprinted 1970. Amsterdam: Ad Orientem.

Al-Ahrī, Abū Bakr al-Quṭbī. 1954. *Ta'rīkh-i Shaikh Uwais (History of Shaikh Uways): An Important Source for the History of Ādharbaijān in the Fourteenth Century*. Translated by J. B. van Loon. The Hague: Mouton.

Anonymous (1). 2006. *The Secret History of the Mongols: A Mongolian Epic Chronicle of the Thirteenth Century*. Edited and translated by Igor de Rachewiltz. Leiden: E. J. Brill.

(2). 1951. *Historie des campagnes de Gengis Khan: Cheng wou ts-in-tcheng lou*. Vol. 1. Translated and edited by Paul Pelliot and Louis Hambis. Leiden: E J. Brill.

(3). 1955. *The Mongol Chronicle Altan Tobči: Text, Translation and Critical Notes*. Translated and edited by Charles Bawden. Wiesbaden: Harrassowitz.

(4). 1970. *The Chronicle of Novgorod*. Translated by Robert Mitchell and Nevill Forbes. New York: AMS Press.

(5). *Mu'izz al-Ansāb*. British Library OR 467.

(6). 1984–89. *The Nikonian Chronicle*. 5 vols. Introduced and annotated by Serge A. Zenkovsky; translated by Serge A. and Betty Jean Zenkovsky. Princeton, The Kingston Press, Inc., 1984–86 (vols. 1–3); ibid., The Darwin Press, Inc., 1988–89 (vols. 4–5). Volume 3.

Aqsarā'ī, Maḥmūd, a.k.a. al-Karīm al-Aqsarā'ī. 1944. *Müsâmeret ül-ahbâr: Mogollar zamaninda Türkiye Selçukları Tarihi*. Edited by Osman Turkan. Ankara: Anjuman Tārīkh Turk.

Babur. 1996. *The Baburnama: Memoirs of Babur, Prince and Emperor*. Translated, edited, and annotated by Wheeler M. Thackston. New York: Oxford University Press in association with the Freer Gallery of Art and the Arthur M. Sackler Gallery, Smithsonian Institution.

Banākatī, Dāvūd. 1969. *Ta'rīkh-i Banākatī* or *Rawḍ al-albāb fī tawārīkh al-akābir wa al-ansāb*. Edited by Ja'far Shi'ār. Tehran: Anjuman-i Āthār-i Millī.

Baybars al-Manṣūrī al-Dawādār. 1987. *Kitāb al-tuḥfah al-mulūkīyah fī al-dawlah al-turkīyah*. Edited by 'Abd al-Ḥamīd Ṣāliḥ Ḥamdān. Cairo: al-Dār al-Miṣrīyah al-Lubnānīyah.

1998. *Zubdat al-fikrah fī ta'rīkh al-hijrah*. Edited by D. S. Richards. Beirut. Bibliotheka Islamica, est. by Hellmut Ritter, in cooperation with Deutschen Morganländischen Gesellschaft, edited by Ulrich Haarmann and Angelika Neuwirth, 42.

Benedict the Pole. 1955. "Narrative of Benedict the Pole." In *The Mongol Mission: Narratives and Letters of the Franciscan Missionaries in Mongolia and China in the Thirteenth and Fourteenth Centuries*. Edited by Christopher Dawson. New York: Sheed and Ward.

Budge, E. W. 1928. *The Monks of Kublai Khan, Emperor of China*. London: The Religious Tracts Society.

Carpini, John of Plano. 1955. "History of the Mongols." In *The Mongol Mission: Narratives and Letters of the Franciscan Missionaries in China and Mongolia in the Thirteenth and Fourteenth centuries*. Translated by a nun of Stanbrook Abbey. Edited by Christopher Dawson. New York: Sheed and Ward.

1900. *The Journey of William of Rubruck to the Eastern Parts of the World, 1235–55, as Narrated by Himself, with Two Accounts of the Earlier Journey of John of Pian de Carpine*. Translated and annotated by W. W. Rockhill. London: Hakluyt Society. https://depts.washington.edu/silkroad/texts/carpini.html

De Bridia. C. 1965. *The Vinland Map and the Tatar Relation*. Translated by R. Skelton, T. Marston, and G. Painter. New Haven: Yale University Press.

Grigor of Akanc (Akner). 1949. *History of the Nation of the Archers*. Edited with an English Translation and Notes by Robert P. Blake and Richard N. Frye. Harvard-Yenching Institute: *Harvard Journal of Asiatic Studies* 12, no. 3/4, 269–399.

Hāfiẓ Abrū, 'Abdallah Khwāfī. 1972. *Dhayl-i Jāmi' al-tawārīkh-i Rashīdī*. Edited by Khānbābā Bāyānī. Tehran: Āsār-i Millī.

Hetoum. 1988. *A Lytell Cronycle*. Edited by Glenn Burger. Toronto Medieval Texts and Translations 6. Richard Pynson's c. 1520 translation of *La Fleur des histoires de la terre d'Orient* (1307). Toronto: University of Toronto Press.

Ibn 'Abd al-Ẓāhir, Muḥyī al-Dīn. 1976. *Al-Rawḍ al-Zāhir fī sīrat al-Malik al-Ẓāhir*. Edited by 'Abd al-'Azīz Khuwayṭir. Riyadh: [n.p.].

1961. *Tashrīf al-Ayyām wa-al-'usūr fī sīrat al-malik al-Manṣūr*. Edited by Murād Kāmil. Cairo: al-Sharikah al-'Arabīyah lil-ṭibā'ah wa al-nashr.

Ibn Aybak al-Dawadārī. 1960. *Kanz al-Durar wa jāmi' al-ghurar*. Vol. 9. Edited by Hans Robert Roemer. Wiesbaden: Franz Steiner.

1971. *Kanz al-Durar wa jāmi' al-ghurar*. Vol. 8. Edited by Ulrich Haarman. Wiesbaden: Franz Steiner.

Ibn Baṭūṭah 'Abdallah. 1958–2000. *The Travels of Ibn Battuta, A. D. 1325–1354*. Translated by H. A. R. Gibb. London: Hakluyt Society.

Ibn Bazzāz Ardabīlī. 1373 / 1994. *Ṣafwat al-ṣafā': dar tarjuman-i aḥval va aqvāl wa karāmāt-i Shaykh Ṣafī al-Dīn Isḥāq Ardabīlī*. Edited by G. R. T. Majd. Tabriz: Intishārāt-i Zaryāb.

Ibn, al-Fuwaṭī. 1995. *Majma' al-ādāb fī mu'jam al-alqāb*. 6 vols. Edited by Muḥammad al-Kāẓim. Tehran: Farhang va Irshād-i Islāmī.

Ibn Ḥajar al-'Asqalānī. 1993. *Al-Durar al-kāminah fī akhbār al-mi'ah wa al-thāminah*. 4 vols. Beirut: Dār al-Jīl.

Ibn al-'Ibrī/Bar Hebraeus, Gregorius Abū al-Faraj. 1890, 1958, [1983]. *Ta'rīkh mukhtaṣar al-duwal*. Edited by Father Anton Salaḥānī. Beirut: Catholic Press. Also reprinted in 1983 in al-Ḥāzimīyah, Lebanon: Dār al-Rā'id al-Lubnānī.

1932. *The Chronography of Gregory Abu'l-Faraj, the Son of Aaron, the Hebrew Physician, Commonly Known as Bar Hebraeus*. Translated by E. A. W. Budge. London: Oxford University Press.

Jamāl Qarshī. 2005 [2007]. See Qarshī, Jamāl.

Joinville, Jean de. 2008. "The Life of Saint Louis." In *Joinville and Villehardouin, Chronicles of the Crusades*. Translated by Caroline Smith. London, New York: Penguin.

1865. *Histoire de Saint Louis*. Edited by Natalis de Wailly. Paris: Jules Renouard. Reprinted Johnson Reprint Company, 1965.

Juvaynī, 'Alā' al-Dīn 'Aṭa-Malik. 1958, 1997. *The History of the World-Conqueror*. Translated by J. A. Boyle. Cambridge, MA: Harvard University Press; Seattle, WA: University of Washington Press.

Juzjānī, Minhāj Sirāj. 1873–87, 1970. *Ṭabaqāt-i Nāṣirī. A general history of the Muhammadan dynasties of Asia, including Hindustan; from A.H. 194 (810 A.D.) to A.H. 658 (1260 A.D.) and the irruption of the infidel Mughals into Islam, by Minhāj-ud-dīn, Abū-'Umar-i-'Usmān*. Translated by H. G. Raverty. Calcutta Asiatic Society, 1873–1887. 2 vols. Reprinted New Delhi, Oriental Books Reprint Corp.; exclusively distributed by Munshiram Manoharlal, 1970.

1342–43 [1963–64]. *Ṭabaqāt-i Nāṣirī*. Edited by 'Abd al Ḥayy Ḥabībī Qandahārī. Kābul: Anjuman-i Tārīkhī Afghānistān.

Kirakos of Gandjak. 1986. *[Patmut'iwn Hayots'] Kirakos Gandzakets'i's history of the Armenians*. Translated by Robert Bedrosian. New York: Sources of the Armenian Tradition.

Kirakos of Ganjak. 1870. *Deux Historiens Arméniens: Kiracos de Gantzac, XIIIe S, Histoire d'Arménie; Oukhtanès D'Ourha, Xe siècle, Histoire En Trois Parties*. Translated by M. Brosset. St. Petersburg: L'Academie Impéeriale des Sciences.

Li, Chih-ch'ang. 1931, 1976. *The Travels of an Alchemist: The Journey of the Taoist Ch'ang-ch'un from China to the Hindukush at the Summons of Chingiz Khan*. Translated by Arthur Waley. London: Routledge. Reprint, Westport, CT: Greenwood Press.

Mirkhwānd, Muḥammad b. Khwāndamīr b. Maḥmūd, a.k.a. Mirkhwānd. 2002–2001. *Rawḍat al-Ṣafā fī Sīrat al-Anbiya' wa al-mulūk wa al-khulafa'*. Ed. Jamshīd Kayānfar. 15 vols. Tehran: Aṣāṭīr.

Mu'izz al-Ansāb. British Library OR 467. See also Anonymous (5).

Mirza, Haydar. (1898) 2008. *A History of the Moghuls of Central Asia: Being the 'Tarikh-i-Rashidi' of Mirza Muhammad Haidar Dughlat*. Edited by N. Elias and translated by E. D. Ross. London: Sampson Low & Co, 1898. Reprint, Leiden and London.

al-Nasawī, Muḥammad b. Aḥmad. 1953. *Sīrat al-Sulṭān Jalāl al-Dīn Mankūbartī*. Edited by Ḥāfiẓ Ahmad Ḥamdī. Cairo: Dār al-Fikr al-'Arabī.

al-Nasawī, Muḥammad b. Aḥmad. 1895. *Histoire du sultan Djelal ed-Din Mankobirti, Prince du Kharezm*. Translated by O. Houdas. Paris: E . Leroux.

Al-Nuwayrī, Aḥmad. 1985–98. *Nihāyat al-arab fī funūn al-adab*. Vols. 27, 29, 30, 31. Edited by Sa'īd 'Āshūr. Cairo: al-Mu'assasah al-Miṣrīyah al-'Āmmah lil-Ta'līf wa-al-Tarjamah wa-al-Ṭibā'ah wa-al-Nashr.

1998. *Nihāyat al-arab fī funūn al-adab*. Vol. 32. Edited by Fāhim Muḥammad 'Alawī Shaltūt. Cairo: Dār al-Kutub al-Miṣrīyah.

1997. *Nihāyat al-arab fī funūn al-adab*. Vol. 33. Edited by Muṣṭafà Hijāzī. Cairo: Dār al-Kutub al-Miṣrīyah.

Olbright, Peter, and Elizabeth Pinks, trans. 1980. *Meng-Ta pei-lu und Hei-Ta Shi-lüeh*. Wiesbaden: Harrassowitz.

Onon, Urgunge, ed. and trans. 1990. *The History and the Life of Chinggis Khan*. Leiden and New York: Brill.

trans. 2001. *The Secret History of the Mongols: The Life and Times of Chinggis Khan*. Richmond, Surrey: Curzon.

Orbelian, Stephannos. 1864. *Historie de la Siounie*. Translated by M. Brosset. St. Petersburg: Académie impériale des sciences.

Paris, Matthew. 1852–54. *Matthew Paris's English History: From the Year 1235–1275*. Translated by the Reverend John Allen Giles. London, H.G. Bohn.

1984. *Chronicles of Matthew Paris: Monastic Life in the Thirteenth Century*. Edited, translated, and with an introduction by Richard Vaughan. Gloucester [Gloucestershire]: A. Sutton; New York: St. Martin's Press.

Polo, Marco. 1938, 1976. *Marco Polo: The Description of the World*. Edited and translated by A. C. Moule and Paul Pelliot. London: G. Routledge. Reprint, New York: AMS Press.

Qāshānī, 'Abdallah b. 'Alī. 1969, 2005. *Ta'rīkh-i pādishāh-i sa'īd ghiyāth al-dunyā wa al-din Uljaytu Sulṭān Muḥammad*. Edited by Māhīn Hambalī. Tehran: Bangāh-i Tarjumah va Nashr-i Kitāb. Reprint, Tehran: Shirkat-i Intishārat-i 'Ilmi va Farhangī.

Qarshī, Jamāl. 2005 [2007]. *Istoriiā︠︡ Kazakhstana v persidskikh istochnikakh*. Edited by Sh. Kh. Vokhidov, B. B. Aminov, A. K. Muminov and M. Kh. Abuseitova. Almaty: Daĭk-Press.

Qazvīnī, Ḥamd Allah Mustawfī. 1983–84. *Ta'rīkh-i Gūzīdah*. Edited by 'Abd al-Ḥusayn Navā'ī. Tehran: Amīr Kabīr.

Qazvīnī, Zayn al-Dīn b. Ḥamd Allah Mustawfī. 1372, 1993–94. *[Dhayl] Zayl-i Ta'rīkh-i Gūzidah*. Edited by Irāj Afshār. Tehran: Bunyād-i Mawqufāt-i Dr. Maḥmūd Afshār Yazdī.

Rashīd al-Dīn, Faḍl Allah. 1994. *Jāmi' al-Tavārīkh*. 4 vols. Edited by Muḥammad Rawshan and Muṣṭafà Musavī. Tehran: Nashr-i Alburz.

1998–99. *Rashiduddin Fazlullah's Jami'u't-tawarikh: Compendium of Chronicles: A History of the Mongols*. 3 vols. Translated and annotated by Wheeler M. Thackston. Cambridge, MA: Harvard University Department of Near Eastern Languages and Civilizations.

1971. *The Successors of Genghis Khan*. Translated by J. A. Boyle. New York: Columbia University Press.

1988. "The Third Portion of the Story of Gāzān Xān in Rašidu'd-Dīn's Ta'rīx-e Mobārak-e Gāzānī." Translated by A. P. Martinez. *Archivum Eurasiae Medii Aevi* 6, 41–127.

Rashīd al-Din, Faḍl Allah. [n.d.] *Shu'āb-i Panjgānah*. MS Istanbul, Topkapi Sarayi III, Ahmet, 2937.

Saint-Quentin, Simon de. 1965. *Histoire des Tatares*. Paris: P. Geuthner. Published by Jean Richard.

Al-Ṣafadī, Khalīl b. Aybak. 1998. *A'yān al-'Aṣr wa A'wān al-naṣr*. 6 vols. Edited by 'Alī Abū Zayd. Beirut and Damascus: Dār al-Fikr al-Mu'āṣir.

Al- Ṣafadī, Khalīl b. Aybak. 1962– . *Al-Wāfī bi-al-wafāyāt* or *Das Biographische Lexicon des Ṣalāḥuddīn Halīl ibn Aibak aṣ-Ṣafadī*. Edited by Hellmut Ritter et al. Wiesbaden: Franz Steiner.

Samarqandī, 'Abd al-Razzāq. (1993) 2004. *Maṭla'-i Sa'dayn va majma'-yi baḥrayn*. Edited by 'Abd al-Ḥusayn Navā'ī. Tehran: Pazhūhishgāh-i 'Ulūm-i Insānī va Muṭāla'āt-i Farhangī.

Shabankarā'ī, Muḥammad b. 'Alī b. Muḥammad. *Majma' al-Ansāb*. 1984. Edited by Mīr Hāshim Muḥaddith. Tehran: Amīr Kabīr.

Shirāzī, Quṭb al-Dīn Maḥmūd b. Mas'ūd. 2010. *Akhbār-i Mughūllān (650–683) dar anbānah-i Mullā Quṭb: az majmu'ah-yi khaṭṭ-i muvarrikh-i 685*. Edited by Iraj Afshār. Qum: Kitābkhānah-yi Āyat-Allah al-'Uẓmà Mar'ashī Najafī.

Smpad, Connetable. 1980. "La Chronique Attribuée au Connétable Smbat." Translated by Gérard Dédéyan. *Documents relatifs à l'histoire des croisades*. Paris: l'Academie des inscriptions et belles-lettres.

Song Lian, et al., compilers. 1976. *Yuan Shi*. "Die Chinesichen Annalen von Ögödei und Güyük—Übersetzung des 2. Kapitels des Yüan-Shih." Translated by Waltraut Abramowski. *Zentralasiatische Studien*, 10, 117–67.

1979. *Yuan Shi*. "Die Chinesichen Annalen des Möngke—Übersetzung des 3. Kapitels des Yüan-Shih." Translated by Waltraut Abramowski. *Zentralasiatische Studien*, 13, 7–71.

1945. *Yuan Shi*. Translated by Louis Hambis. *Le chapitre CVII du Yuan Che: Les généalogies impériales mongoles dans l'histoire chinoise officielle de la dynastie mongole*. Leiden: Brill.

1954. *Yuan Shi*. Translated by Louis Hambis. *Le chapitre CVIII du Yuan Che: Les fiefs attribués aux membres de la famille impériale et aux ministres de la cour mongole d'après l'histoire chinoise officielle de la dynastie mongole*. Leiden: Brill.

1978. *Yuan Shi*. Translated by C. Hsiao. *The Military Establishment of the Yuan Dynasty*. Cambridge, MA: Council of East Asian Studies, Harvard University. Distributed by Harvard University Press.

[n.d.] *Yuan Shi*. Translated by Paul Buell (unpublished) and funded by the University of Massachusetts Amherst. Selections.

Al-ʻUmarī, Ibn Faḍlallah. 1968. *Das Mongolische Weltreich: al-ʻUmarīs Darstellung der mongolischen Reiche in seinem Werke Masālik al-abṣār fī mamālik al-amṣār*. Edited and translated by Klaus Lech. Wiesbaden: Harrassowitz.

Vakhtang VI, King, and Vakhusti, Prince, and anonymous others. 1849. *Histoire de la Géorgie: depuis l'antiquité jusqu'au xix siècle*. Translated by M. Brosset. 5 vols in 4. St. Petersburg: l'Académie impériale des sciences.

Vardan Areweltz. 1989. "The Historical Compilation of Vardan Arewelc'i." Edited and translated by Robert W. Thompson. *Dumbarton Oaks Papers* 43, 125–226.

Vaṣṣāf al-Ḥaẓrah, ʻAbd Allah. 2010. *Tajziyat al-amṣār wa tazjiyat al-aʻsār*. Edited and translated by Joseph Hammer-Purghstall as *Geschichte Vaṣṣāf's: persisch herausgegeben und deutsch übersetz*. New issue by Sibylle Wentker with an introduction by Klaus Wundsam. Vienna: Verlag der Österreichischen Akademie der Wissenschaften.

2009. *Tajziyat al-amṣār wa tazjiyat al-aʻṣār: Ta'rīkh-i Vaṣṣāf*. Edited by Iraj Afshar, et al. Tehran: Talāyah.

1856. *Tajziyat al-amṣār wa tazjiyat al-aʻṣār*. Edited and translated by Joseph Hammer-Purghstall as *Geschichte Vaṣṣāf's: Persisch herausgegeben und Deutsch übersetz*. Vienna: Hof- und Staatsdruckerei.

1346 [1967]. *Taḥrīr-i Ta'rīkh-i Vaṣṣāf*. Edited by ʻAbd al-Muḥammad Āyatī. [Tehran]: Bunyād-i Farhang-i Īrān.

Rubruck, William of. 1990. *The Mission of Friar William of Rubruck: His Journey to the Court of the Great Khan Möngke, 1253–55*. Translated by Peter A. Jackson. London: Hakluyt Society.

Scholarship

Allsen, Thomas T. 2007. "Ögedei and Alcohol." *Mongolian Studies* XXIX, no. 29, 3–12.

2001a. *Culture and Conquest in Mongol Eurasia*. Cambridge: Cambridge University Press.

2001b. "Robing in the Mongolian Empire." In *Robes and Honor: The Medieval World of Investiture*. Edited by Stewart Gordon, 305–13. New York: Palgrave.

1997. *Commodity and Exchange in the Mongol Empire: A Cultural History of Islamic Textiles*. Cambridge: Cambridge University Press.

1997. "Ever Closer Encounters: The Appropriation of Culture and the Apportionment of Peoples in the Mongol Empire." *Journal of Early Modern History* 1, 1–23.

1994a. "The Rise of the Mongolian Empire and Mongolian Rule in North China." In *The Cambridge History of China*, vol. 6, *Alien Regimes and Border States, 907–1368*, Edited by Herbert Franke and Denis Twitchett, 321–413. Cambridge: Cambridge University Press.

1994b. "Two Cultural Brokers of Medieval Eurasia: Bolad Aqa and Marco Polo." In *Nomadic Diplomacy, Destruction and Religion from the Pacific to the Adriatic.* Edited by Michael Gervers and Wayne Schlepp. Toronto Studies in Central and Inner Asia 1. Toronto: University of Toronto Press, 63–78.

1993. "Maḥmūd Yalavač (?–1254), Mas'ūd Beg (?–1289), 'Alī Beg (?–1280); Bujir (fl. 1206–1260)." In *In the Service of the Khan: Eminent Personalities of the Early Mongol-Yüan Period.* Edited by Igor de Rachewiltz, Hok-lam Chan, Hsiao Ch'i-ch'ing and Peter W. Geier, 122–35. Wiesbaden: Harrassowitz.

1989. "Mongolian Princes and Their Merchant Partners, 1200–1260." *Asia Major*, 2, Third Series, 2 vol 2, 83–126.

1987. *Mongol Imperialism: The Policies of the Grand Qan Möngke in China, Russia and the Islamic Lands 1251–59.* Berkeley: University of California Press.

1986. "Guard and Government in the Reign of the Grand Qan Möngke, 1251–59." *Harvard Journal of Asiatic Studies* 46, no. 2, 495–521.

1985 (1987). "The Princes of the Left Hand: An Introduction to the History of the *Ulus* of Orda in the Thirteenth and Early Fourteenth Centuries." *Archivum Eurasiae Medii Aevi* 5, 5–40.

1983. "The Yüan Dynasty and the Uighurs of Turfan." In *China Among Equals: The Middle Kingdom and Its Neighbors, 10th–14th Centuries.* Edited by Morris Rossabi, 243–80. Berkeley and Los Angeles: University of California Press.

1981. "Mongol Census Taking in Rus." *Harvard Ukrainian Studies* 5, no. 1, 32–53.

[n.d.] "Redistribution in the Mongol Empire, Comparisons and Implications," draft of unpublished article. College of New Jersey, Trenton, New Jersey.

Amitai, Reuven, and Michal Biran, eds. 2015. *Nomads as Agents of Cultural Change: The Mongols and Their Eurasian Predecessors.* Honolulu: University of Hawaii Press.

2005. *Mongols, Turks, and Others: Eurasian Nomads and the Sedentary World.* Brill's Inner Asian Library 11. Leiden: Brill.

Amitai-Preiss, Reuven. 1995. *Mongols and Mamluks: The Mamluk-Ilkhānid War, 1260–1281.* Cambridge: Cambridge University Press.

Ando, Shiro. 1992. *Timuridische Emire nach dem Mu'izz al-ansāb: untersuchen zur Stammesaristokratie Zentralasiens im 14. und 15. Jahrhundert.* Berlin: Klaus Schwarz Verlag.

Andrews, Peter Alford. 1999. *Felt Tents and Pavilions: The Nomadic Tradition and Its Interaction with Princely Tentage.* 2 vols. London: Melisende.

Atwood, Christopher P. 2015. "Alexander, Ja-a Gambo and the Origins of the Image of Jamugha in the Secret History of the Mongols." In *Neilu Ouya lishi wenhua guoji xueshu yantaohui lunwenji.* Edited by Teligeng [Terigün] and Li Jinxiu, 161–76. Beijing: Nei Menggu renmin chubanshe.

2014–15. "Chigü Küregen and the Origins of the Xiningzhou Qonggirads." In *Archivum Eurasiae Medii Aevi 21: Festschrift for Thomas T. Allsen in Celebration of His 75th Birthday.* Edited by P. B. Golden, R. K. Kovalev,

A. P. Martinez, J. Skaff and A. Zimonyi, Wiesbaden: Harrassowitz Verlag, 7–26.
2015. "The First Mongol Contacts with the Tibetans." In *Trails of the Tibetan Tradition: Papers for Elliot Sperling*. Edited by Roberto Vitali with Gedum Rabsal and Nicole Willock. Special issue of *Revue d'etudes tibetaines* 31, 21–45.
2013a. "Mongols, Arabs, Kurds and Franks: Rashīd al-Dīn's Comparative Ethnography of Tribal Society." In *Rashīd al-Dīn as an Agent and Mediator of Cultural Exchanges in Ilkhanid Iran*. Edited by Anna Akasoy, Ronit Yoeli-Tlalim, and Charles Burnett, 223–50. London: Wartburg Institute.
2013b. "The Uyghur Stone: Archaeological Revelations in the Mongol Empire." In *The Steppe Lands and the World Beyond Them: Studies in Honor of Victor Spinei on his 70th birthday*. Edited by Florin Curta and Bogdan-Petru Maleon, 315–43. Iaşi: Editura Universităţii "Alexandru Ioan Cuza."
2014. "Historiography and Transformation of Ethnic Identity in the Mongol Empire: The Öng'üt Case." *Asian Ethnicity* 15, no. 4, 514–34.
2008–09. "The Sacrificed Brother in the *Secret History of the Mongols*." *Mongolian Studies* 30, no. 31, 189–206.
2008. "How the Mongols Got a Word for Tribe, and What It Means." *Menggu shi yan jiu* 10, 63–89.
2007a. "The Date of the 'Secret History of the Mongols' Reconsidered." *Journal of Song and Yuan Studies* 37, 1–48.
2007b. "Informants and Sources for the *Secret History of the Mongols*." *Mongolian Studies* 29, 27–39.
2007c. "The Date of the 'Secret History of the Mongols' Reconsidered." *Journal of Song-Yuan Studies* 37, 2–48.
2006a. "*Ulus* Emirs, *Keshig* Elders, Signatures and Marriage Partners: The Evolution of a Classic Mongol Institution." In *Imperial Statecraft: Political Forms and Techniques of Governance in Inner Asia, Sixth-Twentieth Centuries*. Edited by D. Sneath, 141–73. Bellingham: Center for East Asian Studies, Western Washington University for Mongolia and Inner Asia Studies Unit, University of Cambridge.
2006b. "Titles, Appanages, Marriages and Officials: A Comparison of Political Forms in the Zhüngar and Thirteenth-Century Mongol Empires." In ibid., 207–43.
2004. *Encyclopedia of Mongolia and the Mongol Empire*. Library of World History. New York: Facts on File, Inc.
1991. "Life in Third-Fourth Century Cadh'ota: A Survey of Information Gathered from the Prakrit Documents Found North of Minfeng (Niyä)." *Central Asiatic Journal* 35, no. 3/4, 161–99.
Aubin, Françoise. 1975. "Le Statut de L'enfant dans La Société Mongole." *Recueils de la société Jean Bodin pour l'histoire comparative des institutions* 35, 459–599.
1995. "Amirs mongols et viziers persans dans les remous de l'acculturation." *Studia Iranica* 15.

Balazs, Etienne. 1964. "Marco Polo in the Capital of China." In *Chinese Civilization and Bureaucracy: Variations on a Theme*. Etienne Balazc. Translated by H. M. Wright and edited by Arthur F. Wright, 79–100. New Haven: Yale University Press.

Bartol'd. V. V. 1977. *Turkestan Down to the Mongol Invasion*. London: E. J. Gibb Memorial Trust; Philadelphia: Porcupine Press.

Biran, Michal. 2015. "The Mongols and Nomadic Identity: The Case of the Kitans in China." *Mongols as Agents of Cultural Change: The Mongols and Their Eurasian Predecessors*. Edited by Reuven Amitai and Michal Biran, 152–81. Honolulu: University of Hawaii Press.

2009. "The Mongols in Central Asia from Chinggis Khan's Invasions to the Rise of Temür: The Ögedeid and Chaghadaid Realms." In *The Cambridge History of Inner Asia: The Chinggisid Period*. Edited by N. Di Cosmo, J. F. Allen and P. Golden. Cambridge: Cambridge University Press.

2007. *Chinggis Khan*. Makers of the Muslim World Series. Oxford: Oneworld.

2005. *The Empire of the Qara Khitai in Eurasian History*. Cambridge: Cambridge University Press.

2004. "True to Their Ways: Why the Qara Khitai Did Not Convert to Islam." In *Mongols, Turks and Others*. Edited by Reuven Amitai and Michal Biran, 175–99. Leiden: Brill.

Birge, Bettine, and Anne F. Broadbridge. [2018 forthcoming]. "Women and Gender Under Mongol Rule." In *The Cambridge History of the Mongol Empire*. Edited by Michal Biran and Hodong Kim. Cambridge: Cambridge University Press.

Birge, Bettine. 2010. "Sources of Law in Mongol-Yuan China (1260–1368): Adjudication in the Absence of a Legal Code." In *Miscellanea Asiatica: mélanges en l'honneur de Françoise Aubin* [Festschrift in Honour of Françoise Aubin]. Edited by Denise Aigle, et al., 387–406. Sankt Augustin, Germany: Institut Monumenta Serica.

2008. "Law of the Liao, Chin, and Yuan and Its Impact on the Chinese Legal Tradition." In *New Perspectives on Chinese History, Legal History: The Formation and Transformation of Traditional Chinese Legal*. Edited by Liu Liyan, 443–503. Taipei: Academia Sinica-Lianjing.

2003. "Women and Confucianism from Song to Ming: The Institutionalization of Patrilineality." In *The Song-Yuan-Ming Transition in Chinese History*. Edited by Richard von Glahn and Paul Smith, 212–40. Cambridge, MA: Harvard University Press.

2002. *Women, Property and Confucian Reaction in Sung and Yüan China (960–1368)*. Cambridge: Cambridge University Press.

1995. "Levirate Marriage and the Revival of Widow Chastity in Yüan China." *Asia Major* 8, no. 2, 107–46.

Bittles, A. H., et al. 2010. "Consanguinity, Human Evolution, and Complex Diseases," *Proceedings of the National Academy of Sciences of the United States of America*. 107 (Suppl. 1), 1779–86: Evolution in Health and Medicine (January 26), 1779–86.

Blake, Stephen P. 1979. "The Patrimonial-Bureaucratic Empire of the Mughals." *The Journal of Asian Studies* 39, no. 1 (November), 77–94.

Bosworth, C. E. "Salghurids," *EI2*, 8, 978–79.

Boyle, J. A. 1968. "Dynastic and Political History of the Īl-Khāns." In *The Cambridge History of Iran*. Vol. 5: *The Saljuq and Mongol Periods*. Edited by J. A. Boyle, 303–421. Cambridge: Cambridge University Press.

Brack, Yoni [Jonathan]. 2011. "A Mongol Princess Making *ḥajj*: The Biography of El Qutlugh Daughter of Abagha Ilkhan (r. 1265–82)." *Journal of the Royal Asiatic Society* (Third Series) 21, no. 3 (July), 331–59.

2016. "Mediating Sacred Kingship: Conversion and Sovereignty in Mongol Iran." PhD dissertation, University of Michigan.

Broadbridge, Anne F. 2008. *Kingship and Ideology in the Islamic and Mongol Worlds*. Cambridge: Cambridge University Press.

2016. "Marriage, Family and Politics: The Ilkhanid-Oirat Connection." In *Journal of the Royal Asiatic Society*. Special edition, edited by Timothy May and Peter Jackson. [Festschrift for David O. Morgan], 1–14.

Broadbridge, Anne F. and Bettine Birge. [2018 forthcoming]. "Women and Gender Under Mongol Rule." In *The Cambridge History of the Mongol Empire*. Edited by Michal Biran and Hodong Kim. Cambridge: Cambridge University Press.

Buell, Paul D. 1979a. "The Role of the Sino-Mongolian Frontier Zone in the Rise of Chinggis-qan." In *Studies on Mongolia: Proceedings of the First North American Conference on Mongolian Studies*, 63–76. Bellingham, WA: Center for East Asian Studies.

1979b. "Sino-Khitan Administration in Mongol Bukhara." *Journal of Asian History* 13, no. 2, 121–51.

1977. "Tribe, Qan and Ulus in Early Mongol China: Some Prolegomena to Yüan History." PhD dissertation, University of Washington.

1980. "Kalmyk Tanggaci People: Thoughts on the Mechanics and Impact of Mongol Expansion." *Mongolian Studies* 6, 41–59.

1992. "Early Mongol Expansion in Western Siberia and Turkestan (1207–1219): a Reconstruction." *Central Asiatic Journal* 36, no. 1/2, 1–32.

1993a. "Sübōtei Ba'atur (1175–1248)." In *In the Service of the Khan: Eminent Personalities of the Early Mongol-Yüan Period*. Edited by Igor de Rachewiltz, Hok-lam Chan, Hsiao Ch'i-ch'ing and Peter W. Geier, 13–26. Wiesbaden: Harrassowitz.

1993b. "Chinqai." In *In the Service of the Khan: Eminent Personalities of the Early Mongol-Yüan Period*. Edited by Igor de Rachewiltz, Hok-lam Chan, Hsiao Ch'i-ch'ing and Peter W. Geier, 95–111. Wiesbaden: Harrassowitz.

2010. "Some Royal Mongol Ladies: Alaqa-beki, Ergene-Qatun and Others." *World History Connected* 7, no. 1. http://worldhistoryconnected.press.illinois.edu/7.1/buell.html.

Buell, Paul D., and Judith Kolbas. 2016. "The Ethos of State and Society in the Early Mongol Empire: Chingiz Khan to Güyük." In *The Mongols and Post-Mongol Asia: Studies in Honour of David O. Morgan*. Edited by Timothy May. *Journal of the Royal Asiatic Society* 26, no. 1–2 (January), 43–64.

Büntgen, Ulf, and Nicola Di Cosmo. 2016. "Climatic and Environmental Aspects of the Mongol Withdrawal from Hungary, 1242." *Scientific Reports* 2016-5-26, 1–9.

Cahen, Claude. 1988. *La Turquie pre-Ottomane*. Istanbul-Paris: Institut français d'études anatoliennes d'Istanbul : Dıvıt Matbaacılık ve Yayıncılık.

2001. *The Formation of Turkey: The Seljuk Sultanate of Rūm: Eleventh to Fourteenth Century*. Translated by P. M. Holt. Harlow, Essex: Longman.

Cheng, Chih-Shu Eva. 1996. "Studies in the Career of Chinggis Qan." PhD dissertation, School of Oriental and African Studies, University of London.

Clark, Larry V. 1978. "The Theme of Revenge in the *Secret History of the Mongols*." In *Aspects of Altaic Civilization II: Proceedings of the XVIII PIAC, Bloomington, June 29–July 5, 1975*. Edited by Larry V. Clark and Paul Alexander Draghi, 33–57. Bloomington, Indiana: Asian Studies Research Institute, Indiana University.

1978–79. "From the Legendary Cycle of Čingis-qaγan: The Story of an Encounter with 300 Tayičiγud from the Altan Tobči (1655)." *Mongolian Studies* 5, 5–39.

Cleaves, F. W. 1977. "Uighuric Mourning Regulations." *Journal of Turkish Studies* 1: 65–93.

1979–80. "The Biography of Empress Čabi in the Yuan Shih." *Harvard Ukrainian Studies* 1, no. 3/4, 138–50.

December 1956. "The Biography of Bayan of the Barin in the Yuan Shih." *Harvard Journal of Asiatic Studies* 19, no. 3/4, 185–303.

Dardess, John W. 1973. *Conquerors and Confucians: Aspects of Political Change in Late Yuan China*. New York: Columbia University Press.

Dawson, Christopher. 1955. *The Mongol Mission: Narratives and Letters of the Franciscan Missionaries in Mongolia and China in the Thirteenth and Fourteenth Centuries*. New York: Sheed and Ward.

De Nicola, Bruno. 2017a. *Women in Mongol Iran: The Khatuns, 1206–1335*. Edinburgh: Edinburgh University Press.

2017b. "The Role of the Domestic Sphere in the Islamization of the Mongols." In *Islamisation: Comparative Perspectives in History*. Edited by A. C. S. Peacock, 353–76. Edinburgh: Edinburgh University Press.

2014a. "The Queen of the Chagatayids: Orghīna Khātūn and the Rule of Central Asia." *Journal of the Royal Asiatic Society* 26, no. 1–2, 107–20.

2014b. "Patrons or Murids? Mongol Women and Shaykhs in Ilkhanid Iran and Anatolia." *Iran Studies* 52, 143–56.

2014c. "The Ladies of Rum: A Hagiographic View of Women in Thirteenth- and Fourteenth-Century Anatolia." *Journal of Sufi Studies* 3, no. 2, 132–56.

2013. "Ruling from Tents: Some Remarks on Women's Ordos in Ilkhanid Iran." In *Ferdowsi, the Mongols and the History of Iran: Art, Literature, and Culture from Early Islam to Qajar Persia*. Edited by Robert Hillenbrand, A, C, S, Peacock, and Firuza Abdullaeva, 26–136. London: I. B. Tauris.

2010. "Women's Role and Participation in Warfare in the Mongol Empire." In *Soldatinnen: Gewalt und Geschlecht im Krieg vom Mittelalter bis heute*, 95–112. Paderborn: Ferdinand Schöningh.

[De Rachewiltz, Igor.] 2009. *The Early Mongols: Language, Culture and History. Studies in Honor of Igor de Rachewiltz on the Occasion of His 80th Birthday*. Edited by Volker Rybatzki, Alessandra Pozzi, Peter W. Geier and John R. Krueger. Bloomington: Indiana University, The Denis Sinor Institute for Inner Asian Studies.

De Rachewiltz, Igor. 1999. "Was Töregene Qatun Ögödei's "Sixth Empress"?" *East Asian History* 17/18 (June–December), 71–76.

1997. "A Note on the Word Börte in the Secret History of the Mongols." *East Asian History* 13/14, 153–55.

1993. "Muqali (1170–1223), Bōl (1197–1220), Tas (1212–1239), An-T'ung (1245–1293)." In *In the Service of the Khan: Eminent Personalities of the Early Mongol-Yüan Period*. Edited by Igor de Rachewiltz, Hok-lam Chan, Hsiao Ch'i-ch'ing and Peter W. Geier, 3–12. Wiesbaden: Harrassowitz.

1985. "On the Expression Cul Ulja'ur (?= Čol Olja'ur) in #254 of the *Secret History of the Mongols*." *Journal of Turkish Studies* 9: 213–18.

1981. "Some Remarks on Töregene's Edict of 1240." *Papers on Far Eastern History* 23: 38–63.

1971. *Papal Envoys to the Great Khans*. London: Faber and Faber.

1966. "Personnel and Personalities in North China in the Early Mongol Period." *Journal of the Economic and Social History of the Orient* IX, 88–144.

De Rachewiltz, Igor, Hok-lam Chan, Hsiao Ch'i-ch'ing, and Peter W. Geier, eds. 1993. *In the Service of the Khan: Eminent Personalities of the Early Mongol-Yüan Period*. Wiesbaden: Harrassowitz.

DeWeese, Devin. 2014. "Shamanism in Central Asia." *Journal of the Economic and Social History of the Orient* 57, 326–63.

2006. "Cultural Transmission and Exchange in the Mongol Empire: Notes from the Biographical Dictionary of Ibn al-Fuwaṭī." In *Beyond the Legacy of Genghis Khan*. Edited by Linda Komaroff, 11–29. Leiden: Brill.

1994. *Islamization and Native Religion in the Golden Horde*. University Park: University of Pennsylvania Press.

Di Cosmo, Nicola. 1999. "State Formation and Periodization in Inner Asian History." *Journal of World History* 10, no. 1, 1–40.

Di Cosmo, Nicola, and Ulf Büntgen. 2016. "Climatic and Environmental Aspects of the Mongol Withdrawal from Hungary, 1242." *Scientific Reports*: 2016-5-26, 1–9.

Drompp, Michael R. 2007. "From Qatun to Refugee: The Taihe Princess among the Uighurs." In *The Role of Women in the Altaic World: Permanent International Altaistic Conference, 44th Meeting, Walberberg, 26–31 August 2001*. Edited by Veronika Veit, 57–68. Wiesbaden: Harrassowitz.

Dunnell, Ruth. 2014. "The Anxi Principality: [un]Making a Muslim Mongol Prince in Northwest China during the Yuan Dynasty." *Central Asiatic Journal* 57 (Special Tangut Edition), 185–200.

2010. *Chinggis Khan: World Conqueror*. Boston: Longman.

1991. "The Fall of the Xia Empire: Sino-Steppe Relations in the Late 12th to Early 13th Centuries." In *Rulers from the Steppe: State Formation on the Eurasian Periphery*. Edited by Gary Seaman and Daniel Marks, 158–85.

Los Angeles: Ethnographic Press, Center for Visual Anthropology, University of Southern California.

Endicott, Elizabeth. 2014–2015. "The Role of Poison in Mongolian History." *Archivum Eurasiae medii aevi* 21, 103–10.

Endicott-West, Elizabeth. 1989. "Merchant Associations in Yüan China." In *Asia Major*, 3rd ser. Vol. 2, no. 2, 127–54.

Farquhar, D. M. 1990. *The Government of China Under Mongolian Rule: A Reference Guide*. Stuttgart: Franz Steiner.

1985. "Female Officials in Yuan China." *Journal of Turkish Studies* 9, 21–25.

1981. "Structure and Government in the Yüan Imperial Government." In *China Under Mongol Rule*. Edited by John D. Langlois, Jr., 25–55. Princeton, NJ: Princeton University Press.

Fiey, J. M. 1975. "Iconographie Syriac: Hulegu, Dokuz Khatun et ... six ambons?" *Le Muséon. Review d'etudes orientales* 88, 59–68.

Fletcher, Joseph. 1986. "The Mongols: Ecological and Social Perspectives." *Harvard Journal of Asiatic Studies* 46, no. 1 (June), 11–50.

Franke, Herbert. 1980 (1994). "Women under the Dynasties of Conquest." In *La donna nella Cina imperiale e nella Cina repubblicana*. Edited by Lionello Lanciotti, 23–43. Florence: L. S. Olschki. Reprint, 1994 in *China Under Mongol Rule*. Brookfield, VT: Variorum.

Gerhard Doerfer. 1963. *Türkische und Mongolische Elemente im Neupersischen, unter besonderer Berücksichtigung älterer neupersischer Geschichtsquellen, vor allem der Mongolen- und Timuridenzeit*. Wiesbaden: Franz Steiner.

Gießauf, Johannes. 2007. "*Mulieres Bellatrices* oder *Apis Argumentosa*? Aspekte der Wahrnehmung mongolischer Frauen in Abendländischen Quellen des Mittelalters." In *The Role of Women in the Altaic World: Permanent International Altaistic Conference, 44th Meeting, Walberberg, 26–31 August 2001*. Edited by Veronika Veit, 83–92. Wiesbaden: Harrassowitz.

2001. *Die Mongolei. Aspekte Ihrer Geschichte und Kultur*. Graz: Grazer Morgenländische Gesellschaft.

2005. "Der Feind in meinem Bett: Frauen und Steppennomaden in den Quellen des Europäischen Mittelalters." *Acta Orientalia Academiae Scientiarum Hungaricae* 58, no. 1, 77–87. Proceedings of the First International Conference on the Mediaeval History of the Eurasian Steppe: Szeged, Hungary, May 11–16, 2004: Part I (2005).

Gilli-Elewy, Hend. 2012. "On Women, Power, and Politics during the Last Phase of the Ilkhanate." *Arabica* 59, 709–23.

Golden, Peter B. 2002. "War and Warfare in the Pre-Činggisid Western Steppe of Eurasia." In *Warfare in Inner Asian History (500–1800)*, 105–72. Edited by Nicola Di Cosmo, et al. Leiden: Brill.

Gol'man, Mark I. 2007. "The Mongolian Women in the Russian Archives of the XVIIth Century." In *The Role of Women in the Altaic World: Permanent International Altaistic Conference, 44th Meeting, Walberberg, 26–31 August 2001*. Edited by Veronika Veit, 93–96. Wiesbaden: Harrassowitz.

Grupper, Samuel. 1992–94. "A Barulas Family Narrative in the Yuan Shih: Some Neglected Prosopographical and Institutional Stories on Timurid Origins." *Archivum Eurasiae Medii Aevi* 8: 11–97.

Hambis, Louis. 1975. "Un episode mal connu de l'histoire de Gengis-Khan." *Journal des Savants* (January–March), 3–46.

1957. "Notes sur l'histoire de Corée a l'époque mongole." *T'oung-pao* 45: 151–218.

Hambis, Louis, trans. 1954. *Le chapitre CVIII du Yuan Che: les fiefs attribués aux membres de la famille imperiale et aux ministres de la cour mongole d'apres l'histoire chinoise officielle de la dynastie mongole*. Leiden: Brill.

1945. *Le chapitre CVII du Yuan Che: les genealogies imperiales mongoles dans l'histoire chinoise officielle de la dynastie mongole*. Leiden: Brill.

Hambly, Gavin R. G. 1998. "Becoming Visible: Medieval Islamic Women in Historiography and History." In *Women in Medieval Islamic World: Power, Patronage and Piety*. Edited by Gavin R. G. Hambly. New York: St. Martin's Press.

Harms, Roger, M.D., ed. 2004. *Mayo Clinic Guide to a Healthy Pregnancy*. Pymble, New South Wales, and New York: HarperResource.

Ho, Kai-Lung. 2016. "The Office and the Noble Titles of the Mongols from the 14th to the 16th Centuries, and the Study of the 'White History' Čayan Teüke." *Central Asiatic Journal* 59, no. 1, *Migration and Nation-Building in Central and Western Asia: Turkic People and their Neighbors I*. Weisbaden: Harrassowitz, 133–77.

Humphrey, Caroline. 2000. "Appendix: Inside a Mongolian Tent." In *Nomads: Nomadic Material Culture in the Asian Collections of the Horniman Museum*. Edited by Ken Teague, 87–95. London: Horniman Museum and Gardens; Coimbra, Portugal: Museo Antropologico da Universidade de Coimbra.

Herrin, J. 2013. *Unrivalled Influence: Women and Empire in Byzantium*. Princeton: Princeton University Press.

Hillenbrand, Carole. 2003. "Women in the Saljuq Period." In *Women in Islam: From the Rise of Islam to 1800*. Edited by G. Nashat and L. Beck, 103–20. Urbana, IL: University of Illinois Press.

Hisamitdinova, F. G. 2007. "The Place and Role of the Bashkir Woman in Family and Society: The Present and the Past." In *The Role of Women in the Altaic World: Permanent International Altaistic Conference, 44th meeting, Walberberg, 26–31 August 2001*. Edited by Veronika Veit, 98–101. Wiesbaden: Harrassowitz.

Holmgren, Jennifer. 1986 (1995). "Observations on Marriage and Inheritance Practices in Early Mongol and Yüan Society, with Particular Reference to the Levirate." *Journal of Asian History* 20, no. 2., 127–92. Reprinted 1995 in *Marriage, Kinship and Power in Northern China*. Aldershot, Hampshire, Great Britain: Variorum.

1991. "Imperial Marriage in the Native Chinese and Non-Han State, Han to Ming." In *Marriage and Inequality in Chinese Society*. Edited by Rubie S. Watson and Patricia Buckley Ebrey, 58–96. Berkeley–Los Angeles: University of California Press. Reprint, 1995, in *Marriage, Kinship and Power in Northern China*. Aldershot, Hampshire, Great Britain: Variorum.

1990–1991. "A Question of Strength: Military Capability and Princess-Bestowal in Imperial China's Foreign Relations (Han to Ching)." *Monumenta Serica* 39, 31–85.

1985. "The Economic Foundations of Virtue: Widow-Remarriage in Early and Modern China. *The Australian Journal of Chinese Affairs* 13, 1–27.

Hodous, Florence. 2012/2013. "The Quriltai as a Legal Institution in the Mongol Empire." *Central Asiatic Journal* 56, 87–102.

Hope, Michael. 2017. "'The Pillars of State': Some Notes on the Qarachu Begs and the *Keshigten* in th Ilkhanate (1256–1335)." *Journal of the Royal Asiatic Society* 27, no. 2, 181–199. https://anu-au.academia.edu/

2016. *Power, Politics and Tradition in the Mongol Empire and the Ilkhanate of Iran*. Oxford: Oxford University Press.

2012. "The Transmission of Authority through the Quriltais of the Early Mongol Empire and the Ilkhanate of Iran (1227–1335)." *Mongolian Studies* 34, 87–115. www.academia.edu/7225175/The_Pillars_of_State_Some_Notes_on_the_Qarachu_Begs_and_the_Keshikten_in_the_Il-Khanate_1256-1335_.

Hsiao, C. 1978. *The Military Establishment of the Yuan Dynasty*. Cambridge, MA: Council of East Asian Studies, Harvard University. Distributed by Harvard University Press.

Hung, W. 1956. "Three of Chi'en Ta-hsin Poems on Yuan History." *Harvard Journal of Asiatic Studies* 19, 1–32.

Jackson, Peter. 2017. *The Mongols and the Islamic World: From Conquest to Conversion*. New Haven, CT: Yale University Press.

2009. "Mongol Khans and Religious Allegiance: The Problems Confronting a Minister-Historian in Ilkhanid Iran." *Iran*, 47 109–22.

2006. "World Conquest and Local Accommodation." In *The Experience of Crusading 2: Defining the Crusader Kingdoms*. Edited by P. Edbury and J. Phillips, 196–213. Cambridge: Cambridge University Press. Reprinted in Jackson, Peter. 2009. *Studies on the Mongol Empire and Early Muslim India*. Farnham, Surrey, and Burlington, VT: Variorum.

2005a. *The Mongols and the West, 1221–1410*. Harlow, England: Pearson/Longman.

2005b. "The Mongols and the Faith of the Conquered." In *Mongols, Turks and Others: Eurasian Nomads and the Sedentary World*. Edited by Reuven Amitai and Michal Biran, 245–90. Leiden: Brill. Reprinted in Jackson, Peter. 2009. *Studies on the Mongol Empire and Early Muslim India*. Farnham, Surrey, and Burlington, VT: Variorum.

2003. "Hülegü and the Christians: The Making of a Myth." Reprinted in Jackson, Peter. 2009. *Studies on the Mongol Empire and Early Muslim India*. Farnham, Surrey, and Burlington, VT: Variorum.

1999. "From *Ulus* to Khanate: The Making of the Mongol States c. 1220–c. 1290." In *The Mongol Empire and Its Legacy*. Edited by Reuven Amitai-Preiss and D. O. Morgan, 12–38. Leiden: Brill. Reprinted in Jackson, Peter. 2009. *Studies on the Mongol Empire and Early Muslim India*. Farnham, Surrey, and Burlington, VT: Variorum.

1986. "Arpa Khan." *Encyclopedia Iranica*. Vol. 2. Edited by Ehsan Yarshater, 518–19. London and Boston: Routledge and Kegan Paul.

1978. "The Dissolution of the Mongol Empire." *Central Asiatic Journal* 22, 186–244. Reprinted in Jackson, Peter. 2009. *Studies on the Mongol Empire and Early Muslim India*. Farnham, Surrey, and Burlington, VT: Variorum.

1975. "The Accession of Qubilai Qa'an: A Re-examination." *Journal of the Anglo-Mongolian Society* 2, no. 1, 1–10. Reprinted in Jackson, Peter. 2009. *Studies on the Mongol Empire and Early Muslim India*. Farnham, Surrey, and Burlington, VT: Variorum.

Jagchid, Sechin, and Paul Hyer. 1979. *Mongolia's Culture and Society*. Boulder, CO: Westview Press.

Johnson, Linda Cooke. *Women of the Conquest Dynasties: Gender and Identity in Liao and Jin China*. Honolulu: University of Hawai'i Press, 2011.

Kahn, Paul. 1996. "Instruction and Entertainment in the Naiman Battle Text: An Analysis of Paragraph 189 through Paragraph 196 of *The Secret History of the Mongols*." In *Cultural Contact, History and Ethnicity in Inner Asia: Papers Presented at the Central and Inner Asian Seminar, University of Toronto, March 4, 1994 and March 3, 1995*. Edited by Michael Gervers and Wayne Schlepp, 96–105. Toronto Studies in Central and Inner Asia 2. Toronto: Joint Center for Asia Pacific Studies.

Kamola, Stephen. 2013. "The Making of History in Mongol Iran." PhD dissertation, University of Washington.

Kellner-Heinkele, Barbara. 2007. "Abu l-Ghazi Bahadur Khan and the Famous and Infamous Women." In *The Role of Women in the Altaic World: Permanent International Altaistic Conference, 44th Meeting, Walberberg, 26–31 August 2001*. Edited by Veronika Veit, 109–18. Wiesbaden: Harrassowitz.

Kervran, Monique. 2002. "Un monument baroque dans les steppes du Kazakhstan: Le tombeau d'Örkina Khatun, princess Chagatay?" *Arts Asiatiques* 57: 5–32.

Kessler, Adam T. 1993. *Empires Beyond the Great Wall: The Heritage of Genghis Khan*. Los Angeles: Natural History Museum of Los Angeles County.

Kim, Hodong. 2005. "A Reappraisal of Güyük Khan." In *Mongols, Turks and Others: Eurasian Nomads and the Sedentary World*. Edited by Reuven Amitai and Michal Biran, 309–38. Brill's Inner Asian Library 11. Leiden: Brill.

Komaroff, Linda, ed. 2006. *Beyond the Legacy of Genghis Khan*. Leiden: Brill.

La Leche League International. 1991 (January). *Breastfeeding and Fertility*. Publication No. 87.

Landa, Ishayahu. 2018. "New Light on Early Mongol Islamisation: The Case of Arghun Aqa's Family." *Journal of the Royal Asiatic Society*, Series 3, 28:1, 1–24.

2016. "Imperial Sons-In-Law on the Move: Oyirad and Qonggirat Dispersion in Mongol Eurasia." *Archivum Eurasiae Medii Aevi* 22. Edited by P. D. Golden, et al., 161–97.

2016. "Oirats in the Ilkhanate and the Mamluk Sultanate in the Thirteenth to the Early Fifteenth Centuries: Two Cases of Assimilation into the Muslim Environment." *Mamluk Studies Review* 19, 149–91.

Lane, George. 2006. *Daily Life in the Mongol Empire*. Westport, CT: Greenwood Press.

2003. *Early Mongol Rule in Thirteenth-Century Iran: A Persian Renaissance*. London: RoutledgeCurzon.

1999a. "An Account of Gregory Bar Hebraeus Abu al-Faraj and His Relations with the Mongols of Persia." *Hugoye Journal of Syriac Studies* 2, no. 2 (July), 209–33.

1999b. "Arghun Aqa: Mongol Bureaucrat." *Iranian Studies* 32:4 (Autumn 1999), 459–82.

Lam, Yuan-Chu. 2007. "A Khotanese Chaste Wife and Her Biographer in Yuan China." In *The Role of Women in the Altaic World: Permanent International Altaistic Conference, 44th Meeting, Walberberg, 26–31 August 2001*. Edited by Veronika Veit, 123–30. Wiesbaden: Harrassowitz.

Lambton, Ann K. S. 1988. *Continuity and Change in Medieval Persia: Aspects of Administrative, Economic and Social History, 11th–14th Century*. Albany, NY: Bibliotheca Persica.

Langlois, J. D., Jr., ed. 1981. *China Under Mongol Rule*. Princeton, NJ: Princeton University Press.

Lattimore, Owen. 1963. "Chingis Khan and the Mongol Conquests." *Scientific American* 209, no. 2: 55–68.

Liu, Jianyi, and Qu, Dafeng. 1998. "On Some Problems Concerning Jochi's Lifetime." *Central Asiatic Journal* 42, no. 2, 283–90.

Lörincz, L. 1975. "Ein historisches Lied in der Geheimen Geschichte der Mongolen." In *Researches in Altaic Languages*. Edited by L. Ligeti, 117–26. Budapest: Akadémiai Kiadó.

Lupprian, K. E., ed. 1981. *Die Beziehungen der Päpste zu islamischen und mongolischen Herrschern im 13. Jahrhundert anhand ihres Briefwechsels*. Vatican City: Biblioteca apostolica vaticana.

Lyons, Emily, et al. 2009. "Consanguinity and Susceptibility to Infectious Diseases in Humans." *Biology Letters*. 5, 574–76.

March of Dimes. www.marchofdimes.com/professionals/14332_1157.asp

Martin, H. Desmond. 1950. *The Rise of Chingiz Khan and His Conquest of North China*. Baltimore: Johns Hopkins Press.

1942. "The Mongol Wars with Hsi Hsia (1205–27)." *Journal of the Royal Asiatic Society* 3–4: 195–228.

Martinez, Peter. See above in primary sources under Rashīd al-Dīn.

May, Timothy.[2015.] "Commercial Queens." Unpublished article.

2012. *The Mongol Conquests in World History*. London: Reaktion Books.

2007. *The Mongol Art of War: Chinggis Khan and the Mongol Military System*. Yardley, PA: Westholme.

2005. "Sorghaghtani Beki." In *Great Lives in History: the Middle Ages, 477–1453*. Edited by Shelley Wolbrink, 954–56. Pasadena, CA: Salem Press.

Melville, Charles. 2016. "The End of the Ilkhanate and After: Observations on the Collapse of the Mongol World Empire." In *The Mongols' Middle East: Continuity and Transformation in Ilkhanid Iran*. Edited by Bruno de Nicola and Charles Melville, 309–35. Leiden, Boston: Brill.

2010. "Genealogy and Exemplary Rulership in the Tarikh-i Chingiz Khan." In *Living Islamic History: Studies in Honour of Professor Carole Hillenbrand*. Edited by Yasir Suleiman, 129–50. Edinburgh: Edinburgh University Press.

2006. "The Keshig in Iran: The Survival of the Royal Mongol Household." In *Beyond the Legacy of Genghis Khan*. Edited by Linda Komaroff, 135–64. Leiden: Brill.

1999. *The Fall of Amir Chupan and the Decline of the Ilkhanate, 1327–37: A Decade of Discord in Iran*. Papers on Inner Asia, no. 30. Bloomington, IN: Research Institute for Inner Asian Studies.

1997. "Abū Sa'īd and the Revolt of the Amirs in 1319." In *L'Iran face à la domination Mongole*. Edited by Denise Aigle, 89–120. Tehran: Institut Français de Recherche en Iran.

1996. "Dokuz (Doquz) Kātūn." *Encyclopedia lranica*. Vol. 7. Edited by Ehsan Yarshater, 475–76. Costa Mesa, CA: Mazda.

1990a. "Bologān Kātun." *Encyclopedia lranica*. Vol. 4. Edited by Ehsan Yarshater, 338–39. London and Boston: Routledge and Kegan Paul.

1990b. "The Itineraries of Sultan Öljeitü, 1304–16." *Iran* 28, 55–70.

Melville, Charles, and 'Abbās Zaryāb. 1992. "Chobanids." *Encyclopedia lranica*. Vol. 5. Edited by Ehsan Yarshater, 496–502. Costa Mesa, CA: Mazda.

Minorsky, Vladimir, trans. 1982. *Hudūd al-'Ālam, the Regions of the World: A Persian Geography, 372 A.H.–982 A.D.* Cambridge: Trustees of the E. J. W. Gibb Memorial.

Miyawaki, Junko. 1997. "The Birth of the Oyirad Khanship." *Central Asiatic Journal* 41, no. 1, 38–75.

Miyawaki-Okada, Junko. 2007. "The Role of Women in the Imperial Succession of the Nomadic Empire." In *The Role of Women in the Altaic World: Permanent International Altaistic Conference, 44th Meeting, Walberberg, 26–31 August 2001*. Edited by Veronika Veit, 143–49. Wiesbaden: Harrassowitz.

Morgan, David O. 2009. "The Decline and Fall of the Mongol Empire." *Journal of the Royal Asiatic Society* 19, no. 4, 1–11.

2005. "The 'Great Yasa of Chinggis Khan' Revisited." In *Mongols, Turks and Others: Eurasian Nomads and the Sedentary World*. Edited by Reuven Amitai and Michal Biran. Brill's Inner Asian Library, no. 11. Leiden: Brill.

2001. "Ibn Baṭṭūṭa and the Mongols." *Journal of the Royal Asiatic Society* (Third Series), 11, no. 1, 1–11.

1986a (2007). *The Mongols*. Malden, MA: Blackwell Publishing.

1986b. "The 'Great Yāsā of Chingiz Khān' and Mongol Law in the Ilkhanate." *Bulletin of the School of Oriental and African Studies* 49, no. 1: 163–76.

1982. "Who Ran the Mongol Empire?" *The Journal of the Royal Asiatic Society of Great Britain and Ireland* 1, 124–36.

Moses, Larry. 1987. "The Quarrelling Sons in the Secret History of the Mongols." *The Journal of American Folklore* 100, no. 395, 63–68.

Näf, Barbara Frey. 2007. "'Compared with the women the ... menfolk have little business of their own': Gender Divison of Labour in the History of the Mongols." In *The Role of Women in the Altaic World: Permanent International Altaistic Conference, 44th meeting, Walberberg, 26–31 August 2001*. Edited by Veronika Veit, 69–76. Wiesbaden: Harrassowitz.

Okada, Hidehiro. 1972. "The Secret History of the Mongols, a Pseudo-Historical Novel." *Ajia Afurika Gengo Bunka Kenkyu* [*Journal of Asian and African Studies*] 5, 62–63.

Peirce, Leslie P. 1993. *The Imperial Harem: Women and Sovereignty in the Ottoman Empire*. New York: Oxford University Press.

Peirce, Leslie. 2009. "Writing Histories of Sexuality in the Middle East." *The American Historical Review* 114, no. 5, 1325–39.

Pfeiffer, Judith. 2006. "Ahmad Tegüder's Second Letter to Qalā'ūn (682–1283)." In *History and Historiography of Post-Mongol Central Asia and the Middle East: Studies in Honor of John E. Woods*. Wiesbaden: Harrassowitz. 167–202.

2006. "Reflections on a 'Double Rapprochement': Conversion to Islam Among the Mongol Elite during the Early Ilkhanate." In *Beyond the Legacy of Genghis Khan*. Edited by Linda Komaroff, 369–89. Leiden and Boston: Brill.

2003. *Conversion to Islam among the Ilkhans in Muslim Narrative Traditions: The Case of Aḥmad Tegüder*. PhD dissertation, University of Chicago.

Pelliot, Paul. 1935. "Sur un passage du *Cheng-wou ts'ing-tcheng lou*." In *Studies Presented to Ts'ai Yuan P'ei on His Sixty-fifth Birthday*. Vol. II, 907–38. [Beijing]: Peiping Academia Sinica.

1959–73. *Notes on Marco Polo*. 3 vols. Paris: Imprimerie Nationale.

1960. *Notes critiques d'histoire Kalmouke*. Paris: Librairie d'Amérique et d'Orient, Adrien-Maisonneuve.

1923. "Les Mongols et la papauté." In *Revue de l'Orient Chrétien*, XXIII (1922–23), 3–30; XXIV (1924), 225–335; XXVIII (1932), 3–84. Rebound in one volume. Paris: A Picard.

Qu, Dafeng and Liu, Jianyi. 1998. "On Some Problems Concerning Jochi's Lifetime." *Central Asiatic Journal* 42, no. 2, 283–90.

Quinn, Sholeh A., 1989. "*The Mu'izz al-Ansāb* and *Shu'āb-i Panjgānah* as Sources for the Chaghatayid Period of History: A Comparative Analysis." *Central Asiatic Journal* 33, 229–53.

Ratchnevsky, Paul. 1993. "Šigi Qutuqu (ca. 1180–ca. 1260)." In *In the Service of the Khan: Eminent Personalities of the Early Mongol-Yüan Period*. Edited by Igor de Rachewiltz, Hok-lam Chan, Hsiao Ch'i-ch'ing and Peter W. Geier, 75–94. Wiesbaden: Harrassowitz.

1992. *Genghis Khan: His Life and Legacy*. Translated by Thomas Nivison Haining. Oxford, UK: Blackwell.

1968. "The Levirate in the Legislation of the Yuan Dynasty." *Tamura Hakushi shoju Toyoshi ronso* [Asiatic studies in honor of Dr. Jitsuzō Tamura on the occasion of his sixth-fourth birthday], Tamura Hakushi Taikan Kinen Jigyō-kai at Kyoto University, Kyoto, 45–62.

1976. "La condition de la femme mongole au 12e/13e siècle." In *Tractata Altaica: Denis Sinor, sexagenario optime de rebus altaicis merito dedicata*. Edited by W. Heissig, J. R. Kruger, F. J. Oinas, and E. Schütz, 509–30. Wiesbaden: Harrassowitz.

Rawlinson, H. C. 1841. "Notes on a Journey from Tabriz, through Persian Kurdistan, to the Ruins of Takhti-Soleiman, and from thence by Zenjan and Tarom to Gilan, in October and November, 1838, with a Memoir on the Site of the Atropatenian Ecbatana." *Journal of the Royal Geographical Society* 10, 1–158.

Rebanks, James. 2015. *The Shepherd's Life: Modern Dispatches from An Ancient Landscape*. New York: Flatiron.

Remilev-Schlüter, Elena. 2007. "The Role of Women in the Oirat-Kalmyk Society." In *The Role of Women in the Altaic World: Permanent International Altaistic Conference, 44th Meeting, Walberberg, 26–31 August 2001*. Edited by Veronika Veit, 199–209. Wiesbaden: Harrassowitz.

Riasanovsky, Valentin. 1965. *Fundamental Principles of Mongol Law*. Indiana University Publications, Uralic and Altaic Series 43. Bloomington, IN.

Richard, Jean. 1967. "La conversion de Berke et les débuts de l'islamisation de la Horde d'Or." *Revue des études islamiques* 35, 173–84.

Robinson, David M. 2009. *Empire's Twilight: Northeast Asia under the Mongols*. Cambridge, MA: Harvard University Asia Center for the Harvard-Yenching Institute.

Rossabi, Morris. 2015. "The Mongol Empire and Its Impact on the Arts of China. In *Nomads as Agents of Cultural Change: The Mongols and Their Eurasian Predecessors*. Edited by Reuven Amitai and Michal Biran, 215–27. Honolulu: University of Hawaii Press.

1988 (2009). *Khubilai Khan: His Life and Times*. Berkeley: University of California Press.

1992. "The Study of the Women of Inner Asia and China in the Mongol Era." *Gest Library Journal* 5, no. 2, 17–28.

1989. "Kuan Tao-Sheng: Woman Artist in Yuan China." *Bulletin of Sung-Yuan Studies* 21, 67–84.

1979. "Khubilai Khan and the Women in His Family." In *Studia Sino-Mongolica: Festschrift für Herbert Franke*. Edited by Wolfgang Bauer. Wiesbaden: Franz Steiner. 153–80.

Roux, Jean-Paul. 1969. "La veuve dans les sociétés Turques et Mongoles de l'Asie Centrale." *L'Homme* IX, no. 4, 51–78.

Ryan, James D. 1998. "Christian Wives of Mongol Khans: Tartar Queens and Missionary Expectations in Asia." *Journal of the Royal Asiatic Society* (Third Series), 8, no. 3 (November), 411–21.

Rybatski, Volker. 2007. "Female Personal Names in Middle Mongolian Sources." In *The Role of Women in the Altaic World: Permanent International Altaistic Conference, 44th meeting, Walberberg, 26–31 August 2001*. Edited by Veronika Veit, 211–29. Wiesbaden: Harrassowitz.

Sarkozi, Alice. 1978. "Love and Friendship in the *Secret History of the Mongols*." In *Aspects of Altaic Civilization II: Proceedings of the XVIII PIAC, Bloomington, June 29–July 5, 1975*. Edited by Larry V. Clark and Paul Alexander Draghi, 145–54. Bloomington: Asian Studies Research Institute, Indiana University.

Saunders. J. J. 1969. "Matthew Paris and the Mongols." In *Essays in Medieval History Presented to Bertie Wilkinson*. Edited by T. A. Sandquist and M. R. Powicke, 116–32. Toronto: University of Toronto Press.

1971. *The History of the Mongol Conquests*. London: Routledge and Kegan Paul.

Schamiloglu, Uli. 1984. "The Qarachi Beys of the Later Golden Horde: Notes on the Organization of the Mongol World Empire." *Archivum Eurasiae Medii Aevi* 4: 283–97.

2002. "The Golden Horde." *The Turks, II: Middle Ages*. Edited by Hasan Celal Güzel, et al, 819–34. Ankara: Yeni Türkiye.
Schurmann, H. F. 1956. *Economic Structure of the Yuan Dynasty*. Cambridge, MA: Harvard University Press.
Sečenmöngke. 2007. "The Role of Women in Traditional Mongolian Society." In *The Role of Women in the Altaic World: Permanent International Altaistic Conference, 44th Meeting, Walberberg, 26–31 August 2001*. Edited by Veronika Veit, 247–51. Wiesbaden: Harrassowitz.
Sela, Ron. 2003. *Ritual and Authority in Central Asia: The Khan's Inauguration Ceremony*. Bloomington: Indiana University Research Institute for Inner Asian Studies.
Serruys, Henry. 1975. "Two Remarkable Women in Mongolia: The Third Lady Erketu Qatun and Dayicing-Beyiji." *Asia Major* 19, no. 2 (August), 191–245.
1974. "Four Manuals for Marriage Ceremonies among the Mongols, Part 1." *Zentralasiatische Studien* 8, 247–331.
Sneath, David. 2010. "The Headless State in Inner Asia: Reconsidering Kingship Society and the Discourse of Tribalism." In *Representing Power in Ancient Inner Asia: Legitimacy, Transmission and the Sacred*. Edited by Isabell Charleux, Grégory Delaplace, Robert Hamayon, and Scott Pearce, 365–415. Bellingham: Western Washington University.
2007. *The Headless State: Aristocratic Orders, Kinship Society and Misrepresentations of Nomadic Inner Asia*. New York: Columbia University Press.
Shiraishi, Noriyuki. 2006. "Avraga Site: The 'Great Ordū' of Genghis Khan." In *Beyond the Legacy of Genghis Khan*. Edited by Linda Komaroff, 83–93. Leiden: Brill.
Sinor, Denis. 2007. "Some Observations on Women in Early and Medieval Inner Asian History." In *The Role of Women in the Altaic World: Permanent International Altaistic Conference, 44th Meeting, Walberberg, 26–31 August 2001*. Edited by Veronika Veit, 261–68. Wiesbaden: Harrassowitz.
1975 (1977). "The Mongols and Western Europe." In *A History of the Crusades, Vol. III. The Fourteenth and Fifteenth Centuries*. Edited by Harry W. Hazard, Kenneth M. Setton, 513–44. Madison: The University of Wisconsin Press. Reprint, 1977, in *Inner Asia and Its Contacts with Medieval Europe*. London: Variorum.
Smith, John Masson. 2000. "Dietary Decadence and Dynastic Decline in the Mongol Empire." *JAH* 34, no. 1, 35–52.
Soullière, E. 1988. "The Imperial Marriages of the Ming Dynasty." *Papers on Far Eastern History* 37, 15–42.
Spuler, Berthold. 1965. *Die Goldene Horde*. Wiesbaden: Harrassowitz.
1968. *Die Mongolen in Iran*. Berlin: Akademie-Verlag.
1985. "Abesh Khatun." *Encyclopedia Iranica*. Edited by Ehsan Yarshater, I:210. London and Boston: Routledge and Kegan Paul.
Stewart, Julie Ann. 2002. "Wife, Mother, Shamaness, Warrior Woman: The Role of Women in Mongolian and Siberian Epic Tales." In *Continuity and Change in Central and Inner Asia*. Edited by Michael Gervers and Wayne Schlepp, 313–29. Toronto Studies in Central and Inner Asia, no. 5 Toronto: Asian Institute.

Szynkiewicz, Sławoj. 1989. "On Kinship Symbolics Among the Western Mongols." In *Religious and Lay Symbolism in the Altaic World and Other Papers. Proceedings of the 27th Meeting of the Permanent International Altaistic Conference, Wlaberberg, Germany, June 12–16, 1984.* Edited by Klaus Sagaster and Helmut Eimer, 379–85. Wiesbaden: Harrassowitz.

1978. "Le mariage, rite sanctionné par le passé culturel." *Études mongoles et siberiennes* 9, 91–105.

Togan, Isenbike. 2006. "The Qongrat in History." In *History and Historiography of Post-Mongol Central Asia and the Middle East: Studies in Honor of John E. Woods.* Edited by Judith Pfeiffer, Sholeh A. Quinn and Ernest Tucker, 61–83. Wiesbaden: Harrassowitz.

1998. *Flexibility and Limitation in Steppe Formation: The Kereit Khanate and Chinggis Khan.* Leiden, Brill.

Uno, Nobuhiro. 2009. "Exchange-Marriage in the Royal Families of Nomadic States." In *The Early Mongols: Language, Culture and History: Studies in Honor of Igor de Rachewiltz on the Occasion of His 80th Birthday.* Edited by Volker Rybatzki, Alessandra Pozzi, Peter W. Geier, and John R. Krueger, 175–82. Bloomington, IN, The Denis Sinor Institute for Inner Asian Studies, Indiana University.

Vásáry, István. 2009. "The Jochid Realm: The Western Steppe and Eastern Europe." In *The Cambridge History of Inner Asia: The Chinggisid Period.* Edited by N. Di Cosmo, J. F. Allen, and P. Golden, 67–85. Cambridge: Cambridge University Press.

1990. "History and Legend in Berke Khan's Conversion to Islam." In *Aspects of Altaistic Civilizations III: Proceedings of the Permanent Meeting of the Permanent International Altaistic Conference, Indiana University, Bloomington IN, June 19–25, 1987*, 230–52. Richmond, Surrey: Curzon.

Vernadsky, George. 1953. *The Mongols and Russia.* New Haven: Yale University Press.

Vinland Map. See De Bridia, C, in primary sources.

Waley, Arthur. See Li, Chih-Ch'ang, in primary sources.

Weatherford, Jack McIver. 2010. *The Secret History of the Mongol Queens: How the Daughters of Genghis Khan Rescued His Empire.* New York: Crown.

Williams, Henry P. III. 1981. "Marriage and Divorce in the Legal Culture of the Old, the Ottoman and the New Turks." *Journal of Turkish Studies* 5, 131–200.

Wittfogel, K. A., and Feng, Chia-sheng, et al. 1949. *History of Chinese Society: Liao (907–1125).* Philadelphia: American Philosophical Society. Distributed by MacMillan.

Wright, David C. 2007. "The Political and Military Power of Kitan Empress Dowagers." In *The Role of Women in the Altaic World: Permanent International Altaistic Conference, 44th meeting, Walberberg, 26–31 August 2001.* Edited by Veronika Veit, 325–35. Wiesbaden: Harrassowitz.

Yang, Lien-Sheng. 1961. "Hostages in Chinese History." In *Studies in Chinese Institutional History.* Edited by Lien-Sheng Yang, 43–57. Harvard-Yenching Institute Studies 20. Cambridge, MA: Harvard University Press.

Yuan Shi: See Song Lian in primary sources.

Zhao, George Qingzhi. 2008. *Marriage as Political Strategy and Cultural Expression: Mongolian Royal Marriages from World Empire to Yuan Dynasty*. Asian Thought and Culture, Vol. 60. New York: Peter Lang.

2004. "Control through Conciliation: Royal Marriages between the Mongol Yuan and Koryŏ (Korea) in the 13th and 14th Centuries." *Cultural Interaction and Conflict in Inner and Central Asia* 6: 3–26.

Zhao George Q. and Richard W. L. Guisso. 2005. "Female Anxiety and Female Power: Political Intervention by Mongol Empresses during the 13th and 14th Centuries in China." In *History and Society in Central and Inner Asia*. Edited by Michael Gervers, et al. *Toronto Studies in Central and Inner Asia*, no. 7, 17–23.

Zimonyi, István. 2005. "Ibn Baṭṭūṭa on the First Wife of Özbek Khan." *Central Asiatic Journal* 49, 303–09.

Index

The page numbers in bold indicate the death of the respective personalities

Other Titles in the Series

Agricultural Innovation in the Early Islamic World: The Diffusion of Crops and Farming Techniques, 700–1100, Andrew M. Watson

Muslim Tradition: Studies in Chronology, Provenance, and Authorship of Early Hadith, G. H. A. Juynboll

Social History of Timbuktu: The Role of Muslim Scholars and Notables 1400–1900, Elias N. Saad

Sex and Society in Islam: Birth Control before the Nineteenth Century, B. F. Musallam

Towns and Townsmen of Ottoman Anatolia: Trade, Crafts, and Food Production in an Urban Setting 1520–1650, Suraiya Faroqhi

Unlawful Gain and Legitimate Profit in Islamic Law: Riba, Gharar, and Islamic Banking, Nabil A. Saleh

Men of Modest Substance: House Owners and House Property in Seventeenth-Century Ankara and Kayseri, Suraiya Faroqhi

Roman, Provincial, and Islamic Law: The Origins of the Islamic Patronate, Patricia Crone

Economic Life in Ottoman Jerusalem, Amnon Cohen

Mannerism in Arabic Poetry: A Structural Analysis of Selected Texts (3rd Century AH/9th Century AD – 5th Century AH/11th Century AD), Stefan Sperl

The Rise and Rule of Tamerlane, Beatrice Forbes Manz

Popular Culture in Medieval Cairo, Boaz Shoshan

Early Philosophical Shiism: The Ismaili Neoplatonism of Abu Ya'qub Al-Sijistani, Paul E. Walker

Indian Merchants and Eurasian Trade, 1600–1750, Stephen Frederic Dale

Palestinian Peasants and Ottoman Officials: Rural Administration around Sixteenth-Century Jerusalem, Amy Singer

Arabic Historical Thought in the Classical Period, Tarif Khalidi

Mongols and Mamluks: The Mamluk-Ilkhanid War, 1260–1281, Reuven Amitai-Preiss

Knowledge and Social Practice in Medieval Damascus, 1190–1350, Michael Chamberlain

The Politics of Households in Ottoman Egypt: The Rise of the Qazdağlis, Jane Hathaway

Hierarchy and Egalitarianism in Islamic Thought, Louise Marlow

Commodity and Exchange in the Mongol Empire: A Cultural History of Islamic Textiles, Thomas T. Allsen

State and Provincial Society in the Ottoman Empire: Mosul, 1540–1834, Dina Rizk Khoury

The Mamluks in Egyptian Politics and Society, Thomas Philipp and Ulrich Haarmann (eds.)

The Delhi Sultanate: A Political and Military History, Peter Jackson

European and Islamic Trade in the Early Ottoman State: The Merchants of Genoa and Turkey, Kate Fleet

The Ottoman City between East and West: Aleppo, Izmir, and Istanbul, Edhem Eldem, Daniel Goffman, and Bruce Masters

The Politics of Trade in Safavid Iran: Silk for Silver, 1600–1730, Rudolph P. Matthee
The Idea of Idolatry and the Emergence of Islam: From Polemic to History, G. R. Hawting
A Monetary History of the Ottoman Empire, Şevket Pamuk
Classical Arabic Biography: The Heirs of the Prophets in the Age of Al-Ma'mun, Michael Cooperson
Empire and Elites after the Muslim Conquest: The Transformation of Northern Mesopotamia, Chase F. Robinson
Poverty and Charity in Medieval Islam: Mamluk Egypt, 1250–1517, Adam Sabra
Culture and Conquest in Mongol Eurasia, Thomas T. Allsen
Christians and Jews in the Ottoman Arab World: The Roots of Sectarianism, Bruce Masters
Arabic Administration in Norman Sicily: The Royal Diwan, Jeremy Johns
Law, Society, and Culture in the Maghrib, 1300–1500, David S. Powers
Revival and Reform in Islam: The Legacy of Muhammad al-Shawkani, Bernard Haykel
Tolerance and Coercion in Islam: Interfaith Relations in the Muslim Tradition, Yohanan Friedmann
Guns for the Sultan: Military Power and the Weapons Industry in the Ottoman Empire, Gábor Ágoston
Marriage, Money, and Divorce in Medieval Islamic Society, Yossef Rapoport
The Empire of the Qara Khitai in Eurasian History: Between China and the Islamic World, Michal Biran
Domesticity and Power in the Early Mughal World, Ruby Lal
Power, Politics, and Religion in Timurid Iran, Beatrice Forbes Manz
Postal Systems in the Pre-Modern Islamic World, Adam J. Silverstein
Kingship and Ideology in the Islamic and Mongol Worlds, Anne F. Broadbridge
Justice, Punishment, and the Medieval Muslim Imagination, Christian Lange
The Shiites of Lebanon under Ottoman Rule, 1516–1788, Stefan Winter
Women and Slavery in the Late Ottoman Empire, Madeline Zilfi
The Second Ottoman Empire: Political and Social Transformation in the Early Modern World, Baki Tezcan
The Legendary Biographies of Tamerlane: Islam and Heroic Apocrypha in Central Asia, Ron Sela
Non-Muslims in the Early Islamic Empire: From Surrender to Coexistence, Milka Levy-Rubin
The Origins of the Shi'a: Identity, Ritual, and Sacred Space in Eighth-Century Kufa, Najam Haider
Politics, Law, and Community in Islamic Thought: The Taymiyyan Moment, Ovamir Anjum
The Power of Oratory in the Medieval Muslim World, Linda G. Jones
Animals in the Qur'an, Sarra Tlili
The Logic of Law Making in Islam: Women and Prayer in the Legal Tradition, Behnam Sadeghi
Empire and Power in the Reign of Süleyman: Narrating the Sixteenth-Century Ottoman World, Kaya Şahin

Law and Piety in Medieval Islam, Megan H. Reid
Women and the Transmission of Religious Knowledge in Islam, Asma Sayeed
The New Muslims of Post-Conquest Iran: Tradition, Memory, and Conversion, Sarah Bowen Savant
The Mamluk City in the Middle East: History, Culture, and the Urban Landscape, Nimrod Luz
Disability in the Ottoman Arab World, 1500–1800, Sara Scalenghe
The Holy City of Medina: Sacred Space in Early Islamic Arabia, Harry Munt
Muslim Midwives: The Craft of Birthing in the Premodern Middle East, Avner Giladi
Doubt in Islamic Law: A History of Legal Maxims, Interpretation, and Islamic Criminal Law, Intisar A. Rabb
The Second Formation of Islamic Law: The Hanafi School in the Early Modern Ottoman Empire, Guy Burak
Sexual Violation in Islamic Law: Substance, Evidence, and Procedure, Hina Azam
Gender Hierarchy in the Qur'an: Medieval Interpretations, Modern Responses, Karen Bauer
Intellectual Networks in Timurid Iran: Sharaf al-Din 'Ali Yazdi and the Islamicate Republic of Letters, Ilker Evrim Binbaş
Authority and Identity in Medieval Islamic Historiography: Persian Histories from the Peripheries, Mimi Hanaoka
The Economics of Ottoman Justice: Settlement and Trial in the Sharia Courts, Top of Form Metin Coşgel and Boğaç Ergene
The Mystics of al-Andalus: Ibn Barrajan and Islamic Thought in the Twelfth Century, Yousef Casewit
Muhammad's Heirs: The Rise of Muslim Scholarly Communities, 622–950, Jonathan E. Brockopp
The First of the Modern Ottomans: The Intellectual History of Ahmed Vasif, Ethan Menchinger
Non-Muslim Provinces under Early Islam: Islamic Rule and Iranian Legitimacy in Armenia and Caucasian Albania, Alison Vacca
Women and the Making of the Mongol Empire, Anne F. Broadbridge
Slavery and Empire in Central Asia, Jeff Eden
Christianity in Fifteenth-Century Iraq, Thomas A. Carlson

Lightning Source UK Ltd.
Milton Keynes UK
UKHW01n2006180918
329127UK00002B/3/P

9 781108 424899